MW01253499

# Practicing Psychotherapy in Constructed Reality

# Practicing Psychotherapy in Constructed Reality

## Ritual, Charisma, and Enhanced Client Outcomes

Stephen Bacon

LEXINGTON BOOKS

*Lanham • Boulder • New York • London*

Published by Lexington Books
An imprint of The Rowman & Littlefield Publishing Group, Inc.
4501 Forbes Boulevard, Suite 200, Lanham, Maryland 20706
www.rowman.com

Unit A, Whitacre Mews, 26-34 Stannary Street, London SE11 4AB

British Library Cataloguing in Publication Information Available

**Library of Congress Cataloging-in-Publication Data**

Names: Bacon, Stephen, author.
Title: Practicing psychotherapy in constructed reality : ritual, charism, and enhanced
    client outcomes / Stephen Bacon.
Description: Lanham : Lexington Books, [2018] | Includes bibliographical references
    and index.
Identifiers: LCCN 2018005356 (print) | LCCN 2018004078 (ebook) |
    ISBN 9781498552271 (electronic) | ISBN 9781498552264 (cloth : alk. paper)
Subjects: | MESH: Psychotherapy | Psychotherapy—education | Treatment Outcome |
    Professional-Patient Relations
Classification: LCC RC480 (print) | LCC RC480 (ebook) | NLM WM 420 |
    DDC 616.89/14—dc23
LC record available at https://lccn.loc.gov/2018005356

♾ ™ The paper used in this publication meets the minimum requirements of American
National Standard for Information Sciences—Permanence of Paper for Printed Library
Materials, ANSI/NISO Z39.48-1992.

Printed in the United States of America

# Contents

Acknowledgments     vii

Introduction: Real versus Constructed     1

**PART I: THE NEW THERAPEUTIC MILIEU**     **15**

1   Psychology's Inconvenient Truths     17

2   Close Encounters with the Abyss     45

3   Social Constructionism     63

4   A Place to Stand     103

5   The Nomological Net     117

**PART II: ENHANCING THERAPIST EFFECTIVENESS**     **129**

6   Focus on the Therapist     131

7   Beginner's Mind     139

8   Wizards among Us     167

9   Apollonian Power: The Primacy of the Conscious Mind     191

10   Identity     211

11   Heart and Soul     229

12   The Other Royal Road: Social Determinants of Change     257

13   Dionysian Power: Sacred Space and Altered States     275

14   The Spiritual Path     303

**15**   Becoming Remarkable                                         343

**16**   The Way Forward                                             385

Appendix: The Geography of Constructed Reality                      391

References                                                          395

Index                                                               405

About the Author                                                    409

# Acknowledgments

This book challenges many of the basic assumptions of psychology and psychotherapy. In particular, it argues against the inherent power of techniques and systems of thought and recommends replacing a scientific psychology with one that operates in constructed reality. Because these ideas contradict so much within established psychological thought, it has been necessary to tap into fields and expertise that lie outside psychology.

Fortunately my life choices exposed me to a substantial amount of such extrapsychological philosophies. I am particularly grateful to the teachers and companions I encountered while living in a Yoga ashram in the 1970s; they introduced me to the concept of the perennial philosophy—a central organizing factor in this book. My professors in religious studies at the University of Colorado continued this education; many of the central thinkers quoted herein come from courses I took in Boulder. My work with Outward Bound—and the spirited, thoughtful, and compassionate instructors I met there—impressed me with the importance of charisma and the ability to cultivate it though adventurous experiences. The workshops I was privileged to attend—particularly the ones with strategic family systems and Ericksonian focuses—pushed me further down the path.

This book benefited from conversations with and feedback from many people. I particularly want to express my gratitude to David Burger, who has been on this journey with me from the beginning, and Kjell Rudestam, a local psychologist who made especially useful suggestions. I also want to thank my fifteen-year-old son Aidan. He kept asking questions about what I was writing, which was lovely in itself, but it also required me to frequently reframe complicated ideas into a more accessible form.

Finally, as we are all aware, none of this book would have been possible without the contributions and experience of hundreds of clients who have always been my best teachers.

# Introduction

## *Real versus Constructed*

A thought, even a possibility, can shatter and transform us.

—Friedrich Nietzsche, *The Complete Works*
*of Friedrich Nietzsche* (1911)

I first thought of writing this book in 1978 as an undergraduate student. I was completing a double major in religious studies and psychology and one of my religious studies professors assigned a paper on social constructionism. As I wrote my paper on a constructionist perspective on spiritual practice it was impossible not to imagine where such concepts might fit into my other great interest: clinical psychology.

This was, of course, prior to all the good work done by thought leaders such as Kenneth Gergen and the narrative therapy school so I had a kind of fresh look at the whole perspective. It was clear to me that psychology hadn't really taken the time to integrate these ideas into its foundational theories. And that seemed strange to me because the briefest of analyses suggests that psychotherapy operates primarily in constructed reality.

I was sympathetic to clinical psychology's attempts to function as a scientific discipline and, indeed, when I went on to get my doctorate, my major was clinical psychology but my minor was in statistics. I used to tell my friends that after all the hours spent in clinical offices—where everything was ephemeral and could change in a moment depending on the frame and reframe—it was a relief to study statistics where there was a relatively clear sense of right and wrong. Actually, I was joking. I loved the fluidity and spontaneity of the clinical process and found myself stimulated by the ease with which a client's reality—or my own—could turn on a simple phrase or a meaningful experience.

Over time, as my career developed and I had the chance to study with different mentors, work in a variety of settings, and meet hundreds of clients and families, I never really abandoned my sense that under all of the diagnoses, case conceptualizations, and techniques was the raw, unformed material of reality. Sure we could freeze it temporarily with our constructions and our social validations, but the discerning ear could always hear a background rumbling—the presence of chaos and generativity and the always-looming Abyss. More important than simply sensing this underlying presence, my mind was beginning to explore ideas about the new clinical approaches that constructionism might offer.

Thanks to a variety of prescient thinkers, social constructionism is no longer a stranger to clinical psychology and has been integrated in a variety of ways. With all that, psychology continues to ignore just how central constructionism is to its processes and our basic assumptions remain firmly committed to the concept that psychotherapy operates in fundamental reality. Given that choice, the door remains shut in terms of fully engaging with the new possibilities implicit in a constructionist frame.

Fortunately, clinical psychology's own research shows the incongruences and contradictions in that assumption; when reexamined carefully, this research provides substantial support for a constructionist perspective. However, sorting out the assumptions from the deductions requires a bit of careful detective work.

Psychology has done thousands of studies to determine if psychotherapy works and why it works. The conclusions of this research are typically presented simply and directly: psychotherapy is effective. Its success rests on potent techniques. We are continuing our search for more efficient and powerful ways to help people change.

These statements seem quite clear. However, scattered throughout these studies are a series of clues that actually point toward a different set of conclusions. When we follow the clues, we find that what seems apparent is actually shrouded in mystery; and, like the famed "purloined letter," much of the mystery is hidden in plain sight.

The best starting point is the seminal study conducted by Strupp and Hadley; in 1979 they published research showing that "understanding" college professors were able to achieve the same level of therapeutic effectiveness as highly experienced therapists when doing therapy with neurotics. The implications of the study are remarkable and somewhat disheartening for psychology. Essentially the results support the argument that therapist training and experience fail to enhance therapist efficacy.

It can be more interesting, however, to pursue some of the subtler implications of the study. Imagine that this study is replicated but, this time, the performance of the college professors is compared to auto mechanics and the goal is to rebuild an engine. Clearly the mechanics would be vastly superior to the college professors; in fact, if it were a sporting event, the results would be scored 100–0 in favor of the mechanics. The same lopsided results would occur if the study was replicated with cardiologists and the task is to install a pacemaker. Again the results would be cardiologists 100, college professors 0.

The reason we can be confident of these results without actually running the experiment is because we know that the professions of cardiology and auto mechanics depend on the acquisition and possession of privileged knowledge. Privileged knowledge is the specialized knowledge and techniques required to practice the profession. Without training, practice, and experience in the area of privileged knowledge, the tasks of the profession cannot be accomplished. In this sense, the Strupp study went beyond a simple critique of the importance of training and experience; essentially it argued that psychotherapy is a field that operates without privileged knowledge. In professions where there is something to learn, there is an overwhelmingly strong training effect. The lack of any training effect in psychotherapy implies that psychology has nothing to teach in terms of enhancing therapist efficacy.

There is a second interesting implication that comes out of the Strupp study. Recall that the study found that the neurotic clients significantly improved whether they were treated by the licensed professionals or the professors. The "score" of the study was not 0–0 but rather 100–100. Somehow, without knowing any psychological techniques, the professors were able to invent their own, on the spot and in the moment. And since the different professors operated independently, they invented different techniques; in a sense, it was like twenty different "schools of therapy" being created spontaneously. Apparently, as long as these different techniques were seen as credible by the clients, they worked as well as the professionally developed and validated techniques used by the licensed therapists. Virtually everything worked! This suggests another important difference between psychotherapy and cardiology/auto mechanics. In the latter there is only one right answer—or perhaps only a few right answers—and many wrong ways to do things. In psychotherapy—the field without privileged knowledge—there appears to be an infinite number of right ways to operate. And, it is certainly possible that there are no wrong answers.

Was the Strupp study an outlier or did subsequent research replicate its findings? Unfortunately for psychology, the study was not only replicated, other studies pushed its findings even further. In short, while the research documents that therapy regularly achieves a modest positive effect, it also shows that training and experience fail to improve that outcome. Although it is hard to believe, the new life coach, who has taken two weekend workshops, essentially achieves the same results as a PhD scholar with twenty years of experience. Moreover, all the research on client characteristics has also failed to improve outcome. Knowing the typical behaviors of alcoholics, or the stages of grief, or the results of trauma should allow the therapist to be more effective; unfortunately, they do not. Finally, all the books written about all the psychotherapeutic systems—behavioral, psychodynamic, family systems, and so forth—have also failed to improve therapeutic outcomes one bit. In sum, virtually all the research, all the training, all the techniques, and all the theoretical approaches have essentially failed to advance therapeutic efficacy in any measurable way. It appears as if psychology's century-long quest to establish a solid base of privileged knowledge has failed.

This takes us to the next important research finding: the so-called dodo bird conclusion. This conclusion, which comes from the *Alice in Wonderland* quote "Everyone has won and all must have prizes" (Carroll, 1869, p. 34) refers to the finding that all the systems in psychology achieve equivalent positive results. Studies that apparently show the superiority of one school over another—for example, the superiority of psychodynamic therapy over cognitive behavioral therapy—are either due to random chance, experimental design flaws, or, most importantly, allegiance effects. Allegiance effects occur when the experimenter or the treating therapists are personally aligned with one treatment versus the comparison treatment. The dodo bird finding is so robust, and has been replicated so frequently, that one prominent outcome research expert, Bruce Wampold, has actually recommended against further treatment outcome research given that the inevitable result will be: both are effective and neither is more effective than the other.

Frankly, the dodo bird conclusion contradicts common sense. We know that the different schools of therapy use radically different techniques and think about pathology and change from entirely dissimilar perspectives. Is it really probable that they would achieve exactly the same positive effect? From a common sense perspective such a conclusion seems highly unlikely. The other conclusion—that techniques and underlying philosophies add nothing to therapist efficacy—seems just as unlikely. Something happens in the room and it appears to be a technique. If you ask a typical client, they will report something like, "I was depressed and then I learned CBT tools and got better." Or, "I had OCD and the therapist used hypnosis to reduce my compulsions." From such recitations, it appears that the techniques used with clients have independent power and the improvement in client symptoms is due to the efficacy of the techniques.

Regardless of the seeming power of techniques, we already know that they are not the source of change. If techniques had inherent power, then experienced therapists would best the untrained since they know validated techniques. And, of course, the dodo bird conclusion requires us to believe that the differing techniques have exactly the same power—a conclusion that is hard to swallow. In sum, in spite of clients and therapists having the feeling that techniques are responsible for change, the research suggests that the active factor lies elsewhere.

Psychology's primary response to the dodo bird conclusion was the development of common factor theory. This theory postulates that clients change due to a combination of common factors—usually described as a relationship with a wise and caring therapist—and specific factors—techniques and their underlying systems of thought. While the research has essentially demonstrated that the effect size of techniques/specific factors is zero, the field is in denial about these results and continues to hope for a major role for specific factors. In other words, psychology cannot let go of the sense that techniques are the basis of change in spite of the research conclusions. In addition to this feeling that change is due to techniques, there is an additional payoff—if we can find specific factors, then we will have privileged knowledge and can join the other professions who operate on that basis. Hope springs eternal.

Regardless of this clinging to hope for specific factor effects, just about everyone agrees that an effective therapeutic relationship is important for client change. In fact, it is not uncommon to hear therapists assert that they have long believed that "it's all about the relationship." While it is certainly credible to say that the relationship is very important, there are problems with attributing all clinical change to the relationship. The simplest argument comes from the research on the general effectiveness of psychotherapy. We know that psychotherapy is effective; the average treated client is better off than 80 percent of the untreated comparison group. Now, it is clear that many of the untreated have caring relationships with a wise friend or family member. In other words, they have experienced the essence of the therapeutic relationship prior to therapy and this relationship, by itself, does not result in the same positive effect size as formal psychotherapy. The full benefits of psychotherapy appear to require a relationship with an individual who is formally designated as a "healer."

Jerome Frank offers a theory to explain this discrepancy; he points out that the expectations for change are much greater if one receives treatment from a legitimate professional rather than simply having a conversation with a caring and wise friend. Frank goes further and suggests that maximizing change also requires a credible theory about why the client is suffering and a rationale explaining how undergoing the therapeutic procedure will result in improvement. Significantly, he suggests what occurs in the room is more accurately described as a ritual instead of a technique.

Frank's theory integrates all of the major factors revealed by the research results. The Strupp study and the dodo bird conclusion both suggest that virtually anything credible works in terms of helping clients change. Frank accepts that level of fluidity and explicitly defines what makes the interaction credible: the good relationship, the explanation of the problem, and the rationale for the ritual. He explains why the therapeutic experience results in change in spite of the fact that techniques have no inherent power. And his redefinition of what happens in the room—from a technique to a ritual—sustains our feelings about the central importance of that interaction. Finally, Frank's theory explains why psychotherapy can be effective without privileged information; if you appear to be a legitimate healer, and you have a good relationship, and you can get the client to endorse your perspective, virtually anything you propose will work.

Contrast his explanation with psychology's insistence that it has privileged information and inherently powerful techniques that are highly effective at treating specific disorders. Certainly it is understandable to want clinical psychology to be a "scientific" discipline with replicable results that occur independent of practitioner or client. However, when our research results contradict such assumptions, it is incumbent on psychology to seek alternative explanations.

We can take some comfort in the thought that our profession does not face this dilemma alone. Certain other fields—for example, leadership, education, and politics—have the same characteristics. In all of these fields, the beginner can equal the performance of the expert. In addition, much as these fields have tried, they have no privileged knowledge equivalent to the knowledge base of cardiology or auto mechanics. This leads to the obvious question: what makes psychotherapy and leadership different than cardiology and auto mechanics? Fortunately, postmodern philosophy offers a credible explanation.

At the risk of vast oversimplification, postmodernists argue that there are two types of reality: fundamental reality and socially constructed reality. We are all familiar with the concept of fundamental reality. A broken leg and the way to treat it is the same across all cultures. How to build a suspension bridge does not vary depending on whether you are a medieval prince or an Aztec at the time of Cortes. Fundamental reality exists free from social constructions and is *discovered*.

Conversely, most of human culture is *created* and operates in constructed reality. While there are often some connections to fundamental reality, human culture, the definition of self, values, attitudes toward what is good and bad, and meaning are essentially "made up." As a concrete example, the definition of femininity or honor might vary significantly from culture to culture. More relevantly, psychological feelings and experiences are also constructed; for example, romantic love, individuation, and psychological mindedness are central in our culture and may hardly exist in another culture. In this sense, each different culture creates its own social reality. However, this constructed reality feels "discovered and true" not an "arbitrarily invented creation" primarily because all other cultural members accept the same reality and live it to each other. This way in which a constructed view of reality acquires social support is the "social" part in social constructionism.

Like the Jerome Frank theory, constructionism fits well with the research results. In constructed reality, anything that the therapist makes up will work as long as he secures validation from the client. When everything works, techniques can have no independent power. Invent any new system of psychotherapy, if it is credible in our culture, you will soon generate results equivalent to extant systems. Invent new diagnostic categories as well. If you act confidently, you will soon find clients who endorse the new diagnosis as an explanation for what ails them. There are no limits on diagnostic categories, effective treatments, and brand new systems of therapy.

Psychology attempts to make sense of this fluidity by using the tools of science but science breaks down when independent observers fail to measure the same object and when the data change from client to client and from experimenter to experimenter. Science, of course, assumes we are operating in Reality A—fundamental reality—when in fact we are in Reality B—constructed reality. We seek for powerful techniques and keep trying to accumulate privileged information when such seeking is doomed to failure. Our quest is reminiscent of the old story about the search for the keys.

> One dark night, Nazrudin the Mullah was on his hands and knees under a lamp searching for something. A group of his neighbors came over to see what was happening.
> "What have you lost, Nazrudin?" said one of his neighbors.
> "My door key," replied the Mullah.
> The others got down on their hands and knees and searched for the key. After a long unsuccessful search, one said: "We've looked everywhere. Are you sure you dropped it here?"
> Nazrudin looked him in the eye and answered: "Of course I didn't drop it here. I dropped it outside my door."
> "Then why are you looking for it here!" One snapped.
> "Obviously," he said, "Because there's more light here." (Shah, 1996, p. 9)

If we are not going to look "where there is more light," where might we look? Once we have understood that we are in constructed reality and there are no techniques with inherent power and no system that can encompass the chaotic and unstructured nature of constructed reality, we are left with only one option: the therapist. We know that therapists vary in their ability to achieve positive clinical outcomes; some therapists are simply better than others. If this superiority is not due to absorbing privileged information, nor is it due to using powerful techniques, then it must arise secondary to the charisma of the therapist. Charisma, as we use it here, refers to the therapist's ability to embody wisdom and compassion.

In constructed reality, each individual must be initiated into the culture; they must be taught how the culture structures reality. Much of this comes from encounters with other member of the culture; each interaction includes verbal and nonverbal elements that socially validate the shared reality. In addition to these everyday encounters, some members of the culture are relatively more influential than others. Such key figures—parents, teachers, mentors, and leaders—are individuals that we defer to in terms of defining collective reality and in terms of defining who I am and my place in the culture.

Therapists must aspire to be seen as a key figure by the client, at least in the arena of mental health. Accepting that therapy occurs in constructed reality implies that the path to becoming a superior therapist rests on accumulating more charisma so that one is recognized as a key individual. Therapy is a ritual that is guided—or at the least, co-created—by the therapist. Each step of the ritual requires the therapist to invest the moment with meaning, purpose, and validity. Superior outcomes in therapy depend on the capacity to be seen as a key individual—all of it rests on the willingness of the client to accept the guidance of the therapist. Put simply, enhancing therapeutic outcomes is essentially an attempt to enhance one's therapeutic charisma.

At this point, the detective story discussed in the beginning comes to a conclusion. The research results have identified a flaw in psychology's strategies to enhance therapeutic outcomes. As long as we are confusing fundamental and constructed realities, we will continue to put our efforts into a fruitless quest for techniques, schools of therapy, and diagnostic categories that will fail to advance the field. Leaving behind those strategies, and replacing them with an effort to understand the nature of constructed reality is a better road. Understanding constructed reality opens new doors in terms of the development of therapeutic charisma.

While the detective story is completed, the purloined letter aspect of that story remains unresolved. The purloined letter reference implies that something can be hidden in plain sight. In this sense, it should be reiterated that all of the research findings discussed above are well known in the field. It is a small step from the lack of training effects, no privileged information, and the dodo bird conclusion to the realization that psychological techniques have no inherent power.

However, from our continued use of old and failed strategies, it is clear that psychology is in complete denial of the research results. The outcome research should have provoked a profound reexamination of basic assumptions; instead, the field has essentially responded to this provocative set of findings by ignoring them. And isn't it remarkable that the lack of privileged information—after almost a century of attempting to accumulate specialized knowledge—wouldn't be recognized for what it is: a sign that we are pursuing a dead end? Instead, books on techniques and manualized approaches to therapy continue to be published in droves; new systems of therapy are advanced regularly; and virtually every study recommends "further research" as if more research will solve the dilemma.

Psychology prides itself on being *the* research-driven field in the behavioral sciences. Yet, in this case, that commitment to taking research seriously has been abandoned. There is a phrase in psychiatry that applies: *la belle indifference*. Taken from French, *la belle indifference* refers to an absence of concern about a serious problem. Typically *la belle indifference* is generated when accepting reality would cause great psychic discomfort or when it might require a massive shift in worldview or self-perception. Psychology clearly has *la belle indifference* about the research results. Sir Arthur Conan Doyle and Sherlock Holmes comment.

*Gregory (Scotland Yard detective):* "Is there any other point to which you would wish to draw my attention?"
*Holmes:* "To the curious incident of the dog in the night-time."
*Gregory:* "The dog did nothing in the night-time."
*Holmes:* "That was the curious incident." (Doyle, 2000, Kindle Locations 9523–9527)

As Holmes points out, this non-event—the abandonment of our responsibility to take the research seriously—is an important clue. It has not occurred because psychologists are less bright than other professions, nor is it due to unethical self-interest. Rather, the cause arises out of one of the chief characteristics of constructed reality: confusion about what is real and what is constructed.

The fact that much of reality is constructed has been understood by philosophers and spiritual thinkers for thousands of years. While it has been more openly discussed in Eastern philosophy than in the West, this knowledge that our values, beliefs, and cultural truths are constructed has always been limited to the few. In fact, it is sometimes called the "secret knowledge," not because it has been hidden so carefully but because it is difficult to absorb and integrate into one's life. It has also been called "maya" or illusion because there is a sense that humans are virtually "in a trance" when it comes to successfully discerning between the constructed and the fundamental. Accepting constructionism always calls into question the validity of core cultural beliefs; questioning such beliefs leaves the individual potentially confused, adrift, alone, and frightened. Constructionism always takes its adherents to the edge of the Abyss.

Psychology's denial, therefore, is partially due to the need for collective affirmation of Western culture and in part due to fear of the Abyss. The tendency to confound fundamental reality and constructed reality is what supports every culture. The non-event discussed by Sherlock Holmes is the defining characteristic of this confounding. The denial of psychology—the ability to ignore the research and the confirming evidence inherent in the lack of privileged information—could not happen unless psychologists feel that accepting these simple, logical arguments threatens not only core cultural beliefs but also personal faith in a predictable sense of reality.

I recently had a lunch experience that illustrated these principles. I was attending a CE workshop and joined three psychologist friends at the lunch break. They politely asked me to describe my new book. I responded by discussing Strupp, the dodo bird conclusion, the powerlessness of techniques, the absence of privileged information, and the way in which psychotherapy operates in constructed reality. The first psychologist responded with, "I accept the logic of your points and cannot find a way to refute the arguments you have made. However, your conclusions simply feel wrong to me." The second psychologist continued, "I don't accept the Dodo Bird conclusion. My review of the research shows that CBT is vastly superior to other systems." When I replied that the inability of psychology to show training and experience effects—and no privileged knowledge—suggests that his argument was flawed, he responded, "The CBT effects are so well documented that you can be sued if you fail to use those techniques and you may end up losing your license." The third psychologist then responded with, "I've long been convinced that we operate in constructed reality. I've never heard of this idea of privileged information and find it interesting and convincing. I look forward to reading your book." This lunchtime conversation illustrates the range of responses to exposure to the "secret knowledge." The first psychologist simply ignored the results because they felt wrong; the second rejected the results because the implicit conflict with his worldview created fear and aggression; and the third psychologist, who had already walked most of the way down the path, found the discussion interesting and intriguing. In sum, it is harder to deal with the idea of constructed reality than one might imagine, particularly when it implications are focused in the area of your expertise and your livelihood.

These beliefs are so fundamental and pervasive—they feel so natural and correct—that most of us fail to identify them as assumptions. There is a well-known story that illustrates this point.

> There are these two young fish swimming along, and they happen to meet an older fish swimming the other way, who nods at them and says, "Morning, boys, how's the water?" And the two young fish swim on for a bit, and then eventually one of them looks over at the other and goes, "What the hell is water?"

In psychology, "water" refers to the assumption that we simply "know" that all of our reality is fundamental, true, solid, and real; none of our reality is constructed, fluid, ephemeral, and relative. This assumption is so primal and basic that it is difficult to identify when it is operating. Making "water" specific to psychology, it refers to the assumptions that psychology is a science, that techniques have inherent power, that we have already made a great deal of progress, that we are moving in the right direction as a field, and that we are headed for an eventual outcome where we understand pathology, the capacity to change, and the way to treat mental illness. These assumptions feel true. As the lunchtime conversation illustrated, the alternative "feels" wrong. Of course, as psychologists attempting to advance our field we are required to bring our assumptions into conscious awareness. However, fully releasing all of these invalid assumptions can be harder than one might imagine.

This is a book about enhancing therapist efficacy. Unfortunately the research shows that reading books is generally unhelpful in terms of meeting this goal. Moreover, any new book that wishes to make a contribution must be written without a dependence on techniques; techniques are the "great red herring" of books on training therapists. If you take the research seriously, you have to overcome these obstacles.

As might be anticipated, I hope to get around the "ineffectiveness of books" finding by embracing social constructionism; it can be argued that previous books are impotent because they confuse fundamental reality with constructed reality and because they believe in the inherent power of techniques. Second, I intend to focus on the therapist; scientific psychology— which has an implicit commitment to developing techniques that can be used by any trained therapist—tends to neglect the therapist factor. Finally, constructionism includes a strong focus on the client; the client's validation of every proposed ritual is necessary for meaningful transformation and change.

But before we can really discuss how to enhance therapist charisma, we have to agree what "water" is. Without that agreement, we can't talk about solutions to the training/experience/technique dilemma. Even worse, until we understand why we don't even know we are swimming in water—that is, until we understand the impact of our hidden assumptions—we won't even know the right questions to ask.

Lest this seem somewhat overwhelming or, even worse, an exercise in philosophical abstractions, we are rescued by a number of common sense factors. First, postmodern concepts have been taught in universities for at least half a century; most college graduates and many members of the culture are familiar with the basic ideas and have integrated them into their worldview. Second, therapists are experts in the concept that we all construct models of the world that are somewhat arbitrary and that can lead to good or bad outcomes. More specifically, a great deal of therapy looks like: "I understand that you see the situation as if it's 'X,' perhaps your life would work better if you see it as 'Y'." Third, while it may be true that all of the various schools of therapy achieve equal therapeutic outcomes, it is also clear that they frame the nature of the world, psychopathology, and therapeutic work quite differently. This book attempts to demonstrate that these differences between the therapeutic schools can be seen as thoughtful attempts to highlight and delineate some of the major geographic markers of constructed reality. If one understands the essential assumptions of each major school, there can be a readiness to understand differing viewpoints on constructed reality.

Finally, while therapy as it is currently practiced is only a bit over a century old, philosophers, priests, shamen, and all types of healers have been helping people understand how to heal trauma, evolve and mature as individuals, and ultimately live the good life for thousands of years. When Jerome Frank developed his theory, he intentionally made it broad enough to include how people change and how they are healed over all times and cultures. Aldous Huxley coined the term "perennial philosophy" to describe philosophical and psychological themes that arise repeatedly across human experience. The dilemma that psychology currently faces is not a new dilemma for the perennial philosophy. When psychologist Sheldon Kopp wrote a book entitled *If You Meet the Buddha on the Road, Kill Him*, he was referring to the principle that taking abstractions too literally can minimize both human progress and the attempt to discern truth. In sum, philosophers of various stripes have been critiquing literalism—believing we are in fundamental reality when we are actually in constructed reality—for generations. Integrating some of these older answers into our current research and outcome dilemma can be helpful in pointing the way.

That said, at the end of the day this is a clinical book with concrete suggestions aimed at actually enhancing therapeutic outcomes. It may appear that we have to detour down a few philosophical byways to understand "water" and the nature of our implicit assumptions. But I attempt to minimize the detours, to use common sense language, and to ground examples in clinical cases from my own practice and others.

Take a moment to stop and speculate. Assume that we are operating in constructed reality, a fluid and amorphous environment where the rules and values of the culture are made up, an environment which is held in place by social consensus, and an environment that can be meaningfully altered by key, charismatic individuals. Given this profound change in perspective, how might you train new psychologists? And how would you help existing psychologists move from average performance to superior performance?

The purpose of this book is to speculate on what is possible when we accept that psychotherapy operates in constructed reality. And, since the concepts of constructionism are already intertwined in every aspect of our lives and in every therapeutic encounter, it is relatively easy to use clinical examples and outcomes to support and extend the speculation. Thomas Kuhn tells us: "Though the world does not change with a change of paradigm, the scientist afterward works in a different world. . . . I am convinced that we must learn to make sense of statements that at least resemble these" (1962, p. 120). In this sense, the purpose of this book is to invite the reader to enter a different world—a world of new possibilities, a world that opens the doors to enhanced therapeutic outcomes.

This book divides itself into two separate but interconnected halves. The first half of this book, *The New Therapeutic Milieu*, advances the argument that psychology is operating in constructed reality not in fundamental reality. This first half also provides a description of the nature of Reality B. The second half of the book, *Enhancing Therapist Effectiveness*, focuses on developing a Reality B model of training that allows therapists to profit from study and experience. In addition, the second half of the book includes many vignettes and case examples all of which are presented and analyzed from a constructionist perspective. While the theoretical presentations contained in the first half of the book are necessary to analyze the research and present the theory behind Reality B, most of us learn better from stories and narratives. In this sense, the second half not only focuses on presenting a model for enhancing therapist outcomes, it also allows the paradigm shift presented in the first half to assume a human form. It's appropriate to say that the first half is about the nature of "water" and the second half explores the ways that understanding water can enhance clinical outcomes.

And, since we are about to explore the nature of water—and the secret knowledge—let us close with a relevant quote from the movie *The Matrix*.

Have you ever had a dream, Neo, that you were so sure was real? What if you were unable to wake from that dream, Neo? How would you know the difference between the dream world and the real world?

—Morpheus (Silver, Wachowski, & Wachowski, 1999)

*Part I*

# THE NEW THERAPEUTIC MILIEU

Mundus vult decipi; ego decipiatur (The world wishes to be deceived; therefore let it be deceived)

—Petronus, *The Book of Quotations* (1907)

# Chapter 1

# Psychology's Inconvenient Truths

"You will not apply my precept," he said, shaking his head. "How often have I said to you that when you have eliminated the impossible, whatever remains, *however improbable*, must be the truth?"

—Sir Arthur Conan Doyle, *The Sign of the Four*,
Sherlock Holmes (1890)

Psychological research is famous for studies that confirm common sense and generate expected results: trauma in early life leads to higher risk for pathology in later life, abusing your spouse verbally or physically puts your marriage at risk, the children of the elite have better options and outcomes than the children of the poor, and so on. But there are a series of research results from the therapy outcome literature that are completely unexpected; when they are taken seriously, these results have radical and disturbing implications.

The study that embodies these results most succinctly occurred almost forty years ago. In 1979 Han Strupp and Suzanne Hadley published a study showing that "understanding" college professors were able to achieve the same level of therapeutic effectiveness as "highly experienced," licensed therapists when doing therapy with neurotics. This study created quite the intellectual storm. Its direct implication was that psychological training and experience were insignificant. The possible inferences went even further. Since experienced therapists have access to specialized professional knowledge—for example, they understand the nature and characteristics of anxiety and depression better than the lay person—it implies that this special knowledge fails to contribute to outcomes. Since the experienced therapists know psychotherapeutic techniques—and the professors do not—it implies that psychotherapeutic techniques fail to contribute to outcomes. And, since the

17

experienced therapists understand psychological theories like psychodynamic psychotherapy and cognitive behavioral therapy (CBT), it implies that all that has been studied, researched, and written about those areas also fail to contribute to therapy. Put another way, it argues that a person who has read a book on life coaching can hang out a shingle and get the same outcome as a licensed therapist with twenty years of experience in the room. It argues that a recovering alcoholic who has gone to some Alcoholics Anonymous (AA) meetings can match the outcomes of the psychologist with years of experience treating substance abuse.

These ideas are appalling for psychotherapy; essentially they remove most of the rationale for calling it a profession. Given the gravity of the implications, one would think that the Strupp results would generate numerous studies attempting to refute its conclusions; after all, if the conclusions are allowed to stand, they would fundamentally disrupt virtually all of psychology's[1] claims. Interestingly, while there has been some research looking at the Strupp claims, in comparison to the search for new techniques, for example, the examination of the effects of training and experience has been somewhat limited and circumscribed. However, there are sufficient studies to draw conclusions about whether the Strupp results are accurate. And, unfortunately for psychology, the answer is "yes, the results have been sustained."

Some of the most important studies in the experience area are meta-analyses; meta-analyses combine the results from many studies using statistical models in an attempt to achieve more accurate conclusions. Leon, Martinovich, Lutz, and Lyons (2005) summarize these meta-analysis results as follows.

> As part of the classic meta-analysis by Smith and Glass (1977) demonstrating the overall effectiveness of psychotherapy, these researchers examined whether years of experience as a therapist correlated with outcome. The authors found that years of experience correlated -.01 with effect size (Smith and Glass, 1977). In their 1980 meta-analysis of 485 studies, the correlation was again zero (Smith, Glass & Miller, 1980). Shapiro and Shapiro (1982) conducted another meta-analysis in response to the criticisms made of the meta-analysis of Smith et al. Sample therapists had an average of three years of experience. Despite improvement in their meta-analysis, these researchers again failed to find a correlation between years of experience and effect size. (p. 417)

These and other meta-analyses were referred to in the following quote from the "Bible" of the therapy outcome literature, *Bergin and Garfield's Handbook of Psychotherapy and Behavioral Change.*

> [O]verall, the meta-analytic reviews of psychotherapy that have provided correlational data find little evidence for a relationship between experience and outcome. (Lambert & Ogles, 2004, p. 169)

Statisticians and behavioral science researchers are always quick to point out that correlation does not equal causation. Sometimes when there is a positive correlation between two factors the causal connection is actually due to a third factor. However, the converse finding—the absence of a connection or correlation—is often more convincing. In this case, the various meta-analyses examined a large number of client outcomes and analyzed those outcomes against therapist experience. The larger the sample size, the more sensitive the research in terms of finding even small effects. In this sense, the complete absence of an experience effect is meaningful and convincing and, of course, troubling.

The next edition (2013) of *Bergin and Garfield's Handbook of Psychotherapy and Behavioral Change* took another look at the question of experience. Hill and Knox, in their review of the experience and training literature, noted that while there have been a number of studies of therapist experience that showed small positive experience effects, there have been other studies showing no effect and even a few studies showing the superiority of beginners. These contradictory findings are fairly normal in the outcome literature and are usually interpreted as evidence that there are weak or no effects. In support of that, Hill and Knox cite the two recent, larger studies which directly address the question.

Two recent analyses of very large numbers of therapists perhaps provide the most definitive evidence about therapist experience. Wampold and Brown (2005) found no effects for therapist experience level (years of practice) when they analyzed the outcomes of 6,146 clients seen by 581 therapists in a managed care setting (all therapists were postdegree). Similarly, Okiishi et al. (2006) found no effects of therapist experience level (pre-internship, internship, post-internship) on the speed of client improvement in their study of more than 5,000 clients seen by 71 therapists at a university counseling center. (Hill & Knox, 2013, p. 797)

At this point the available evidence suggests that the "no experience" finding of the Strupp study has been sustained.

The training effect literature is weaker than the experience literature but has many of the same characteristics. In the same summary article, Hill and Knox cite studies showing small positive effects of training and other studies showing no effects. They go into some detail describing a study by Anderson et al., essentially replicating Strupp, which found that graduate students from other disciplines got the same results as clinical psychology graduate students when doing therapy. This weak and contradictory literature led to the following conclusion: "The results of these studies certainly do not provide direct evidence for the effectiveness of training; in fact, they call into question the very necessity of this training" (2013, p. 799).

Scott Miller is a psychologist who has played a central role in terms of looking at the implications of the therapy outcome literature. Here is his summary of the effects of training.

> Findings from a large, long-term multinational study of behavioral health practitioners confirm that therapists desire to—and see themselves—as continually improving throughout their careers.
>
> When researchers examine the evidence, however, they find little proof of increasing expertise. As just one example, in a comparative study of licensed doctoral-level providers, pre-doctoral interns, and practicum students that appeared in last spring's Journal of Counseling and Development, Scott Nyman, Mark Nafziger, and Timothy Smith found "the extensive efforts involved in educating graduate students to become licensed professionals result in *no observable differences* in client outcome."
>
> The problem isn't that professionals are failing to acquire new knowledge or skills: the problem is that what's learned is unrelated to improved outcomes. (Miller & Hubble 2011, p. 30)

And here is Miller's summary of both training and experience effects across the professional spectrum.

> You can't do better therapy by attending workshops and you can't improve your therapy skills while doing therapy. (Thomas, 2014, p. 1)

The literature has essentially sustained the initial findings of the Strupp study. The subsequent half century of research finds weak or no effects for therapist experience or therapist training on client outcomes.

Now, that we have briefly reviewed the experience and training literature, let us look at some of the additional implications of the Strupp study. Experienced therapists know techniques, they have studied the differing philosophies of the schools of therapy, and they have been trained in specific information about diagnostic categories and client characteristics. In other words, they are trained and experienced in the specialized professional knowledge that defines the field of psychology. Obviously, the inability of this knowledge to enhance outcomes suggests that this knowledge holds very little or no value for client improvement. This hypothesis is even more appalling than the first. It is one thing to argue that training and experience provide no benefit, but it is another thing to postulate that all the accumulated theories, techniques, and specialized knowledge should be discarded. This leaves psychology as an empty container; virtually all the ideas and research are judged as irrelevant and the field is required to essentially start from scratch.

To examine this upsetting hypothesis, let's look at the research from a different angle. Historically, for psychology the most pressing question has been "does psychotherapy work?" Happily the thousands of studies that have been done on that question have answered it in the affirmative: psychotherapy is, in fact, effective. Scott Miller comments:

> The average treated client in most studies published over the last 40 years is better off than 80 percent of those that do not have the benefit of treatment. By the way, such results are not limited to tightly controlled randomized clinical trials but apply to practitioners in real-world settings. A soon-to-be published study examined the outcomes of practicing clinicians (working, for the most part, in California) and found they either met, or exceeded, the outcomes reported in randomized clinical trials. The therapists in the study were a diverse group (professional counselors, psychologists, social workers, marriage and family therapists, and psychiatrists) working in diverse ways (using a variety of approaches) with a diverse population. Unlike most randomized clinical trials, the clients weren't limited to a single diagnosis. Co-morbidity was the rule, not the exception. The bottom line is that most therapists do good work. (Walt, 2007)

The next most pressing question has to do with the superiority of one approach over another. Is psychodynamic therapy superior to CBT, for example? In general, one would expect one school of therapy to be better than another. After all, they are based on vastly different assumptions and the techniques differ significantly as well. In spite of this logic, however, the research results reveal the unexpected. Returning to Bergin and Garfield's Handbook, Lambert and Ogle (2004) summarize:

> Although there are a large number of therapies, each containing its own ratio-nale and specific techniques, there is little evidence to suggest the superiority of one school over another. (Lambert & Ogles, 2004, p. 171)

This finding of no significant differences between schools and treatments has been found again and again. It is humorously referred to as the dodo bird effect.

> The conclusion of most, but not all, of these reviews is similar to that drawn by Luborsky, Singer, and Luborsky (1975) who suggested a verdict similar to that of the Dodo bird in Alice in Wonderland: "Everyone has won and all must have prizes." . . . However, meta-analytic methods have now been extensively applied to large groups of comparative studies, and these reviews generally offer similar conclusions, that is, little or no difference between therapies. (Lambert & Ogles, 2004, p. 161)

This is not limited to general outcome studies but also includes techniques that are especially designed for specific populations. Scott Miller summarizes:

Also, and more importantly, when the appropriate analyses of the research are done between so-called "evidence-based practices" and any other approach that's intended to be therapeutic—now listen to that—any approach that's intended to be therapeutic, you don't find any difference in outcome between those approaches. I know this can be hard to believe given the current zeitgeist. Unfortunately, at the state and federal oversight level, and for an increasing number of clinicians, it has somehow become "known" that certain treatments work best for clients with certain diagnoses. For people diagnosed with so-called "Borderline Personality Disorder," Dialectical Behavior Therapy is the "best practice" when, in fact, available evidence indicates that it works as well as everything else. . . .

Now, I'm not saying that DBT is not effective or that therapists shouldn't learn about it, or other approaches. Rather, the point here is something that most therapists know intuitively: all approaches work with some people some of the time. The challenge for the practicing clinician is, therefore, not figuring out what approach works for which diagnosis, but what will work for this person sitting with me on this day at this stage in their life. (Walt, 2007, pp. 81–87)

These conclusions are vigorously debated by practitioners who are eager to find specific treatments for specific disorders, so-called evidence-based treatment. While these practitioners can point to some studies that demonstrate that one technique is better than another for very specific situations, once these techniques are compiled into a manual and formed into an empirically derived system, that complex system performs equivalently to other complex systems such as cognitive or psychodynamic. Hubble, Duncan, Miller, and Wampold, in their review of manualized treatment programs, state:

Notwithstanding, after more than 40 years of research, evidence that specific ingredients are needed for resolving particular disorders remains conspicuously missing. The conclusion is inescapable: "Psychotherapy does not work in the same way as medicine." . . . Bluntly put, the existence of specific psychological treatments for specific disorders is a myth. (Duncan, Miller, Wampold, & Hubble, 2010, Kindle Locations 1023–1027)

Finally, some optimistic psychologists argue that we are always on the brink of finding a new technique that will embody all of the principles of human change and lead to a breakthrough in personal growth and healing. As an example, take Eye Movement Desensitization and Reprocessing (EMDR); especially when EMDR was first developed there were multiple stories of seemingly wonderful outcomes. Over time that has faded and the research shows that EMDR is no more effective than many other approaches for trauma. Perhaps, however, the next approach will be able to sustain the sizeable positive outcomes. Maybe mindfulness, when it is fully understood, will be the breakthrough technique. After all, it has been in use for thousands of years.

It is always possible that a wonderfully effective new technique might be discovered. Research results can never prove that the next technique won't stand up; research results can never determine the future and research results can never extinguish hope. But after seventy-five years of sustained work, it appears likely that the next creative technique, no matter how wondrous, will also prove unable to differentiate itself from the extant techniques. Wampold comments:

> Clinical trials comparing two treatments should be discontinued. Much money has been spent on clinical trials, with the same result: "Both treatments were more effective than no treatment, but there were no differences in outcomes between the two treatments." Continued research that looks at new variations of old treatments will yield little that can be transported to systems of care to improve the outcomes of clients. (Wampold 2010, Kindle Locations 2089–2092)

In conclusion, this question of "which approach is better" has been addressed in hundreds and hundreds of studies. Psychologists have been much more interested in this question than the questions about training and experience effects. Many of the studies have been conducted by practitioners who hope that their new ideas and techniques will make a contribution and move the field forward. Others simply hope to confirm that psychotherapy is a science; after all, if anything one does gets equal positive results, that result implicitly suggests psychology is not "science-based." In sum, the practitioners conducting these studies have been highly motivated and unceasing in their creative proposals for new and better ways to help clients change. And with all that effort, we are still stuck with the outcome that pretty much any credible effort to help a client change gets the same result.

Let's return to the "dodo bird" effect. While psychology has been in almost complete denial about addressing the lack of training and experience effects, there has been quite a lot of discussion about this "all treatments are essentially equivalent" concept. The primary response to these findings has been the development of common factors theory. Essentially this theory postulates the existence of "nonspecific" or "common" factors in therapy that are shared by all schools of therapy—factors which are essentially responsible for therapeutic change. The therapeutic alliance is the most oft cited common factor which Lambert and Ogles (2004) describe as "a therapeutic relationship that is characterized by trust, warmth, understanding, acceptance, kindness, and human wisdom" (p. 181). Put in simplest terms, the typical psychologist—when confronted with the dodo bird conclusion—might say, "Well, I always knew it was all about the relationship."

While many psychologists are quick to accept this argument, they fail to follow it to its logical conclusion. Common factors theory argues that clients

get better because of the power of the therapeutic alliance (nonspecific factors) plus the power of "specific factors." Specific factors are essentially all
the factors—techniques, knowledge of diagnostic categories, specialized
training, etc.—that collectively compose psychology's privileged knowledge
and the specific contributions of each school of therapy. In sum, therapists
might say that it's "all" about the relationship but very few of them actually
believe that all the specific factors are completely ineffective. If they believed
that, they would need to stop reading books, attending workshops, and giving
and receiving supervision.

If it's "all about the relationship," one quickly arrives at the placebo theory
of psychotherapy. This theory argues that if a client is motivated to get better
and approaches any helper who seems to be legitimate, the ensuing psychotherapeutic work will result in a significant and reliable therapeutic improvement. The expectation of success and the credible context create the positive
change. There is no "specialness," no magic in therapy; the belief one is
going to get better—given a credible encounter—makes one better. Therapy
is a kind of "sugar pill." Lambert and Ogles (2004) comment:

> [O]ne might conclude that the benefits of therapy are not caused by the specific
> treatments, but rather by a generalized placebo effect (i.e., that psychotherapists
> are merely "placebologists"). (p. 150)

This may be a logical conclusion but it is a hundred miles away from what
psychologists actually mean when they say, "It's all about the relationship."
Virtually no one is ready to throw away most of the work of the past century
and assert that everything actually done in the room is a credible placebo
whose specific form is insignificant.

At the risk of generating some math anxiety, common factors theory
is easily expressed with basic algebra. Where CF = common factors and
SF = techniques, theoretical orientation, and knowledge that is specific to a
particular school.

$$CF_{(the\ relationship)} + SF_{(unique\ to\ the\ school)} = Total\ Effect\ Size$$

Since the Total Effect size of every school is equal, we get the next formula.

$$CF_{(the\ relationship)} + SF_{(unique\ to\ one\ school)} = CF_{(the\ relationship)} + SF_{(unique\ to\ another\ school)}$$

Subtracting the common factors, we get.

$$SF_{(unique\ to\ one\ school)} = SF_{(unique\ to\ another\ school)}$$

This simple bit of algebra shows that the dodo bird effect implies that the effect size due to specific factors of any school of therapy is exactly equal to the effect size due to specific factors of any other school.

There are two possibilities here: either the specific factors are important and significant (greater than zero) or the specific factors equal zero. The idea that the specific factors are important immediately runs into a logical issue. More specifically, how can the schools of therapy achieve equal results when their assumptions and techniques differ so significantly? For example, psychodynamic psychotherapy emphasizes the power of the unconscious mind while cognitive behavioral approaches formally deny it. One would think that one of those schools is correct—or at least closer to reality—and that their results would, therefore, be superior. But even on this most basic assumption about the importance/irrelevance of the unconscious, the research results say, "no significant differences." Similarly, the humanistic/existential schools are based on assumptions about the inherent health and completeness of each human being. Contrast that with the psychodynamic school which prioritizes the core importance of human trauma and psychopathology. Shouldn't this large difference in assumptions result in outcome differences? Finally, systems theories see individuals as embedded in and strongly affected by families and larger systems. If in fact humans are social animals whose every choice is affected by social context, shouldn't that approach get better outcomes than schools that look solely at the individual? Finally, recall that the dodo bird effect is not limited to the four major schools of psychotherapy; the Wampold recommendation for no more comparative outcome studies includes the observation that thirty or forty "minor" psychotherapy schools also get exactly the same positive effect. In sum, given these substantial differences in philosophy, techniques, and specific knowledge, it is highly unlikely that the effect sizes would be exactly equal to each other.

When you add the finding that training and experience do not contribute to increased effectiveness the conclusions become clear. If the systems actually contributed to the effect size, via different but equivalent principles, then people who studied the systems would be more effective than change agents who have not studied the systems. Trained therapists should best the untrained if the systems have anything concrete to offer. However, the research does not demonstrate that superiority. And, recall the literature summary from Wampold above, "Bluntly put, the existence of specific psychological treatments for specific disorders is a myth."

The dodo bird effect goes past Strupp and implies that the power of techniques is not responsible for change. This in turn suggests that understanding the worldview of each system—for example, the nature of the psyche according to systems theory—also fails to contribute. And, finally, even specific knowledge about clients—how alcoholics differ from "normies," for example—also fails to contribute.

Before attempting to integrate these conclusions, it is useful to perform one more analysis, this one from the perspective of differing professions. Each profession or trade is defined by its own privileged knowledge; generally this knowledge consists of techniques and specialized information that is unavailable to a lay member of the culture. Typically, this privileged knowledge is so important that one cannot function in the profession without it. And it is large enough that the practitioner cannot master it completely during training; it requires years of practice and continued effort to become an expert practitioner. Take the simple example of a car mechanic. A lay person will be unable to rebuild an engine without training. And there are so many cars with so many features—that is, the extent of specialized knowledge is large—that the master mechanic will always best the beginning mechanic. If we were conducting research on the effects of training as a mechanic, it would be easy to demonstrate an enormous effect size from training and an equally large effect size from experience.

Most professions and trades have these qualities. A lay person can't calculate the thrust necessary to put a satellite into orbit; one must be a trained physicist or engineer. A lay person can't design a new CPU or evaluate the strengths and weaknesses of the existing CPUs on the market. A researcher in these fields might ask a question like "which training model works best for learning to be a mechanic?" but they would never waste time asking if training is better than no training. The answer is so obvious that it is unnecessary to even ask the question.

Now imagine that we are taking a look at training effects in high school math teachers. For this exercise, imagine that they are all competent mathematicians; that is, they have already mastered math at a high school level and we are only looking at their teaching abilities. How is learning to teach different than learning to be a cardiac surgeon?

First, in teaching—as opposed to the professions we have reviewed thus far—a lay person will do just fine. If one knows high school math, training is not required to teach students the subject. Moreover, beginners will probably equal experienced teachers and in some cases their performance might surpass that of the experienced. We are all familiar with the brand new teacher who is so fired up and so connected to the students that they do an excellent job right off the bat. We all know teachers who have retired from their previous job and teach for the love of teaching who also do an exceptional job without any specialized training in how to be an educator. And we all know experienced teachers whose years in the field fail to guarantee superior performance. In sum, education seems to belong in a completely different category than the first fields we reviewed.

And there are a number of other fields similar to teaching. For example, leadership, organizational management, and sales are all fields where training is neither necessary nor documented as effective. Moreover, in those fields, experience fails to guarantee superior performance.

If we were to speculate on the differences between the two types of professions—the ones with training effects and the ones without—we might come up with theories like: the first group of professions are concerned with mastering the material world and the second group is concerned with complex human interactions. One could also argue that the first type of field fits the scientific model and the second type is incompatible with it. In this book, we are going to use the terminology of professions that operate in fundamental reality versus professions that focus on socially constructed reality. The next two chapters will be devoted to defining and understanding the difference between those two terms.

What are the implications for psychotherapy of this analysis of professions? First psychology has been endeavoring to become a field of the first type. All the research, all the diagnostic categories, all the theoretical models, and all the development of techniques are an attempt to manufacture privileged knowledge that will serve to differentiate the psychological professional from the lay person. Second, the research results prove that psychology has failed to accumulate meaningful privileged knowledge in spite of all this effort. Third, psychology presents itself to the public as a profession with privileged knowledge and the public talks about psychology in that manner. For example, the public believes that training and experience enhance outcomes and that there are specific treatments for specific disorders. Fourth, even when psychologists know the research, the dodo bird effect, and psychology's similarity to teaching and leadership, its practitioners also believe that it is a first type profession that can be explored and enhanced through the scientific method.

Accepting these facts requires the reader to move from a Reality A perspective to Reality B. In Reality A, the assumptions of psychology—that it is a scientific profession with significant privileged knowledge—hold true. In Reality B psychology is revealed as a type 2 profession that will require a different kind of paradigm. Two factors give rise to optimism. First, psychotherapy works. Second, the research clearly shows that some therapists get significantly better results than others. Taken together these two factors imply that we can take a model that is already working, make it better, and then train therapists to enhance their results.

However, these possible outcomes rest on an important first step: we must accept that we are in Reality B. As long as the vast majority of psychology's resources are focused on a futile attempt to prove that we are a type 1 profession—that we operate in the material world and that our primary tool is the scientific method—we will continue to repeat the lack of progress that characterizes psychology at this point. Scott Miller describes our current level of evolution:

> During the last few decades, more than 10,000 "how to" books on psychotherapy have been published. At the same time, the number of treatment approaches has mushroomed, going from around 60 in the early days to more than 400. There are presently 145 officially approved, manualized, evidence-based treatments for 51 of the 397 possible DSM diagnostic groups. Based on these numbers alone, one would be hard-pressed not to believe that real progress has been made by the field. More than ever before, we know what works for whom. Or do we?
>
> Comparing today's success rates with those of 10, 20, or 30 years ago is a way of finding out. One would expect that the profession is progressing in a manner comparable to the Olympics. Its fans know that during the last century, the best performance for every event has improved—in some cases, by as much as 50%. What's more, excellence at the top has had a trickle-down effect, improving performance at every level. The fastest time clocked for the marathon in the 1896 Olympics was just 1 min. faster than the time currently required just to participate in the most competitive marathons like Boston and Chicago. *By contrast, no measurable improvement in the effectiveness of psychotherapy has occurred in the last 30 years.*
>
> The time is come to confront the unpleasant truth: our tried and true strategies for improving what we do have failed. Instead of advancing as a field, we've stagnated, mistaking our feverish pedaling on a stationary bicycle for progress in the Tour de Therapy. (Miller, Hubble, & Duncan, 2007, p. 31)

We're going to need to accept the research results and the analysis of professions, work to understand the fact that psychology operates in Reality B, and use those insights to enhance our results.

Let's take a closer look at the widespread denial inside psychology about these results. Consider for a moment just how profound the denial of psychology has been. The research results are not secret; the Strupp study was widely discussed back in 1979, the Bergin and Garfield quotes are from the most well-known summary of outcome research, and Miller and his colleges have been disseminating his primary conclusions via books, articles, workshops, and keynote speeches. It takes only a moment of reflection to perform the analysis of professions and recognize that psychology essentially has no privileged knowledge. Given how easy it is to put these arguments together, the inability to do so suggests that there are powerful forces in the collective and individual psyche that resist such conclusions. Identifying and understanding those forces are an important first step toward mastering Reality B.

## BUILDING AND SUSTAINING WORLDVIEWS

Man can seldom—very, very, seldom—fight a winning fight against
his training; the odds are too heavy.

—Mark Twain, *Europe and Elsewhere* (1923)

It is common knowledge that humans are expert at ignoring information that
would contradict a comfortable worldview. In fact, the comic and political
commentator, Bill Maher, finds this human tendency so amusing that he
makes it a central part of his comedic approach. Maher calls this tendency
to filter out disconfirming information "living in the Bubble." To Maher, the
Bubble is a cognitive filter which allows "Republicans" to maintain stable
political beliefs and to discount any facts which might threaten those beliefs.

Winston Churchill once said in wartime, "the truth is protected by a bodyguard
of lies." In America today, Republican voters are protected by a bodyguard of
"duh"—a thick shell of super hardened bullshit, a membrane so tough that the
only thing that gets in is FOX news and the only things that come out are mis-
spelled signs and babies.

Has this ever happened to you: you go home for Thanksgiving and your uncle
from Ohio is there, who you thought was normal, but soon the discussion turns
to politics and he says, "that Barack Obama wants to use the UN to seize our
guns and give them to his Negro army of ACORN volunteers." And you think,
"What! Where is he even getting this stuff?"

Trying to get today's Republican to accept basic facts is like trying to get
your dog to take a pill. You have to feed them the truth wrapped in a piece
of baloney, hold their snouts shut and stroke their throats. And even then, just
when you think they've swallowed it, they spit it out on the linoleum. Gore
called his project "24 hours of reality" and that's the problem. Half the country
doesn't believe in reality. (Maher, 2011)

Obviously a Republican commentator might argue that Democrats have
an equivalent bubble and they would certainly have a point. For the purposes
of this book however it is not Republicans versus Democrats; rather, it is
Maher's witty yet painfully accurate description of how people resist learning from experience. Could something equivalent be operating in the therapy
room and be responsible for therapists' inability to learn from thousands of
hours of direct contact with patients?

Fortunately, Nobel Prize winning psychologist Daniel Kahneman has writ-
ten a book which precisely addresses this question. The title of his book is
*Thinking, Fast and Slow* but it easily could have been entitled *How People
Build Comprehensive Realities from Limited Data; then Rationalize Them,*

*and Finally Deny All Contradictory Information*. In his book, Kahneman gives a number of examples of how the "Bubble" functions.

His first example consists of a consultation with a Wall Street wealth management firm. This firm was both prestigious and successful and literally had hundreds of millions of dollars under management. End of year bonuses for the specific money managers were awarded based on each manager's performance for the year. Prior to his formal consultation meeting with the firm's executives, Kahneman was given the performance data for the top twenty-five money managers over the past eight years.

Unfortunately for the managers, Kahneman's statistical analyses revealed a zero correlation between performance from one year to the next. In other words, his statistics proved that the advisors had no skill at all at stock picking and money management and their results were solely due to chance. The quote below, where Kahneman reports these results to the firm's top executives, is a perfect example of a "Bubble," of people filtering information in a way that leaves their current view of reality intact and unaffected by the new information. Kahneman began by asking the executives to estimate the correlation between performance and the managers.

> They thought they knew what was coming and smiled as they said "not very high" or "performance certainly fluctuates." It quickly became clear, however, that no one expected the average correlation to be zero.
>
> Our message to the executives was that, at least when it came to building portfolios, the firm was rewarding luck as if it were skill. This should have been shocking news to them, but it was not. There was no sign that they disbelieved us. How could they? After all, we had analyzed their own results, and they were sophisticated enough to see the implications, which we politely refrained from spelling out. We all went on calmly with our dinner, and I have no doubt that both our findings and their implications were quickly swept under the rug and that life in the firm went on just as before. The illusion of skill is not only an individual aberration; it is deeply ingrained in the culture of the industry. Facts that challenge such basic assumptions—and thereby threaten people's livelihood and self-esteem—are simply not absorbed. The mind does not digest them. (Kahneman, 2013, p. 216)

This is a perfect description of the "Bubble"—of living life with active filters which preclude one from learning from experience. Kahneman is arguing that the filters automatically kick into effect when there is a threat to "livelihood and self-esteem." Accepting this new information that the firm and its advisors are a complete fraud and that they add nothing of value to the management of their clients' wealth is an unacceptable truth. Before proceeding and allowing Kahneman to explain the mechanisms of filtering, it is helpful to look at another example of the "Bubble" in a different context.

Kahneman reports that he had a job in the Israeli army as a psychology officer where he was responsible for evaluating candidates for officer training. He and others in his group would watch the candidates run through field exercises designed to show leadership, being a team player, perseverance, feedback skills, and so on. After observing these exercises, Kahneman and his colleagues would meet, discuss their results, and make their recommendations about the suitability of each candidate for officer training.

> Because our impressions of how well each soldier had performed were generally coherent and clear, our formal predictions were just as definite. A single score usually came to mind and we rarely experienced doubts or formed conflicting impressions. (Kahneman, 2013, p. 211)

They received feedback later about how the candidates were doing and were surprised to find that their rankings were almost completely incorrect; the officers' subsequent performances essentially had a negligible correlation with Kahneman's predictions. He reports that they were initially depressed about these results but quickly recovered. The army still required them to use the obstacle field and rank the new candidates. And again, the quality of leadership seemed apparent to Kahneman. In spite of the information that their estimates had low correlations with actual performance, he had the same confidence that his results could be trusted.

Once again we see the operation of the Bubble: the fact that performance on the field exercise had little or no power to predict officer effectiveness was disregarded due to the seductive clarity of the present experience. The key word here is "seductive." Kahneman goes to some pains in a different part of his book to describe the human tendency to confidently generalize from one small piece of information to large conclusions. It's as if the mind has a tendency to build worlds that are coherent and make sense. If we don't have enough information to accurately predict or describe a world, we will still act as if we have enough. Apparently, we have a compulsion to build a complete worldview regardless of how little we know and ultimately, in spite of how inaccurate our world turns out to be. And after this world is built—regardless of how shaky its foundations might be—we have great confidence in it. Not only are we sure of its implications, but the longer we work with it, the more it dominates our perspective. Over time we lose the ability to see the data from any other point of view.

In order to explain these Bubble effects, Kahneman presents a two part model of the mind which he calls System 1 and System 2. System 1 corresponds to "thinking fast" and System 2 corresponds to "thinking slow." System 2 is easier to describe and understand. It specializes in effortful, analytical, mathematical, logical, and rational reasoning—hence, thinking "slow." Kahneman states:

> System 2 allocates attention to the effortful mental activities that demand it, including complex computations. The operations of System 2 are often associated with the subjective experience of agency, choice, and concentration. (Kahneman, 2013, p. 21)

Later in this book we will review some key parts of the work of Allan Schore, noted neuroscientist, who also has a two part model of the mind. In Schore's model, Kahneman's System 2 corresponds to what he calls "left brain" activity. Schore goes further and suggests that left brain corresponds to Conscious Mind. As one would expect, in Schore's terminology, Kahneman's System 1 corresponds to "right brain" and Unconscious Mind.

Kahneman himself studiously avoids those terms from neuroscience and psychodynamic psychotherapy; he notes, "The use of such language is considered a sin in the professional circles in which I travel," (p. 28) and limits himself to more objective descriptions of System 1 and System 2. The first thing Kahneman says about System 1 is that it "operates automatically and quickly, with little or no effort and no sense of voluntary control" (p. 20). System 1 is responsible for quick assessments of danger versus safety, friend versus enemy, desirable versus undesirable. It stores stereotypes, assumptions, associations, and snap judgments and effortlessly overlays them on the world.

Kahneman believes that System 1 was evolved to fulfill an evolutionary purpose of keeping us safe both physically and emotionally. The physical safety is straightforward: System 1 is biased toward determining threatening versus unthreatening situations quickly and effortlessly. Kahneman presents a great deal of research showing that this threat assessment isn't rational and reasonable; rather, System 1 is designed to overweight the threat of every situation and irrationally prioritizes the sure thing and avoidance of pain over healthy risk taking.

Not only does System 1 keep us safe from physical dangers, it also keeps us emotionally safe and relatively free from anxiety by developing a worldview that is cohesive and predictable. Kahneman describes the worldview creation aspect of System 1 as follows.

> The main function of System 1 is to maintain and update a model of your personal world, which represents what is normal in it. The model is constructed by associations that link ideas of circumstances, events, actions and outcomes that co-occur with some regularity, either at the same time or within a relatively short interval. As these links are formed and strengthen, the pattern of associated ideas comes to represent the structure of events in your life, and it determines

your interpretation of the present as well as your expectations of the future. (Kahneman, 2013, p. 71)

This worldview function is every bit as important as the risk avoiding function; human beings become paralyzed and terrified when directly exposed to chaos and unpredictability. The sense that "anything can happen" creates profound anxiety in most people. The belief that the world is unordered and unpredictable can even create paralysis and a fugue state. It is something to be avoided at all costs. Kahneman comments:

> The sense-making machinery of System 1 makes us see the world as more tidy, simple, predictable, and coherent than it really is. The illusion that one has understood the past feeds the further illusion that one can predict and control the future. These illusions are comforting. They reduce the anxiety that we would experience if we allowed ourselves to fully acknowledge the uncertainties of existence. We all have a need for the reassuring message that actions have appropriate consequences, and that success will reward wisdom and courage. (Kahneman, 2013, pp. 204–205)

The beneficial functioning of System 2 is obvious; that kind of effortful thinking allows humans to plan, to calculate and estimate the future more rationally and carefully, and to figure out connections and patterns which are not apparent to the "jump to conclusions-oriented" System 1. Regardless of these strengths, Kahneman calls System 1 the "hero" of his book. He believes that in spite of System 1's weaknesses and flaws, it dominates human judgment and decision-making. Furthermore, while humans pride themselves on identifying with System 2 functioning, and consider themselves rational and reasonable, in truth, the vast majority of our judgments and decisions about the world are determined by System 1. And, while System 2 occasionally overrules System 1, far more often System 2 simply lets the judgments of System 1 slide by.

Even more significantly, System 2 functions as a justifier of the System 1 assessments. Kahneman literally believes that "[i]n the context of attitudes, however, System 2 is more of an apologist for the emotions of System 1 than a critic of those emotions—an endorser rather than an enforcer" (Kahneman, 2013, p. 103). In sum, the worldview formation process stands rationality on its head. Instead of starting with a rational and logical weighing of the alternatives and then forming a conclusion, people make the judgment based on System 1's feelings and then use System 2's logic and left brain rationality to justify the decision. This is sufficiently important to be reemphasized. Kahneman believes that people form cohesive and irrational worldviews based on System 1 "gut feelings" and then, afterward, use their rational and articulate System 2 to justify them. We paper over our irrational assumptions with rational justifications.

To further illustrate the contrast between System 1 and System 2, Kahneman uses the example of an optical illusion. Consider the figure below.

As one might expect, all three dogs are the same height, a fact which can easily be verified by a ruler. It is one of the functions of System 1 to make

**Figure 1.1**   Image created by Aidan Barcia-Bacon.

quick judgments about relative size. And System 1 insists that the dog on the right is much larger than the dog on the left. Even after System 2 measures the figures and verifies that they are equal, System 1 continues to see the size of the figures as different. It is a simple example of how one can know a fact through the operation of System 2 and continue to "feel" as if a different "fact" were true via System 1. The System 2 findings do not automatically supersede the System 1 "truth" even when it clearly describes reality more accurately. Very few people can "see" the dogs as the same height.

Of course, the drawing is not simply an example, it is also an analogy. Just as one cannot "see the truth" about the dogs even after applying the ruler, similarly the financial advisors were unable to absorb the truth about their lack of skill in spite of the convincing statistics. And Kahneman specifically noted how the psychology officers, including himself, were unable to abandon the sense that their field exercises predicted leadership even after they had solid feedback proving that their predictions were inaccurate.

Even in the simple example of the optical illusion above, it is almost impossible to absorb a System 2 finding when it is in contradiction with System 1. Given that difficulty, what chance is there that an individual can discount a System 1 certainty when the facts are more ambiguous and complicated than a ruler and an optical illusion. How often does a Democrat succeed at converting a Republican through a System 2-type discussion? And, more relevant to our analysis, how easy is it to let go of the feeling that one's psychotherapy system of choice—be it psychodynamic, systems, or humanistic-existential—accurately and completely describes the inner world of the psyche? The even more compelling question concerns the value of experience. How easy is it to absorb that experience fails to make me a better therapist when experience improves performance in so many other areas of my life. The feeling that experience improves my performance trumps the System 2 rationality of the research results.

The research findings may be logical and compelling but, because of the power of System 1, I cannot absorb them. Although the research facts have been well known for many years, they have yet to be integrated into either psychology training models or psychology practice models. And, without great personal effort, it is likely that this lack of integration will continue.

Let us add one final example from the psychotherapy field. Barry Michels is the co-author of the best-selling psychotherapy book *The Tools*. In the first chapter of his book, Michels describes his view of the psychotherapy bubble in a way that illustrates the power of System 1 in psychotherapy supervision. His example brings to mind the old saying "if all you have is a hammer, then everything is a nail." Michels has approached his two supervisors about a new client, Roberta, who wants help dealing with an uncomfortable feeling. Notice how Michels' supervisors insist on fitting all data into their preexisting model.

I described Roberta's demand to them. Their response confirmed my worst fears. They had no solution. Worse, what seemed to me like a reasonable request, they saw as part of her problem. They used a lot of clinical terms: Roberta was "impulsive," "resistant," and "craved immediate gratification." If I tried to meet her immediate needs, they warned me, she would actually become more demanding. Unanimously, they advised me to guide her back to her childhood—there we would find what caused the obsession in the first place. I told them she already knew why she was obsessed. Their answer was that her father's abandonment couldn't be the real reason. "You have to go even deeper into her childhood." I was fed up with this runaround: I'd heard it before—every time a patient made a direct request, the therapist would turn it back on the patient and tell him or her to "go deeper." It was a shell game they used to hide the truth: when it came to immediate help, these therapists had very little to give to their patients. Not only was I disappointed, I had the sinking feeling that my supervisors were speaking for the entire psychotherapeutic profession—certainly I'd never heard anyone say anything else. I didn't know where to turn. (Stutz & Michels, 2012, p. 4)

Note that Michels talks about a "shell game to hide the truth." This is not a statement about poor ethics, it is clear that Michels sees his supervisors as sincere people. Rather it is a statement about an implicit blindness which becomes apparent when one looks at a System 1 decision from a System 2 standpoint. Michels has come to believe that experienced psychotherapists—his respected supervisors—have created a worldview that takes any input from the client and slots it into preexisting categories. In this example, the existing categories are psychodynamic and he is urged to go deeper into the client's childhood experiences whether this approach works or not. He also describes how the implicit worldview discounts information about what works and what doesn't. And Michels has almost no chance of helping his supervisors see their limitations; System 1 makes them comfortable with their choices and perspectives.

The parallels between the different Bubble stories are fairly obvious. The varying worldviews are established with the primary goal of making the worldview creator feel safe and making his world predictable and comfortable. However, instead of admitting the real purpose, the worldviews are sold, marketed, and rationalized as being true, accurate, and effective maps of reality. Maher's Republicans claim they evaluate political facts and come to educated and enlightened conclusions; Maher believes they pretend to be rational but are using their worldview to be stable, safe, and comfortable. The money managers say they are using their skills to invest their clients' wealth and achieve returns that an unskilled investor could not match; analyses show that their skills are nonexistent and they are using market variability to hide their ineffectiveness. The Israeli psychology team claims to have insight into potential officer effectiveness but ignores the fact that their field exercises are poor metaphors for leadership. And the senior psychotherapists are more interested in maintaining their positions and opinions than in actually meeting the needs of their clients or addressing the real concerns of their supervisee. Interestingly in all four examples the actual situations are so ambiguous that it is hard to prove that the worldview creators are ineffective and fraudulent. Predicting good officer candidates, having the right political opinion, managing money in an up and down market, and defining real therapeutic change are all tricky. The worldview creators can easily justify their positions as rational and accurate. And one can imagine that it would be almost impossible to win an argument with the worldview creators about the validity of their positions, especially when abandoning their positions would hurt their livelihood or status or create a sense of chaos and anxiety.

As a way to summarize this section, let us imagine that a psychologist who has expertise in ethics has been asked to write an *Informed Consent Form* for all clients who are about to invest their hard-earned savings at the Wall Street firm which Kahneman mentions. The form might look something like this.

- You acknowledge that I have told you that I have no greater skills in managing your money than any lay person.
- However, because I can speak the "language" of a stock market expert, your System 1 will be led to believe that I am superior to you at money management.
- While this won't increase your financial returns, it is likely you will have a decrease in market-related anxiety "believing" that you have put your money in the hands of an "expert."

While this form fits the facts as Kahneman presents them, it will feel completely untrue to the money managers. In spite of the facts, they "know" they understand the market and they believe they bring real value to their clients. These beliefs are sustained by the fact that the markets generally go up over time, allowing the managers to "mistake luck for skill." The parallels between an upwardly biased market and the fact that most clients get better regardless of therapist, approach, and techniques are obvious.

As part of our summary, an equivalent *Informed Consent Form* can be written for psychology. Imagine that you are the director of training at a clinical psychology program. It is the first day for the new class of graduate students and they are at their first class in Systems and Theories of Psychotherapy. Because you take both the research findings and the Code of Ethics seriously, you have prepared an *Informed Consent Form* which might go something like this.

- We will teach you psychotherapy systems which will appear to be good maps of how to change people but we acknowledge that familiarity with these maps won't actually make you a more effective therapist.
- We will teach you about characteristics of different client populations but that knowledge won't actually make you a more effective therapist.
- We will provide you with hundreds of hours of client contact and supervision but those hours won't make you a more effective therapist.
- And, even though you sign this informed consent and acknowledge the accuracy of our warnings, because of the effects of System 1, part of you will continue to believe that our training program has made you a more effective therapist.

Obviously such an *Informed Consent Form* will never be produced on the first day of training for new graduate students. While Kahneman's argument that it is hard to absorb new facts when they threaten one's successes, sense of self, and livelihood is certainly true, that is not the main reason we will never see this *Informed Consent Form*. Rather, it is due to the overwhelming power of System 1.

In spite of the research findings, no clinical director would advance such a *Form* because all of psychology's systems, theories, training experiences, and supervision continue to "feel" as if they make an enormous difference even though the facts refute the feelings. Kahneman calls System 1 the "hero" of his book. Since it is obviously not the "hero" because of its accuracy, we must assume that it is the "hero" because of its power—because it allows us to function in a world permeated by chaos and danger. Few humans could get out of bed in the morning if they had to face the threats and uncertainties of their world without the comfort that System 1 provides.

I have great sympathy for our imaginary clinical director. I am one of those people who cannot see the three dogs in the optical illusion as being the same size even after I measure them. Similarly, it is very difficult for me to feel and believe that all of the psychology books that I have read and studied have failed to help me be a better therapist. Just like Kahneman's military psychology team, each time I read the "masters" in psychology—whether they be Jung, Haley, or whomever—I feel enriched, educated, strengthened, and enlightened. In spite of all those System 1 feelings, however, I do feel a responsibility to integrate the powerful and compelling research findings into my worldview.

At this point, whenever I am presenting this material in a workshop to professionals, I always stop and take questions. Remember, regardless of how convincing the research findings are to System 2, System 1 absolutely refutes them because they do not "feel true." Then, as Kahneman argues, people use System 2 arguments to prove their System 1 feelings are the "real truth."

Failing that, they will replicate the money managers in the example above and simply disregard the findings.

The first argument that is usually advanced in a workshop is that the research is so primitive that the real effects of training, experience, and psychotherapeutic systems have simply been missed. It is, of course, rather incongruent to argue that the outcome research proving therapy works should be accepted but the same research that shows training and experience do not contribute should be discounted. These critics get into the indefensible position of liking research when it supports what they believe and discounting it when it violates their System 1-related gut feelings. This argument is particularly embarrassing for psychologists who pride themselves on being science and research-based mental health professionals.

Moreover, everyone agrees the research works perfectly well when it is measuring psychological factors that are robust. For example, all the research show strong effects when it comes to documenting that trauma, poverty, and early substance abuse predict many problems later in life. The research is not too "primitive" to pick up on the effects of therapy; rather, the unique effects of specific psychological systems are too small to be documented. In addition, the research clearly demonstrates that some therapists are much more effective than others. If the research supports differential therapist effects, how can it be too primitive? Clearly the research is sophisticated enough to find robust effects when they actually exist. We need to trust that the absence of findings when it comes to the effectiveness of experience or psychotherapeutic systems is just as accurate and trustworthy.

The next argument is that trained and experienced therapists add value to their clients' lives in terms of an almost immeasurable dimension of richness or depth or core-level quality and the outcome research only focuses on crude outcomes. This critique seems to hold some validity: who can really argue that a Jungian client, who has been watching his dreams and perceiving his life as a mythological adventure is not, in some manner, living a "richer" life than the cognitive-behavioral client who has simply become a bit more "rational." Unfortunately, when this argument is extended it implies that any enriching experience is capable of improving people and that enriching people enhances therapeutic effectiveness. If enrichment is that powerful, this argument implies that people who love the outdoors are superior to those who avoid nature; people who have their life enriched by going to church are better than non-churchgoers; artists—who dialog with the forces of creativity—are healthier than non-artists; and people who meditate on the past via making scrapbooks are superior to non-scrap bookers. Clearly, while many things in life—including Jungian dream analysis—may enrich one's depth or worldview when measured from that particular standpoint, these "enriching" experiences do not contribute directly to enhancing therapeutic effectiveness.

Regardless of the logic of the Reality B argument, many therapists reply that it just doesn't feel true especially because they are sure that their clients have gotten better on multiple occasions. Of course, in this they are correct; therapy typically has a modest positive effect. But that is not the point being argued. Clients do get better but their improvement is not due to systems, training, or experience. Accepting Reality B requires abandoning faith in techniques not abandoning faith in client improvement. Becoming a superior therapist rests on attributing the reason for change to the relevant factors and letting go of the ones that make no contribution.

Next, the workshop attendees simply state that they know that they are better therapists than they were when they started and they are sure that they have learned important things that benefit their clients from their hundreds of hours of experience. This feeling is shared by the money managers who "know" they are more effective because they have witnessed the machinations of the market in detail and close up for many years. First of all, both the therapists and the money managers have, indeed, had many experiences denied to the normal person. In most cases, they are richer as human beings for having these experiences. In truth, the money managers "know more" about the market—just like the experienced therapist "knows more" about people—but that increased knowledge does not translate to enhanced effectiveness. If I studied the history of Rome, I would know more about Roman history but that increased knowledge is unlikely to make me a more effective therapist. As argued above, the filtering process causes the increased knowledge to be organized in such a way that it validates unhelpful theories and is unavailable as outcome-enhancing learning. In sum, the experience of therapists in the room has in some ways enriched the therapist as a person but that enhancement does not translate into increased effectiveness.

The next objection is to the concept that "techniques don't work." Psychologists point out that they have read hundreds of studies that show that techniques are effective and, often, the techniques are shown to be superior to a standard treatment. For example, new psychological techniques for treating headache pain not only must demonstrate that they are effective but often they must also show that they are more effective than a standard treatment such as progressive muscle relaxation. If these studies are accurate, and techniques not only work but some techniques are much better than others, then there is evidence for "specific factors" in psychotherapy and it can be argued that psychotherapy operates in fundamental reality.

Of course we already know that there are no training or experience effects that the dodo bird finding demonstrates that there are no specific factors, and that Strupp and other studies show that psychology is a field that operates without privileged information. Moreover, the Wampold quote about the futility of further comparative outcome studies argues that the apparent superiority of one technique over another disappears when the research results are examined more carefully.

This careful reexamination is based on three factors; the preeminence of one technique over another is due to: 1) poor research design, 2) chance/replication problems, and 3) allegiance effects. The first two are self-explanatory, allegiance effects deserve more discussion. Allegiance effects occur when the authors of the study and/or the therapists in the study are more committed to one treatment over another. Many studies have shown that therapists get better results when they believe in the treatment that they are using. In the vast majority of outcome studies, the therapists either prefer one treatment over another or know that the authors have a preference. In sum, once poor design, chance, and allegiance effects are accounted for, the apparent superiority of one technique over another disappears.

In spite of these arguments, some attendees continue to make a concerted attack on the dodo bird conclusion; given that there are studies that show the superiority of one technique over another, the Wampold explanations fail to convince them. This argument would have more credibility if the lack of privileged knowledge is not so apparent. Fields with privileged knowledge always have strong training and experience effects; we have no such effects. Whether we like it or not, we have failed to establish privileged knowledge in psychotherapy. Techniques with inherent power are privileged knowledge; the lack of privileged knowledge means that Wampold is correct and the dodo bird verdict is sustained.

Finally we should recall that the actual statement is not "techniques don't work," but rather "all techniques work." The specific statement being evaluated is "learning and practicing techniques does not result in enhanced therapist efficacy." In spite of the hundreds of studies showing one technique is better than another in a specific situation, the fundamental conclusion— *techniques have no inherent power*—remains intact.

Naturally, there is always the hope that the next technique that is discovered may be the one that finally establishes the existence of specific factors. If this is Reality A, then this hope is well founded. Unfortunately, psychotherapy operates in Reality B. We are not being asked to give up hope of becoming more effective. We are being asked to stop looking for effectiveness in the wrong place. In giving up our devotion to developing new techniques, we open the door to developing other aspects of the field.

The *Informed Consent Form* should not be taken as a humorous reference to the foibles of psychologists but rather as a literally accurate document from the standpoint of the contributions of psychotherapeutic theory and training to therapist effectiveness. The fact that it is true from the perspective of therapeutic effectiveness does not make it true from the standpoint of personal enrichment. Studying what brilliant writers have postulated about human pathology, development, and health can be a personally enriching experience but not an effectiveness-enhancing experience. Confusing these two concepts—enrichment and effectiveness—tends to stifle our hunger to become more effective. If I come home every day knowing I have helped people and feeling that I have touched the "core of being human," I am not likely to critique my psychotherapeutic system. If it isn't broken, why fix it? Moreover, if my peers report similar feelings, why should I doubt myself? Scott Miller (2011) comments:

> Compounding the problem of isolation is the well-documented tendency of clinicians to overestimate their level of skill and effectiveness. In one study, a representative sample of psychologists, social workers, psychiatrists, and marriage and family therapists from all 50 states were asked to rank their clinical skills and effectiveness compared with other mental health professionals with similar credentials. Respondents, on average, ranked themselves at the 80th percentile—a statistical impossibility. It gets worse: fewer than 4 percent considered themselves average, and not a single person in the study rated their performance below average. (Miller & Hubble, 2011, p. 26)

Regardless of these feelings, however, it is simply true that experience, mastery of systems, and expertise in techniques do not improve therapist effectiveness. It is polite to call this an "inconvenient truth." In fact, integrating this truth leaves most therapists in a profoundly difficult place. Letting in that all my training and experience are for naught, that I am not superior to the "life coach" who hung out his shingle after two weekends of training, that I have been misled about what works and why it works, that I have participated in advancing that misconstrual with my clients: these are disturbing implications.

This chapter has presented the research results and advanced Kahneman's explanation for why these results have been disregarded. For the purpose of this book, however, the research is simply the jumping off point; the actual focus is on the *implications* of the research.

And there is one primary implication: if we are not going to enhance our results through techniques, specialized information, and schools of psychotherapy, we are forced into a focus on the therapist. Science, by definition, searches for techniques and tools that are replicable—that any qualified practitioner can employ effectively. Abandoning techniques implies abandoning replicability; psychology needs to search for experiences and approaches that make the practitioner more powerful and influential regardless of what they do in the room. Scott Miller comments:

> After all, the research showed the treatment did work, regardless of model. This led us to discover, or rediscover, that the most neglected variable in outcome is

the therapist. We've investigated methods, we've investigated clients in their pathology, but we haven't turned our attention to the clinicians. And yet, the amount of variability attributable to the individual provider trumps technical factors by eight or nine times. We began to measure outcome and found that some clinicians were better than others—consistently better. (Millham, 2011, p. 34)

It is important to understand why Kahneman's explanation for the denial of the profession has featured so prominently in this chapter. Recall the illusion of the differing sizes of the three figures in the drawing above. We are programmed to see them as different, and most of us will still see them as different regardless of how many times we take out our ruler and measure them. The research results have been clear for forty years but the profession continues to ignore them. This book attempts to take the results seriously and discuss the implications of doing psychotherapy in constructed reality. Time and again this discussion will generate the same results as the figure: it will seem logically true but it will feel completely false. Readers will find that the subsequent material in this book requires an ability to avoid being seduced by System 1 simplicities and a concurrent ability to tolerate incongruent feelings.

It is now time to define the differences between Reality A and Really B. Everyone is familiar with the characteristics of Reality A—fundamental reality—but Reality B—constructed reality—is more mysterious. As part of enhancing therapist effectiveness it is necessary to develop a kind of map or geography of constructed reality. That is the purpose of the next two chapters.

## NOTE

1. Psychology will be used in the text as synonymous with clinical psychology and psychotherapy. Clearly there are other branches of psychology—for example, physiological psychology—which function differently than psychotherapy and which encompass different bodies of knowledge. The oversimplified use of the word "psychology" is simply for literary purposes.

# Chapter 2

# Close Encounters with the Abyss

> The bow of God's wrath is bent, and the arrow made ready on the
> string, and justice bends the arrow at your heart, and strains the bow,
> and it is nothing but the mere pleasure of God, and that of an angry
> God, without any promise or obligation at all, that keeps the arrow
> one moment from being made drunk with your blood.
>
> —Jonathan Edwards, *Colonial Prose and Poetry* (1901)

Everyone feels the insidious presence of the Abyss. Buddha tells us that the
existence of suffering is the first noble truth. All humans are aware that negative change is much more powerful, much more rapid, and much more long-
lasting than positive change. Asking why negative and traumatic experiences
are so powerful seems like a waste of breath. It is obvious to virtually every
adult human that life is neither safe nor predictable. Every loss reminds us
that we live suspended above the Abyss and our precarious hold can crumble
at any moment. Every experience of trauma, illness, and injustice recalls this
threat and each one of these experiences eviscerates our state of denial and
our hope that life is meaningful, safe, and rewarding.

The Jonathan Edwards epigraph powerfully conveys the sense of danger
and doom that is part of every human life. Reading Edwards—feeling his
threatening passion—impels the reader into a sense of anomia, of falling into
the Abyss. And even the things that protect us—work, friends, family, religion, etc.—may fail us in the face of the Abyss. Even epiphanies—with all
their healing, connecting power—can be transformed into ephemeral shadows by the experience of loss, death, disappointment, and failure.

All of these sorts of negative events can be called anomic experiences.
Nomos means ordered, constructed, or lawful. Anomic refers to experiences
which are perceived as destroying order, meaning, safety, or stability; it is

the state of being lost, confused, unsure of how to orient or which way to go. Most traumatic experiences result in some form of anomia. The stability and safety of the world has been ripped asunder and what remains is a threatening, chaotic exposure to a reality which is at best indifferent to the self and often hostile. This chapter examines the anomia lurking just outside the sense of consciousness. It is waiting, barely held at bay by culture, daily routine, and social support.

## THE DENIAL OF DEATH

> And so faintly you came tapping, tapping at my chamber door, That I scarce was sure I heard you—here I opened wide the door;—Darkness there, and nothing more.
>
> —Edgar Allan Poe, *The Complete Poetical Works of Edgar Allan Poe* (1866)

This concept of the "denial of death" is central to the motivation of all human beings. Without functional denial in place cultures break down and individuals lose a sense of meaning and purpose in their daily activities. In *The Social Construction of Reality*, Burger and Luckmann (1966) point out:

> The hardest thing that a culture has to deal with is the imminence of death. Cultures are required to invent elaborate schemes including afterlife, etc. that function to keep people motivated and compliant even though there is proof all around that they are going to die. (p. 101)

Burger and Luckmann go on to argue that the reality of imminent death continues to break through regardless of how many elaborate structures are created by the culture. For purposes of this book, however, all that is important is to note that everyone at some level has some anxiety about their own imminent death. Everyone who functions in a motivated way is practicing some form of denial—usually characterized as "healthy" denial since it results in cooperative and motivated behavior. But nothing completely removes the sense of fragility and ephemerality caused by the presence of death.

The absence of healthy denial is considered mental illness. Post-traumatic stress disorder is a mental health diagnosis which is given when an individual's denial of death has been stripped away from him violently and suddenly. In a formal sense, the diagnosis occurs when one experiences death or a near-death experience to themselves or those nearby. Symptoms include flashbacks, anxiety, depression, purposelessness, anomie, anhedonia, and hypervigilance. Not surprisingly, these are the essentially the same symptoms anyone would have if they believed that their death is truly imminent. No one would call these symptoms a "mental health" problem if they were exhibited by a group of people about to be executed as part of a genocidal rampage. Instead, the symptoms would be considered normal and understandable. In fact, it is considered perfectly healthy and normal if one continues to have these symptoms for a certain period of time—which varies according to the culture and the scope of the trauma—following a brush with one's mortality. PTSD symptoms are only classified as abnormal and as a mental health diagnosis when we believe that people have had sufficient time to recover. In this sense, the entire diagnosis is socially constructed; that is, it only exists when the social norms say that the victims should have reestablished their sense of healthy denial of death. We want them to be as in denial as all the rest of us so they can get back to the business of living.

Perhaps the most important book which addresses these issues is *The Denial of Death* by Ernest Becker. In this Pulitzer Prize–winning book, Becker argues that the primal motivator in all human activities is the fear of death. According to Becker, this fear is so paralyzing that all human experience, culture, institutions, and so on are an elaborate construction designed to deny the reality of our eventual demise. In the following quote, Becker (1997) lays out the essential thesis of his book.

The prospect of death, Dr. Johnson said, wonderfully concentrates the mind. The main thesis of this book is that it does much more than that: the idea of death, the fear of it, haunts the human animal like nothing else; it is a mainspring of human activity—activity designed largely to avoid the fatality of death, to overcome it by denying in some way that it is the final destiny for man. (p. xvii)

Sam Keen, who wrote the introduction to the book, summarizes Becker's ideas from a slightly different perspective.

The world is terrifying. To say the least, Becker's account of nature has little in common with Walt Disney. Mother Nature is a brutal bitch, red in tooth and claw, who destroys what she creates. We live, he says, in a creation in which the routine activity for organisms is "tearing others apart with teeth of all types—biting, grinding flesh, plant stalks, bones between molars, pushing the pulp greedily down the gullet with delight, incorporating its essence into one's own organization, and then excreting with foul stench and gasses the residue." The basic motivation for human behavior is our biological need to control our basic anxiety, to deny the terror of death. Human beings are naturally anxious because we are ultimately helpless and abandoned in a world where we are fated to die. "This is the terror: to have emerged from nothing, to have a name, consciousness of self, deep inner feelings, an excruciating inner yearning for life and self-expression—and with all this yet to die." (Keen, 1997, p. xii)

With these two quotes, Becker (1997) begins to give Jonathan Edwards a run for the money in terms of evoking a sense of the Abyss. And Becker sees no easy solution. He does recommend psychotherapy and argues that it can result in a removal of one's delusions. Unfortunately, the new awareness simply leads to a further encounter with one's own mortality and one's existential despair.

> If you get rid of the four-layered neurotic shield, the armor that covers the characterological lie about life, how can you talk about "enjoying" this Pyrrhic victory? The person gives up something restricting and illusory, it is true, but only to come face to face with something even more awful: genuine despair. Full humanness means full fear and trembling, at least some of the waking day. When you get a person to emerge into life, away from his dependencies, his automatic safety in the cloak of someone else's power, what joy can you promise him with the burden of his aloneness? When you get a person to look at the sun as it bakes down on the daily carnage taking place on earth, the ridiculous accidents, the utter fragility of life, the powerlessness of those he thought most powerful—what comfort can you give him from a psychotherapeutic point of view? (pp. 58–59)

Becker believes that the fear of death answers the question about why humans are so vulnerable to trauma and loss. When the curtains are rent and the Abyss yawns beneath one's feet, it is no wonder that people change so rapidly, radically, and profoundly. And, of course, with few exceptions, the sudden immersion into the anxiety implicit in one's own mortality results in depression, terror, and decompensation.

Why do we not feel this anxiety constantly? Becker believes that we do feel it—at least as background anxiety—but most humans are denied the full experience on a daily basis because we build worldviews that shelter us from the Abyss. He argues that the constructed world is based on the hero myth and goes to some effort elaborating on its details. In the sense that Becker postulates an invented world, developed to hide humans from the truth, he has much in common with the writers of the film *The Matrix*.

*Morpheus:* The Matrix is everywhere. It is all around us. Even now, in this very room. You can see it when you look out your window or when you turn on your television. You can feel it when you go to work . . . when you go to church . . . when you pay your taxes. It is the world that has been pulled over your eyes to blind you from the truth.
*Neo:* What truth?
*Morpheus:* That you are a slave, Neo. Like everyone else you were born into bondage. Into a prison that you cannot taste or see or touch. A prison for your mind. (Silver, Wachowski, & Wachowski, 1999)

Becker's vision of the construction of the human culture is literally different than the invented reality of the Matrix and its war with the Machine World. But the two worlds are equivalent in the way they limit clear thinking, choices, and, ultimately, freedom. Like Morpheus, he recommends "waking up" and facing the truth about human existence. And as in the Matrix, "waking up" transforms the lovely world of illusion into the gritty, painful world of conscious responsibility.

Since Becker wrote his book in 1976, the fragility of the constructed world has become even more apparent. The ensuing half century has been the era of postmodernism, a deconstructive philosophy which has as its aim the tearing down of illusory assumptions. The remainder of this chapter could have the subtitle "Worse than Becker Thought" in the sense that each section of this chapter will present another angle on the Abyss.

## EATING THE APPLE OF KNOWLEDGE: SELF-AWARENESS AND THE FRAGILITY OF IDENTITY

When I was a child, I spoke as a child, I understood as a child, I thought as a child: but when I became a man, I put away childish things.

—1 Corinthians 13:11

There is a positive stance toward change in most developing young people. At each stage of growth we can look back at previous assumptions and understandings about life and see that they were based on oversimplifications and fallacies. Obvious and humorous examples include young people outgrowing Santa Claus or the Easter Bunny. Just as obviously, developing teenagers start questioning the black and white teachings of their childhood and ask questions like "I understand that honesty is important, but when is it right to tell a lie?" or "Is it best to follow my own vision or to serve others?" Children, teens, and young adults are always outgrowing ideas like "my parents are all knowing and infallible," "my town is the best place in the country," or "I am deeply in love and am going to marry my girlfriend." The vast majority of individuals have the experience of changing certain beliefs as they mature; hence, the following are common statements: "I've outgrown those beliefs," "I used to feel that way but experience changed me," and, the most famous "you'll feel differently when you're older."

In this sense, virtually all people see their younger selves as conditioned, programmed, concrete, and limited. They see their current selves as comparatively sophisticated, awake, realistic, and mature. Because human beings do much of their cognitive development post birth, it is inevitable that everyone has an evolutionary slant toward the development of consciousness and learning. Everyone is predisposed to seeing even deeply held beliefs as mutable, malleable, and potentially naïve.

Of course, many people slow down or even halt this process of examining their beliefs as they get older; however, even this relative stability does not negate the feeling that they were foolish and confused when younger in comparison to their current wisdom and knowledge. There is an implicit sense that what we believe now is ephemeral and that we may soon outgrow it. In this sense, everyone is a born philosopher seeking to wake up to what truly is, to find out one's true nature, and to throw off all external programming. And, of course, one of the effects of conducting any kind of genuine philosophical inquiry is that a person becomes less certain of what he knows. Many people recall Plato's famous critique of Socrates: "this man, on one hand, believes that he knows something, while not knowing anything. On the other hand, I—equally ignorant—do not believe that I know anything." When one has the experience of repeatedly rejecting a formerly deeply held belief, it is normal to start questioning whether one's current firmly held beliefs are truly solid. And, since these beliefs are tightly intertwined with the concept of the self, it is appropriate to say that we all are predisposed to doubt the solidity of our present self.

Therapy is often described as a process of growing more conscious and self-aware. By and large, in most types of psychotherapy the client reports that they are discarding old beliefs and behaviors and replacing them with more functional ones. This is all well and good, but it also implies that the new beliefs are also transient and temporary and can easily be replaced by even more evolved beliefs. Again one starts running into a more transitory and fragile sense of self—a self that seems to be solid at this moment but also one which is ready to evolve into another self after more self-examination or therapy or experience. From this point of view, the oft-heard critique of people who participate in therapy seems particularly telling: "why bother doing therapy when it is just like peeling an onion? After every new layer is discovered, there's another layer just like it underneath and so on forever."

This criticism argues against the benefits of insight. The critic is pointing out that one should not "waste time gazing at your navel when you're never going to finish the process; instead get to work on something really important like making money." But even this clichéd criticism of psychotherapy reveals a consciousness embedded in the common sense wisdom of the culture, an implicit awareness that the self is ephemeral and plastic. The criticism could safely be recast as: "why bother looking for the self when it doesn't exist as a solid object and what you do find will only be solid for a brief period of time." In sum, the critics of psychotherapy—of self-awareness and consciousness development—implicitly adopt a philosophically sophisticated position not too different than Plato's or the no-self stance of a Buddhist.

If the fragility of the self is so apparent even in common culture, it becomes even more obvious when one undertakes an intentional philosophical search. Virtually all philosophical inquiry questions the common ways of seeing and recommends looking below the surface, throwing off assumptions, identifying and removing blind spots, and having the courage to accept the truth. Take the following simple philosophical tool from an Indian scripture called the Vedas.

> Thus has the Shruti (scriptures) spoken of Atman; "That Thou art." Of the illusory world, born of the five physical elements, the Shruti says: "Neti, neti" (not this, not this). (Avadhuta Gita)

This passage recommends using *Neti, Neti,* or "not this, not that," as a core philosophic practice. Essentially the practitioner is asked to examine everything in his life to determine whether it is real. If not, it is to be discarded and the next assumption examined. According to the Vedas, at the end of a sustained examination, nothing with form will be left and, therefore, *Tat Twam Asi* (Thou Art That).

Contrast this with a relatively modern form of philosophy: Existentialism. Sartre, one of the most well-known existential writers, penned a novel called *Nausea* where his protagonist had reached such a state of consciousness and awareness that even the hearing of a word with its implicit concepts, assumptions, and innate programming could generate a sense of nausea. Camus, another well-known existentialist, wrote a novel called *The Stranger* where the protagonist shows indifference to common human taboos such as murder and imprisonment. The protagonist exemplifies someone who is so awake and free that they understand that all taboos are conditioned and programmed; no meaning arises out of the event itself except as a person chooses to endorse that meaning. If one is allowed a bit of poetic license, one can imagine an existentialist who has completed her philosophical inquiry. She is poised at the edge of the universe with undifferentiated chaos all around her and a sense of nausea pervading her being. As Sartre says, "I exist, that is all, and I find it nauseating" (Sartre, 2013).

Buddhism offers a well-known analysis relating to the fragility of the self that is incumbent in one of its most famous techniques: mindfulness meditation. Mindfulness meditation is a simple practice: one sits quietly, watches the breath, and practices an awareness of whatever thoughts, feelings, sensations, memories, etc. flow across the field of awareness. The only conscious effort is to practice awareness; all that comes into consciousness, therefore, arises on its own. Every thought, feeling, sensation, etc. is generated by non self; none of them come from "you" because "you" are simply being quiet and aware.

The beginning meditator finds his mind wandering away from the breath and often forgets he is meditating. He starts thinking the thoughts and feeling the feelings and his identity shifts from the aware observer to the thinker/feeler. However, as soon as he recalls he is meditating, the individual focuses back on his breath and pure awareness.

The obvious implication of mindfulness meditation for self and identity is that we are not our thoughts, feelings, sensations, and everything else we identify as self; rather, we are essentially pure consciousness and pure awareness. To the Buddhist, all thoughts, feelings, and so on are other-generated and compose what they call "non self" or "false self."

And, in truth, the Buddhists have a point. If all that I control, my conscious self, is just watching, then everything else must be non self. My beloved identity is simply a series of seductive thoughts, feelings, and sensations that pose as my true nature. Of course, the Buddhists believe that this thought experiment is not sufficient to disprove the false self; they urge people to actually practice mindfulness meditation and discover for themselves whether they are truly the observed thoughts or something else. But even this simple description of mindfulness shows the fragility of the self-concept when it is examined with any kind of systematic process.

Both common sense experience and structured philosophic inquiry lead us to doubt the existence of a permanent and solid Self; instead we find a Self is characterized by shakiness versus solidity and fragility versus durability and permanence. Returning to Kahneman's System 1, one can see that the human sense of safety, predictability, and stability is more sustained by denial than by awareness—more supported by a need for security rather than resting on factual support. Little wonder that we can change so quickly in a negative direction when our sense of self is so fragile and rests on such a weak foundation.

## CULTURAL RELATIVITY

Infinite are the paths and infinite the opinions.

—Ramakrishna, *The Gospel of Sri Ramakrishna* (1910)

Relativity is one of the defining aspects of the Abyss. Perhaps the most obvious example of this relativity arises from an examination of the almost infinite variability of human culture.

It is an ethnological commonplace that the ways of becoming and being human are as numerous as man's cultures. Humanness is socio-culturally variable. . . . While it is possible to say that man has a nature, it is more significant to say

that man constructs his own nature, or more simply, that man produces himself.
(Berger & Luckmann, 1966, p. 49)

In the quote above, Berger and Luckmann ask the reader to address the radical implications of cultural diversity in a serious manner; essentially they are saying that *people who live in different cultures are educated and conditioned so differently that they literally inhabit different realities.* Imagine yourself as a member of an indigenous Native American culture who lives with the expectation of communication with a Buffalo or a Coyote spirit and who believes that every action in life is being reviewed by those spirits. Every day this individual hears stories of people he knows having such communications. The shaman of the tribe is capable of curing illness because he has the ability to visit the "land of the dead" and return safely. And the people of the tribe have numerous documented experiences where the shaman's power has cured illness in much the same way that a modern Westerner experiences antibiotics.

What Westerner really understands the reality of a Japanese Samurai in the sixteenth century in terms of suicide? In that culture, it was not only permitted but required in certain situations. And how can a post-feminist American woman understand the spiritual duties and obligations of an East Indian woman in the nineteenth century?

These differences are not simply values or sex roles or spiritual beliefs, rather they encompass something far more profound and foundational. Alan Watts comments:

We seldom realize, for example that our most private thoughts and emotions are not actually our own. For we think in terms of languages and images which we did not invent, but which were given to us by our society. (Watts, 1966, pp. 53–54)

Where does the unique "I" stop and the culturally created "I" begin? How much of all that "I 'freely choose'" has actually been "chosen by 'me'" and how many of those choices are programmed? Clearly our personhood is intricately interwoven with our cultural identity. Edward Saour (1929) concurs and states:

No two languages are ever sufficiently similar to be considered as representing the same social reality. The worlds in which different societies live are distinct worlds, not merely the same world with different labels attached. (p. 209)

How powerful are these differences and distinctions? Emotions are often thought to be cross cultural; in our emotions, we are all equally and commonly human. However, Gergen (2009) cites an Ifaluk example of an emotion called "fago" which calls this into question. Gergen argues that the Ifaluk use the word to indicate compassion, sadness, admiration, and homesickness. Like Saour, he concluded that the Ifaluk are actually feeling something different than Westerners—not simply a Western feeling with an Ifaluk label.

With this brief discussion of an emotion that has no Western correlate, Gergen supports his contention that emotions are culturally determined; even when it comes to feelings, there is no solid shared affective reality that bridges one culture to another. In this sense, when one accepts the idea that different cultures equal different realities, then there is no longer a sense that any particular reality is truly "real." Given that every culture believes that their own view is solid and implicitly superior to all other cultural views, no culture can actually have an innate claim on the "true view" of reality. As we deconstruct our cultural programming and assumptions, we can sense the chaos that lies beneath our feet, the sense that everything could have been different. Thomas Hylland Eriksen (2010) comments:

> The single most important human insight to be gained from this way of compar-
> ing societies is perhaps the realization that everything could have been different
> in our own society—that the way we live is only one among innumerable ways
> of life which humans have adopted. . . . Anthropology may not provide the
> answer to the question of the meaning of life, but at least it can tell us that there
> are many ways in which to make a life meaningful. (p. 327)

Understanding the implications of this sort of chaos, cultures take various steps to protect their members from the deviant and competing worldviews of other cultures. A culture cannot afford the idea that its view of reality—its values, laws, standards, and mores—are simply created by a series of complex and arbitrary interactions between geography, technology, history, and so forth; instead, the culture is constrained to argue that it's worldview has a solid and indisputable basis. The worldview of a culture is always presented as the "Truth," the map that provides an accurate description of the territory. In most cultures, this "map" is "holy" and contains the essential truths about how it really is, the immutable laws about the nature of reality. Often this map comes from a divine source; there are myths and stories about the role of the Gods in the origin of the People. Sometimes there is a prophet who speaks with the power of the divine; sometimes there is a covenant between God and His People underlying the map. What is important is some documenta-
tion that the view of Reality is derived from or endorsed by a Higher Power.

Another way to infuse the cultural map with authority is the claim that it is a much more accurate map of reality. Western cultural beliefs are superior to indigenous cultures because science has generated a map that is superior to the superstitious maps that came before. Capitalism is "proven" to be the best way to motivate people to work together. And democracy is the "right" way for people to govern themselves.

When subjected to basic psychological analyses, these arguments about our map being "more accurate" or "derived from the one True God" simply sound like an insecure person desperately seeking stability and validation. Given this level of desperation, it is not surprising that the competing views of other cultures are often labeled "insane." This particular label not only serves to protect extant cultural members, it simultaneously implies that one might go crazy if she accepts a different view of reality. There's a nice example of this attribution of insanity from the blockbuster movie *Avatar*. Jake, *Avatar*'s protagonist, is attempting to become a member of another culture. Most members of the indigenous culture are resisting this idea but the shamaness becomes a somewhat unwilling supporter due to the occurrence of certain spiritual signs. However, even with this support, note the nature of her invitation to Jake:

> "It is decided. My daughter will teach you our ways. Learn well, 'Jakesully,' and we will see if your *insanity* can be cured." (Cameron, 2009, emphasis added)

As mentioned above, from the perspective of a centered member of one culture, the beliefs of another culture are literally "insane." This fragment of dialog illustrates just how threatening a competing view of Reality can be and just how important it is not to be polluted by a competing Reality. Calling something "insane" is a synonym for "absolutely dangerous," "toxic if touched," "destructive if consumed." The shamaness, at least, is deeply convinced that an individual cannot be healthy—or, in some ways, be allowed to exist—unless their heretical beliefs are purified.

Since we are discussing the need for a culture to defend itself against the belief system of a competing culture, it is perhaps even more instructive to review the reaction to *Avatar*, especially from the more conservative or "Apollonian" segment of the media. There is a useful typology, originally made popular in Western culture by Nietzsche, called the Dionysian/Apollonian continuum. While these terms can be used variously by different writers, for the purposes of this book Apollonian is defined as an orientation toward what is ordered, lawful, responsible, self-sacrificing, future-oriented, logical, rational, and structured. Dionysian refers to an orientation which is spontaneous, present-oriented, hedonistic, creative, intuitive, and passionate. Apollonian types accept authority, are comfortable in hierarchical systems, and seek certainty from externals. Dionysian types promote ideas such as "following your own wisdom or feelings," internal authority, and being true to oneself. Obviously, Dionysians are comfortable and even eager to embrace change and Apollonians are distrustful and wary of change.

James Cameron, the award-winning writer and director of the Hollywood film, *Avatar*, contrasts two cultures: the first is a caricaturized version of a capitalistic, post-industrial culture which sees the natural world as a place to be exploited for its material wealth; the second is a technologically primitive culture which, however, embraces and embodies a worldview where everything is connected and interdependent. The story line is fairly predictable: wounded hero meets princess from an innocent culture; they fall in love but he makes mistakes which alienate him from his woman. He redeems himself via an act of courage, then leads the fight where the pure but powerless culture—David—overcomes the rich but evil culture—Goliath.

Most viewers considered *Avatar* a cutting edge film in terms of special effects and an entertaining retelling of one of the standard Hollywood themes. Viewers rewarded it financially by making it the highest grossing film of all time. However, in spite of all of those accolades and rewards, religious and political conservatives attacked the film relentlessly. Epithets virtually rained from the sky as the film was called variously "un-American," "ungodly," "anti-capitalistic," "anti-US military," "anti-white," "New Age," "polytheistic," and a hundred other critiques. Many of these critical reviewers cautioned readers against seeing it and especially cautioned the impressionable—young people—against viewing the film.

While the attacks were partly due to the implicit liberal values espoused by the film—*Avatar* is strikingly pro-environment and politically progressive—the level of attacks was too high for a simple political or values disagreement. There was a level of fervor in the attacks—a fervor perhaps better characterized as terror; it felt like the conservative commentators were fighting for their lives. It seems that the Apollonian critics fully agreed with the shamaness in the film: *Avatar* espoused a worldview that was "insane," a worldview that was capable of destroying the consciousness of an unprepared or immature viewer, a worldview capable of destroying "the American Way of Life."

Lest this seem like an overreaction from the conservative press, recall that the whole point of this chapter is to point out the fragility of the Real. In *Avatar*, Cameron was arguing that the worldview of the other culture—their sense of reality—is superior to our own. Since the truth of one's cultural superiority—and the resulting stable sense of reality—is always delicate and hanging by a thread, the conservatives were correct that *Avatar* was a dangerous movie with a dangerous message. Of course, in truth this was simply a movie and the competing culture was an invented fantasy. However, the volume and ferocity of the attacks do imply that a real threat to the worldview existed. And it is appropriate for a culture to defend itself vigorously when its worldview is threatened.

Returning to the concept of the need of a culture to define itself as superior: as long as a culture considers itself the "apex" culture—and virtually all cultures do in one way or another—that culture is immunized against reality pollution from another culture's worldview. When I believe that my cultural viewpoint is more "advanced" than yours, my worldview is safe. Western culture was safe in this manner throughout the end of the nineteenth century and believed that its dominance could not be challenged by the inferior, "primitive" cultures that formed its competition.

**Figure 2.1** Edvard Munch. The Scream. Pastel on board. 1895. © 2012 The Munch Museum/The Munch-Ellingsen Group/Artists Rights Society (ARS), New York.

**Figure 2.2 Two Tahitian Women.** Gift of William Church Osborn, 1949 to The Metropolitan Museum of Art. Public Domain.

With the advent of the twentieth century, that simple superiority began to be challenged from many angles. Between 1893 and 1910 Edward Munch painted a series of four impressionist paintings entitled *The Scream*. This work embodied the alienation and suffering of modern man. As time went on, it became a symbol for all Western suffering. Western life is good on the surface but examine it more closely and one finds poverty, crime, world wars, the Holocaust, the Depression, and Nuclear War. Hundreds of other writers, social scientists, poets, and artists joined Munch in depicting the dark and problematic side of Western culture. In sum, the implicit superiority of Western culture began to show cracks around the edges; the simplistic confidence of empiricism began to be threatened.

In 1928 Margaret Mead researched and wrote a book which was to become the single most famous text in anthropology at the time: *Coming of Age in Samoa*. This book affected Western culture in multiple ways; for purposes of our argument, however, it was a credible and powerful discussion of the concept that other cultures have the capacity to develop healthy human beings; in fact, in some cases these humans are healthier than the equivalent members of our culture. More specifically, it documented how Samoan culture was superior to Western culture in terms of sexuality, relationships, and the ability to be present in life. This book, and the hundreds of subsequent books, pictures, and research projects emphasizing ways in which other cultures are superior to Western culture, fundamentally challenged facile Western assumptions about dominance. The Gaugin painting to the right can be seen as symbolic of these healthier alternatives to the Western way of being. This shifting of consciousness is documented in the following quote from Lily King (2015).

> Anthropology at that time was in transition, moving from the study of men dead and gone to the study of living people, and slowly letting go of the rigid belief that the natural and inevitable culmination of every society is the Western model. (p. 36)

Munch, Mead, and all their compatriots did succeed at threatening the superiority of Western culture. Of course, it is also true that Western culture continued to argue for its position as the apex culture via references to two important factors: its adherence to the scientific model and its dominance in the area of technology. However, even with these outstanding factors, the claim to be the apex culture was no longer undisputed. After the early twentieth century, ethnology, cultural anthropology, and the daily life experience of other cultures implicitly challenged the stability of our own worldview. Our culturally derived sense of reality generally continues to feel solid but, when examined, it is clear that it is built on sand. Its stability dissolves under simple ethnographic analysis.

Modern anthropology demonstrates that all humans live in cultures based on constructed realities. As Western culture evolved, doubts began to grow about our identity as the apex culture and the sense of the fragility of our cultural reality grew proportionally. The corresponding backlash against other cultures documents one way in which this growing fragility is experienced in the culture. Most importantly, however, is the fact that any thoughtful and reflective reader can feel the insubstantiality and ephemerality of our culturally created reality.

## DENIAL VERSUS DEPTH

> Comfort is no test of truth. Truth is often far from being comfortable.
>
> —Swami Vivekananda, *The Complete Works of Swami Vivekananda* (1907)

This chapter has focused on the existence of the Abyss, the Abyss as the underlying reason for anxiety, and the Abyss as the explanation of the rapid deterioration in psychological functioning seen so often in conjunction with bad news. Becker tells us: "To live fully is to live with an awareness of the rumble of terror that underlies everything." This chapter has expanded Becker's focus on death by including two additional aspects of the Abyss. The first demonstrates that the sense of Self is fragile and ephemeral; the second shows that all culturally based views of reality are constructed and relative. Death waits for us all and makes a joke of all we accomplish here. You, as person, do not truly exist; you only "feel" you exist. Finally, everything you have been taught and believe about reality is simply "made up"; it changes from culture to culture. Death, no Self and no Reality: this is the nature of the Abyss.

Living with these truths requires a level of denial. In this sense, denial can be a wonderful thing. At the least, it can be highly functional. Most of the clinical problems brought into therapy can be discussed and resolved without direct reference to the Abyss; in fact, if the therapist insisted that every dilemma be framed existentially, many clients would react with dismay, distress, and rejection.

For therapists, however, denial is massively counterproductive. If a therapist is in existential denial, how can she fully understand client depression or anxiety? This, of course, is the old argument of existential psychology; unless a therapist has the depth to face and integrate her own existential terror, she will be handicapped when it comes to helping a client with his terror. It is possible to ignore this existential argument when psychology believes that techniques have power. From this point of view, any well-trained therapist can successfully employ effective techniques; personal depth might be helpful but it is not required. However, when techniques have no inherent power—and the focus shifts to the charisma of the therapist—the existential argument gains new credibility.

To make this sense of the Abyss more concrete, Yalom offers an example of a client with a recurring nightmare.

Another patient had a recurrent nightmare that dated back to early childhood and now, in adulthood, resulted in severe insomnia—in fact, in a sleep phobia, since he was terrified of going to sleep. The nightmare is unusual in that the dreamer himself suffered no harm. Instead, his world melted away, exposing him to nothingness. The dream:

I am awake in my room. Suddenly I begin to notice that everything is changing. The window frame seems stretched and then wavy, the bookcases squashed, the doorknob disappears, and a hole appears in the door which gets larger and larger. Everything loses its shape and begins to melt. There's nothing there any more and I begin to scream. (Yalom, 2008, Kindle Locations 4994–4998)

Or take this second example from Kurt Reinhardt.

Something utterly mysterious intervenes between him and the familiar objects of his world, between him and his fellowmen, between him and all his "values." Everything which he had called his own pales and sinks away, so that there is nothing left to which he might cling. What threatens is "nothing" (no thing), and he finds himself alone and lost in the void. But when this dark and terrible night of anguish has passed, man breathes a sigh of relief and tells himself: it was "nothing," after all. He has experienced "nothingness." (Yalom, 2008, Kindle Locations 5045–5048)

Without understanding the Abyss—without being in dialog with the primal terror inherent in chaos and death—the therapist will never completely understand the power of constructed reality. Constructed reality is built on the foundation of the Abyss. When cultural conditioning and all programming are deconstructed by mindfulness and discernment, the philosopher arrives at the edge of the Abyss.

The Abyss in not simply a foundation, it is a dynamic force. It is appropriate to state that constructed reality is in dialog with the Abyss. The Abyss is always attempting to break through the shelter of constructed reality. In fact, these Abyss "breakthroughs" are often seen as the source of psychopathology; certainly Carl Jung and James Hillman make such breakthroughs central in their models. Paradoxically, both Jung and Hillman also argue that the Abyss can have an opposite effect; the right type of interactions with the Abyss can lead to inner peace and wisdom.

In sum, even though psychologists may not directly discuss the Abyss with clients on a daily basis, they need to be comfortable with its presence to understand anxiety, decompensation, and existential issues. This familiarity has always been necessary but it is even more important once it is understood that techniques lack inherent power. Constructionists need to understand the Abyss to understand the nature of constructed reality. Indeed the fluid and ever-changing dialog between Abyss and culture—between mortality and self—creates the milieu for psychotherapy. Finally, denial may be functional at certain times for individuals and for the culture in general; however, it has little utility for therapists who want to enhance outcomes. *The Empire Strikes Back* tells us:

*LUKE:* I'm not afraid.
*YODA:* Ohhh . . . you will be, you will be. (Lucas & Kershner, 1980)

# Chapter 3

# Social Constructionism

All that we see or seem
Is but a dream within a dream.

—Edgar Allan Poe, "A Dream Within a Dream," 1849

Social constructionism is a relatively new discipline with roots in a variety of approaches including philosophy, sociology, psychology, ethnology, and literature. It is fairly easy to define. The "constructionism" part of the term refers to the idea that reality is constructed not discovered. The "social" part refers to the idea that these created realities are supported, affirmed, and reconfirmed in every social interaction with another member of the same culture.

It is easy to illustrate some of the main ideas of constructionism with a simple picture.

This is a picture of a cliff randomly shaped by time and erosion. Imagine you walk past it and do not notice anything special—just another rock outcropping. However, the next time you pass by, you are with a friend who remarks that the cliff is actually a sculpture of a face or perhaps the mask of an ancient God. From that point forward, it will be very difficult for you to ever see it as just another rock outcropping.

The first question has to do with discovery versus construction or creation. Since we know that the outcropping was formed randomly, it is obvious that the "face" was not "discovered"; rather it was constructed by the pattern-creating part of the mind. This process, which is formally called *Pareidolia*, is operated by Kahneman's System 1. After one has seen the cliff as a face, it will be difficult to see it as a random outcropping again. There is a sense that the face "really exists." And, since it was first experienced in a social context, and your friend also has the sense the face "really exists," there

**Figure 3.1**    Photo Credit: https://weirdtwist.wordpress.com/2012/11/13/faces-in-rocks/.

is social reinforcement about viewing reality this way. Hence, we have the *Social Construction of Reality* which is, of course, the title of Berger and Luckmann's famous book.

Note how easy it is to deconstruct this creation. Simply cover the upper part of the photo (the nose and eyes) and the face disappears and all that is left is a randomly eroded rock outcropping. In sum, constructionists believe that "reality" is essentially random—the Abyss. Until we bring the focus of System 1 onto it, it remains chaotic and unorganized. Once System 1 perceives a pattern, reality is constructed into whatever pattern has been projected onto it. This pattern has a great sense of solidity and truth; even though there is no essential "face" in the rock, it feels as if there is. This realness can be greatly enhanced if we get another person—or the entire culture—to agree that this is the way we are going to perceive this rock outcropping. Finally, with the right methodology, the construction can be deconstructed and the perceived object (or idea) dissolves back into random and chaotic material.

Frankly, it is always difficult to believe that constructionists are actually arguing what they are arguing. Can they really be serious when they say that we have created everything, that it is all, in the end, just invented? However, an examination of the following quote from Vivian Burr, a leading social constructionist, shows just how serious she is about the provocative implications of her ideas.

> Since the social world, including ourselves as people, is the product of social processes, it follows that there cannot be any given, determined nature to the world or people. There are no essences inside things or people that make them what they are. . . . It is important to stress the radical nature of the proposal that is being put forward here. (Burr 2003, 5–6)

Later in her book, she expands this point further.

> Social Constructionism, then, replaces the self-contained, pre-social and unitary individual with a fragmented and changing, socially produced phenomenon who comes into existence and is maintained not inside the skull but in social life. (Burr, 2003, p. 104)

Burr and the other constructionists are literally saying that "it's all made up." Our culture is invented; our identity is the process of negotiation between ourselves and others; and the specter of our inevitable death creates an underlying sense of anxiety that motivates us to reify the constructs. It only seems real because everyone around us has an implicit agreement with us to act like it is real. It is the *Emperor's New Clothes* on steroids.

Look at the quotes above. Burr is saying that reality is essentially a chameleon, capable of shifting into whatever form we collectively desire—whatever we choose through consensus. And then the magic occurs. Once we agree on the form, due to System 1's ability to imbue worldviews with a sense of permanence, we will all have a shared "gut" feeling that our invented reality is solid. Of course, in truth, this agreement never really changes the nature of the world; it continues to be a fluid, fragmented and changing medium that takes shape briefly and then collapses again into the raw building blocks of chaos. The constructionists are essentially arguing that life is more akin to an LSD experience of fluidity, hallucination, and dissolution than the commonly accepted reality of routine, expectations, conventions, and solidity.

The full implications of this viewpoint are profound and difficult to understand and accept; however, it is relatively easy to understand a limited constructionist view when it comes to social roles. Any educated person knows that, for example, a woman's sexual attractiveness varies according to which culture she inhabits and which historical period. Burr (2003) comments:

> It is often pointed out that, a couple of hundred years ago, a woman of ample proportions and pale skin was the epitome of desirable femininity. The change to today's preference for a slender, tanned body is hard to understand within the view of sexuality as hard-wired and fixed but makes a good deal of sense once we locate sexuality within a socially shared meaning system that is intimately bound up with social structure and the economy. In times when access to the material resources for sustaining life was perhaps even more divided by class than today, a well-fleshed body, who skin declared that its own had never needed to toil in the fields, spoke of wealth and comfort. (p. 43)

This knowledge that our collective sense of sexual attractiveness is socially constructed is relatively easy to absorb. Next, Burr (2003) takes us another step further and asks us to look at "motherhood," a concept where it is more difficult to discern the social constructions. In the following quote, Burr looks as the definitions of "good" versus "bad" motherhood and resulting feelings of depression, empowerment, and choice.

> A woman may complain of depression, feeling that she cannot cope with her life. Perhaps she feels that she is a bad mother because she frequently loses her temper with her young children, or that she is an inadequate daughter because she is reluctant to care for her own elderly mother. But in re-casting the problem at a societal level rather than at the level of the individual a different analysis emerges. Such an analysis may suggest that the woman sees herself as oppressed rather than depressed. The discourses of motherhood, femininity, family life and so on actively encourage women to engage in practices which are not necessarily in their own psychological, social and economic best interests. Thinking of oneself as oppressed rather than depressed fosters a different view of oneself. (p. 122)

Social constructionists can get truly radical when they argue that feelings themselves do not arise internally from an essential self but rather exist in the space between people. In the following quote, Gergen cuts to the heart of our sense of self by arguing that internal feelings and the sense of an "inner life" was essentially invented (constructed) only a few hundred years ago.

> It was only in the following century (the 1700's) that people began to construct themselves as having "feelings." And, over the centuries that followed, we have steadily increased the number of events and processes that we attribute to the mental world. It is now estimated that in English we have over 2000 words referring to the inner world of the self. Is it not totally clear to us today that each of us has thoughts, emotions, motives, desires, wants, needs, ideas, will-power

and memory? To be without these ingredients of the mind, we would be something less than human. (Gergen, 2009, p. 82)

Of course, what Gergen is arguing here is that these "ingredients of the mind" which we define as essential to being human simply didn't exist in Western culture prior to the 1700s and don't exist in a number of other cultures both historical and current. This is such a radical concept to any modern Westerner—especially mental health professionals—that it is almost unthinkable. Who would I be if I didn't understand myself in terms of my feelings and my inner life? How do people in other cultures and time periods have a sense of self without these reference points?

This final point was illustrated by my own experience at a workshop with Joseph Campbell in the 1980s. During this workshop, which was organized around the Tristan and Isolde myth, Campbell made the provocative statement that the primary contribution of Western culture was the invention of the concept of romantic love. This statement rocked my sense of reality. I tried to imagine a culture where "falling in love" was not a central experience of being human. Of course I had heard long before about arranged marriages, and imagined what it might be like if one only had a choice of three females from the adjoining tribe of hunter/gatherers, but actually letting in that most human cultures have functioned without the concept of romantic love literally made me feel unstuck and adrift. Romantic love was so central to my own sense of identity that the idea of operating without it made me feel a bit like Sartre, a bit nauseous.

Social constructionists refuse to limit their analyses to social roles and psychological feelings; they insist that the power of constructionism extends to basic processes such as illness and pain. Gergen (2009, p. 105) points out that athletes in the midst of a competition experience little or no pain even when sustaining major blows and broken limbs. Soldiers who see a wound as a ticket to safety often experience euphoria instead of pain when injured. Women in certain other cultures—for example, Micronesia—have so little labor pain that doctors can only identify contractions with a hand on the abdomen. Finally, deeply religious individuals, when attempting to identify with the "passion of Christ," experience pain as an elevated spiritual rapture. In sum, pain is much more constructed than might be expected.

I can easily imagine getting euphoric about pain when a wound is a passport to get out of the danger of war; I had already met a number of veterans who had this exact experience and it seemed credible to me. Moreover, I had personally experienced the level of pain control embodied in the athletic references. I was shocked, however, to imagine that Micronesian women live in a reality that precludes contraction-related pain during childbirth.

In sum, the Social constructionists are intent on exposing the chaotic and arbitrary nature of the world that underlies our seemingly solid and consensually supported worldview. They want to strip away the easy assumptions and the safe and stable models and replace them with an awakened consciousness that cuts through assumptions and social programming. In the right person, this increase in consciousness can be stimulating and liberating. For an individual who is less sure of herself, exposure to such ideas can be terrifying and destabilizing.

## SCIENCE AND POSTMODERNISM

One hears only those questions for which one is able to find
answers.

—Friedrich Nietzsche, *The Gay Science* (1882)

Social constructionism is not content with helping the individual understand the degree to which his daily experience and cognitions are socially constructed; it also critiques the shared worldviews of the culture and specially focuses on assumptions related to meaning and progress. To understand what the constructionists are critiquing, it is important to review the evolution of meaning over the last 500 years of Western culture.

More specifically, from the standpoint of implicit meaning and authority, Western culture can be divided into three periods: 1) pre-modern (from the beginning of the historical record through Galileo), 2) modern (from Galileo through World War I), and post-modern (World War I through the present). Pre-modern Western culture derives its authority and validity from revelation as documented in the scriptures and as interpreted by religious authorities. Modernism is identified with empiricism and science; progress, meaning, and ultimate truth will be attained by rationality and scientific discovery. Postmodern Western culture believes that whether there is ultimate truth or not, humans can't attain it in a pure form; instead, there are personal, functional, and relative truths. Authority is based on inner experience and existential choices.

Obviously constructionism is one of the leading components of postmodernism. And, just as empiricism criticized the authority of the church and its revelation, constructionism offers its critiques on the power and authority of science. In order to appreciate the constructionist critique of science, it is important to understand that what we call "science" needs to be divided into two parts. The first part, which for this discussion can be called "functional science," has to do with creating maps and models about fundamental reality and about making things work. The second part, which can be called "faith-based science," has to do with science's authority and its "promise" of happiness, security, and abundance in the future.

The benefits of functional science are easy to describe and understand. Humans are adaptive and have been highly motivated and successful throughout history in terms of developing enhanced technologies which contribute to our security and comfort. The invention of metal tools, the domestication of the horse, and developments in architecture and ship building all occurred before the articulation of the scientific method, yet they all embody the highest level of creativity, problem solving, hard work, and perseverance. To make anything work, or work better, one needs to observe phenomena, come up with a theory about it, test the theory, and then modify the theory based on the results. Science did not invent this method; it is inherent in figuring anything out or developing any technology.

The faith-based aspect of science is more subtle and more difficult to understand. Recall that the popular articulation of the scientific model was created by eighteenth-century empiricists. These empiricists had a fairly straightforward view of the universe. They saw it as a complicated machine that could be taken apart and understood via hard work and rational thought. The fruits of understanding this complicated machine would include cheap energy, advanced technology, increase in wealth, improved social justice and a decrease in poverty, control of disease, and an extended life span. They had not heard of the uncertainty principle, chaos theory, and the fact that Schrodinger's cat can be simultaneously alive and dead. They certainly would have agreed with Einstein's famous quote: "God does not play with dice."

Kahneman would probably point out that this empirical theory of the universe was almost certainly generated by System 1 and then justified by System 2. System 1 loves the idea that the universe is some kind of immensely complicated mechanism whose laws can be discovered and whose principles can be mastered. This theory has all the characteristics that System 1 is drawn to: it is simple, comprehensive, and makes the future predictable and safe. Remember that System 1 is so seductive and powerful that even sophisticated and educated members of Western culture—who also might intellectually understand uncertainty and chaos—will find it hard to reject this simplistic, mechanistic model of the universe.

It is also important to note that for the modern layman, faith-based science is structured in a manner which is highly similar to the structure of premodern religion. The first similarity is that the view of the universe espoused by the seventeenth-century empiricists is no more accurate—and just as faith based—as any religious claims of the nature of reality that are derived from revelation or scripture. The empiricists simply advanced a theory which seemed reasonable to them and that theory—because it has been endorsed by virtually every member of the culture—seems like an accurate description of the universe. It has become reified in the cultural consciousness. Almost all Westerners "implicitly believe" that the universe is a complicated machine, that science is making significant progress in figuring it out, and that "sometime in the future" the machine will be fully mastered and all of the promises of science will come to fruition.

The second similarity between science and religion is the idea of a priestly caste—a group of special people that are closer to God than normal people. These are people that can intercede with the divine, provide guidance to lay people, and ultimately hasten our arrival at the final goal. They speak a special language indecipherable to the common man and have powers and abilities beyond the norm. There is a humorous reference to these concepts of a priestly case from Duck Breath Theatre who popularized these ideas in their famous NPR comedy sketches featuring "Dr. Science." The introduction to the show always began with:

> "He knows more than you do." (because he has) "a Master's Degree . . . in *science!*"

Similarly, at the end of *Raiders of the Lost Ark*, Indiana Jones is assured that the ark, with all of its divine power, is in safe hands because:

*Maj. Eaton:* We have top men working on it now.
*Indiana:* Who?
*Maj. Eaton:* Top . . . men. (Marshall & Spielberg, 1981)

Like priests speaking Latin, scientists speak a special tongue unavailable to the common man. They make pronouncements and predictions that cannot be understood by the lay person because of a lack of training and innate ability; instead they need to be accepted on faith. This special status is internalized in the culture through common use phrases such as "it doesn't take a rocket scientist to figure this out."

They are particularly trusted because they have a "sacred" method that ensures their leadership is free from blemishes: they have taken "vows" to be rational and impartial and to use the objective scientific method that ensures fairness and purity. In fact, the term "scientific" has become synonymous with rational, impartial, trustworthy, and reality based. People may lie but science is innocent and pure.

Recall what we expect from science—what are its implicit promises? Because of science, someday we will travel to the stars. We will eventually vanquish all disease and increase the lifespan. There will be abundant free energy and advanced technologies that will lift everyone out of poverty and ensure justice and peace for all mankind. All mental health disorders will be cured and human conflict will be minimized. If this sounds like the Garden of Eden or a terrestrial version of Heaven, the similarities are not accidental.

The faith-based aspects of science and modernism bear striking similarities to the promises of religion and premodernism. There are assumptions about the nature of the universe that must be taken on faith and never questioned; there is a priestly caste of gifted and semi-divine people who will facilitate our arrival at the final goal and who can be trusted to solve all problems; and there is the eventual outcome of reestablishing the Garden of Eden on earth.

Constructionists making such an argument about the implicit values and structure of science are usually attacked on three fronts. The first is the concept that in premodern cultures, the religious authorities hinder the advancement of knowledge by forbidding inquiry into areas that threaten the religious worldview. Copernicus and Galileo are often cited examples. However, it is not hard to counter this by pointing out that people in power in every culture always have a vested interest in controlling the evolution of technology and knowledge. Current examples include the "science" around the health risks of tobacco or the validity of climate change.

And in the area of medicine and mental health, there are numerous examples of the control of the evolution of knowledge. For example, pharmaceutical companies have paid the most prestigious physicians and journal editors to endorse their products and approaches and have controlled the direction of scientific research simply by funding one approach and defunding another. Even the "impartial and rational" scientific method has been manipulated by powerful members of the culture. A recent article (Lexchin, Bero, Djulbe, & Clark, 2003) found that double blind studies of new medications were 30 percent more likely to find significance if the studies were funded by the pharmaceutical company that developed the drug versus independent investigators. How did the funding source affect the purity implicit in the double blind model?

The second critique of the constructionist position is more compelling: "How can one doubt the efficacy and power of science when: 1) it has achieved all these advances and 2) each piece of knowledge builds on previous discoveries?" The worth of science is validated by the wonderful things it has created and the body of knowledge that has been developed. The internet and antibiotics prove that science is powerful and effective.

The key to responding to this critique is to separate the implicit human desire to adapt, create, and make one's life easier from the faith-based aspect of science. One can understand this most easily by examining the same claims from the vantage point of a premodern culture. For example, when Cortes arrived in Mexico with the intention of conquering the country for the Spanish king, he made almost identical claims that his technology validated his philosophy and religious beliefs. When he approached a native tribe, he would tell them that they should submit to him and his God because all of his advanced technology—ships, guns, armor, etc.—was the result of worshipping the one true God. He never claimed that his culture had these advanced technologies because they had been lucky in their geopolitical fortunes, or had a fruitful interaction with the Orient or because humans are generally adaptive and inventive. Cortes truly believed that his culture's advanced technology was due to the Grace of his God. Similarly, modern technological advances are simply the next stage of technological innovation and are not due to the vision of seventeenth-century empiricists that the Universe is a complicated machine.

The final argument is based on the concept that science promotes rationality and rationality will eventually unlock all the secrets of the universe. This is an appealing idea if one accepts the idea that "God does not play with dice" and that there are simple cause-and-effect connections in the Universe. Unfortunately it seems that the closer we examine the universe, the less it appears to follow simple cause/effect rules. Consider the following quote by Moreno (2012) about the futility of applying a simple Enlightenment model to modern scientific challenges.

> By the late 19th century some philosophers theorized that, given enough time and money, the scientific community would be able to come up with a unified system of knowledge of the whole of reality. That endpoint may never actually come, of course, but it was the product of a thought experiment about the demonstrated power of actual experiments, a kind of ideal terminus of knowledge. Certainly the Darwinian revolution give reason to believe this could be done in the biological world, and even today physicists are aiming for unified theory of the cosmos.
>
> But what we seem to be discovering is that, as we dig into the weeds of the nature of reality, reality is ever more stubborn about giving up the secrets. Nowhere is this recalcitrance more apparent than in genetics and neuroscience. The more we learned about the human genome, the more important proteins of turned out to be, and the more we learned about brain cells, the more we've realized how important the connection between brain cells are (something the philosopher and psychologist William James told us in 1890!).
>
> . . . Just to take the case of neurological disorders like autism, it's quite clear that like cancer, the conditions brought under that large rubric have diverse biological roots. A couple of years ago a well-known geneticist told me that he is sure Asperger's syndrome is genetically quite distinct from the spectrum of autism disorders, for example. So, again, it's often the case that the next step gets harder and more expensive. At the same time, the external variables that cause multiple genetic switches to be turned on and off are so numerous, subtle and hard to control that few disease risks can be confidently predicted. Even "designer babies" wouldn't change that. (Moreno, 2012)

This is a new way of seeing. The universe does not appear to be a complex machine which can be disassembled and understood via sufficient rational study and experiments. Rather it is a fluid, dynamic system marked by chaos and unpredictability that resists rational explanation and control. Michael Crichton, in his well-known movie, *Jurassic Park*, took on this exact question. In the movie, geneticists have recreated dinosaurs from recovered DNA and the park developer has brought in independent scientists to review the park before opening it to the public. One of the scientists is an advocate of Chaos Theory and Crichton uses the plot and the dialog to contrast a rationalistic scientific view with a view influenced by chaos theory; in other words, he creates a dialog between the modern perspective and the postmodern. Examine the following quotes from the "chaostician" brought in to review the park and note his disparagement of the empirical model of reality.

*Dr. Ian Malcolm:* Gee, the lack of humility before nature that's being displayed here, uh . . . staggers me.

Later in the film, as all parties recognize the limitations of rational control over nature, that is, the dinosaurs have gotten loose and are killing people, the chaostician continues.

*Dr. Ian Malcolm:* God help us; we're in the hands of engineers.
*Dr. Ian Malcolm:* [realizing that the park is out of control] Boy, do I hate being right all the time! (Kennedy & Molen [Producers] & Spielberg [Director], 1993)

Constructionists make a powerful case undermining the innate assumptions of faith-based science. In actuality, science gets much of its credibility from System 1's "will to believe" and most of the rest of it from its archetypal and structural identity with religion. With science deconstructed, modern man is both more free to perceive reality from any perspective and more prone to experience the raw sense of an underlying chaos. While this can be terrifying, it also frees up opportunities for fresh approaches to thinking, creating, and innovating.

## CONSTRUCTIONISM AND PSYCHOLOGY

God had created the world in play.

—Ramakrishna, *The Gospel of Sri Ramakrishna* (1910)

Kenneth Gergen is perhaps psychology's leading exponent of constructionism. From that perspective he actively critiques many of psychology's basic assumptions. One of his primary critiques is nosology; Gergen is clear that diagnosis in mental health is far more suspect than diagnosis in medicine. Perhaps the single most famous diagnostic category "embarrassment" was the American Psychiatric Association's 1974 debate on homosexuality. Prior to this meeting, homosexuality had been considered a mental illness and it had its own diagnostic category. By a vote of 5854 to 3810, this category was removed and millions of Americans were "cured" overnight (Madigan, 2012, p. 966). If the vote had been a bit different, homosexuals would still be considered mentally ill, a conclusion that in the present would be considered absurd. Both the current sense of "absurdity" and the pre-1974 categorization as "illness" illustrate the constructed nature of diagnoses.

Gergen tends to focus on the proliferation of diagnoses from the several dozens in *Diagnostic and Statistical Manual of Mental Disorders I* (*DSM I*) to the hundreds in the *DSM V*. More specifically, Gergen (2009, pp. 48–49) points out that the increase in the number of diagnostic categories is almost perfectly correlated with the number of practicing mental health professionals. The more mental health professionals, the more diagnoses. Is this increase in categories due to careful scientific discovery of underlying mental health structures or is the increase due to mental health professionals attempting to expand their market and enhance the power of their guild? Every new *DSM* release gives rise to the question "do the new categories pathologize normal human functioning?"

Of course, once these categories are created they become self-sustaining. First, practitioners invent the categories and "market" them to clients. Clients hear about the new category and start organizing and reporting their symptoms in the new context. This leads other mental health professionals to endorse the new category and so on ad infinitum. We are not discovering a new diagnostic category, we are creating it.

Nosology in mental health illustrates the arbitrariness of psychopathology. Are there really 20 categories of mental illness, or 60, or 300, or 600? The only correct answer is that there are as many as the *DSM* committee believes there are and that number is not based on any independently verifiable foundation. In medicine, an X-ray confirms a broken bone and a blood test confirms diabetes; but there are no such real world correlates with mental health diagnoses.

And the systems of psychotherapy are also based on similarly invented constructs. Let us take the basic psychodynamic belief that current dysfunctional behavior is secondary to a past trauma. The response to this trauma forms a "complex" which must be removed by revisiting the past experiences and working through them. To the psychodynamic therapist, these are real events that caused real traumas. They are not imaginations or invented memories. However, what if the psychodynamic therapists are not working with real events from the past but instead are working with co-created constructions of the past?

Gergen (2009, pp. 40–41) particularly cites the work of Donald Spence, the author of *Narrative Truth and Historical Truth*. Essentially Spence argues that the past that is recreated is not the actual, historical past. Rather, the therapist and the client have worked over the past and developed a new memory which is more conducive to problem resolution and future growth. Apparently resolving the invented trauma is as conducive to change as resolving the historical trauma.

While this may lead to a desirable therapeutic outcome, it raises significant questions. Can psychology be a science, based on facts and observations that can be independently confirmed by separate practitioners, if it argues that what really happened in the past is not the sine qua non of healing. Can the science of psychology afford to accept the idea that the key to healing is what the client feels and believes occurred in the past, not what actually occurred? Irvin Yalom argues that the question is moot: the historical past has escaped all of us long ago.

> Psychoanalytic revisionists make an analogous point and argue that reconstructive attempts to capture historical "truth" are futile; it is far more important to the process of change to construct plausible, meaningful, personal narratives. The past is not static: every experienced therapist knows that the process of exploration and understanding alters the recollection of the past. In fact, current neurobiological research tells us that every time we access an old memory we automatically alter it according to our current context, and the revised memory is then returned to long-term storage in place of the original memory. (Yalom & Leszcz, 2008, p. 187)

This description of how analytic therapists co-create a constructed past and then heal it can be applied to other psychological systems. Cognitive therapists elicit (co-create) irrational beliefs and then replace them with more functional ones. Systems therapists co-create an existing description of a family system that they define as dysfunctional and then create an alternative that allows the identified patient and, hopefully, the family to move to a more healthy and empowered position. Equivalent arguments can be made for the other schools of psychotherapy. In sum, Gergen is arguing that a therapist following any psychological system begins by co-creating a pathological world and then replaces it with a more functional one. From this point of view, every psychological system is essentially reframing—an initial frame that defines the origins of pain and pathology and a subsequent frame that provides relief and resolution. And, clearly, all of the differing frames are constructed and co-created; in fact, the variability between the systems—and the fact that they all work—exposes certain important principles that underlie the research results.

Integrating the two research findings—that therapy works but that techniques have no inherent power—can be confusing. We know that knowledge of specific techniques don't add to therapeutic efficacy because if they did, therapists trained in techniques would be superior to untrained therapists, therapists who have practiced techniques for long (experienced) should be superior to the less experienced, and some techniques (psychological systems) should be superior to others. Since none of these statements are true, knowledge of techniques does not add to therapeutic efficacy.

But something happens between client and therapist during the therapy hour; they discuss something and they have interactions and all of these experiences can be mistaken for techniques. In fact, that is the classic error made by most therapists: I performed a technique and, since the therapy had a positive outcome, my technique must be responsible for the results. However, the preceding discussion documents that "what happens" is constructed, co-created, and highly variable. It doesn't matter what frame is offered, as long as the client is invested in the frame and the therapist is seen as credible. Therapeutic reality is so constructed that the client will improve even if offered wildly divergent ideas of why they are suffering from "you are the identified patient in your dysfunctional family system," to "your symptoms are the results of trauma in your childhood," to "you need to replace your irrational assumptions about self and the world with rational ones."

Fully accepting that "techniques lack inherent power" is not simply accepting the research results, it means accepting that what masquerade as techniques are an infinite variety of constructed realities limited only by the investment of the client and the creativity and respectability of the therapist. The positive effect is achieved by the relationship and the process of constructing and deconstructing worldviews; it is not achieved by applying scientific principles to fundamental reality.

## CROSS-CULTURAL PSYCHOLOGY AND DEVIANCY

If God did not exist, it would be necessary to invent him.

—Voltaire, *Familiar Short Sayings of Great Men* (1887)

Other constructionists have taken Western mental health concepts to task from a cross-cultural point of view. The most serious critiques argue that Western mental health is simply another form of cultural imperialism. Consider the following description of the worldview of a Maori from New Zealand:

For the Maori, the person is invested with a particular kind of power, called Mana, which is given to the person, by the gods, in accordance with their family status and birth circumstances. This Mana is what enables the person to be effective, whether in battle or in their everyday dealings with each other. This power, however, is not a stable resource, but can be enhanced or diminished by the person's day-to-day conduct. For example, their power could be reduced if they forget one of the ritual observances or commit some misdemeanor. A person's social standing, their successes and failures and so on, are seen as dependent upon external forces, not internal states such as their personality or level of motivation. For the Maori, accounting for oneself in terms of external forces such as Mana means that all mental life and subjective experience will be read off from this framework. (Burr, 2003, p. 138)

This worldview is radically different from the psychodynamic emphasis on the importance of childhood trauma or the cognitive behavioral assumptions about emotional distress resting on cognitive misconstruals. Given the seemingly radical (to Westerners) Maori worldview and how it differs from the standard psychological systems, is it any wonder that a Maori would make the following critique of the usefulness of a Western map of mental health.

Psychology . . . has created the mass abnormalization of Maori people by virtue of the fact that Maori people have been . . . recipients of English defined labels and treatments. . . . Clinical psychology is a form of social control . . . and offers no more "truth" about the realities of Maori people's lives than a regular reading of the horoscope page in the local newspaper. (Lawson-Te, 1993, pp. 25–30)

What makes the frames, theories, and typologies of psychology superior to those of indigenous peoples? Is there evidence that our ideas of mental health produce healthier young people, or adults who are more centered and grounded, or seniors who are more connected to the culture? Moreover, are the Western maps of symptoms and causes sufficiently robust to operate across divergent cultures?

Berger and Luckmann explicitly believe that the Western map of mental health breaks down when it is applied cross culturally. To make their point, they argue that mental health symptoms differ so profoundly across cultures that one culture's "symptom map" looks silly from the perspective of another. Of course, in making this argument, they not only caution against applying Western mental health maps to people from another culture, they also use the cultural variability of symptoms as further proof that mental health symptoms are culture-specific. And, if the psychological systems are culture-specific they must be constructed.

The rural Haitian who internalizes Voudun psychology will become possessed as soon as he discovers certain well defined signs. Similarly, the New York intellectual who internalizes Freudian psychology will become neurotic as soon as he diagnoses certain well-known symptoms. Indeed, it is possible that, given a certain biographical context, signs or symptoms will be produced by the individual himself. The Haitian will, in that case, produce not symptoms of neurosis but signs of possession, while the New Yorker will construct his neurosis in conformity with the recognized symptomatology. This has nothing to do with "mass hysteria," much less with malingering, but with the imprint of societal identity types upon the individual subjective reality of ordinary people with common sense. (Berger & Luckmann, 1967, p. 179)

Constructionists believe that it is easy to demonstrate the culturally bound nature of psychological maps and constructs. If the psychological maps are ethnocentric, what right do Western mental health experts have to assert that their maps are an independent and scientifically based description of human functioning versus Western cultural imperialism? Medicine argues that its principles apply to all human bodies, can psychology claim the same?

In their own attempt to examine psychology from a cross-cultural point of view, Berger and Luckmann suggest that there is a need for "psychological services" in every culture. However, in this statement Berger and Luckmann are not endorsing the universal healing or empowering nature of Western psychological services. Instead, in the quote below, they argue that psychotherapy has the primary purpose of helping reprogram or recondition people who are deviant—people who are having problems achieving functional roles in the culture.

Therapy entails the application of conceptual machinery to ensure that actual or potential deviants stay within the institutionalized definitions of reality, or, in other words, to prevent the "inhabitants" of a given universe from "emigrating." It does this by applying the legitimating apparatus to individual "cases." Since, as we have seen, every society faces the danger of individual deviance, we may assume that therapy in one form or another is a global social phenomena. Its specific institutional arrangements, from exorcism to psychoanalysis, from pastoral care to personnel counseling programs, belong, of course, under the category of social control. What interests us here, however, is the conceptual aspect of therapy. Since therapy must concern itself with deviations from the "official" definitions of reality, it must develop a conceptual machinery to account for such deviations and to maintain the realities thus challenged. This requires a body of knowledge that includes a theory of deviance, a diagnostic apparatus, and a conceptual system for the "cure of souls." (1966, pp. 112–113)

Successful therapy establishes a symmetry between the conceptual machinery and its subjective appropriation in the individual's consciousness; it resocializes the deviant into the objective reality of the symbolic universe of the society. There is, of course, considerable subjective satisfaction in such a return to "normalcy." The individual may now return to the amorphous embrace of his platoon commander in the happy knowledge that he is "found himself," and that he is right once more in the eyes of the gods. (1966, p. 114)

One can read this statement as a delegitimizing of psychology—an argument that the primary goals of psychology are related to social control instead of personal growth and maximizing human potential. Naturally this argument makes a great many therapists bristle. The vast majority of psychotherapists did not choose their careers to help clients become "better adjusted." Such terms raise the specter of the novel *1984* with its nightmares of coerced drug treatment and mandatory conditioning (Orwell, 1964). Most psychologists joined the profession to help their clients be more free, to learn to think for themselves, and to make choices that align with their inner truth.

What Berger and Luckmann do offer, however, is a wider perspective on the causes of client distress. Because Berger and Luckmann start from the perspective of multiple cultures —all of which face the dilemma of how to "sell" their view of reality to individual members—they offer the word "deviants" to describe all the individuals who fail to integrate into a culture. And they allow for a great deal of variability in terms of the causes of that deviancy. Some individuals are not raised by functional parents. Others fail to integrate because of poverty, racism, sexism, or trauma. Some become deviants because the rewards of being "well-adjusted" are not sufficiently enticing. From this point of view, for example, clients with anxiety disorders can be seen as individuals who are not satisfied with the way the shared worldview predicts the future; depressed people are individuals who don't believe the worldview offers a path to fulfill their hopes and dreams; and sociopaths are individuals who failed to buy into the cultural worldview's concepts about justice and the rewards of delayed gratification.

Berger and Luckmann argue that every culture fails to fully integrate a certain percentage of its candidates. Imagine that the most successful cultures integrate 97 percent of their candidates and less successful cultures only integrate 85 percent. Is this 12 percent difference due to a relative imbalance in neurotransmitters in the low functioning culture? Is the prevalence of "mental health disorders" 12 percent higher in any given culture? When examined from a cross-cultural perspective, such explanations quickly break down. Berger and Luckmann are arguing that the simple act of trying to integrate into any given culture will result in some failures. Moreover, the failures are not necessarily best conceptualized as psychopathology or deficits in brain chemistry.

The concept of "deviancy" results in another interesting implication. Since cultural constructions are supported by all members of the culture endorsing the same basic worldview, deviants are considered the biggest threats to the acceptance of that worldview. And, as has been argued above from a variety of points of view, the disintegration of the prevailing cultural worldview results in anxiety, depression, lack of motivation, and antisocial behaviors. In this sense, deviants are always considered primary threats to cultural stability. If they cannot be reeducated and reintegrated, they need to be marginalized, minimized, and expelled. If they continue to try and make their presence felt

and their views heard, they need to be incarcerated or even killed. The homeless, the impoverished, and the mentally ill can be tolerated up to a point,
but if they become too prominent, a community will take action to minimize
their impact. Lower class suffering—those who live on the "wrong side of
the tracks"—is also tolerated as long as the deviants stay in their own place.

Since, by definition, conformity supports more conformity and deviancy
spawns more deviancy, all those who work with deviants are at risk in terms
of losing confidence in the solidity of their own worldview. There are a number of theories of therapist burnout ranging from compassion fatigue to lack
of personal power to working too hard or too long to mental health problems
in the provider. All of these theories underestimate or ignore the raw impact
of seeing one deviant after another—day in and day out—on the solidity and
stability of one's worldview.

The most common response to this over exposure to deviancy is to develop
a theory that minimizes the credibility of the deviant attack. If the deviant is
an equal-status human being, her implicit attack on my worldview is likely
to have a strong effect on me. If somehow I can make her into a subhuman
being, then her deviancy is much less threatening. Obviously the simplest
way to make her subhuman is to define her as sick: I have normal neurotransmitters; she has sick neurotransmitters. I have normal abilities to form human
attachments; she is so damaged that she is incapable of forming human
attachments. Ronald Siegel, a Buddhist therapist, comments:

> Related to this point is the near universal tendency, in our quest to be helpful
> or feel competent, to develop facile, simplistic, or reductionistic understandings
> of our patients' difficulties. "It's a reaction to childhood sexual abuse," "It's
> because of his narcissistic father," "She's a borderline," and countless other con-
> clusions help us to feel more secure as therapists while overlooking our patients'
> complexity. (Siegel, 2012, p. 141)

Surrey and Jordan, also Buddhist therapists, comment in a similar vein.

> When therapists feel uncertain or inadequate in therapy sessions, we sometimes
> find ourselves turning to theory or distancing ourselves with diagnostic labels.
> This grasping after fact and reason can take us away from our client and increase
> the sense of aloneness for both. (Surrey & Jordan, 2012, p. 170)

While such conceptualizations do protect the worldview of the psychotherapists, they also have a number of negative outcomes. Obviously they minimize the rapport between therapist and client; it is hard for a client to feel
close to a therapist who covertly needs to see the client as "sick" to avoid
being infected by his deviancy. Moreover, theories of client "illness" always
act as filters to the information available to the therapist. Once a person

is seen as ill, the illness frame filters all incoming information in terms of diagnoses and cures; we lose the ability to see the person as whole, complex, multifaceted, and equal to ourselves.

The obvious solution to this dilemma of the encounter with the deviant is to have therapists who have already come to peace with the constructed nature of their own identity and culture and who, therefore, are not threatened by deviants and their implicit challenge to the prevailing worldview. Such therapists do not need to see deviancy as "sick" to avoid their own anxiety; rather, relative to standard therapists, they can hear messages from deviant clients with less filtering and less discounting.

Returning to the Berger and Luckmann quote and its argument that therapists are social control agents, in many cases helping a client integrate into the culture is often a meaningful goal and sometimes the primary goal. In most cases, an individual must first belong to the culture in order to achieve higher order goals like individuation, positive relationships, or spiritual development. Urging clients to find a way to integrate into the culture is not a default violation of personal rights; it is usually the only available road to becoming fully human. However, cultural integration—"joining up"—or, indeed, any other therapeutic goal is more easily achieved if the therapist is confident in her own worldview and unconcerned that she might be polluted by the client's deviancy. And, finally, the requirement to join up can be politically complex if the culture only offers the "deviant" client a subservient, oppressive, or limited role.

In sum, a closer examination of psychology quickly reveals its constructed nature. The most obvious examples are diagnostic categories which rise and fall at the whims of a committee. The inability of Western psychology to move across cultural boundaries adds to the argument that it is constructed. Moreover, the process of co-creating a pathological frame in order to resolve the dilemma with a healing frame is clearly rooted in constructed reality. Finally, Berger and Luckmann's points about deviancy and social control imply that at least a portion of psychotherapy is oriented toward helping clients accept a culturally constructed worldview.

## FUNDAMENTAL REALITY VERSUS CONSTRUCTED REALITY

The world has not gone one step beyond idolatry yet.

—Swami Vivekananda, *The Complete Works of Swami Vivekananda* (1907)

The constructionist idea that "it's all made up"—that it is constructed rather than discovered—is absolutely offensive to many members of western culture. Even bright teenagers can summon simple arguments that support the concept that there is an objective reality that is shared and must be recognized. The concept that there is a concrete reality that actually exists is, not surprisingly, called realism. And constructionism is forced to accommodate to the arguments of realism in a variety of ways.

Certain constructionists endorse relatively radical beliefs and point out that reality is always constructed and no two individuals can ever share reality perfectly. They have many arguments supporting this concept; one of the most simple and easy to understand is derived from the phrase "the map is not the territory." Coined by the famous general semanticist, Alfred Korzybski, the phrase means that regardless of the objective reality of the outside world, it cannot be encountered directly. Rather, the "real world" outside is represented internally as a "map." This map varies from person to person depending on their conditioning, experience, and culture; in that sense, there is no fully shared reality, only our individual perspectives on it. And, my belief that my map is accurate, and yours is not, leads to confusion, poor communication, and conflict.

Regardless of whether such models make philosophic sense, there is a common sense divide between constructed reality and fundamental reality. This book has used the pragmatic definition where fundamental reality equals the material world—for example, trees and houses—and constructed reality refers to our individual and cultural interpretations of the world, the other, and ourselves. While this simple definition can be critiqued from a number of angles, it provides a useful set of categories and can easily be applied to psychotherapy.

This moves us directly to the primary question: how much of the psychological world is constructed and how much is based on fundamental reality? As one might expect, the constructionists argue that much more is constructed than is commonly believed and the realists counter with the idea that the more we discover, the more we will understand that the universe really is a complicated machine and we really can rationally decipher the intricacies of the machine.[1]

At present, in psychology, this realist argument is probably best represented by the ongoing discoveries in neuroscience and genetics. It often feels as if those advances are so interesting, compelling, and consequential that they are poised to unlock the essence of human psychology. Following that course, David Eagleman, a neuroscientist, recently wrote a book called *Incognito* (2012) where he argues that human beings have much less conscious control over their life and decisions than is normally assumed. In the book, he offers a variety of examples which show how little conscious control the individual actually has over his feelings, cognitions, and behaviors. Among other topics, Eagleman reviews split brain research, effects of different kinds of brain damage, and a variety of unconscious predictors of choices and decision-making. The following case involving a brain tumor is typical of the material presented in his book.

A middle-aged man, Alex, came to the attention of his wife, Julia, when he began to develop a strong interest in child pornography.

> And not just a little interest, an overwhelming one. He poured his time and energy into visiting child pornography websites and collecting magazines. He also solicited prostitution from a young woman at a massage parlor, something he had never previously done. This was no longer the man Julia had married, and she was alarmed by the change in his behavior. At the same time, Alex was complaining of worsening headaches. And so Julia took him to the family doctor, who referred them on to a neurologist. Alex underwent a brain scan, which revealed a massive brain tumor in his orbitofrontal cortex. The neurosurgeons removed the tumor. Alex's sexual appetite returned to normal.
>     . . . The lesson of Alex's story is reinforced by its unexpected follow-up. About six months after the brain surgery, his pedophilic behavior began to return. His wife took him back to the doctors. The neuroradiologist discovered that a portion of the tumor had been missed in the surgery and was regrowing— and Alex went back under the knife. After the removal of the remaining tumor, his behavior returned to normal. (pp. 154–155)

Eagleman argues that this type of evidence and the other examples in his book demonstrate that people have far less control over themselves than they imagine. In fact, he even goes so far as to argue that there is no actual free will; instead all choices, behaviors and the sense of self are simply biology.

> The crux of the question is whether all of your actions are fundamentally on autopilot or whether there is some little bit that is "free" to choose, independent of the rules of biology. This has always been the sticking point for both philosophers and scientists. As far as we can tell, all activity in the brain is driven by other activity in the brain, in a vastly complex, interconnected network. For better or worse, this seems to leave no room for anything other than neural activity—that is, no room for a ghost in the machine. To consider this from the other direction, if free will is to have any effect on the actions of the body, it needs to influence the ongoing brain activity. And to do that, it needs to be physically connected to at least some of the neurons. But we don't find any spot in the brain that is not itself driven by other parts of the network. Instead, every part of the brain is densely interconnected with—and driven by—other brain parts. And that suggest that no part is independent and therefore "free." (p. 166)

Eagleman presses the point even further and postulates that every example of criminal behavior or abnormal functioning is fundamentally due to brain damage or cognitive dysfunction. We may not currently possess the technology to diagnose, predict, and understand the nature of this dysfunction, but this technology is on the way. And the implications of his arguments and examples are that brain damage is concrete, real, difficult to modify, and most responsive to surgical and medical interventions.

> As the neuroscientist Wolf Singer recently suggested: even when we cannot measure what is wrong with the criminal's brain, we can fairly safely assume that something is wrong. His actions are sufficient evidence of a brain abnormality, even if we don't know (and maybe we'll never know) the details. As Singer put it: "As long as we can't identify all the causes, which we cannot and will probably never be able to do, we should grant that for everybody there is a neurobiological reason for being abnormal."
>     . . . The bottom line of the argument is that criminals should always be treated as incapable of having acted otherwise. The criminal activity itself should be taken as evidence of brain abnormality, regardless whether currently measurable problems can be pinpointed. (p. 177)

This argument, of course, suggests that all significant dysfunction, whether it violates the legal code or not, is nonvolitional; in that sense, we should be compassionate toward the misbehaving person because, in truth, they lacked the ability to operate in an ethical manner.

There are several obvious problems with Eagleman's arguments. First, the concept that all criminal behavior is the result of an abnormal brain suggests that we have a clear definition of criminal behavior. Since such definitions are socially constructed, this argument runs into trouble from the very beginning. For example, if having an abortion is criminal behavior, does a change in the law mean that we have cured a brain abnormality? Similarly, most all of us would agree that murder is one of our most criminal acts; if anything should define the abnormal brain, it should be murder. Now, certainly we do not consider soldiers to be murderers. Yet in guerilla war-type conflicts many soldiers report killing innocent civilians either through misconstruals, in the fog of war, or in the heat of battle. Do all these soldiers possess abnormal brains? Do the brains become "abnormal" after the murder occurs?

Examine Eagleman's arguments from the standpoint of criminal behavior across race.

> One in every three black males born today can expect to go to prison at some point in their life, compared with one in every six Latino males, and one in every 17 white males, if current incarceration trends continue.
>     These are among the many pieces of evidence cited by the Sentencing Project, a Washington, D.C.-based group that advocates for prison reform, in a report on the staggering racial disparities that permeate the American criminal justice system. (Knafo, 2013)

Using Eagleman's arguments, these statistics prove that there are severe brain abnormalities in black males, moderate abnormalities in Latino males, and milder rates of abnormalities in Caucasians. I doubt that Eagleman intended to argue that blacks have more brain damage, yet that finding jumps out of the data.

Contradictions such as the above often occur when fundamental reality and constructed reality are confused. Eagleman is a neuroscientist; he believes his work is based in fundamental reality. His primary error is not racism; rather, it is assuming that categories like "criminal behavior" or "mental health" are fundamental reality categories, when, in fact, they are constructed categories. In Eagleman's defense, psychology presents its categories and diagnostic manuals as if they are based in fundamental reality. Unfortunately, given that they are constructed, errors similar to Eagleman's occur frequently.

The "lack of free will due to all neurons being interconnected" argument is also shaky. Eagleman would need to prove that every psychic event ever experienced were all exaggerations and lies. Jack Kornfield (1993, p. 52) describes an experience that occurred in a Hospice program. Apparently the children of a dying sixty-five-year-old were sitting outside his room during a visit when they received the information that their father's brother had just been killed in a car accident. They debated whether to tell him, worrying that it might upset him. When they went in to see him, he said:

> "Don't you have something to tell me?" . . . "Why didn't you tell me that my brother died?" Astonished, they asked how he had found out. "I've been talking with him for the past half hour."

He offered some parting words to each child and died within the hour. And here is another such story from a different angle.

> Another young American man, who knew nothing of spiritual life, had a dream of a Tibetan lama while sick in the hospital. Two years later, while traveling in Nepal, he met the very lama who appeared in his dream. This lama smiled and said, "I have been expecting you." (Kornfield, 1993, p. 233)

Such stories are relatively common. Even if many of them can be debunked, is it likely that every one of them is a fantasy? Moreover, every psychic who ever helped a police department find a clue to a crime would need to be discredited. All of these examples embody experiences where individuals have access to information that could not have come from interconnected neurons. Even one valid example of this kind of experience destroys Eagleman's arguments.

Finally, we come to the concept that Eagleman's arguments strongly support the worldview that the Universe is an intricate machine and that science will eventually discover the machine's secrets. This chapter has already shown the difference between this kind of "faith-based" science and the basic scientific method which functions to make human life easier and more productive.

All of those points being made, Eagleman's arguments—and the arguments of other realists—certainly suggest that there is something "out there" that limits constructionism's ability to create new realities out of thin air. Could even the most gifted therapist create a sufficiently powerful intervention with Alex that would result in a decrease in his pedophilia? Most of us would answer that question in the negative; the pathological effects of the brain tumor were so significant that they were likely to negate the power of even the most brilliant therapist. Reality would trump constructionism.

And, obviously, there are many other examples similar to that of Alex and his brain tumor. Eagleman is arguing against the effect size of constructionism and all psychological interventions in favor of the power of the structural and biochemical realities of the brain. In this sense he is united with the bio-psychiatrists who, at their most extreme, believe that medications are vastly more effective than psychotherapy when it comes to altering dysfunctional human behavior. Finally examine the following quote from a psychiatrist who works on a daily basis with the mentally ill. While he is sympathetic to constructionism, he points out its limitations.

However, this vein of research has been tarred by its own crude ideology. If scientism can falsely turn ethical and political issues into matters of disease, and grossly exaggerate what we know about the nature of mental illness, Foucault and his acolytes are prone to an antithetical failing: radical social constructionism. Madness, they would have us believe, whether it is schizophrenia, post-traumatic stress disorder or anorexia, is not grounded in any biological reality. Greedy commercial interests and a repressive society, they claim, have falsely transformed human differences and personal choices into psychiatric disorders.

Arguments of this sort can be morally compelling, for they appeal to the liberal ideal of toleration and argue for the civil rights of stigmatized minorities. However, no one is a Foucauldian in an emergency room. I was a medical resident in psychiatry when I first studied Foucault's arguments, and I got the distinct impression that his "madness" was often just a metaphor with which to challenge authority, not much related to the shaking, hallucinating teenager that I would soon return to on the wards.

To me, Foucault and his followers seemed impossibly naïve, even complacent. Had they ever encountered severe obsessive-compulsive disorder or suicidal depression? Had they ever seen a manic patient take lithium and be restored? Psychiatrists might be blinded by their commitments as insiders, but this academic view seemed sustainable only by remaining on the outside looking in. (Makari, 2016)

Makari appeals to common sense. constructionism is well and good but in the trenches of psychiatric care, arguing that "it's all made up" disrespects the way in which mental illness plays out in daily life; more specifically, he argues that the gravity of certain mental health symptoms overpower constructionist arguments.

While there is a certain attraction to the argument that florid symptoms indicate that the individual's problems must be rooted in fundamental reality, it is easy to offer many examples of florid symptoms occurring in constructed reality. For example, inexperienced sailors on a small sailboat might encounter gale conditions when making a blue water passage. Convinced they are about to die, the beginners might cry, scream, and throw themselves to the deck. Moreover, they could become disoriented, enter a fugue state, or urinate on themselves. Conversely, the captain, who is aware that weathering the gale is well within the capacity of the sailboat, shows no symptoms of anxiety or decompensation. Constructed reality is emotionally equivalent to fundamental reality for most members of the culture and the "shaking, hallucinating teen" might be living in his own version of hell. The presence of florid symptoms does not prove that the causes of the distress must be rooted in fundamental reality.

In fact, it is easy to argue that most of our symptoms of psychological distress are derived from constructed reality. The goals of life—happiness, contentment, achieving social respect, living the good life—are all constructed and vary from culture to culture. Depression, anxiety and many other psychological conditions arise as the individual compares their social status and success against their expectations. Advocates against racism, sexism, and classism argue that the biopsychiatric tendency to see all psychological symptoms in terms of bad genetics and biochemistry stigmatizes individuals in liminal groups; furthermore, they believe such theories indicate both poor thinking and bad science.

It is relatively easy to propose a simple theory that includes the contributions of both fundamental reality and constructed reality. Imagine life is like a foot race. First, one must have the capacity to run in the race. Getting to the starting line with that capacity is a question for fundamental interventions. Alex's brain tumor would have precluded running the race. Therefore he needed an intervention in fundamental reality—surgery—to get to the starting line. However, the race itself is run in constructed reality. Managing expectations, dealing with social forces, cultivating hopefulness and motivation, reducing cognitive misconstruals—all of these factors primarily operate in constructed reality.

Is the race analogy perfect? Of course not; there are constructed reality factors that are relevant in terms of getting to the starting line and fundamental factors that influence the running of the race. However, the primary analogy—that functionality in fundamental reality is necessary but not sufficient—holds true. Another way to look at this is through reviewing the simplistic hope that "eventually drug therapies will become so effective that they will eliminate mental health problems." This expectation, which is clearly rooted in the "faith-based" aspect of science—ignores the fact that a functional body and brain do not guarantee immunity to depression, anxiety, and trauma nor do they guarantee happiness and contentment in life. In sum, some form of psychotherapy—or an equivalent technology that focuses on constructed reality—will always be incorporated into human culture regardless of scientific and medical advances. Biopsychiatrists who belittle the value of psychotherapy are simply confused.

That said, constructionism often states its case as if there are no limits on its power to reshape reality. In truth, fundamental reality places actual limits on the ability to change and grow. The arguments proposed by Eagleman, Makari, and other realists are supported by common sense. It seems clear that there are effect sizes from brain injuries, congenital problems, environmental toxins, and all manner of interactions between the human and his physical, genetic, and biochemical environment.

Just as obviously, there are effect sizes due to constructing reality. Determining the exact relationship between these two forces would take an entire book in itself and, again, that is not the purpose of this book. Until that issue is worked out, it should simply be stipulated that Reality exists and that it will sometimes function to limit the constructionist's attempt to create new social and meaning-based "truths."

However, in general, those reality-based limits are much smaller and less important than Eagleman and his colleagues would have you think. Remember that System 1 tends to see all reality as fundamental reality. This suggests that the current line dividing fundamental reality from constructed reality will always be skewed toward overestimating the percentage of experiences that are determined by fundamental reality. As a closing metaphor, review the following example from Frank Farrelly. In this vignette, Farrelly discusses an intervention with a schizophrenic. Since schizophrenia is widely considered to be a highly biologically based disorder, it is an ideal diagnosis to demonstrate the effectiveness of a socially constructed intervention.

A female catatonic patient who had been completely mute for six months was a problem to the ward staff. I was convinced that she was putting on a big act, that she had even extinguished her startle response, and that though she gave no sign that she was aware of anyone around her, she could be made to talk relatively easily. I made a bet of two dollars with some of the staff . . . that I could provoke a clearly articulated English sentence from her along with appropriate congruent affect—an integrated response—within one week's time.

My reasoning was twofold: 1) she was treating us like pieces of furniture and not even acknowledging our existence as persons, and thus I (along with several other staff members, chosen carefully for their weight) would treat her as a piece of furniture and sit on her for 10 three-minute "lap sitting trials" per day for a week. 2) I reasoned that even though she was obviously "mentally diseased," nonetheless as I said to the staff, "the thigh bone is connected to the backbone, which is connected to the head bone, which is connected to the tongue bone, and she's gonna talk when her thighs feel squashed enough." My bet was, the conflicts in her thighs would outweigh those in her head.

The "lap sitting trials" were begun and were immediately sequential. On the fourth trial she pushed hard, but that nonverbal response, even though it demonstrated clearly that she was returning from her limbo, did not count. On the sixth trial she burst out laughing, pushed hard on the staff member's back, and clearly enunciated, "get the hell off my lap." So much for mute catatonia: if six months of it can be counter conditioned after only 18 minutes of innocuous lap sitting, it obviously cannot be that serious a condition. (Farrelly & Brandsma, 1981, pp. 121–122)

## BIOPSYCHIATRY AND THE MEDICAL MODEL

A thing is not necessarily true because a man dies for it.

—Oscar Wilde, *The Portrait of Mr. W. H.* (1889)

If the faith-based assumptions of science are constructed and psychology is constructed, then what of biopsychiatry? Is it an example of realism or is it as constructed as psychotherapy?

The proliferation of psychiatric diagnoses has already been discussed in a previous section. However, there is a particularly interesting history to the evolution of the *DSM* that is relevant here. In the 1970s, psychiatry was in crisis. Most psychiatrists had functioned as Freudian analysts, providing therapy to neurotic patients. However, the burgeoning fields of psychology and social work were also supplying therapists who were in direct competition with the psychiatrists. Besides, the rest of the medical field looked down their noses at psychiatrists, claiming that they were unscientific and weren't "real" doctors. Finally certain medications, such as early antidepressants and antipsychotics, had had a major impact on the field and their advocates were promoting them as the future of psychiatry and mental health treatment. As a result of these factors, certain leaders in psychiatry decided to shift the focus of the profession from unconscious childhood conflicts to brain science.

Psychiatrists began to refer to themselves as psychopharmacologists, and they had less and less interest in exploring the life stories of their patients. Their main concern was to eliminate or reduce symptoms by treating sufferers with drugs that would alter brain function. (Angell, 2011b, p. 2)

They adopted a conscious strategy to move psychiatry back into the mainstream of medicine. The medical director of the American Psychiatric Association (APA), Melvin Sabshin, declared in 1977 that "a vigorous effort to remedicalize psychiatry should be strongly supported, and he launched an all-out media and public relations campaign to do exactly that" (Angell, 2011b, p. 2). The primary vehicle for this remedicalization was the upcoming *DSM III* release. The first two *DSM*'s were psychodynamic and little known outside the profession. But this new version was going to be different. Robert Spitzer, a leading psychiatrist, fully intended to use the *DSM III* to rebrand psychiatry.

Spitzer set out to make the *DSM-III* something quite different. He promised that it would be "a defense of the medical model as applied to psychiatric problems," and the president of the APA in 1977, Jack Weinberg, said it would "clarify to anyone who may be in doubt that we regard psychiatry as a specialty of medicine." (Angell, 2011b, p. 2)

In addition to legitimizing psychiatry, the *DSM* had a second goal: providing a justification for psychotropic medications. Essentially, Spitzer and his committee members created diagnostic categories that were not only arbitrary but specifically oriented toward the psychotropic medicines that were in current favor. For example, following is a first person account of the creations of "Panic Disorder" and "Generalized Anxiety Disorder."

David Sheehan worked on the DSM-III task force. One night in the mid-1970s Sheehan recalls, a subset of the task force got together for dinner in Manhattan. "As the wine flowed," Sheehan says, the committee members talked about how Donald Klein's research showed that imipramine blocked anxiety attacks. This did seem to be pharmacological evidence of a panic disorder that was distinct from other kinds. As Sheehan puts it:
    Panic disorder was born. And then the wine flowed some more, and the psychiatrists around the dinner table started talking about one of their colleagues who didn't suffer from panic attacks but who worried all the time. How would we classify him? He's just sort of generally anxious. Hey, how about "generalized anxiety disorder"? And then they toasted the christening of the disease with the next bottle of wine. And then for the next thirty years the world collected data on it. (Stossel, 2014, p. 191)

As the last sentence implies, neuroscientists, who take the *DSM* seriously (as they must since they are hardly experts in nosology), would be looking for structures and processes in the brain common to generalized anxiety disorder (GAD) patients. This arbitrary shift in the *DSM* results in a big shift in the direction of the neuropsychological research. And, of course, since seekers often find what they seek, this contribution may, in fact, have created (constructed) neurobiological advances.

The problem, of course, is that *DSM III* looked like a serious diagnostic manual but since it had been essentially cobbled together by the committee—without being based on research or scientific findings—the diagnoses were arbitrary and overlapping. One therapist would diagnose a client as depressed, the next one would say he had an anxiety disorder, and the third might believe it was a personality disorder. In sum, the manual did not generate reliable diagnoses and, although the subsequent editions of the *DSM* have endeavored to improve the situation, the present *DSM* suffers from equally significant problems with reliability.

More importantly, however, the arbitrary manner with which the diagnoses were created argued that they had little validity; that is, they did not reflect any underlying or fundamental conditions that caused or contributed to the mental health disorder. Standard medicine is proud that their diagnosis of, for example, diabetes, is supported by confirmatory blood tests. In psychiatry, however, in spite of over a half century of looking, not one diagnosis has been linked to an underlying biological condition. There are no scans or blood tests for anxiety, depression, or schizophrenia.

> What these pages do not say is that despite 50 years of Herculean efforts, the invention of electron microscopy, the advent of radiolabeling techniques, the revolution of molecular biology, and the merger of computers with neuroimaging machines, no reliable biological marker has ever emerged as the definitive cause of any psychiatric "disease." What many fail to appreciate is that biochemical imbalances and other so-called functional mind diseases remain the only territory in medicine where diagnoses are permitted without a single confirmatory test of underlying pathology. (Sparks, Duncan, & Miller, 2006, p. 91)

The medical model upon which psychiatry is based requires a reliable and valid diagnosis (confirmed by objective tests) which then leads to a treatment which results in amelioration of symptoms or a cure of the condition. We have already seen the problems with diagnosis, what about the efficacy of the psychotropic drugs that form the basis of treatment?

Approximately 11 percent of Americans take an antidepressant—that amounts to over 30 million people. The outcome research documents results that are virtually identical to the psychotherapy research: 75 percent of these people report modest, positive improvement in their symptoms. (Sparks, Duncan & Miller, 2008) The problem, unfortunately, is that recent research reviews have shown that virtually all of that improvement is due to placebo effect.

But ever since a seminal study in 1998, whose findings were reinforced by land-
mark research in *The Journal of the American Medical Association* last month,
that evidence has come with a big asterisk. Yes, the drugs are effective, in that
they lift depression in most patients. But that benefit is hardly more than what
patients get when they, unknowingly and as part of a study, take a dummy pill—
a placebo. As more and more scientists who study depression and the drugs that
treat it are concluding, that suggests that antidepressants are basically expensive
Tic Tacs. (Begley, 2010, p. 1)

Moreover, if we have actually identified and treated the 11 percent of the
population that is actually depressed, one would expect to get a decrease in
depression nationwide. Instead we have the following findings.

Looking at recent scientific studies, Moncrieff (2001) concluded that despite
their increasing use, antidepressants give no indications that they have lessened
the burden of depressive experiences. Her observation was partially fueled by an
inspection of prevalence rates over a 40-year-period. That analysis showed that
rates of depression had not changed since the 1950s. The most recent National
Comorbidity Study Replication (Kessler et al. 2005) confirms Moncrieff's
assessment that rising antidepressant rates have made hardly a dent in depression prevalence. Antidepressants, Moncrieff reasoned, are overrated. Others
have come to the same conclusion, citing that the difference in outcome between
antidepressants and placebos is much smaller than the public has generally been
led to believe. (Sparks, Duncan, & Miller, 2006, p. 92)

Why has the ineffectiveness of antidepressants only recently come to light? It
appears that the research literature supporting antidepressants was tampered
with through various means. First and foremost, the drug companies have a
huge, vested interest in the success of antidepressants. Not surprisingly, they
have been guilty of hiding studies that showed antidepressants were no better
than placebos, of hiring psychiatrists to serve as their spokesmen at major
conferences, and of conducting studies without adequate research design
(Sparks, Duncan, & Miller, 2008). Moreover, even the well conducted studies
were primarily done with passive versus active placebos. Since antidepressants have side effects, the research subjects could tell whether they were
getting the "real" medication or the sugar pill. When antidepressants are
compared to other medications that have side effects—active placebos such
as atrophine (which causes dryness of the mouth)—there are almost no studies that showed a clinically significant benefit for antidepressants.

And what of the oft-touted model of "chemical imbalance": the well-
publicized theory that depression is due to a serotonin deficit at the synapses
of the brain and that this condition is remediated by antidepressants? It turns
out that this seemingly solid theory—which is usually advanced as "scientific
fact"—simply fails to stand up.

In the first place, the theory originated as a speculative jump from some suggestive research findings.

> Unfortunately, the serotonin-deficit theory of depression is built on a foundation of tissue paper. How that came to be is a story in itself, but the basics are that in the 1950s scientists discovered, serendipitously, that a drug called iproniazid seemed to help some people with depression. Iproniazid increases brain levels of serotonin and norepinephrine. Ergo, low levels of those neurotransmitters must cause depression. (Begley, 2010, p. 5)

This was certainly an interesting finding, and deserved to be followed up, but it was hardly proof that a deficit in serotonin or norepinephrine at the synapses caused depression. That theory particularly falls apart when one examines subsequent research. For example:

> Direct evidence doesn't exist. Lowering people's serotonin levels does not change their mood. And a new drug, tianeptine, which is sold in France and some other countries (but not the U.S.), turns out to be as effective as Prozac-like antidepressants that keep the synapses well supplied with serotonin. The mechanism of the new drug? It *lowers* brain levels of serotonin. "If depression can be equally affected by drugs that increase serotonin and by drugs that decrease it," says Kirsch, "it's hard to imagine how the benefits can be due to their chemical activity." (Begley, 2010, p. 5)

And this finding was not limited to tianeptine; it was easy to replicate it across a variety of drugs including opiates and amphetamines.

> Kirsch was also struck by another unexpected finding. In his earlier study and in work by others, he observed that even treatments that were not considered to be antidepressants—such as synthetic thyroid hormone, opiates, sedatives, stimulants, and some herbal remedies—were as effective as antidepressants in alleviating the symptoms of depression. Kirsch writes, "When administered as antidepressants, drugs that increase, decrease or have no effect on serotonin all relieve depression to about the same degree." What all these "effective" drugs had in common was that they produced side effects, which participating patients had been told they might experience. (Angell, 2011b, p. 7)

And, finally, the biggest problem with the theory is that, as far as it can be measured, neurotransmitter function seems to be normal in people with depression; moreover, many people with low levels of neurotransmitters show no signs of depression.

> But the main problem with the theory is that after decades of trying to prove it, researchers have still come up empty-handed. All three authors document

the failure of scientists to find good evidence in its favor. Neurotransmitter function seems to be normal in people with mental illness before treatment. In Whitaker's words:

Prior to treatment, patients diagnosed with schizophrenia, depression, and other psychiatric disorders do not suffer from any known "chemical imbalance." However, once a person is put on a psychiatric medication, which, in one manner or another, throws a wrench into the usual mechanics of a neuronal pathway, his or her brain begins to function . . . *abnormally.* (Angell, 2011b, p. 5)

There is compelling evidence that disproves the "chemical imbalance" theory and equally compelling evidence that documents that antidepressants are no better than active placebos. Given these facts, how did psychiatry and the public become so convinced that the truth is otherwise? The simple answer is: money and the influence it can buy.

Most thoughtful citizens are aware that legislators at both the federal and state level are significantly influenced by money and power. It is not as well known that pharmaceutical companies have similarly used their financial assets to corrupt the "science" around the biological basis of mental illness and the efficacy of the psychotropic drugs used to treat them. Given the payoffs from the pharmaceutical companies, it is hard to see how they could have resisted. Not only are 11 percent of all Americans on antidepressants but "[t]he new generation of antipsychotics, such as Risperdal, Zyprexa, and Seroquel, has replaced cholesterol-lowering agents as the top-selling class of drugs in the US" (Angell, 2011a, p. 2). In short, the market for psychotropic drugs is worth billions and billions of dollars. If you were a pharmaceutical company executive, wouldn't you spend money to ensure that there is "scientific support" for your product?

And spend money they have. First they went after the research. It was documented above that double blind studies conducted by pharmaceutical companies were a third more likely to find significance than studies done by independent researchers. The companies also hid many studies that found no difference between their new products and standard drugs and placebos. More insidiously, however, they made a concerted effort to determine who were the most prominent members of the psychiatric community and took effective steps to get these people on their payroll. Angell (2011) documents an extensive campaign by big pharma to influence the field via the following steps: 1) hiring key opinion leaders as consultants, 2) making donations to patient advocacy groups, educational organizations, and professional organizations, and 3) influencing university and medical school departments. For example, review the analysis below of the pharmaceutic industry's influence at the university.

Finally, to claim, as Preston does, that university research is "clean" reflects a lack of understanding about how industry money gets spent. The majority of drug company trials are conducted by university research institutions. Industry money constitutes a significant portion of the dollars that flow into academic research, supporting researchers and general operations.

    Antonuccio et al. (2003) detail the vast reach of the pharmaceutical industry—from Internet, print, and broadcast media, direct-to-consumer advertising, "grassroots" consumer-advocacy organizations, and professional guilds to medical schools, prescribing physicians, and research—even into the boardrooms of FDA. They conclude, "It is difficult to think of any arena involving information about medications that does not have significant industry financial or marketing influences." (Sparks, Duncan, & Miller, 2006, pp. 97–99)

Up to this point, we have concentrated on the efficacy of antidepressants. What of other classes of psychotropic drugs? Sparks, Duncan, and Miller (2006) present some rather disturbing information about the interaction between psychotropic drugs and the course of treatment in schizophrenia. Citing studies that compare first world treatments' outcomes for schizophrenia—where the treatment virtually always includes antipsychotic medication—with third world treatments—which rarely include antipsychotics—they note that the outcomes are much better in the third world paradigm. Patients who either never took medication or who weaned themselves off medication had shorter courses of psychosis, spent less time in hospitals, and were more likely to be employed and have adequate social networks.

This research raises the alarming possibility that the medications used in the treatment for schizophrenia are actually having a negative effect. Psychiatrists who are concerned with this possibility cite a number of arguments. First, historically conditions such as schizophrenia were once self-limiting and episodic whereas now the conditions are chronic and lifelong. Second, some psychiatrists speculate that the psychotropic drugs have long-term effects on neural functioning probably as the result of the body attempting to adjust to the effects of the medications through negative feedback—a process where the brain essentially attempts to nullify the drug's effects. Third, the drugs have powerful side effects which, in turn, require treatment by other powerful drugs creating an unpredictable set of drug interactions. Many patients with serious mental health conditions are placed on five or six drugs simultaneously. Finally there is some evidence that these kinds of drug cocktails gradually lead to prefrontal cortex atrophy (Angell, 2011). Obviously, this would be an extremely alarming situation if these arguments are sustained. At this point, however, these are simply speculations, albeit speculations with enough grave implications that they ought to be taken seriously by all mental health practitioners.

The purpose of this section is not to perform a full review of all the information about psychiatry and the medical model or the effectiveness of psychotropic medication. Such a review would require listing all the rebuttals to the findings above offered by the defenders of psychiatry and the pharmaceutical industry. In addition, all the major diagnostic categories would require review including ADHD and bipolar disorder. This type of endeavor would require a full book in its own right and that is not the purpose of this text.

However, this brief review of biopsychiatry does demonstrate that there is substantial evidence that the medical approach to mental health is as constructed as the psychological approach. The history of the evolution of the *DSM* supports the constructed nature of diagnoses. The misrepresentation of the research shows that the impartiality of the scientific method has been breached. The scientific vow to approach all facts with a critical perspective has been repeatedly flouted. And the effects of money and advertising on the profession and the public show that the ability of the powerful to influence science is as strong now as it was in the days of the medieval church and Galileo.

For the constructionist, the most interesting aspect of biopsychiatry is not the question, "do medications work?" Rather, the most relevant question is: "how is biopsychiatry framed?" The primary implicit claim of biopsychiatry is that medications treat the cause of psychiatric disorders. More specifically, psychotropics treat mental illness like antibiotics treat an infection. The problem with this claim is that there is no accepted theory about the biological basis of mental illness nor is there any objective test that can determine the presence or absence of mental illness. Exceptions exist—such as the brain tumor discussed in the last chapter—but mental illness is essentially diagnosed by interpreting deviant feelings and behaviors. And we are unclear about whether the factors underlying deviancy are based in fundamental or constructed reality.

Realists will argue that it is only a matter of time before more is discovered about the biological basis of mental illness and that the more florid diagnoses—for example, schizophrenia and bipolar—are the most likely to be influenced by fundamental reality factors. This may be proven true over time—no one has a crystal ball about such matters—but it is also true that fully exploring constructed reality will reveal that more is constructed than we currently believe. The important point is that, at present, we fail to have a biological theory that explains mental illness and we have no objective measurements that differentiate normal from deviant. In sum, without an accurate theory about the biological basis of each diagnosis, we cannot claim that the medications treat the cause of the mental illness.

The second implicit assumption—that psychotropic medications effectively suppress mental health symptoms over long periods of time—also has problems. This claim is similar to the effectiveness of insulin with diabetes; insulin doesn't treat the cause of diabetes but it controls symptoms over the life span. This claim is easier to support. Anxiolytics do control symptoms of anxiety; unfortunately their continued use results in tolerance and withdrawal effects so they fail to ameliorate the anxiety over long periods. Amphetamines are effective at enhancing focus and attention, not simply with ADD clients but with humans in general. It is an open question whether their effectiveness fades over time as the body attempts to regain homeostasis. Major tranquilizers are effective at suppressing psychotic, bipolar, and dementia symptoms; the issue with these drugs is that the suppression of significant agitation and anxiety also suppresses the ability to think, feel, and function. The cost benefit analysis of such suppression continues to provoke meaningful discussion. In sum, biopsychiatry is effective at short term control of symptoms but has difficulty demonstrating that its drugs are helpful over long periods of time; moreover, the side effects can be significantly problematic.

A third way to look at the framing of psychotropic medications is a bit more radical; moreover, it is unpopular both with the pharmaceutical companies and with the psychiatric community. This perspective simply states that a variety of drugs can create states that can be helpful in terms of dealing with psychiatric symptoms. From this perspective, alcohol is probably the most useful drug discovered by humans. At correct doses it effectively treats social anxiety, is conducive to relaxation, and creates positive states of disinhibition and euphoria. Opiates, for certain people, are terrific anxiolytics and also create euphoria and a mild bump in energy. Hallucinogens are useful for getting people out of a rut and have been effective at treating everything from depression to PTSD to marital dysfunction. No one would want to work in a psychiatric emergency room without access to major tranquilizers and the helpfulness of amphetamines and benzodiazepines is already documented above. Interestingly, one of the best ways to rank the usefulness of drugs is to examine their price "on the street." Opiates, alcohol, marijuana, hallucinogens, and amphetamines are worth quite a lot. Major tranquilizers are worth a little and antidepressants have no street value.

While it is true that some psychiatrists pragmatically adopt this more radical view—and will use anything legal to create therapeutic change in their patients—the field as a whole cannot accept such a model. A psychiatrist who says something like "I decided to add Adderall to the antidepressant because I wanted the patient to experience a boost in energy," would likely get in trouble because this pragmatic approach fails to honor the medical model of the "medication fits the diagnosis." Such an approach might help the patient but it would open psychiatry to a kind of "theory-free," Wild West kind of environment where psychiatry would lose much of its scientific justification.

There are equivalent problems with defining psychiatry as a field where doctors primarily prescribe drugs that help suppress psychiatric symptoms over the short term. While it can be argued that this model is more accurate than the prevailing medical model, accepting the short term model would diminish the respect for the field and the respect for the value of medication. Moreover, many of the placebo benefits of medications would be lost. The willingness to tolerate side effects would go down; some patients would refuse to take medications with significant side effects if they didn't believe that these medications were treating the cause of their mental illness. When the statement: "you have clinical depression and will need to stay on antidepressants the rest of your life" is no longer seen as accurate, the value of biopsychiatry will plummet.

In sum, biopsychiatry uses drugs that operate in fundamental reality and create real responses in patients. The constructed aspect of psychiatry is the concept that psychotropics treat the biological cause of mental illness and the related concept that the medications successfully control symptoms over long periods of time. In spite of these issues, psychiatry continues to be a highly useful adjunct in mental health treatment; however, psychotherapeutic practitioners need to deconstruct certain "scientific" assumptions and stay aware of the actual effects of medications.

Most importantly, we need to cultivate discernment regarding the empirical view that the universe is a complicated machine and that mental health problems can be solved once we dissemble the complex biomechanisms of the human brain. The faith-based assumption that "one day we will have great medications that will cure all mental illnesses," will never come to fruition given that so many of our illnesses are created and sustained by challenges, problems, and injustices in constructed reality. Understanding the seductive allure of faith-based science opens the door to a realistic assessment of the positive and negative effects of psychopharmacology.

## RELATIVISM, CHAOS, AND ANOMIA

Existential writers like Kurt Vonnegut (2010) make fun of the human need for foundations and meaning.

"In the beginning, God created the earth, and he looked upon it in his cosmic loneliness."

And God said, "Let Us make living creatures out of mud, so the mud can see what We have done." And God created every living creature that now moveth, and one was man. Mud as man alone could speak. God leaned close to mud as man sat, looked around, and spoke. "What is the purpose of all this?" he asked politely.

"Everything must have a purpose?" asked God.
"Certainly," said man.
"Then I leave it to you to think of one for all this," said God.
And He went away. (p. 264)

That is the precise dilemma that one experiences following repeated exposure to constructionists, cultural anthropologists, Buddhists, and postmodern
thinkers: the world has been deconstructed leaving no solid place to stand.
Reality has become Humpty-Dumpty and nothing can put it together again.
When constructionism and postmodernism are taken seriously, the world as
we know it no longer exists. Gergen relates a story of two students enrolled
in one of his seminars. They were so disturbed by constructionism—calling it
immoral and nihilistic—that they actually complained to the Provost.

> "Without any truth, how can we ever be sure of anything?" They asked; "with-
> out sound reasoning, how are we to survive; and without a firm view of moral
> good, what is worth doing?" Everything they believed worthwhile seemed
> destroyed by the seminar. (Gergen, 2009, p. 31)

Although Gergen does not directly comment upon this, I suspect that he was
probably happy to have some students who had listened carefully enough to
be disturbed by the nature of the material presented in his class. Often constructionism and the supporting material presented in this chapter are seen as
so upsetting that they are received by the listener in a manner similar to the
heads of the investment firm in the Kahneman vignette: they offered polite
comments, vacant stares, and essentially communicated their belief that the
material was so overwhelming that it must be discarded immediately. Put
simply: *if constructionism and all its implications are fully integrated into
one's worldview, such integration requires a complete and radical rewriting
of one's core beliefs.* Moreover, such acceptance can result in being treated
like a "deviant." Individuals who have pierced the veil of constructed reality
become threats; and true threats to the social order must be marginalized at
best and expelled at worst.

Postmodernism not only deconstructs one's worldview, all values based on
that worldview also come into doubt. Values connect to emotions and pas-
sions, and constructionism threatens all of these. Gergen comments:

> Perhaps the most heated attack against constructionist views is directed against its
> moral and political posture. As it is said, constructionism has no values; it seems
> to tolerate everything and stand for nothing. Worse, it discourages a commitment
> to any set of values or ideals; all values are "just constructions." Constructionism
> fails to offer any social criticism or directions for change. I first became aware
> of the bitterness of this critique during a lunch with a Jewish philosopher friend.

As I tried to explain constructionist ideas to him, he responded with anger, and announced he could no longer eat with me. My constructionist ideas, he said, did not condemn the Holocaust. In effect, constructionists would simply go along with the Nazis. Such tolerance is morally repugnant. Another hour of dialogue was needed to re-cement our friendship. (2009, p. 167)

One who truly integrates these ideas finds herself adrift in the ocean of relativism and chaos with no solid sense of right and wrong. It should come as no surprise that this view of reality—a deconstructed, deprogrammed kind of freedom—has been repeatedly rediscovered and discussed across history and culture, particularly in religious and philosophical spheres. It is sometimes called the "secret knowledge" in mystical traditions. It is secret not because it has been hidden; on the contrary, it is discussed in one form or another in almost all spiritual traditions. Rather, it is secret because it is simultaneously repellant to most people in the culture and can be used for exploitation by others.

A modern example of a group who embodied some of these constructionist dilemmas is Bagawan Shree Rajneesh and his dynamic meditation movement. Rajneesh believed and preached a philosophy of deconstructionism and liberation. Since his analyses proved that all values and conventions were the result of social programming, real liberation required his followers to feel, think, and act in a way that showed they were beyond this programming. His most famous meditation technique, dynamic meditation, asked the practitioner to directly experience the chaotic and unformed nature of the universe; from the outside this looked like people walking in circles while making spontaneous movements and meaningless sounds. His practitioners flouted traditional rules and preached that operating outside of social boundaries was a path to liberation. They used drugs, had promiscuous sexual encounters, practiced limited levels of violence in certain situations, encouraged displays of material wealth, and were free to do virtually anything that demonstrated that their consciousness was unaffected by traditional programming.

Not surprisingly, Rajneesh's movement was controversial from the beginning; resulted in many stories of individuals who were traumatized and/or violated; had just as many stories of narcissists and sociopaths being drawn to and exploiting the movement; and finally attracted the attention of the police who essentially terminated the community.

Clearly the full implications of constructionism are always dangerous, both to the social order and to the individuals who practice the beliefs. When "all that is holy" can be attacked and discounted, the attackers may win, but they enjoy a pyrrhic victory. They may be right but what good can come from their analyses and discussions?

For the psychotherapist, the dilemma is obvious. Constructionist ideas may feel more accurate than existing beliefs but there is danger in their adoption.

Psychotherapists already wrestle with their "right" to change clients and to urge one course of action above another. It is true that many therapists argue that a psychologist's "right" to make a recommendation is derivative: the client gives power to the therapist as a byproduct of coming into the office and asking for help. Even with this qualification, constructionism operates to undercut a therapist's ability to urge one direction over another; all of the therapist's values become questionable and there is neither a safe center nor any solid position that allows the exercise of power and choice in guiding clients. Constructionism may be liberating, but at the end of the day it leaves us more battered and confused than we were at the beginning.

Returning to the movie *The Matrix* (1999) at one point the protagonist is confronted by the wisdom figure Morpheus and asked whether he really wants to wake up and see Reality as it is. Along with this invitation, however, Morpheus includes an implicit warning: waking up will not be comfortable. It will have its terrifying moments and the awakened self loses stability, certainty, and predictability.

> This is your last chance. After this, there is no turning back. You take the blue pill—the story ends, you wake up in your bed and believe whatever you want to believe. You take the red pill—you stay in Wonderland and I show you how deep the rabbit-hole goes. (Silver, Wachowski, & Wachowski, 1999)

At this point, the reader might be feeling two opposing emotions. On the one hand, there can be a level of intoxication, exhilaration, and freedom as a result of the constructionist analysis. If everything is "made up," the therapist has access to levels of creativity and spontaneity unavailable to the practitioner who continues to be entranced by cultural conditioning and professional programming. On the other hand, the constructionist is never far from the cold winds of the Abyss. Along with freedom and empowerment come simultaneous doubts. If it's "all made up" then what does anything matter? What can I do that makes any kind of difference? And where is the meaning in all of it?

## NOTE

1. For a detailed discussion of constructionism versus realism in psychology, please see Held's *Psychology's Interpretive Turn*. Held not only contrasts modern and postmodern perspectives on psychology, she devotes a great deal of attention to various theorists who have attempted to articulate the stance of this book: reality is both constructed and fundamental. This is an easy, common sense answer; however, as Held points out, holding this position becomes challenging when one explores all the philosophical implications of blending the opposites.

# Chapter 4

# A Place to Stand

Give me the place to stand, and I can move the earth.

—Archimedes, *The Works of Archimedes* (1897)

The last two chapters provide a description of Reality B. The Abyss, with its chaos and meaninglessness, is the primary experience. In response, humans construct social realities aimed at reducing anxiety and providing stability. System 1 and social reinforcement make constructed reality feel like fundamental reality. Awareness of this process leads to the promise of postmodernism: fluidity and freedom; unfortunately, these gifts come with the dark corollaries of relativism, absence of core values, and a sense of being adrift in chaos. Particularly for therapists, who are involved in making judgments and effecting change, it is vital to have a place to stand—a sense of some sort of meaning running through the chaos.

Looking for the threads of meaning pervading existential chaos is one of the primary purviews of the discipline of existential theology. Paul Tillich, arguably the most prominent existential theologian of the twentieth century, particularly focused on the intersection of chaos and meaning. His most intellectually rigorous work is his Systematic Theology, but fortunately for us, he also wished to make his ideas accessible to the lay person. Hence he preached regularly and wrote a series of shorter books designed for the man-in-the-street. Tillich was a contemporary of Becker and was in his prime in the post–World War II environment of existential doubt, burgeoning postmodern thought, and the implicit despair inherent in the recent deaths of millions of human beings.

One of his shortest books, entitled *Dynamics of Faith* (1957), is particularly relevant to the existential challenges posed by postmodernism. Examine the opening paragraph of the book.

Faith is the state of being ultimately concerned: the dynamics of faith are the dynamics of man's ultimate concern. Man, like every living being, is concerned about many things, above all about those which condition his very existence, such as food and shelter. But man, in contrast to other living beings, has spiritual concerns—cognitive, aesthetic, social, political. Some of them are urgent, often extremely urgent, and each of them as well as the vital concerns can claim ultimacy for human life or the life of the social group. If it claims ultimacy it demands the total surrender of him who accepts this claim, and it promises total fulfillment even if all other claims have to be subjected to it or rejected in its name. (p. 1)

In his first paragraph, Tillich presents the basic principles which run throughout his book. Man is a "meaning-creating" animal. Meaning for Tillich is operationalized as "ultimate concern." He argues that every human has an ultimate concern—whether they are conscious of it and can articulate it or not. This certainly dovetails nicely with Kahneman's sense that System 1 operates continuously to make coherent sense of reality and existence. Kahneman would probably argue that humans cannot disable System 1 and function without this coherent map of Reality. In that sense, he would agree that man is the "meaning-creating" animal.

This ultimate concern often evolves as one moves through life. It can be oriented toward the "vital concerns" like food and shelter but, as those concerns are satisfied, it reorients toward higher level concerns—concerns connected to safety, accomplishments, recognition, ideals, and spirituality. Most importantly, the ultimate concern "demands total surrender"; for example, if success or money is one's ultimate concern, one will work day and night, and sacrifice relationships and even health, in the name of fulfilling one's goal. The ultimate concern implicitly promises ultimate happiness. To one who is pursuing an ultimate concern, there is the sense that while one is pursuing it they are on a "right" path and that, upon achieving it, they will experience happiness, safety, and total fulfillment.

In addition to placing meaning and the unconditional concern at the center of man's being, Tillich is providing a new definition for the word "faith." It is not, as it is normally defined, a belief in something without proof; rather, it describes the relationship between the individual and his ultimate concern. The hope is that if the ultimate concern is fulfilled, one will be happy, content, and living life correctly. Obviously such beliefs have to be "faith based" since no one can promise—with authority—that fulfilling any goal will result in perfect happiness and contentment. Yet individuals implicitly have this faith that their ultimate concern will provide these things. Recalling all the times one has said, "if I can just . . ." (get the job, have the relationship, pass the test, own the house, recover from the disease), virtually everyone has a personal experience of an encounter with their own ultimate concern.

Tillich's next proposal is that ultimate concerns can be ranked on a hierarchy of authentic versus idolatrous faith. Not surprisingly, he emphasizes the common sense arguments that shallow and ephemeral ultimate concerns will lead to disappointment and confusion. While they lead to disappointing ends, a material ultimate concern still makes the demands of any ultimate concern—sacrifice of our entire life. However, these ultimate concerns cannot and will not deliver on their implicit promises of happiness and fulfillment. Obviously Tillich's arguments are backed up by hundreds of stories and anecdotes with messages like: "money and success won't make you happy. Don't follow their siren songs to the ruination of your life."

Of course, these sorts of ultimate concerns are not idolatrous at certain moments in a person's life. One definition of a successful passage of the adolescent/adult transition is that the young person acquires a desirable mate and finds work that is respected by others and fairly compensated. Achieving those goals is often the ultimate concern of a young person in the midst of their transition to adulthood. These concerns only become "idolatrous" if a person continues to elevate them above all others after she has achieved them and the developmental passage has been completed successfully. An obvious example is a classic midlife crisis where a man leaves his marriage, gets a red sports car and a girlfriend who is twenty years his junior. He is confused about how to move forward so attempts to recreate an earlier success. That success was healthy when he was twenty-five but is idolatrous now. Similarly, it is often on one's path to achieve a certain level of financial security for oneself and one's family; however, the fixation on security, and the continued working to save more and more in the fruitless pursuit of perfect safety, is idolatrous.

In this sense, Tillich's system of authentic versus idolatrous faith is hierarchical and evolutionary. He believes that every ultimate concern, when it is encountered and experienced with a healthy and present attitude, leads to a higher level ultimate concern. Staying in any stage too long opens one to idolatry. Interestingly, it can also be argued that attempting to skip ahead creates another form of idolatry. In psychotherapy, for example, a victim of violence, injustice, or abuse is enjoined to work through their fear and anger before trying to achieve understanding, compassion, and forgiveness. Some clients, who are being urged by well-meaning others to jump ahead to forgiveness without regaining personal safety and personal power, inappropriately move into what might be called an idolatrous forgiveness, a forgiveness where the client tries to feel and act forgiving while unresolved emotions hinder her ability to achieve authentic compassion for the perpetrator.

Given that Tillich believes that to be human is to have an ultimate concern, he essentially sees man as *homo religiosus*. Are the rationalist, the scientist, and the atheist—who formally disavow all versions of God—just as "faith based" as the theist? Tillich argues in the affirmative, of course. The dedication of the rationalist to clarity and fearlessness in thought, of the scientist to discovering truths about the Universe, and the atheist to removing all cultural programming are clearly ultimate concerns in Tillich's view. He would, of course, argue that these are transitory ultimate concerns; ultimate concerns that are valid at one point in the developmental cycle, ultimate concerns that need to evolve to a higher level as one grows in wisdom and awareness. Be that as it may, Tillich not only includes the rationalists, scientists, and atheists, he even includes the skeptics and the cynics.

Becker (1997), writing from a much different perspective, agrees with Tillich that all heartfelt philosophies double as religious systems. He believes that society attempts to create meaning by reenacting a hero system—a living myth that points toward the infinite. In this sense, Becker argues that every society has a religious theme even if—as in communism—the society is formally atheistic. The "heroic" vision of an egalitarian society appears to be idealism but, to Becker, it is simply another way to deny death. What Tillich calls ultimate concerns, Becker sees as ultimate rationalizations and ultimate denial. But both agree that every idealized social system attempts to point beyond itself and, hence, is "religious."

Tillich continually emphasizes the "ultimate" in the term ultimate concern. Ultimacy implies spiritually and Tillich is not shy about using religious language to grasp the essence of the relationship to the ultimate concern.

> [E]verything which is a matter of unconditional concern is made into a God. . . .
> Success as ultimate concern is not the natural desire of actualizing potentialities,
> but as readiness to sacrifice all of the values of life for the sake of a position
> of power and social predominance. The anxiety about not being a success is an
> idolatrous form of the anxiety about divine condemnation. Success is grace; lack
> of success, ultimate judgment. (p. 44)

In introducing religious language into the discussion, Tillich deepens the emotional response to the concept of the ultimate concern. He argues that every ultimate concern is a God to the one who is committed to it, to the one who has faith in it. Similarly, the individual experiences success as "grace," a free and spontaneous outpouring of well-being, support and a sense of righteous endorsement that one is on one's path. Finally, lack of success is experienced as "ultimate judgment" that the person is a failure. The failure to achieve one's ultimate concern casts one into darkness and despair and results in a profound sense of self-abnegation. Think of certain investors who threw themselves out the window during the market crash of the 1920s. They would still have had a middle class life style but they preferred death over accepting the loss of their idolatrous ultimate concern.

Tillich's path—as we have discussed it so far—is hierarchical: one ascends an increasingly spiritual and idealistic path with one ultimate concern leading to the next. Tillich however is not content with such a simple model and introduces the concept that every part of the path toward the ultimate is equivalent to every other point. In other words, his model is both hierarchical and flat.

He introduces his nonhierarchical view with the idea that when one walks an authentic path, the first step on the path participates in the terminus just as much as the middle or the last step on the path. Since one can never fully arrive at the ultimate, every step on the path, no matter how near or far, partakes equally in the final goal.

Moreover, the path itself is not simply a "sign" that points toward the ultimate; rather, it is a "symbol" that participates in the ultimate. This difference between sign and symbol is central to Tillich. To illustrate this, he uses the symbol of the national flag. On the battlefield a soldier might risk death to dash out into the open and retrieve a fallen flag. Members of a nation experience visceral anger and a sense of violation when their flag is burned or debased. Contrast that with a sign; write "United States of America" on a large piece of plywood and put it out in the open in a battlefield. One cannot imagine a soldier risking his life for this piece of plywood with writing on it. Both the flag and the plywood signify America yet only one is a symbol that participates in it, only one participates in an ultimate concern that calls on one to risk one's life.

Tillich states that symbols do not last forever; they rise and fall with the vagaries of the individual and the collective unconscious. But while they are living symbols, they not only point to the ultimate concern; in some sense, they are the ultimate concern. Being fully present with a symbol of the ultimate is equivalent to having an experience of the ultimate. And it is not an intellectual experience like one would have with a sign or a rational discussion, it is a full, centered experience of the total person.

With his discussion of symbols, Tillich "flattens" his hierarchical path. Since every symbol along the path fully participates in the terminus of the path, it stands to reason that an eighteen-year-old who is experiencing romantic love is having a spiritual experience that is equivalent to a fifty-five-year-old on a week-long meditation retreat. At this point, the Tillichian path becomes paradoxical. It continues to be hierarchical in that one advances developmentally on the continuum of idolatrous/authentic but it is also "flat" in that any person walking at any point on the path has the opportunity to participate equally in the ultimate. The paradoxical nature of the path gives room for the opportunities to learn, grow, and evolve, but also endorses the power of being fully in the present and the sense that the ultimate is always only a breath away.

Not coincidentally, in defining his path as both hierarchical and flat, Tillich provides the foundation for a paradoxical view of the therapeutic relationship—a relationship that is both one up and egalitarian. In other words, the therapist in the relationship can be a hierarchically superior guide and, simultaneously, honor the essential equality with the client. Similarly he can paradoxically feel that his judgment is more accurate than the client's at one moment while, in the next moment, deferring to the inner wisdom of the client in terms of determining her own path.

This also supports the common therapeutic idea that therapy essentially consists of functioning as midwife to the client's inner truth. In Tillich's hierarchy, the true faith of every individual participates fully in the ultimate and hence, is "holy." In this sense, the therapist is required to orient treatment around the ultimate concern of the client. If it is idolatrous, the therapist's work is to expose the futility of such a path and, eventually, to help the client orient to something more real and rewarding. This also implies that each person has a unique path that exists for them alone. The ultimate presents in many ways depending on the nature and needs of the client. The therapist is required to honor this uniqueness and to structure the therapy to serve the client's true ultimate concern.

## FAITH AND DOUBT

First, believe in the world—that there is meaning behind everything.

—Swami Vivekananda, *The Complete Works
of Swami Vivekananda* (1907)

Tillich's system begins with the definition of man as a meaning-creating animal and then analyzes the path as authentic/idolatrous and paradoxically hierarchical and flat. This is helpful to therapists in that it allows them to use judgment—"this choice or feeling is more authentic"—while still deferring to the client's own truth—"we are being guided by your inner wisdom." So far, so good. However, since Tillich's path points toward the ultimate, it immediately raises the classic issue: is there really an ultimate or are we simply programmed to invent an ultimate secondary to our fear of death and meaninglessness?

Tillich addresses this basic question by developing new definitions of both faith and doubt. Instead of seeing them as contradictory forces, he believes that one is a necessary complement to the other.

All this is sharply expressed in the relation of faith and doubt. If faith is understood as belief that something is true, doubt is incompatible with the act of faith. If faith is understood as being ultimately concerned, doubt is a necessary element in it. It is a consequence of the risk of faith. (pp. 17–18)

With this quote, Tillich moves away from the traditional definition of faith as a belief in something without proof to faith as a relationship to the ultimate concern. And he specifically states that in a relationship with an ultimate concern there is an ecstatic and transcendental quality of choosing and committing but there is an equivalent force of doubt and risk. With Tillich's Faith, one is never completely safe. Because we live in the world we are subjected to the powers of nonbeing which are the heritage of everything finite. Regardless of how committed or wholehearted one is in the choosing of the ultimate concern, the experience of doubt is just around the corner. And as one experiences doubt, one is required to choose daringness and courage in the face of possible failure.

A concrete example helps to illustrate Tillich's arguments about the symbiotic union of doubt and faith. Martin Buber was famous as an existential philosopher and a Jewish theologian. He had a series of repetitive dreams, which he named the *dream of the double cry*. The dreams were set in a kind of primitive world. They begin differently but include an event—like an animal attack—that must be resisted.

> Then suddenly the pace abates: I stand there and cry out. In the view of the events which my waking consciousness has I should have to suppose that the cry I utter varies in accordance with what preceded it, and is sometimes joyous, sometimes fearful, sometimes even filled both with pain and with triumph. But in my morning recollection it is neither so expressive nor so various. Each time it is the same cry, inarticulate but in strict rhythm, rising and falling, swelling to a fullness which my throat could not endure were I awake, long and slow, quiet, quite slow and very long, a cry that is a song. When it ends my heart stops beating. But then, somewhere, far away, another cry moves towards me, another which is the same, the same cry uttered or sung by another voice. Yet it is not the same cry, certainly no "echo" of my cry but rather its true rejoinder, tone for tone not repeating mine, not even in a weakened form, but corresponding to mine, answering its tones—so much so, that mine, which at first had to my own ear no sound of questioning at all, now appear as questions, as a long series of questions, which now all receive a response. The response is no more capable of interpretation than the question. And yet the cries that meet the one cry that is the same do not seem to be the same as one another. Each time the voice is new. But now, as the reply ends, in the first moment after its dying fall, a certitude, true dream certitude comes to me that now it has happened. Nothing more. Just this, and in this way—*now it has happened.* (Buber, 2014, p. 1)

Buber had the dream in this form several more times until, at last, the dream took on a new form. It began in the same way—primitive setting, animal attack, and a cry—but this time there was no answer, no response.

> Awaited, it failed to come. But now something happened with me. . . . I exposed myself to the distance, open to all sensation and perception.

And then, not from a distance but from the air round about me, noiselessly, came the answer. Really it did not come; *it was there*. It had been there—so I may explain it—even before my cry: there it was and now, when I laid myself open to it, it let itself be received by me. I received it as completely into my perception as ever I received the rejoinder in one of the earlier dreams. If I were to report with what I heard it I should have to say "with every pore of my body." As ever the rejoinder came in one of the earlier dreams this corresponded to and answered my cry. It exceeded the earlier rejoinder in an unknown perfection which is hard to define, for it resides in the fact that it was already there.

When I had reached an end of receiving it, I felt again that certainty, pealing out more than ever, that *now it has happened*. (Buber, 2014, p. 1)

At the conclusion of this series of dream experiences Buber had the obligation to make sense of them and to integrate them into his life. He was free to see them as the result of social conditioning and spiritual expectations and dismiss them as essentially meaningless. Conversely, he could interpret them as a connection with the "wholly other"—with the ultimate—and take it as an affirmation of his spiritual identity. Following an experience like this dream series, there is no higher authority one can call on to determine whether they should be dismissed as a conditioned response or accepted as an affirmation of the ultimate. And whichever way Buber chooses to interpret them, he will be picking one form of ultimate concern over another: the ultimate concern embodying deprogramming and aloneness or the ultimate concern embodying the numinous.

If he chooses to dismiss the dreams as the result of social programming, he is simultaneously affirming his essential alienation—his aloneness as he moves through the world of the absurd. In *Denial of Death* (1997), Becker comes to just this conclusion. After deconstructing all culture and meaning as inventions designed to stave off the terror of mortality, Becker rests in the honesty of his analysis and in his courage to abandon all comforting illusions.

The prison of one's character is painstakingly built to deny one thing and one thing alone: one's creatureliness. The creatureliness is the terror. Once admit that you are a defecating creature and you invite the primeval ocean of creature anxiety to flood over you. . . . What does it mean to be a self-conscious animal? The idea is ludicrous, if it is not monstrous. It means to know that one is food for worms. This is the terror: to have emerged from nothing, to have a name, consciousness of self, deep inner feelings, an excruciating inner yearning for life and self-expression—and with all this yet to die. . . .

The man with the clear head is the man who frees himself from those fantastic "ideas" . . . and looks life in the face, realizes that everything in it is problematic, and feels himself lost. And this is the simple truth—that to live is to feel oneself lost—he who accepts it has already begun to find himself, to be on firm ground. Instinctively, as do the shipwrecked, he will look round for something to which to cling, and that tragic, ruthless glance, absolutely sincere, because it is a question of his salvation, will cause him to bring order into the chaos of his life. These are the only genuine ideas; the ideas of the shipwrecked. All the rest is rhetoric, posturing, farce. He who does not really feel himself lost, is without remission; that is to say, he never finds himself, never comes up against his own reality. (pp. 87–88)

To Becker, everything past the feeling of the shipwrecked, the lost, is "rhetoric, posturing, farce" (1997, p. 89). He has made his choice, made his leap of faith, and embraced the ultimate concern of being free, free to experience the Abyss without remission. Conversely, as Buber affirms the meaning of the dreams as a connection with the ultimate and an affirmation of his spiritual nature, he achieves a place to stand, a spiritual center which forms the foundation of his decisions, choices, and values.

Buber's dreams are simply one example of an experience which in the final analysis must be accepted as an affirmation of the ultimate or dismissed as programming. Other examples include watching the face of a sleeping child, falling in love, walking on the beach at sunset, experiencing the season of spring, having a peak experience that all things are connected and you are a part of everything, or being moved and inspired by a sermon or a spiritual talk.

Once one has followed the analyses in chapters 2 and 3, and seen the Abyss and the constructed nature of reality, that person is forced into a decision: Tillich or Becker—an alignment with the ultimate or some form of abiding in the Abyss. Both choices embody ultimate concerns. More importantly, both choices are intertwined with doubt. Becker can never be certain—twenty-four hours a day—that no meaning runs through life and that the best one can do is have an existential acceptance of chaos. Tillich and Buber are never without doubt that their lofty ideals are mere constructs—invented ideas created to shelter them from the cold winter night of the Abyss.

This dilemma is related to the concept of free choice as developed by Sartre and other existentialists. However, Sartre diverges from Tillich in that he believes that the connection/alienation dilemma has been settled; he has examined the alternatives and, to him, it is clear that we are alone. "Every existing thing is born without reason, prolongs itself out of weakness, and dies by chance" (Sartre, 2013). Accepting our aloneness, Sartre believes that the best one can do is to impose meaning on essential meaninglessness by "choosing." "Life has no meaning a priori. . . . It is up to you to give it a meaning, and value is nothing but the meaning that you choose" (Sartre, 2007, p. 51). Orson Welles also accepts basic aloneness and talks about creating the illusion of connection.

We're born alone, we live alone, we die alone. Only through our love and friendship can we create the illusion for the moment that we're not alone.

Buber and Tillich disagree. They accept that there is a case to be made for alienation but argue that it is not clear that aloneness is the "truth" and connection is "manufactured" through an act of will. Tillich and Buber believe connection is as much a part of the human experience as aloneness and alienation. They reject Sartre's confidence that connection and meaning only exist in constructed reality. They grant that Sartre's choice between the alternatives is as valid as their own but deny that it represents higher truth or a more accurate picture of reality.

The existentialists argue that their choice is not only supported by experience, it also takes a high degree of courage to accept it—to continue moving bravely forward in spite of one's aloneness and a fundamental meaninglessness. To frame love and connection as illusion is to leap courageously into a life of existential despair. If it is this hard, it must be true. Conversely, adopting Tillich's perspective is seen as an escaping to a manufactured and seductive comfort because one lacks the moral character to face one's essential alienation.

Buber and Tillich respond that choosing to see life as meaningless is, in actuality, the coward's option. Affirming connection and purpose require an active stance—a stance that consciously resists the seductive whisperings of narcissism and self-centeredness. Is it easier "to be my brother's keeper" or to surrender to the fear that we are always alone? For the conscious individual at the edge of the Abyss either choice is ultimately challenging and either choice requires boundless courage.

The only easy choice is to remain unconscious—to deny the constructed nature of reality. It is easy for atheists to reject spirituality as they point out the logical inconsistencies of spiritual metaphors. Similarly it is easy for the believer—using the old definition of "faith" as "belief"—to assert what he has been taught since childhood, the comforting credo endorsed by all who surround him. In sum, the first choice is awake versus asleep—accepting constructed reality as "real" or rejecting all that is programmed. Only those who arrive at the edge of the Abyss actually make a spiritual choice.

There is an interesting and important contribution to this dilemma from recent work in the field of evolutionary theory. For decades school children have been taught Darwin's dictum of the survival of the fittest. This principle has bearing on our Buber/Becker dilemma. If humans are genetically selected for selfishness—and those who are focused on "getting mine" reproduce at higher rates than the more altruistic—then evolution votes in the direction of Becker. Buber is simply trying to paper over a competitive, disconnected world with a sweet-smelling, consolatory theory.

However, new advances in evolutionary theory are replacing the simple principle of survival of the fittest. Edward Wilson, one of the authors of the new theory, states that we have actually been selected for both altruism and for selfishness. According to his analysis, since humans are highly social and tend to band together and form groups, there is competition and evolutionary selection at both the group level and the individual level.

> Probably at this point, during the habiline period, a conflict ensued between individual-level selection, with individuals competing with other individuals in the same group, on the one side, and group-level selection, with competition among groups, on the other. The latter force promoted altruism and cooperation among all the group members. It led to innate group-wide morality and a sense of conscience and honor. The competition between the two forces can be succinctly expressed as follows: Within groups selfish individuals beat altruistic individuals, but groups of altruists beat groups of selfish individuals. Or, risking oversimplification, individual selection promoted sin, while group selection promoted virtue. (Wilson, 2015, pp. 32–33)

The Buber/Becker debate concerns whether humans are essentially alone or essentially connected. Wilson makes the case that humans are evolved to feel both selfishness and altruism simultaneously and profoundly. This concept is highly similar to Tillich's argument that one can never choose connection without doubting its final truth and never choose alienation without being besieged—at least occasionally—by a sense of unity. Wilson's evolutionary theory has interesting parallels with Tillich's hierarchy in that early developmental concerns about individual success evolve into more other-centered goals later on. Of course Maslow's and Kohlberg's hierarchies have similar developmental steps.

Wilson himself is quite clear that, for him, this altruism/selfish duality does not imply anything spiritual. One of his books is entitled *The Meaning of Human Existence* and his primary argument is that the altruism is more an accident of evolution than evidence of connection. When the Dalai Lama states, "Our ancient experience confirms at every point that everything is linked together, everything is inseparable," Wilson shakes his head and recommends studying evolution more carefully. Yet at other parts of the book, Wilson comments that he chooses to behave altruistically and uses climate change as the concrete example. Wilson believes that the human race is in the midst of an evolutionary challenge; without sufficient individuals choosing their altruistic side, we are headed for a rough future.

Wilson's pragmatic choosing of altruism leads fairly directly to an equivalent choice in psychotherapy. Therapists, when working with clients, rarely or never support the decision to disconnect, to go it alone, and to refuse relationship with others. This choice to be alone is almost always framed as "the client did not have the courage and ego strength to choose to connect. They took the easy way out—to stay armored and alone." Conversely overcoming the fear of the other and saying "yes" to authentic connection is seen as embodying healthy risk taking, consciousness, and love.

The importance of this "choice point" in psychotherapy should not be underestimated. While the consensus of a helping profession to choose connection over alienation hardly "proves" that connected is the "right answer" in terms of Buber's dilemma, it does suggest that therapy, healing, and personal development are inextricably intertwined with the "connected" choice. Psychotherapists begin with an implicit assumption about the value of helping others. On a pragmatic level, as well as a spiritual one, they have already made their choice.[1]

At the end of the day, there can be no certainty. Each individual has their own experience of Sartre's nausea, Wilson's compelling arguments, and Buber's dreams. Expecting definitive answers requires regression to the old definition of faith: something that is believed without proof. There can be no proofs here. Instead there is only faith, activated by courage in the face of non-Being, and accompanied by breakthroughs of doubt and existential despair. Tillich (1957) comments:

> Out of the element of participation follows the certainty of faith; out of the element of separation follows the doubt in faith. And each is essential for the nature of faith. Sometimes certainty conquers doubt, but it cannot eliminate doubt. . . . Since the life of faith is life in the state of ultimate concern and no human being can exist completely without such a concern, we can say: Neither faith nor doubt can be eliminated from man as man.
>
> . . . Doubt is overcome not by repression but by courage. Courage does not deny that there is doubt, but it takes the doubt into itself as an expression of its own finitude and affirms the content of an ultimate concern. Courage does not need the safety of an unquestionable conviction. It includes the risk without which no creative life is possible. (pp. 100–101)

While there will never be a "proof" of God that eliminates doubt, the power of the ultimate concern will always stand at the end of the day. Tillich argues that it is necessary to embrace one ultimate concern to debate the truth of another. At the end of the day, man is always endorsed as the meaning-creating animal.

> [F]aith is not a phenomenon beside others, but the central phenomenon in man's personal life, manifest and hidden at the same time. It is religious and transcends religion, it is universal and concrete, it is infinitely variable and always the same. Faith is an essential possibility of man, and therefore its existence is necessary and universal. . . . Faith stands upon itself and justifies itself against

those who attack it, because they can attack it only in the name of another faith. It is the triumph of the dynamics of faith that any denial of faith is itself an expression of faith, of an ultimate concern. (pp. 126–127)

## NOTE

1. This does not imply that therapists avoid discussing existential aloneness with clients or that they believe that anyone who experiences alienation is on the wrong path. Since connection and alienation are both fundamental human experiences, they necessarily exist in the psyche of every human and therapists recognize their essential validity. However, when it comes to recommending that a client attempt to live life as an isolated being suspended alone in an eternal sense of nausea and meaninglessness, therapists inevitably step back and recommend instead that the client cultivate a sense of connection, love, and meaning. Obviously the manner with which this is accomplished varies from client to client and timing is central, but the commitment of the therapist to alleviate suffering makes their essential choice inevitable.

*Chapter 5*

# The Nomological Net

If you have built castles in the air, your work need not be lost; that is where they should be. Now put the foundations under them.

—Henry David Thoreau, *Walden* (1854)

In order to use constructionism and Tillich's hierarchy in a clinical context, it is helpful to articulate a formal model—to describe Reality B explicitly. Constructionists of course, always begin with the concept of a creative chaos—the raw stuff of life which can be formed into diverse realities and cultures. A culture, and by extension, a personal identity, needs to stabilize this material to create an environment where reality is predictable and safe. This stabilizing force is often visualized as a "Net"—a series of strands and cross hatchings which connect one to the rest of the culture and which stabilizes reality. The analogy can be made to a hillside of raw earth bereft of plants because it has been graded recently. The hillside is stabilized with an anti-erosion net until the roots of the seeded plants can take over the job; a net of fiber or plant roots is required to restrain the relatively fluid hillside from changing and altering shape with each rain storm.

By extension, each individual exists at the center of her own net with strands going off in every direction. The purpose of this net, of course, is to sustain the nature and structure of one's personality across experiences, social encounters, and time. As demonstrated in the earlier chapter on the Abyss, identity is fluid and plastic, a fact which, when fully experienced, is equivalent to falling into the Abyss. Stabilizing this fluidity is necessary for a sense of personal safety and for social functioning.

The individual's strands connect to virtually everything relevant to his life: his body, his family, other individuals, his bank account, and important

117

cultural ideas like the nature of government and religion. The strands are of varying thicknesses and strength and change with the passage of time and in the context of different experiences. Tillich, of course, would argue that one of the primary strands is related to the person's ultimate concern. This net appears to be solid but is always inherently fragile; as Becker argues, the anxiety related to the existence of the Abyss is always prepared to break through and to transform a person's experiences and feelings in a rapid, irresistible, and terrifying direction. Gilligan compares the Net to a concept of overlapping filters. Simply replace "filter" with "thread" in the following quote.

> There are many types of reality filters: neurological, cultural, familial, personal, social, and so on. The body is a filter, family is a filter, educational background is a filter, the social context is a filter. All are gateways through which consciousness flows, translating information/energy into classical and human form. Each filter has multiple dimensions—for example, a specific filter may carry beliefs, histories, images, verbal languages, rules, images, defining narratives—and each dimension can be set in many ways. For example, in your intimacy map you may believe that you're unlovable, or that you can enjoy intimacy, or that intimacy is never fulfilling. . . . Of course, there are many filters operating at many levels, so we don't want to fall into the solipsistic trap of assuming that your conscious thoughts singularly create the whole universe. You belong to a culture, a family, a gender, social groups, and so forth. All these different levels of identities are in play, each with their own filters, so the process is complex. (Gilligan, 2012, p. 23)

And narrative therapists in particular see this Net as instrumental and fundamental to the definition of self. My self is not in me; rather, it exists in the space between me and my entire environment—with everything in dialog with me. "Who am I?" is best answered socially.

> During the early 1930s, Mikhail Bakhtin, who was a Russian psychologist and linguist, suggested that we are direct contributors to each other's identity. Bakhtin described a relational view of the self when he stated that "[I] get a self that I can see, that I can understand and use, by clothing my otherwise invisible (incomprehensible, unutilizable) self in the completing categories I appropriate from the other's image of me" (Clark & Holquist, 1984, p. 79). Bakhtin's belief is that the other plays a central role in constituting the individual's self. And without the ongoing relationship to the other, our selves would be invisible, incomprehensible, and unusable. The other gives us meaning and a comprehension of our self so that we might possibly function in the social world (Liapunov & Holquist, 1993). The knowledge we have of ourselves appears in and through social practices—namely, interaction, dialogue, and conversation with others' responses. (Madigan, 2012, Kindle Locations 1634–1647)

For purposes of this book, we will call this net, the "Nomological Net" with Nomos referring to the principle of order or law. The job of the therapist is to help the client move from his current identity—his current position in the Net—to a new one which is relatively free of symptoms, or more vital and meaningful, or an evolutionary step along one's path.

The Net is stabilizing and the Abyss is destabilizing. The Net is Apollonian and the Abyss is Dionysian. The Net holds it all together and the Abyss dissolves everything into primal chaos. When Abyss is used in this manner it implies all of the forces of entropy: change, death, and developmental processes.

The forces of the Abyss are usually characterized as terrifying and disintegrative but, paradoxically, they can also be seen as freeing, liberating, and empowering as well. Dionysian can be chaotic and destructive but change is also necessary for adaptability, growth, development, and life itself. The Abyss is a living contradiction. Typically, when the Abyss breaks through the shielding aspect of the Net, the result is grief, confusion, meaninglessness, and terror. Recall the beginning of the chapter on the Abyss which emphasized the relative power of negative life experiences.

Contrast that with Joseph Campbell's view of the Abyss: "It is by going down into the abyss that we recover the treasures of life. Where you stumble, there lies your treasure" (Kain, 2011, p. 112). In that same vein, Buber repeatedly urges seekers to leap into the Abyss to achieve spiritual fulfillment. Rumi tells us, "The cure for pain is in the pain." And Jung, Hillman, and Merton believe that psychopathology—while admittedly associated with pain and suffering—when explored appropriately will often serve as a road into meaning. This concept, that the breakthrough of the Abyss into normal life can lead to epiphanies, spiritual experiences, and guidance, is precisely the opposite of its typical reputation as a terrifying and demoralizing experience. In this sense, the Abyss functions as an oracle.

The individual who can confront the Abyss directly has a power beyond most of us humans, a freedom which surpasses those who fear it and try to contain it. One of the classic definitions of a shaman—a definition which crosses cultures and time—is the person who can visit the "other world" or "the world of the dead" and return bearing gifts to the world of the living. In this sense, the Abyss—when manifest as Dionysian or creative energy—is the source of all that is new, fresh, progressive, and adaptive. The Hindus characterized the dark side of the Abyss as Kali and Shiva: destroyers of ignorance, divine forces which cut through all that holds us back. They are terrifying and liberating simultaneously; it simply depends on whether one can find a place to stand that is sufficiently solid, such a vantage point allows one to experience the raw material of life and change with exhilaration and liberation instead of terror. The same force that terrifies us and cuts through ignorance can also open the door to truth and inner peace.

Opposed to these forces are the forces of stabilization. This Apollonian force is embodied by the conservative effort to keep it all together, to resist falling apart, to preserve what is good. This force is particularly familiar to family systems therapists who call it homeostasis: the tendency of a system to revert to a previous form after being buffeted by the winds of change. The power of the Abyss requires an equally powerful counterforce: homeostasis is not a mild elasticity which is easy to overcome. It is resistant, persevering, and powerful. The "light" side of the Apollonian stance manifests as preserving what is best and making life predictable and fair, for example, it is particularly important in the context of raising children. The dark side is easily seen in the righteousness and anger of a "conservative" who, when confronted by something beyond his control, chooses actions which extend from fury and indignation to assassination and execution. Destabilization is a very serious matter when one lacks a sufficiently strong place to stand; terror, doom, and a sense of imminent death are common results when one is exposed suddenly and unwittingly to the Abyss.

While Apollonian forces are useful and necessary in a healthy culture or family, stability is the enemy of the effective therapist. Stability implies a continuation of the symptoms which brought the client into treatment. And of course, not only will the client operate to stabilize her own position but it is often true that the culture itself will work to stabilize the individual. The therapist's job is to be a provocateur, an unbalancing influence that helps the individual alter the shape and nature of her Nomological Net into something more effective, workable, and functional. Putting this in terms of Tillich's system, the therapist moves the client from an idolatrous fixation to a more functional and fluid relationship with her ultimate concern.

From this description it is easy to conceptualize an individual's Nomological Net as strong or weak—hyper stabilized or fluid. A hyper stabilized identity is rigid with fear; the individual senses the looming Abyss and clutches on for all they are worth. Conversely a fluid Net allows a person to adapt easily to the inevitable changes and developmental processes that characterize life. A so-called unstable person—an individual who has labile moods and flits from one center point to another—only appears fluid; in reality, their apparent instability is in itself a hyper stability. Typically the more unstable, the more difficult it will be for such a person to change appropriately and in alignment with an ultimate concern.

In addition to this hyper stable/fluid dimension, there is another dimension worth considering: cultural integration versus alienation. From a constructionist point of view, the primary task of child rearing is to inculcate the worldview of the culture. Success or failure in this regard can vary widely across individuals, religions, social classes, and so on. To be a successful member of the culture, one must not only "speak the language" in every sense of the word, one must also believe that cooperating with others, deferring to higher status people, and working hard will eventually result in happiness. In a general sense, while there may be many subcultures, each of which can be differentiated from the primary culture in varying ways, at the end of the day there is one primary choice: become a member of the tribe or live as an outsider. And, of course, to motivate individuals to "join up" there are various incentives as well as implicit and explicit penalties and punishments if one chooses to be an outsider.

Individuals vary by how well they are integrated into the culture from "pillars of the community," to the "upwardly mobile," to normal individuals. And then there are the outsiders: the disabled, the rule breakers and sociopaths, and the liminal. On the outer edge of the culture live those who have never integrated—the homeless, the severely mentally ill, and the oppressed—and those who were in the tribe but have been pushed toward the fringes—the underemployed, the recently divorced, and the disabled. All of those who live on or near the edge are in daily dialog with the Abyss; often they are suspended in it full time. And, of course, one would expect that many of those at the edge of the culture have hyper stabilized identities.[1]

Tillich's analysis adds a vertical dimension; individuals are not only measured in terms of the center or being near the edge, they are also measured hierarchically in terms of the true/idolatrous nature of their ultimate concern. Often the person at the center of the culture is the same person who is the most idolatrous. It is easy to become attached—idolatrous—when one is successful by cultural definitions. The New Testament quote about it being as difficult for a rich man to enter heaven as for a camel to pass through the eye of a needle is relevant here.

Nietzsche's continuum of Apollonian versus Dionysian will be central to many discussions in this book. Everything that supports the solidity and stability of the net is Apollonian; all that is conducive to change, fluidity, and creativity is Dionysian. Apollonian change is gradual, logical, and expected. Conversely, Dionysian change is often discontinuous, abrupt, and occurs via altered states. Since psychotherapists are primarily focused on change, the Apollonian forces of stability usually provide resistance and the Dionysian forces of personal growth are usually allies. Of course, there are many healthy forms of Apollonian change and, as we will discuss below, psychology is often more comfortable with championing gradual and expected change that implicitly supports the Net than the sometimes jarring and unsettling process that often characterizes Dionysian change.

All of the concepts discussed in this section taken collectively form a geography of constructed reality. The most important concept is the constant,

ongoing dialog between the Abyss and the Net. An awareness of the dialog between these primary forces and a graceful ability to work with their
nuances can be symbolized by the concept of dancing with the Abyss.

## THERAPY AS RITUAL

Truths are illusions of which one has forgotten they are illusions.

—Friedrich Nietzsche, *The Complete Works*
*of Friedrich Nietzsche* (1911)

The research tells us that what we do in the room with clients works; virtually every system and every technique generates the expected mild, positive
effect. Given this unity of outcomes, there have been a number of common
factors theories that attempt to identify the shared elements across approaches
that are most responsible for change. We have already reviewed the most
famous common factors theory—the concept that a healthy therapeutic relationship underlies all change.

Something happens in the room beyond the relationship. Traditionally
these interactions are called "techniques"; however, with the literature
explicitly supporting the concept that techniques have no inherent power, we
require a more comprehensive common factors theory that fits with a constructionist analysis. Fortunately, Jerome Frank proposed just such a theory
over fifty years ago.

When he initially proposed his theory, Frank was attempting to articulate a
model of change that could unite modern psychotherapy with other models of
change across cultures and history, models as diverse as shamanism, spiritual
mentoring, and faith healing. Writing in his classic work, *Persuasion & Healing*, Frank proposed that all therapy, whether modern, shamanic, or spiritual,
has four factors in common.

In our view, all psychotherapies share at least four effective features.

- An emotionally charged, confiding relationship with a helping person;
- A healing setting;
- A rationale, conceptual scheme, or myth that plausibly explains the
  patient's symptoms;
- A ritual or procedure that requires the active participation of both patient
  and therapist and that is believed by both to be the means of restoring the
  patient's health. (Frank & Frank, 1993, pp. 40–43)

Frank's model begins with the most well-known factor, the therapeutic
alliance. He then veers toward constructionism when he implies that the

explanation for the symptoms can essentially be anything, even a myth. For Frank, it is important to note that the explanation is not required to be "true"; instead, he simply requires that it is acceptable and plausible. Finally, he addresses the concept of "technique" and replaces it with "ritual."

This use of the concept of "ritual" was prescient given that the research evidence that techniques aren't responsible for change was weak at the time Frank developed his theory. It seems clear that he used the concept "ritual" in part because he was developing a model broad enough to include shamanic healing, but it was still an idea that was well ahead of its time. Finally, he concludes his model by emphasizing the power of belief and expectations.

Modern common factor theorists have integrated the research results with Frank's model and become much more assertive in their use of the concepts of myth and ritual. Their sense of "myth" includes two of its most common definitions: something that isn't true and something that provides a meaningful foundation for experience and choices. In the following quote, Anderson, Lunnen, and Ogles (2010) explain their understanding of myth and psychotherapeutic rationales.

> To be persuasive, any intervention must first be meaningfully linked with shared communal beliefs (Wampold, 2007). As Frank and Frank (1998) noted, "The power of any therapeutic rationale to persuade is influenced by the culture from which it derives. In devout cultures, religious rationales may have the greatest therapeutic power. In our secular society, such power derives from science" (p. 590). In short, models must possess a rationale that strikes at the heart of what it means to be a person within a particular place and time. (Kindle Locations 3909–3915)

Like constructionists, Anderson et al. are relatively unconcerned about the literal truthfulness of the explanation; as long as it is meaningfully linked to communal beliefs, it will work. This is a radical break from standard clinical psychology where the explanations offered to the client are seen as truthful and accurate. In the common factors model clinicians are enjoined to adjust their own beliefs to the worldview of the client. In addition, if the clinician determines that the client shares a prevailing mythic belief—for example, that anxiety or depression has roots in childhood trauma—then they are free to expand the client's investment in that worldview by exploring it in depth. There are few limits on what can serve as an explanation. Clearly the farther outside prevailing beliefs, the more work the therapist needs to do to support the mythic explanation.

The next major aspect of the common factors theory is the procedure or ritual. The research has made a significant contribution in that it has virtually made it impossible for thoughtful research consumers to tout the benefit of techniques and "specific factors." Recall that Wampold took an even more radical stance and argued that the issue of the power of techniques is such a dead end that "clinical trials comparing two treatments should be discontinued."

On the surface, this appears to be a radical idea: cease all research into new techniques and abandon the hope that the next procedure will be more effective. The fact that virtually everything works steals the sense of permanence and solidity from techniques. Of course, client suffering remains real but the explanation for the suffering is a construct and the ritual/procedure is a construct. Constructionists understand that the power to change is never in the technique; it always exists in the presentation of the therapist and the endorsement of the client. Once again, the client is not changing because a powerful technique has been employed that correctly fits the specific diagnostic problem; rather, any procedure that is invested with meaning will serve as a change agent. Anderson et al. comment:

> Ritual or technique is the means by which a given cultural myth or therapeutic rationale is enacted. Where myth or rationale explains why, ritual or technique shows how. In the field of psychotherapy, practice and research have long been dominated by therapeutic technique. At the same time, it may be said, paraphrasing Winston Churchill, that never has a subject that contributes so little to outcome received so much professional attention and approbation. As reviewed elsewhere in this volume, no differences in effectiveness have been found among treatment approaches intended to be therapeutic. . . . In other words, therapeutic techniques are placebo delivery devices (Kirsch, 2005). . . . At this point, suffice it to say that techniques work, in large part, if not completely, through the activation and operation of placebo, hope, and expectancy. (2010, Kindle Locations 3948–3960)

This is a wildly constructionistic view of psychotherapy. It doesn't matter what is done as long as it is accepted by client and therapist and both believe that the ritual will lead to change or improvement. Virtually everything works as long as it is done with the right attitude. In sum, selecting the correct procedure is not the secret; rather it is imbuing the procedure with numinosity.

While these arguments about ritual are well supported by both the research results and logic, they do run into the problem that arises with all constructionist explanations: how can a therapist authentically support a ritual with the same allegiance that they would have with a technique? This is particularly important given that the research has shown—not surprisingly—that therapists get better outcomes when they believe in the approach that they are using. In the following quote, Anderson et al. directly address this question and argue that they can achieve this faith and inspiration by aligning with the client's "narrative truth" and by abiding with their own "core beliefs."

Awareness that contemporary healing practices are infused with the culture's mythology does not necessarily diminish one's ability to participate in and use them in treatment . . . (j)ust because a therapist might have an awareness of treatment as myth does not reduce the therapist into a detached and cynical critic who is playing a charade. As noted throughout, effective therapy requires emotional investment and commitment to some shared cultural values. That is, the therapist who cannot summon a passionate commitment to his or her core beliefs will ultimately fail to engage the patient in an emotionally charged relationship. The therapist's own emotion and commitment serve to weave treatment myth, treatment principles, and ritual into a powerful and persuasive communication that, in turn, enhances the therapeutic relationship. . . . Knowledge that these values are culturally dependent need not be a forbidden fruit that bans the therapist from participation in his or her own culture, nor from conducting good psychotherapy! For many therapists, adherence to their practices seems to be based on both literal and historical sense. Therapists may believe just as stridently that only the client's narrative construction is true in its own right. With regard to the latter, narrative truth is no less real than the physical and historical reality, such as in the prior discussion of placebo effects. (2010, Kindle Locations 4157–4176)

This answer returns us to the end of the chapter on constructionism and directly raises the question of the need for a "place to stand." For example, when psychology is framed as a discipline that operates in fundamental reality—and, hence, has techniques—the question of meaning and belief are secondary. If I know a technique that has the power to reduce your anxiety or relieve your depression, then it is ethical for me to share it with you and easy for you and me to believe in it.

Conversely, the moment I operate in a "technique-free" zone—in constructed reality—huge problems arise in the area of meaning and belief. Anderson et al. point us in the right direction with their references above to "core beliefs" and the "client's narrative truth." Fortunately, Tillich has already taken us further down that road when he references the client's "ultimate concern." Standing with Tillich, the constructionist therapist can argue that a given ritual is meaningful because it participates in advancing the client's evolutionary path—the hierarchical aspect of Tillich's model. For example, when a constructionist therapist tells a client that the way to get over her rape-related PTSD is to help other survivors, this frame can be advanced with full sincerity. The knowledge that the therapist might have said instead, "The best way to release your anxiety is to go on a Buddhist meditation retreat and experience that your 'true self' was always untouched by the rape," fails to diminish the therapist's authenticity or their commitment to the injunction.

Finally, it is worth examining Frank's understanding of the therapeutic relationship. He notes that the therapy requires "a healing setting." The healing setting literally refers to an office or hospital, but in a larger sense, it also refers to a license, an education, and a title like "doctor" or "life coach." In discussing the healing setting Frank is endorsing the concept of the implicit hierarchy between the therapist and the client. I come to the healing setting because that's where the magic happens. The therapist is a denizen of the magic or sacred space and, hence, implicitly has great powers.

But, of course, these are only outer symbols; the real sense of respect is derived from the projected confidence of the therapist and the ability of the therapist to explain the dilemma both clearly and in a manner that pushes the conceptualization of the client into a new dimension. In so doing, the therapist demonstrates greater consciousness than the client; in so doing, they appear "charismatic."

Frank's model helps differentiate the therapeutic relationship from normal relationships. I can have a relationship with a wise and caring friend, and their counsel can be helpful to me, but our relationship lacks hierarchy—they are not my superior. Conversely, in a therapeutic setting I have a relationship with a wise and caring therapist who, by definition, is one up on me. Whether techniques have inherent power or not, when I go to a therapist for healing— and visit her in a healing setting—I assume that she will have something special to offer me. And without that specialness both the explanation for my problem and the prescribed ritual will fall flat. Understanding that hierarchy is necessary in order to achieve good outcomes is central; when knowledge of techniques does not confer implicit respect, the therapist must pay attention to their own charisma. Put another way, the therapist is special because of who she is, not what she knows.

## THE NEW THERAPEUTIC MILIEU

One must still have chaos in oneself to be able to give birth to a dancing star.

—Friedrich Nietzsche, *Thus Spake Zarathustra* (1896)

With this chapter, we conclude the description of Reality B: the new therapeutic milieu. Our journey began with the therapy outcome research results. The findings that beginners are as effective as experts and the lack of innate power in techniques indicates that therapy operates outside of conventional assumptions about reality. The huge denial—Maher's "Bubble"—about the import of these findings was addressed by Kahneman's work with System 1. He argues that it is characteristic of the most powerful part of the mind to create worldviews that are oversimplified and inaccurate in order to impose apparent order on the terrifyingly chaotic world. He also pointed out that these inaccurate worldviews are vigorously justified and defended using System 2—the rational and analytic part of the mind.

This "terrifying chaotic world" has three major components: Buddha's "old age, sickness, and death"; the shifting, insubstantial, and ephemeral nature of the Self; and the implicit sense that the values, beliefs, and vision of reality espoused by one's "home culture" are constructed and made up. Collectively these three form the Abyss—the place of chaos, terror, and meaninglessness. Its presence is obvious and apparent; we all feel like we are one small slip—in our health, fortunes, or luck—away from disaster and defeat. In order to co-exist with the ever present terror, most humans cultivate some form of denial. For many of us, this denial works fairly well, but all of our actions, choices, and feelings continue to be in dialog with the underlying Abyss.

Constructionism is as old as thought. It is the inevitable result of any kind of self-reflection and is present in one form or another in every culture. Constructionism is a core component of the "perennial philosophy," an essential and inevitable critique of facile assumptions about reality. Apollonian forces always resist constructionism, understanding its implicit and explicit threat to the social order and to healthy denial.

The concept of constructed reality is always in dialog with its partner, fundamental reality. Regardless of the arguments of philosophers, the human experience rests in the sense that we live in a shared world that is actually real. This world of "trees and houses" stands in contrast to the constructed world of concepts like "masculinity and honor." Higher order discernment separates the one reality from the other.

Mild constructionism does not require an encounter with the Abyss. To understand that feminine beauty is relative and culturally determined is an insight that cuts through certain levels of social programming but it does not shatter one's sense of reality. In contrast, constructionism taken to its logical extreme always leads to the edge of the Abyss and leaves the seeker exposed to meaninglessness and anomia. Psychotherapists who develop a powerful relationship with the concepts of the ephemerality of the Self and cultural relativity will arrive at this edge.

Genuine seekers eventually have need of a "Place to Stand"; members of a helping profession, who require a sense of meaning and purpose to guide clients in distress, are particularly dependent on finding a center. Tillich tells us that all such places to stand—his model, and other spiritual/philosophical models—share two key components: faith—where faith is defined as a relationship to an ultimate concern—and doubt. Humans are impelled into relationship with an ultimate concern by their essential nature. If Tillich had lived to read Kahneman, he might argue that System 1 is not only required to create worldviews but those worldviews have a central connection to an ultimate concern.

The worldview is not simply an individual matter; it is interwoven with all significant others and also tied in with cultural assumptions. This interweaving defines the Nomological Net. It is the job of all Apollonian forces to defend the current structure of the Net and only allow permissible evolution—such as a child becoming an adult—and resist more radical alterations. Since psychotherapists are agents of change, the profession is implicitly Dionysian and is essentially provocative and revolutionary. That said, Apollonian forces are always seeking to coopt the Dionysian and it is clear that there are a great many Apollonian forces operative in psychology itself.

Finally, Frank's common factors theory—especially the more provocative, modern version of it—defines therapeutic growth as a process which begins with a mythic explanation and creates change through rituals. Without the shelter of active and innately powerful techniques—or the privileged knowledge which defines most professions—enhanced therapeutic efficacy rests on therapist charisma—the ability of the client to see the therapist as a key figure with the power to define the rules of constructed reality. The essence of change is not dependent on what the therapist knows but on who the therapist is.

All the theoretical factors are now in place: the research results, Kahneman's System 1 and its need to create worldviews, the terrifying Abyss with the implicit need for denial, pragmatic constructionism with its attendant fundamental reality and constructed reality, Tillich's "place to stand," the Nomological Net, and the therapeutic environment espoused by common factors theory. These factors show the path from Reality A to Reality B.

More specifically, they define the new therapeutic milieu. Its geography now has shape and form. Its implicit rules and principles govern the possibility of therapeutic change. This has meaningful implications for how therapists can be trained and for how they can improve over their professional lifespan; in sum, it outlines a path that leads to enhancing therapist efficacy.

# NOTE

1. Obviously social justice plays a large role in becoming a liminal member. There are no completely "just" societies; hence there will always be individuals and groups that are liminal members secondary to injustice.

*Part II*

# ENHANCING THERAPIST EFFECTIVENESS

The strongest and sweetest songs yet remain to be sung.

—Walt Whitman, "November Boughs. A Backward Glance O'er Travel'd Roads," 1888

# Chapter 6

# Focus on the Therapist

I am larger, better than I thought; I did not know I held so much goodness.

—Walt Whitman, *Selections from the Prose and Poetry of Walt Whitman* (1898)

Now that we have a shared sense of what "water" is, we can move directly to the primary concept of the book: enhancing therapist effectiveness. The central focus of these enhancement strategies will be the very arena that the research discounts: therapist experience. We all feel powerfully affected—indeed, sometimes, transformed—by our encounters with our clients and their lives. Regardless of how convincing the research results may be, accepting the conclusion that my clinical experience fails to make me more effective remains unsettling. In this sense, it is entirely appropriate to make experiences in the room the key contributor to enhancing therapist efficacy.

While many, many books have been written extoling the privilege of working with clients, the power of the experiences in the room, and the transformative impact on the therapist, these same books labor at a significant disadvantage. Most of these books implicitly or explicitly endorse scientific psychology and its pursuit of powerful techniques and replicability. Privileged knowledge necessarily diminishes the specialness of the therapist; when one has techniques that have independent power, the individual therapist is simply a technician. In this sense, scientific psychology is always the enemy of directly cultivating therapist charisma.

Being effective in constructed reality requires a shift from this outer focus on privileged knowledge and technical mastery to an inner focus on qualities that mark the therapist as a gifted and special individual. Duncan, Miller,

Wampold, and Hubble (2010) comment on the centrality of the inner qualities of the therapist:

> For one thing, this volume brings the psychotherapist back into focus as a key
> determinant of ultimate treatment outcome—far more important than what the
> therapist is doing is who the therapist is. (Kindle Locations 385–386)

Once it is acceptable to change the focus of the search from techniques to cultivating therapist charisma, a new range of possibilities arises. Traditionally,
when psychology looks at what occurs in the room, the focus is on how the
techniques impact the client. What if the focus shifts to how the experiences
in the room facilitate or diminish therapist charisma?

This may seem unethical; after all, the entire purpose of being in the room is to
serve the client's needs. But when we are focusing on being more effective, the
actual emphasis should be on how the time in the room enhances the therapist.
And, of course, an enhanced therapist is more capable of serving client needs.
Once we give ourselves permission to make such a shift, the strategy is fairly
straightforward: therapists need to see their time in the room as a "practice" that
leads to their own empowerment. At the same time, they must continue to be committed to the ethical concept that therapy is all about serving the client's needs.

Putting these two seemingly incongruent concepts together is simpler than
it might appear. Take the example of Mother Teresa working with the poor
in Calcutta. There are dual levels of reality present in her actions regarding
"helping the poor." One the one hand, Mother Teresa was attempting to
develop programs and interventions that would assist needy individuals. On
the other hand, she was aware that she was performing her good deeds in
order to purify her heart and to serve her God. In that sense, she was helping
poor people in one reality and cleansing her own ego in another reality. Her
work was focused on helping others but was simultaneously a spiritual practice oriented toward her own evolution.

These dual levels of reality are fairly common and typically occur when a
set of outer activities that achieves one goal simultaneously results in inner
activities that achieve a different goal. Perhaps the most famous example of
this is meditation. The external results are tranquility, lower blood pressure
and stress reduction. In the right context, the inner results can be a sense of
existential peace, bliss, and enlightenment. The Christian psychologist works
with clients and simultaneously follows the will of God. The Buddhist psychologist works with clients and attempts to experience "no Self."

The focus on how the time in the room either facilitates or diminishes
charisma requires a brief definition of charisma. As used herein, charisma
refers to the ability of the client to perceive the therapist as a key individual
who has the authority to define reality. Recall that constructed reality is

held together by the Nomological Net, a structure which varies from culture to culture. Every culture has key individuals who are "empowered" to define the nature of reality—the Net—for the individuals in the culture. Examples are parents, teachers, mentors, and leaders. A therapist must aspire to be perceived as such an individual if they are going to be a superior clinician.

There are two primary factors which characterize charisma. The first is wisdom—the ability to discern what is fundamental from what is constructed. The second is compassion—the "I-Thou" relationship formed at the edge of the Abyss. This "pursuit of charisma" may seem egocentric especially in contrast with the selfless approaches of Mother Teresa or the Buddhist psychologists discussed above. This is particularly true because the common usage of charisma often confuses the concept with the kind of narcissistic behaviors found in the wealthy, the famous, and the powerful. In contrast, however, therapeutic charisma tends to be humble and self-effacing without losing the ability to be direct and confrontive when appropriate.

This second half of the book is characterized by multiple clinical vignettes and examples. The vignettes in the clinical section may appear familiar; they may look like concrete examples that illustrate the application of certain techniques. This appearance is likely to be amplified by the fact that many of the vignettes are taken from other books which teach techniques. In truth, however, they have been chosen because practicing these approaches with the correct consciousness can lead to enhanced therapist charisma. We should remember that anyone can copy a shamanic technique; it is both rarer and more useful to use the technique to awaken one's inner shaman.

The clinical examples have another purpose; they offer concrete examples of the differences between Reality A and Reality B. Examine the following quote from Stephen Lawhead (1988).

> Perhaps it is how we are made; perhaps words of truth reach us best through the heart, and stories and songs are the language of the heart. (p. 164)

As is well known, stories often convey the essence of an idea better than abstract reasoning. Most of us will be able to get a better feel for constructed reality through stories and narratives versus expository writing. The Abyss is also better understood through concrete examples, particularly its paradoxical nature of being simultaneously chaotic and terrifying and numinous and oracular. This is not a minor point; reviewing multiple vignettes is probably the only way to get a sense of where the fundamental stops and the constructed begins. Moreover, seeing therapeutic results as a product of myth and ritual instead of techniques and privileged knowledge also requires concreteness, practice, and repetition.

# PRAGMATICS

He who would learn to fly one day must first learn to walk and run
and climb and dance; one cannot fly into flying.

—Friedrich Nietzsche, *Beyond Good and Evil* (1886)

What needs to change so that the daily practice of psychotherapy becomes
transformative? Every therapy experience that makes a therapist into a bigger
person—one with more charisma—has the potential to be transformative. We
all have moments with clients where we encounter fear and move through
it, or have profound heartfelt connections, or deep epiphanies. Having the
average amount of such moments makes one an average therapist. Our focus
needs to be on having above-average amounts if we wish to be superior
therapists.

Simply being a seeker of such experiences creates an immediate positive
result. When I believe that a technique changes the client, then I seek to be
a master of powerful techniques. When I believe that my charisma is the
definitive factor, then I seek charisma. With few exceptions, workshops and
trainings teach us that the power is in the client or in the technique. Replacing
that focus with an intention to use every opportunity in therapy to enhance
charisma makes an enormous difference.

The second key factor that allows the psychotherapy experience to generate charisma is the attempt to master the dialog and the interfaces between
therapy and constructed reality. This book has repeatedly argued that it is
difficult to grasp the effects and power of constructed reality in our lives.
We are programmed to act as if everything occurs in fundamental reality.
Passing through the exact same therapeutic interactions—but experiencing
and understanding them from a constructed reality perspective—is transformative. For example, the work of therapeutic wizards has frequently been
studied with the hope of distilling their techniques; we expect that copying
their techniques will allow us to replicate their results. Unfortunately, as we
have discovered, this approach—which would work well in fundamental
reality—fails time and again in the psychotherapeutic world. Studying Milton Erickson has not resulted in a thousand students replicating Erickson's
results. Perhaps these disappointing outcomes occurred because his actual
results were simply due to Ericson's charisma; as a key individual he simply
needed to ask for a client behavior to achieve change. We have been distracted by what he did and missed who he was. Focusing on what actually
works enhances charisma.

A second example comes out of Frank's common factors model. What if
a therapist actually perceived every explanation for the client's problem as
a cultural or individual "myth" and every intervention as a co-created and

co-endorsed "ritual"? What kind of freedom and flexibility arise out of those understandings and how might that enhance a therapist's charisma?

These two factors—directly and deliberately seeking charisma and experiencing all therapeutic interactions in the context of constructed, as opposed to fundamental, reality—are the central strategies underlying the approach of this book. But we can make it even more specific. A map or geography of constructed reality can be developed using the principles articulated in the first half of the book. The two primary features of this map of constructed reality are the Nomological Net and the Abyss. The two have an ongoing dialog with each other. The Net gives form and stability to human culture and individual identity. The Abyss—with its implicit chaos and meaninglessness—attempts to break through the shelter of the Net. The Apollonian forces attempt to support the Net and resist the Abyss while the Dionysian forces of the Abyss threaten with terror and alienation but also beckon with creativity and spontaneity.

Psychotherapeutic systems can be described in terms of their position in the Net-Abyss dialog. For example, they can emphasize the Net aspect of constructed reality in which case they will prioritize success in the world, controlling emotions, and fulfilling expectations. Apollonian therapies such as CBT and reality therapy are examples of such systems.

The Abyss, of course, is always attempting to break through the shelter of the Net; these breakthroughs manifest externally as death, aging, and illness and internally as symptoms and pathologizing. Depth psychology and affective therapies focus on such breakthroughs; ultimately they work with the concept that this "shadow material" contains hidden meanings and guidance.

Where the Net stops—the edge of the Abyss—is the provenance of altered states. Hypnosis, group therapies, and retreats operate in this domain. Finally some individuals attempt to "leap into" the Abyss in search of the numinous and the oracular. This is the purview of the transpersonal therapies and the spiritual traditions.

In sum, an individual's place in constructed reality can be defined by her proximity to the Net or the Abyss and the nature of the interaction with these two forces. Similarly, the major schools of psychotherapy can also be defined by their place in constructed reality and by their relationships to the Abyss and the Net. One can frame participation in the different schools of therapy as an evolutionary experience where the therapist and her clients move from a more Net-centered focus to a more Abyss-centered one.

Traditional psychotherapy recommends either a focus on one school of therapy—mastering it on a deep level—or a kind of self-selected eclecticism. However, if the point of doing therapy is to enhance charisma, it is more useful to accept the challenge of every aspect of the Net-Abyss dialog; in short, there is benefit in mastering the essence of every system. For most therapists, one part of the Net-Abyss dialog will be more comfortable and other parts more challenging. Accepting challenges generates charisma. Forcing oneself to operate out of one's comfort zone—concentrating on the area where one is weakest—is called the deliberate practice model. Mastering one's weaknesses enhances charisma.

Similarly, pushing further up the evolutionary chain than one might find comfortable is also helpful in terms of charisma enhancement; having a sense that there is no part of constructed reality that is "off-limits" generates the kind of charisma associated with any explorer of distant worlds.

Each chapter in the clinical section has been chosen to illuminate one facet of constructed reality or another. Not surprisingly, the first clinical chapter is concerned with differentiating between fundamental reality and constructed reality. The second chapter—on therapeutic wizards—defines the goal of the book; it discusses the power and effectiveness of the archetypal charismatic therapist. Following are chapters on Apollonian therapies, the fluidity of the Self, and breakthroughs of the Abyss. Constructionism places a high value on the contributions of the client—after all, the client creates his own reality as much as the therapist does—so there is a section on going beyond client-centered therapy and working with the ultimate concern. Finally, as the individual elects to have a more direct experience of the Abyss, there are chapters on altered states and Dionysian therapies. Moving from the Net-centered therapies to the Abyss-centered therapies is called the evolutionary model.

The third model, Mindful Development, is both the most obvious and yet, in some sense, the most challenging. Psychology has a long tradition of recommending personal growth for both beginning and experienced therapists; if I can resolve my own issues and cultivate depth and an internal richness, I ought to be a more effective therapist. Generally this has taken the form of participation in personal therapy as part of a psychotherapy training program. While it is logical to expect that therapists who have had more personal therapy will be superior to less exposed therapists, the research on this question has failed to find support for this supposition (Macran & Shapiro, 1998). In short, personal psychotherapy fails to enhance charisma.

This inability of simple personal growth experiences to enhance charisma should not be discouraging; rather it suggests that only the most powerful life events will be helpful. The Mindful Development practice focuses on identifying such events and utilizing them consciously in service of becoming a more effective therapist.

The fourth approach to enhancing therapist charisma is called dancing with the Abyss and has some similarities to an intentional mindfulness practice. The essence of this approach is to be as aware as possible of the nature of reality, of the dialog between the Net and the Abyss, and of the presence of meaning in the form of the ultimate concern.

There is always a dynamic tension between Apollonian and Dionysian. Almost every approach outlined in the clinical section can be performed from an Apollonian stance or a Dionysian one. One intervention can leave the Net intact and create incremental and predictable change or, conversely, it can generate altered states, be discontinuous, and create experiences of "being a different person," "living in a new reality," and "waking up from a sleep." Feeling the presence of the Net and the Abyss as one crafts and carries through interventions changes the therapist as well as the client. Holding a sense of being outside the Net and connected to the Abyss opens doors to enhancing clinical outcomes.

There is another dance that is also central: the dialog between the ultimate concern of the client and the ultimate concern of the therapist. At the end of the day, all charisma flows from the ultimate concern and every ritual is a co-creation between the therapist/client and their ultimate concerns. Cultivating charisma can often sound like an ego-centered activity. Realizing that it is centered in the ultimate concern addresses that issue. The research demonstrates that client factors are much more important in predicting outcome than therapist factors. Recognizing this means that at the end of the day, serving the client's ultimate concern is always the priority.

Clearly the Net and the Abyss are always in dialog with each other. The Net is paradoxically supportive yet constraining; the Abyss is terrifying yet numinous and oracular. Feeling all of these forces moving together is the essence of the dancing with the Abyss model.

Finally, a note of caution: once one accepts the implications of Reality B, the recommendations and observations contained in the following clinical chapters are fairly straightforward. However, fulfilling these recommendations requires sustaining a sense of the fluidity of reality. This puts one in direct conflict with Kahneman's System 1 and its power to reify reality into a safe worldview. Recall that Kahneman called System 1 the "hero" of his book and documented numerous examples of his own and others' difficulties surmounting its power to confuse and confound. Eastern religions go on and on about the power of Maya—illusion—to seduce and trap even the most prepared. Staying awake—not going back to sleep—is a major challenge. Rumi comments:

> Sit, be still, and listen,
> because you're drunk
> and we're at
> the edge of the roof.

# Chapter 7

# Beginner's Mind

What has been is what will be,
And what has been done is what will be done,
And there is nothing new under the sun.

—Ecclesiastes 1:9

The Reality B model implies that the therapist must work to loosen, lighten, remove, and realign the threads of the Nomological Net which currently define the identity of a client who is experiencing suffering and dysphoria. This suggests that the therapist must be capable of seeing the client's identity as fluid, changeable, malleable, and plastic. Naturally the client will not be much help here. If the client could see himself as a person with many resources and options—a person capable of adapting to changing situations—it is unlikely that he will present for therapy.

In terms of fluidity and adaptability, most of the extant psychological systems tend to be as unhelpful as the client's own self-image. The medical model, with its emphasis on psychiatric diagnosis and labeling, tends to support the threads of the Net and add new threads, some of which are very strong. Being labeled a depressive, a personality disorder, or learning disabled is not likely to help the client or the therapist see him as fluid, changeable, or full of options. Similarly being seen as prone to irrational cognitions or an alcoholic or an incest survivor rarely makes one more mobile. In sum, labeling virtually always works to stabilize the client in the current position. Moreover, as Burger and Luckmann point out, therapists who work with "deviants" all day, every day, have their own sense of vulnerability to the Abyss and their own need to apply labels to clients which help mark them as different and "not like me." Obviously a label or diagnosis makes the individual into an object as opposed to a person; the object's doubts, feelings, and confusions now belong to someone "broken" or "different" and are less likely to infect or spoil me. The first step toward understanding and working with a constructionist approach is to sense all of the forces—within the client certainly—but also from the culture, the profession and, of course, from inside the therapist—which act to stabilize the client's identity.

If one takes the research seriously, and fully accepts that our well-developed psychological systems are not useful maps in terms of increasing therapeutic effectiveness, then it is clear that generally accepted concepts such as the trauma of childhood experiences, irrational thinking, and diagnostic categories are not helpful when framing cases and developing interventions. Instead of using these systems, as each client enters the office, the psychologist needs to be free to perceive him through whatever perspective she finds most appropriate at the moment. This freedom can be empowering in that one no longer has to see people though the AA lens of "alcoholic/addicts" or the psychodynamic lens of "narcissism," yet it can also be confusing or even terrifying to try and operate without the ability to lean on generally accepted psychiatric concepts.

One of the most powerful explorations of this concept of seeing people and situations without preconceptions comes from Shunryu Suzuki's book, *Zen Mind, Beginner's Mind*, where he states: "In the beginner's mind there are many possibilities, but in the expert's there are few" (2010, p. 1). Suzuki's statement arises directly out of the Zen practice of meditation. In this practice, every event, feeling, and cognition is to be experienced as it exists, without judgment, prejudice, or reference. Each experience is whole in itself and complete in the present moment. There is no cataloging and there are no typologies that summarize data. Each experience is fresh, unique, and unlike any other. The ability to operate from this perspective is what he calls "beginner's mind."

He contrasts this with "expert mind" which interprets every experience in the context of a limited number of preconceived categories. Being restricted to a few options in predefined categories limits the therapist's creativity and her ability to see the client as unfettered. In psychotherapy—which operates in constructed reality—loss of options is virtually always counterproductive.

Contrast that with expert mind operating in fundamental reality. Fundamental reality is relatively predictable and solid. Eliminating options that don't work or work poorly simply makes one more efficient and effective. In such cases, expert mind generates reliable and superior results. Unfortunately, much as we may wish otherwise, psychotherapy—and constructed reality—operate outside the purview of expert mind.

More specifically, every extant psychological system is a form of expert mind. These systems force the practitioner into seeing the client as the victim of a pathological family system, or traumatized, or unable to think "rationally." In the midst of the presuppositions created by the various systems, the uniqueness of the present moment is lost. It is helpful to let these assumptions go. And the research that the systems do not add value in terms of therapist effectiveness reassures us that discarding their theories will not be harmful.

The good news is that this concept of beginner's mind has been present in Western culture for almost half a century and is more or less woven into our shared reality. Ever since Ram Dass wrote *Be Here Now*, and Eckhart Tolle extended the concept with *The Power of Now*, much of Western culture has been infused with the idea that the wise and healthy person is the one who can be truly present, truly "show up." This concept has never been that hard for people to understand because the vast majority of people have at least some experiences where they are actually present, without self-consciousness, and only paying attention to what is occurring in that moment. Examples of this sort of consciousness are easily found: the basketball player who is making a move for the basket, the musician who is immersed in the song, the scientist who becomes one with his theory, and, yes, the therapist who is fully paying attention to the client in front of her. In Reality B language, at these moments, the person is temporarily unconcerned with the threads that stabilize his identity—he is not self-conscious—and simply operates as the situation requires in the context of the present moment. For the athlete, the game is the context; for the musician it is the song, and so forth.

Tara Brach (2012), a Buddhist therapist, uses the term "mindfulness" to describe this same process.

> In the simplest terms, mindfulness is the intentional process of paying attention, without judgment, to the unfolding of moment-to-moment experience. It is the opposite of trance, a word I use to describe all the ways in which we—therapists and clients alike—live inside a limiting story about life. (p. 37)

In this short quote, Brach pulls together the Reality B perspective in a few simple lines. Strive to be present and mindful. There are forces around the therapist and within the therapist which will distract and confuse one—forces which act to put the therapist in an impotent trance, forces which are limiting. These forces need to be recognized and the therapist needs a practice to minimize their influence.

The first step toward becoming a Reality B therapist is to differentiate constructed reality from fundamental reality. Operating in constructed reality requires mindfulness and beginner's mind—the ability to show up in each moment without preconceptions. This enhances creativity and facilitates relationship; the client feels seen and is allowed to freely change and grow without preconceived and predefined limitations. While it takes an act of discernment and courage to release expert mind—to release the standard psychological worldview—the results of the outcome research and the constructionist analyses support the leap from Reality A to Reality B.

## DIAGNOSES AND PRECONCEPTIONS

> No one is sane, straight along, year in and year out, and we all know it. Our insanities are of varying sorts, and express themselves in varying forms—fortunately harmless forms as a rule.
>
> —Mark Twain, *Mark Twain's Letters* (1917)

Nothing interferes with mindfulness quite as effectively as labeling and diagnosis. Formal categorizing pushes us into expert mind with all of its implicit assumptions about pathology, prognosis, dynamics, and associations to past clients with the same diagnosis. And this is not limited to the therapist; most clients come to therapy with either a formal diagnosis from a mental health professional, a diagnosis bestowed by family, friends or self, or a set of codified assumptions that might as well be a diagnosis. For example, the client may say: "I'm anxious because everyone in my family is anxious," or "my psychiatrist told me I have a biochemical imbalance and I will need to take medications for the rest of my life to be normal," or "I'm the black sheep in my family and, because of that, I have a fear of success."

As a general rule the therapist should make every effort to keep the client's identity fluid and malleable and resist these kinds of explanations and interpretations, at least inside her own mind. Naturally, it is rarely helpful to confront the client and point out that these explanations create more harm than good. Instead, as Brach advises, they should be regarded as a kind of hypnotic induction where the client, the culture, and the profession are attempting to ensorcel the therapist to the point where they cannot imagine the client as having another identity. A chronic depressive has little chance of long-term change and a recovering abuse victim has little opportunity for real independence. A clinical example will illustrate the point.[1]

A 15-year-old, high school freshman was referred to me for treatment of anorexia. Six months prior she had been hospitalized for several weeks when her weight had dropped down to 74 pounds. Post discharge, the parents had set up a team of a therapist, a nutritionist, a psychiatrist, and a medical doctor to treat her disorder. My initial interview with the parents suggested that all of these professionals were experienced with eating disorders, had conducted themselves in a competent and professional manner, and had extended themselves to the young woman in terms of being generous with their time and had treated her in a friendly and kind manner. In sum, she had a good team and was receiving top notch treatment for the anorexia.

The client had responded by repeatedly lying to her parents and all members of the team. She had water-loaded prior to weigh-ins, sewn weights surreptitiously into her clothes, been angry and aggressive with her parents whenever they brought up her eating choices, exhibited significant anxiety around eating high fat food, and in every way demonstrated resistance to treatment. She had cursed at her mother, pushed her, and the parents had been forced to call the police on several occasions to control the teen. She was sent to see me after telling her parents she couldn't relate to the previous therapist although the nutritionist, the psychiatrist, and the medical doctor were continuing to serve on the team.

In my first interview, I told the young woman that, while she clearly had an eating disorder in the technical sense, and while her parents and the medical doctor were obliged to check her weight and to keep her safe, it would be more useful for her to understand her condition as resulting from a particular part of her personality. Using some other information from the interview and her history, I suggested that she had an atypical eating disorder was caused and maintained by her great capacity for single-minded focus and a corresponding ability to ignore everything except her intended goal. In this case, she had decided that eating pure food was going to enhance her physical health and athletic prowess. Her single minded focus resulted in ignoring other factors like the simple truth that her diet was putting her health at risk.

I also told her that she had long felt that no one else really understood her and mentioned that she was accustomed to making decisions on her own. She had a long history of academic and athletic excellence and she had confused achieving "pure health" with achieving her high end goals. In sum, I framed her eating disorder as a positive part of her personality that had gotten somewhat out of control.

She immediately warmed to this interpretation and told me that everyone else had been talking about how serious it was to have an eating disorder and telling her that she needed to accept that she was going to have to struggle with it for years. Moreover, she had been informed that healing was going to take a great deal of perseverance, work, and effort, and that she was going to be a "patient" for a long time to come.

I responded that because her eating disorder was "atypical" and came from the best part of her personality, it had a much better prognosis than normal eating disorders. If she wanted to try, she could show her parents and the team that she could vanquish her eating disorder relatively quickly, using the same tools and motivation which had led to her exceptional successes in the athletic and academic realms.

She quickly began to gain weight, reported that her charge around eating food with a high fat content was mostly gone, and her emotional blow ups with his parents diminished markedly.

This case illustrates how easily certain clients can move when the therapist can free himself from the internal blinders created by diagnoses and conventional treatment protocols. Clearly this young woman had a severe eating disorder with a significant risk to her health, a strong aversion to certain classes of food, and marked emotional agitation manifested as aggression toward her parents and lying to the team. The team was justified in diagnosing the young woman with anorexia and such disorders usually do require years of treatment. The severity of her presentation made it difficult to avoid seeing the client as the embodiment of her pathology. This is the exact moment when the therapist most needs to see the identity of the client as fluid and malleable.

There was special pressure on me from both the parents and some other members of the treatment team because, of course, the young woman told everyone that her new psychologist had informed her that she "didn't have an eating disorder." The pressure from the culture and the profession to reify the identity of the client is real and palpable. Operating from a constructionist point of view, where frames are seen as useful/useless instead of true/false is a radical approach to diagnosis and treatment; inevitably, it will create resistance and backlash. The initial resistance may be experienced inside the therapist but the atypical frames and interventions will often create resistance from every direction imaginable. There really are cultural, professional, and individual forces—Apollonian elements—that attempt to stabilize individual identity. They continue to operate even when the identity is dysfunctional and creates pain in the client and those around her. Clients, their significant others, and involved professionals sincerely desire positive change but they feel compelled to fight a new frame if it takes an unusual form, especially when it is accompanied by an atypical, unsanctioned explanation.

This leads directly into the question of how real and accurate my explanation was versus the standard explanation of the treatment team. Constructionists would argue that neither explanation was true. Obviously, in this case, mine was more "useful" in that it had a positive impact in a relatively short time. From a Reality B perspective, it was also more useful because it was designed with fluidity of identity in mind. It was not "true" that her eating disorder was a result of using the same strategies previously employed to achieve academic success, but when I suggested the idea, the client was happy to embrace it. In this new frame she was no longer sick; rather, she was a goal-achieving idealist on a "pure food diet" who had gone a bit too far. That was a problem she could understand, accept, and correct. Conversely, she resented and resisted the frame of being a patient recovering from an eating disorder.

Naturally both the parents and the other professionals distrusted her quick and fairly effortless improvement because they saw her as an eating disorder and "everyone knows" that progress with such disorders is slow and has many reversals. The professionals had even more difficulties with her improvements than the parents because, as experts, they "knew" that these improvements were false and ephemeral and that she would quickly relapse. The more expert, the more they saw her eating disorder identity as stable and resistant to change.

It was clear that the teen could not "stomach" the eating disorder explanations that had been offered from various professionals. She wanted to see herself as a winner who had been striving for something great. In Tillich's language, the "pure food" diet participated in her ultimate concern. She saw herself as strong, brave, unconventional, and independent. Conversely, the eating disorder frame saw her as deeply wounded, dependent on support and counsel from others, and only capable of slow recovery. In that sense, the teen experienced any possible alignment with the eating disorder model as a step backward into childhood dependency and as a violation of her commitment to her ultimate concern. Her resistance was noble, not pathological, and she saw cooperation with and acceptance of the professional model as a personal violation. She justified all her lying, aggression, and resistance from this point of view.

When Tillich and ultimate concern are introduced, we leave the world of pure constructionism and enter the Tillichian reality of idolatrous versus true ultimate concerns. In this sense, whatever intervention moves the client further along toward her own authentic ultimate concern is truer for her. Tillich might argue that my intervention was not only more "useful," it was also better aligned with her ultimate concern and, hence, more valid. Put more concretely, doing anything that facilitated the teen's independence and success was aligned with her ultimate concern. In sum, while constructionism allows almost any alternative frame that ensures client's fluidity, Tillich's model sharply limits the choices. Beginner's mind does not stand alone; it always coexists with the concept of the ultimate concern.

Beginner's mind is not simply a spiritual concept; a number of prominent therapists have urged trainees to be cautious about having implicit assumptions about clients. For example, in the following quote Milton Ericson recommends seeing the client as the "thing in itself."

I think we should all know that every individual is unique. . . . There are no duplicates. In the 3 1/2 million years that man has lived on earth, I think I'm quite safe in saying there are no duplicate fingerprints, no duplicate individuals. Fraternal twins are very, very different in their fingerprints, their resistance to disease, their psychological structure and personality.

And I do wish that Rogerian therapists, Gestalt therapists, transactional analysts, group analysts, and all the other offspring of various theories would recognize that not one of them really recognizes that psychotherapy for person #1 is not psychotherapy for person #2. I treated many conditions, and I always invent a new treatment in accord with the individual personality. I know that when I take us out to dinner, I let the guests choose what to eat, because I don't know what they like. I think people should dress the way they want to. I am very certain that all of you know that I dress the way I want to. (Erickson laughs.) I think that psychotherapy is an individual procedure. (Zeig, 1980, p. 104)

While the language is different, Erickson is obviously encouraging his students to begin every encounter with a new client with beginner's mind. Again, in the mental health world, expert mind is all about diagnostic categories and expectations that tend to stabilize a client in their pathology. The resulting set of standard treatments often slow down treatment progress. Such treatments are implicitly oriented toward creating a stable and predictable reality—a reality that only changes slowly, a reality that keeps both professionals and clients from feeling destabilized.

## THE SEDUCTIVE NATURE OF TECHNIQUES

I was in a printing house in Hell, and saw the method in which knowledge is transmitted from generation to generation.

—William Blake, *The Marriage of Heaven and Hell* (1790–1793)

Belief that techniques are contributing to client improvement is one of the greatest threats to beginner's mind. The research, of course, completely discounts the inherent power of techniques. If they are responsible for change, then the therapist who knows more of them, or is better trained in them, or has practiced them more, should be superior. And, of course, the research reports no differences between the technically savvy and the beginner.

Even with this understanding it is hard not to feel as if the power lies in techniques; when I do CBT with a client and they get better, it feels like they were helped by the technique. Not only do I feel it but the client also believes it. They tell their friends and family members that CBT really worked for them and recommend the technique to others with similar problems.

In addition, therapists like to have a variety of tools so that they can try another approach if the first one doesn't work. Therapists often say, for example, that "family systems didn't work with the client but hypnotherapy was much more effective." Such statements simply feel true. But, of course, they aren't.

In the following clinical example we examine an unusual technique that, like standard talk therapy, appears to be responsible for client improvement. Yet in this case, the technique is so unusual—so outside of normal limits—that it is relatively easy to believe that another factor is responsible for improvement besides the technique.

Some years ago, I was introduced to a retired OB/GYN who had set up his own private psychotherapy practice. His specialty was unusual in that he used hypnosis to identify and exorcise malevolent spirits. Apparently he had stumbled upon this model through working with many patients in hypnosis. I had a number of friends, acquaintances, and clients tell me that they had consulted him and they shared their outcomes with me.

Not surprisingly, some of these people were put off by his belief in spirit possession. However a number of the people reported that in spite of their skepticism, the experience had been extremely positive for them. Apparently the doctor identified the presence of malevolent spirits by ideomotor signaling; in other words, he put his clients into a hypnotic trance and then asked the unconscious mind to involuntarily raise a finger if they were possessed. Then, through continued use of the ideomotor signaling, the doctor would help the client access the resources required to remove the spirit. The doctor would confirm the removal with more ideomotor signaling and then predict that things would be much better now that the entity was exorcized.

Subsequent to this process, the clients typically experienced feelings of lightness and relief. They also reported a significant reduction in their presenting symptoms. A few said they felt better than they had in years or even "I feel like a whole new person." Of course, others reported no positive results and stated that the entire experience had made them uncomfortable.

The first thing that must be granted is that the physician achieved better results, and achieved them more rapidly, than the average psychologist. How many of us generate such powerful results in just one or two sessions? Setting aside the problems of inducing clients to believe in the existence of malevolent entities, the doctor's effectiveness was certainly impressive.

Like many stories of rapid change, the first question is often: "Are the changes durable?" Clearly the rapidity and the power of the changes are worth respect, but are they sustainable? Given that the exorcized client will tend to have a hard time getting social validation from friends and families, the powerful changes will have more trouble sustaining themselves than more conventional change strategies. My family is more likely to support my beliefs that I am different after ten sessions of insight-oriented talk therapy than they are likely to support my belief that I am different because a new age healer told me I was Charlemagne in my last life. Unless of course I am in a new age cult and all my friends believed that they were famous people in their last lives.

What makes this exorcism discussion both interesting and confusing is that it highlights the lack of clear boundaries between fundamental and constructed reality. This is especially true because Apollonian forces consistently blur the two together and then declare that there is no constructed reality—only fundamental reality. Irving Yalom, the renowned existential therapist, addresses these issues in the quote below.

> The superego, the id, the ego; the archetypes, the idealized and the actual selves, the pride system; the self system and the dissociated system, the masculine protest; parent, child, and adult ego states-none of these really exists. They are all fictions, all psychological constructs created for semantic convenience, and they justify their existence only by virtue of their explanatory power. . . .
>
> Does this mean that psychotherapists abandon their attempts to make precise, thoughtful interpretations? Not at all. Only that they recognize the purpose and function of an interpretation. Some interpretations may be superior to others, not because they are "deeper" but because they have more explanatory power, are more credible, provide more mastery, and therefore better catalyze the will.
>
> When I present this relativistic thesis to students, they respond with such questions as "Do you mean that an astrological explanation is also valid in psychotherapy?" In spite of my own intellectual reservations, I have to respond affirmatively. If an astrological or a shamanistic or a magical explanation enhances one's sense of mastery, and leads to inner, personal change, then it is valid (keeping in mind the proviso that it must be consonant with one's frame of reference). There is much evidence from cross-cultural psychiatric research to support my position; in most primitive cultures only the magical or the religious explanation is acceptable, and hence valid and effective. (Yalom, 2008, Kindle Locations 4852–4867)

In this quote, Yalom emphasizes the fluid nature of the psychotherapeutic world. It is fluid, of course, because it operates in constructed reality. Yalom validates astrology in his quote and, by implication, he also validates the exorcism therapy. Saying he validates it does not imply that he thinks exorcism or astrology are real from a fundamental reality perspective; he means that they are real and valid because they have the capacity to alter a client's Net and personal identity. And they have the same capacity to alter the Net as other constructs: id, ego, and so on. Exorcism is considered "unreal" in the context of Western constructed reality, but it is real to the clients that go through the procedure and they are as changed by the "unreal" procedure as they are by a socially validated one like "childhood trauma."

Essentially Yalom argues that spirit exorcism is as experientially true as any standard psychotherapy technique. And he goes further; his explanation allows us to understand that the clients are changing not because of the innate power of an exorcism, or standard talk therapy, or astrology but because the procedure "enhances one's sense of mastery, and leads to inner, personal change." It is true because they experience it as true. The client has the final say about what is real.

Entities are not real—at least not in Western culture. Therefore exorcism cannot be a technique in the way the term is used in fundamental reality.

In the exorcism we have an effective procedure—probably more effective than standard talk therapy in terms of immediate change—that cannot be a technique. If it works, and it is not a technique, than what can it be?

Previously we reviewed the common factors model proposed by Jerome Frank. In that model, he substituted the concept of "ritual" in place of technique. He used ritual not only because it included the shamanic healings common across so many cultures but also because he understood that modern clients were changing for the same reasons. Techniques were not the active ingredient; ritual was just as central to change in the psychologist's office as it was around the medicine man's fire.

Ritual can be defined as "a series of outer experiences that create a shift in inner reality." The secret, of course, is that the therapist and the client must have an implicit or explicit agreement that the passage through the outer experiences will, in fact, cause the inner shift. Some of the differences between technique and ritual are well illustrated by the marriage ceremony. The goal of the marriage ceremony is clear: the couple is moving from an identification as single people into their new identities as married people. In the marriage ceremony, the details can be altered substantially and the result is unaffected. For example, the ceremony is just as powerful regardless of what music is played and how the couple are dressed; moreover, the ceremony is equally moving whether it is Jewish, or Christian, or secular. Conversely when it comes to a technique like the right way to build a house, there is only one way—with a few small variations—to get the corners square and the walls vertical. In a technique, if you change the details significantly, the outcome will fail.

In a marriage ritual, the result is amplified when there is social consensus that the couple is "really married." The audience meaningfully participates in the effectiveness and power of the ritual. In building the house, the corners are equally square whether one person sees it or a hundred people witness it. Phillip Dick tells us: "Reality is that which, when you stop believing in it, doesn't go away" (Dick, 1996, p. 261). Obviously, he is referring to fundamental reality and techniques.

In terms of therapeutic rituals, Yalom and Frank tell us the minimum requirements for success. A charismatic and caring therapist offers (or co-creates) a frame that explains why the client is suffering and why moving through a certain procedure will change the client in the desired direction. The client must be receptive to this explanation and motivated enough to undertake the procedure. Since this is constructed reality, the procedure itself has no innate power; rather, it is invested with the power of change by the intentions of the therapist and the client. And, when the client moves through the procedure, their belief that it will change them becomes a self-fulfilling prophesy and they are changed. As Yalom says, "then it is valid (keeping in mind the proviso that it must be consonant with one's frame of reference)."

Yalom calls all the psychological constructs "fictional": "They are all fictions, all psychological constructs created for semantic convenience, and they justify their existence only by virtue of their explanatory power." In calling these fictional, Yalom is stating that these concepts are not true from a fundamental reality perspective. But what about their truth in constructed reality? From that perspective, how can a ritual be fictional? There are no "fictional" marriage ceremonies; there are only moving and meaningful marriage ceremonies and, sometimes, flat and insincere ceremonies. Rituals are not judged as true or false; rather they are judged as meaningful or meaningless and effective change procedures or ineffective change procedures.

The success of the exorcism procedure also points toward the "placebo effect." A placebo, of course, is a powerless treatment or drug; it generates an effect because the clients are led to believe that it actually is a powerful treatment or drug. Placebo is easy to understand with sugar pills and drugs in fundamental reality; however, things become more complex when it comes to psychotherapy and constructed reality.

First of all, the concept of placebo only makes sense in fundamental reality where there are "authentic" interventions and "faux" interventions. In constructed reality there can be no placebo because there is no innate power in techniques and no "faux" interventions. In constructed reality every change of belief is "real." This has led to problems with psychotherapy research. Following the medical model, some psychotherapy researchers have attempted to compare new psychotherapeutic interventions with faux psychotherapy interventions. The problem, of course, is that when the "faux" interventions are sufficiently developed to be credible, they work as well as the experimental intervention. And when they are degraded enough to be inert interventions, the experimental subjects are aware that they are faux interventions.

Placebo experiments in fundamental reality allow researchers to separate out active or specific effects from belief/expectation effects. The interesting aspect, of course, is how powerful the placebo effects can be in certain research studies. Recall that the antidepressant literature found that virtually all the antidepressant effects from the drugs came from placebo effects. As we know, sometimes these belief or placebo effects are so strong that they allow the experimental subject to change somatic effects as well as feelings and attitudes. Clearly, in the case of placebo studies, constructed reality is interwoven with fundamental reality.

Saying that all therapy is placebo and therapists are placebologists sounds like a good way to summarize therapy in constructed reality; in truth, the phrase creates confusion and misunderstandings. Since placebos only exist in fundamental reality and therapy takes place in constructed reality, the phrase literally makes no sense. Even worse, it implicitly suggests that therapy is occurring in fundamental reality and its power is due to placebo. Placebo, of course, is linked to misconstruals, intentional lying, and a sense that the elicited effect is, in some sense, unreal, artificial, or insubstantial. These are unhelpful, confusing, and inappropriate associations.

Contrast that saying to the title of a book on neurolinguistic programming written by Bandler and Grinder in the 1970s called *The Structure of Magic*. The fluid and rapid change seen in the exorcism intervention did appear to have magical qualities. Using a "magic" metaphor for conscious work in constructed reality highlights the Dionysian opportunities that emerge when one lets go of a belief that therapy operates in fundamental reality. In other words, it's better to call therapists in constructed reality "magicians" than "placebologists." But of course it is not the ritual—not the exorcism intervention—that has the magical qualities. Rather, it is the nature of constructed reality to be conducive to "magical" change. After all, if it is all made up, how hard can change really be? The magic is in the milieu, not the intervention.

Beginner's mind is consciousness designed to work effectively with all aspects of constructed reality. Expert mind is superior in fundamental reality. Myth and ritual are the building blocks of change in constructed reality; science and techniques rule in fundamental reality. Discerning the difference between the two opens the therapist to the magical qualities of change implied by the Bandler/Grinder title. While it is true that this book emphasizes acquiring charisma—a process which can be intentional and require hard work—it is also true that simply letting in that everything is possible with little effort in constructed reality ushers in a sense of effortless power. In this sense, awareness trumps effort. Rumi tells us:

> You wander from room to room
> Hunting for the diamond necklace
> That is already around your neck!

## FRAMING AND TRUTH

> What is originality? To see something that has no name as yet and
> hence cannot be mentioned although it stares us all in the face. The
> way men usually are, it takes a name to make something visible for
> them.

> —Friedrich Nietzsche, *The Gay Science* (1882)

Another significant threat to sustaining beginner's mind is the question about the truth of any intervention. Yalom has already argued that all interventions are based on "fictions," but that can hardly be the only word on the subject. While it is true that constructed reality implies that concepts are invented—and the therapist gains lots of room to maneuver from this approach—it is also important to find that "place to stand" to enhance therapeutic power.

Every intervention with a client includes an implicit negotiation between therapist and client about the validity of the explanations of the current state—usually a state of suffering—and the recommended path forward. Clearly the explanation and the path forward must feel "real" to the client. And they must also feel "real" to the therapist to maximize authenticity and charisma. Yet in a constructed reality, what is real, what feels real, and what is simply a construct manufactured to reach a desired goal?

The arbitrary nature of any frame is relatively easy to demonstrate with virtually any case study. In the following example from my practice, this discretionary nature of the frame is particularly easy to see because the frame is "politically incorrect."

A 49-year-old, divorced, female physical therapist presented with complaints of depression and anxiety. She explained that she had been raised from birth to take care of others and now, with both of her children launched into the world, she felt there was no longer any purpose in living. She had some interest in a few men but minimized any hopes and expectations that she had in the romantic arena.

Her caretaking strategy was validated and she was invited to explore the possibility that fulfillment of her complete life potential required her to have the ability to form her own individual vision of happiness. In response, she identified several events in her family of origin which required her to give up any hope of personal happiness in order to live to serve others. She agreed that these old mislearnings ought to be discarded if she was going to have any chance at personal happiness. Since she had a natural albeit somewhat muted attraction to men, it was easy for her to accept the idea that the ability to conduct a healthy romantic relationship would signify that her core wound—her lack of permission to pursue her own happiness—had been healed.

The client went on a series of dates through an Internet dating service. While she, of course, processed the dates using normal criteria such as degree of attraction, common values, and fun, she also carefully monitored her own behaviors and feelings in terms of her "primal wound," her necessity to live only to serve others. She finally found someone who both pleased her and allowed her to operate as a free and unwounded woman in the relationship. She not only felt much better in general, she also expressed the belief that her experience had healed her in that: "My ability to give and receive love this way means that I have given up my sense that I live only to serve others."

Telling a woman that she needs to heal herself by finding a boyfriend is clearly "politically incorrect." In addition, advising a woman who has a tendency to lose herself in the service of others to enter a relationship is fraught with peril; how many women have complained that romantic relationships require them to give excessively to their lovers. From this point of view, the fact that this frame proved successful—and the client was clear that loving someone helped her get over an obsessive need to serve others—is an unexpected result.

Conversely, it is easy to defend the frame. The client clearly equated romantic relationships with meeting her own needs; for her, intimate relationships were for her and normal relationships were about serving others. Apparently she saw a romantic relationship as representative of mutuality and other relationships as a commitment to one-way service. Hence, the politically incorrect frame served her well.

Exploring additional alternatives, it is easy to imagine that other therapists would prefer to work directly with her "service-oriented" relationships. They would follow up on her feelings of exploitation and process those experiences. Another approach might involve exploring why she was so "conflicted" about relationships in general. This perspective might recommend a period of aloneness—both in terms of serving and romance—and investigate the feelings that arise as a result. In sum, it appears that at least three, if not fourteen, different approaches would have worked well in this situation.

And that is virtually always the case. If one grants that all the schools of therapy would see this woman differently, and proscribe different treatment frames, and all would achieve roughly equivalent results, then Yalom's dictum that all frames are "fictions" certainly makes sense. Beginner's mind embraces the meaning-creating potential of many, many different frames. Abandoning the concept of the "best" or "most accurate" frame is a necessary first step for the Reality B therapist.

This can be summarized as: "everything works/nothing really works." Virtually all positive frames work in terms of their potential to help clients but none of them work in the sense that they embody ultimate truth or inherent power. This may be obvious to many therapists but it can still be challenging to retain this level of fluidity as one works in real time with a client. We all have Apollonian tendencies which require us to believe that the worldview we are co-creating with the client is fundamentally real; at this point, we lose access to all competing realities. Beginner's mind always cultivates awareness of the ephemeral nature of every frame even while endorsing the functional usefulness of a frame in the here and now.

That said, are there any frames that are superior to others? Jerome Frank tells us that the one that is most compelling to the client is the best. Tillich argues that the one that heals an idolatrous ultimate concern or evolves an existing one is the best. And the research discusses the power of therapeutic allegiance effects; when the therapist believes in the frame, therapy becomes more efficacious. These three approaches are, in fact complementary. An elegantly designed frame will include all three.

Finally, let's look at one more case study, this one from Milton Erickson, to further explore beginner's mind. A seventeen-year-old girl was having trouble leaving home to go to college. It appeared that she was socially sensitive and withdrawn because her breasts had failed to develop. She had already received endocrine therapy to no avail. She was so emotionally labile that hospitalization was being considered; in fact, when Erickson went to her home to treat her, she was hiding behind the sofa.

Erickson found she was a good hypnotic subject and made a number of suggestions to activate her endocrine system and to channel attention—in some unspecified manner—to her breast area.

> This series of suggestions had the multiple purpose of meeting her ambivalence, puzzling and intriguing her, stimulating her sense of humor, meeting her need for self-aggression and self-derogation, and yet doing all this without adding to her distress. It was done so indirectly that there was little for her to do but accept and respond to the suggestions.
>
> I suggested to her that, at each therapeutic interview, she visualize herself mentally in the most embarrassing situation that she could possibly imagine. This situation, not necessarily the same each time, would always involve her breasts, and she would feel and sense the embarrassment with great intensity, at first in her face, and then, with a feeling of relief, she would feel the weight of embarrassment move slowly downward and come to rest in her breasts. I gave her the additional posthypnotic suggestion that, whenever she was alone, she would regularly take the opportunity to think of her therapeutic sessions, and she would then immediately develop intense feelings of embarrassment, all of which would promptly "settle" in her breasts in a most bewildering but entirely pleasing way.
>
> I explained that she could, in addition to handling her academic work adequately, entertain herself and mystify her college mates delightfully by the judicious wearing of tight sweaters and the use of different sets of falsies of varying sizes, sometimes not in matched pairs. She was also instructed to carry assorted sizes in her handbag in case she decided to make an unexpected change in her appearance, or, should any of her escorts become too venturesome, so that she could offer them a choice with which to play. Thus her puckish activities would not lead to difficulties.
>
> I first saw her in mid-August and gave her weekly appointments thereafter. The first few of these she kept in person, and they were used to reiterate and reinforce the instructions previously given her and to ensure her adequate understanding and cooperation. After that, she kept, by permission, three out of four appointments "in absentia." That is, she would seclude herself for at least an hour and develop, in response to post hypnotic suggestion, a medium to deep trance state. . . . The other appointment she kept in person, sometimes asking for information, sometimes for trance induction, almost always for instructions

to "keep going." Occasionally she would describe with much merriment the reactions of her friends to her falsies.

She entered college in September, adjusted well, received freshman honors, and became prominent in extracurricular activities. During the last two months of her therapy, her visits were at the level of social office calls. In May, however, she came in wearing a sweater and stated with extreme embarrassment, "I'm not wearing falsies. I've grown my own. They are large medium size. Now tell them to stop growing. I'm completely satisfied." (Haley, 1993b, pp. 113–115)

The first point that leaps out from this anecdote is Erickson's refusal to engage with the level of pathology apparent in this history. The teenager was hiding behind furniture in a primitive and regressed manner. She was obsessed with a sexually related body part. This level of anxiety and obsession suggests serious pathology, perhaps a personality disorder or perhaps a pre-psychotic condition. His intervention, which focused on her sense of humor, did literally nothing to address this underlying pathology. Offering Erickson's treatment plan at a professional case conference would leave the presenter open to the accusation that he had underestimated the severity of her disorder. Of course, the success of Erickson's intervention not only validates his choice to ignore the diagnostic implications, it also calls into question the utility of Apollonian schemas such as diagnosis and a fixed attitude toward pathology.

His basic frame was twofold and embodies his well-known utilization approach. Accept her obsessive focus on her breasts but make certain therapeutic alterations. First, combine the breast focus with her strong sense of humor. Second, let the breast focus become a form of mind/body healing—as I meditate on the breasts, they develop in a natural and healthy manner.

Are these the only right frames? Clearly not. Erickson would have done just as well using a feminist approach that helped the woman understand that she is not her breast size. Or he could have explored her upbringing with the aim of discovering the source of her excessive social anxiety and providing an alternative set of responses.

Is hypnosis different than the other techniques already discussed? Not from a research point of view; hypnosis has failed to prove that it is consistently better than any other psychotherapeutic technique. His results may have been magical but not because his technique—hypnosis—was magical.

But hypnosis is different than standard talk therapy techniques because it involves altered states. Altered states exist at the edge of the Net—the place where the Net ends and the Abyss begins. Altered states are essentially Dionysian in comparison to the Apollonian style of standard talk therapies. Especially when altered states are combined with a highly charismatic therapist, more rapid change is possible. Put in Jerome Frank language, a therapeutic ritual that includes hypnosis is a ritual that implicitly justifies and supports rapid and profound change. All that may be true but recall that some therapists—the more charismatic ones—are better regardless of what techniques they use and the "altered states" nature of hypnosis does not guarantee that average therapists become superior if they attain expertise in hypnosis.

That said, while Erickson takes great pains in his case presentation to directly avoid taking credit for her eventual breast development, there is certainly the implication that the therapy may have contributed to it. Recall the earlier discussion about the line between fundamental reality and constructed reality: as a general principle, reality is more constructed than normally believed because of the tendency of Apollonian forces to perceive all reality as fundamental reality. The implications of this case study—that the mind-body connection is more powerful than traditional medicine postulates—is an argument that our bodies also participate in constructed reality. As we think, so our bodies become.

Returning to the question about framing and truth: our two clinical examples illustrate that many, many different approaches would have led to equally successful outcomes. Interestingly, once the stories are told, for many of us the explanations become "real"; not only do the frames seem correct, it feels like they are the only possible way to see the situation.

On the one hand, this reification is simply the result of Kahneman's System 1 and its tendency to create simplified worldviews and assume that everything exists in fundamental reality. But there is another factor at work as well: the shared and co-created commitment to healing that exists in the space between therapist and client. Tillich tells us that every place on the path points toward the terminus of the path. He argues that each of these moments become symbols that participate in the ultimate goal. In this sense, all authentic healing has a feeling of being ultimately real. Put in the language of the Abyss, the frames in therapy are literally fluid and interchangeable—they participate in the chaotic aspect of the Abyss—but they are simultaneously and paradoxically real and truthful—they participate in the numinous aspects of the Abyss.

## ASSUMPTIONS ABOUT CHANGE

Assumptions about change are deeply imbedded in the culture. In order to give form to these assumptions, I searched the internet[2] for quotes connected to change and then selected a number that seemed representative.

"Growth is a painful process."

—Wilma Mankiller

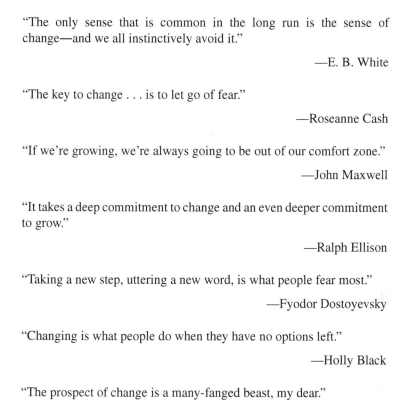

"The only sense that is common in the long run is the sense of change—and we all instinctively avoid it."

—E. B. White

"The key to change . . . is to let go of fear."

—Roseanne Cash

"If we're growing, we're always going to be out of our comfort zone."

—John Maxwell

"It takes a deep commitment to change and an even deeper commitment to grow."

—Ralph Ellison

"Taking a new step, uttering a new word, is what people fear most."

—Fyodor Dostoyevsky

"Changing is what people do when they have no options left."

—Holly Black

"The prospect of change is a many-fanged beast, my dear."

—Christopher Moore

All of these quotes have one thing in common: they caution that growth and change are demanding, slow, hard, and painful. The association between pain and change is so ingrained that it is rarely questioned. Yet the smallest reflection leads to the more accurate conclusion that change is sometimes hard, sometimes easy—sometimes quick and painless and sometimes requires courage and perseverance. Why this default idea that change is so difficult?

The answer is straightforward: in every culture, Apollonian forces operate to sustain the Net. Their first job is to support the concept that constructed reality is actually fundamental reality. The second major priority is to resist change and promote stability. Given that there are Apollonian forces in psychology, it stands to reason that therapists will be trained to conceive of change as difficult, slow, demanding, and sometimes impossible. This may seem counter intuitive—that a field dedicated to change and healing would be limited by encouraging assumptions that such change is unlikely and challenging—but this simply reflects the power of Apollonian forces.

The quotes above demonstrate that the resistance to change is not limited to the mental health field, it is a principle that is pervasive in the culture. Examining the quotes, one can easily see the standard Apollonian stance toward change: it is a long, slow, painful, and difficult process requiring sacrifice, perseverance, and courage. The literary record is full of inspiring quotes aimed at encouraging individuals to stay committed to the change and growth process in spite of fear and obstacles. Many therapists, coaches, and motivational speakers are fond of telling individuals to keep on going, that they are in "good company" in terms of their fear of moving forward. They promise that if the individual perseveres, a brighter future lies just ahead. Sometimes they complement these encouraging statements with not-so-subtlety veiled threats that refusal to change leads to lost opportunities, a wasted life, or even a kind of "soul death."

Current ethics in psychology require psychologists to begin the therapeutic relationship by giving the new client an *Informed Consent Form*. The form has a number of components; the part most relevant to our discussion is the heart of the form where the psychologist is required to explain the risks and benefits that are implicit in the process of psychotherapy. Following are excerpts taken from the *Sample Informed Consent Form* from the American Psychological Association Insurance Trust.

> Psychotherapy is not easily described in general statements. It varies depending on the personalities of the psychologist and patient, and the particular problems you bring forward. There are many different methods I may use to deal with the problems that you hope to address. Psychotherapy is not like a medical doctor visit. Instead, it calls for a very active effort on your part. In order for the therapy to be most successful, you will have to work on things we talk about both during our sessions and at home
>
> Psychotherapy can have benefits and risks. Since therapy often involves discussing unpleasant aspects of your life, you may experience uncomfortable feelings like sadness, guilt, anger, frustration, loneliness, and helplessness. On the other hand, psychotherapy has also been shown to have benefits for people who go through it. Therapy often leads to better relationships, solutions to specific problems, and significant reductions in feelings of distress. But there are no guarantees of what you will experience.
>
> . . . Therapy involves a large commitment of time, money, and energy, so you should be very careful about the therapist you select.

Note how well the *Informed Consent Form* specifies the assumptions about change noted above. Therapy is going to be hard work. It is painful and you will experience uncomfortable feelings. It is slow and takes large commitments of time, money, and energy. And, because there may be resistance or interference from a variety of factors, the outcome is far from certain.

In fact, you should know that psychotherapy is not a powerful process with a guaranteed result but rather a more modest intervention that only helps occasionally. This form is the client's first introduction to the concept of psychotherapy; it appears to be designed more to inhibit change than to encourage it.

The following amusing, but revealing, joke about psychologists makes some of the same points as the *Informed Consent Form*.

*Question:* How many psychologists do you need to change a light bulb?
*Answer:* One, but the light bulb has to want to change.

The implication in this joke is that psychotherapy is a weak process that needs cooperative and enthusiastic participation by the client in order to be effective. Compare that to a more robust intervention such as an antibiotic prescribed for a bladder infection. In the case of the powerful intervention, antibiotics, the desired outcome will occur whether the patient has a cooperative attitude or not. In other words, the need for cooperation from the client highlights the weakness of the psychotherapeutic effect and implies that, compared to robust interventions, the effect size of psychotherapy is relatively small.

Western culture assumes there is a solid self—with an established sense of identity—that is confronting this opportunity to change. There are lots of theories about how this self is formed—genetic/biochemical contributions, early life traumas, learned and modeled behaviors, etc.— but all the theories support one's inner experience that "I exist," "I am a solid person," and "I am a stable person across time and place." It is assumed that change threatens the stability and comfort zone of this self and, therefore, change is associated with the pain of letting go, releasing the secure sense of self, and stepping into the unknown. The concept of "resistance" in psychotherapy—the feeling that the client is slowing or stopping change and thereby supporting the self as it currently exists— has been central to teaching and understanding therapy since the inception of the field.

This sense of the solidness of the self can be extended to the idea that real change is impossible. At moments of despair—with themselves, their loved ones or their clients/patients—people become susceptible to the fear that "people never really do change." Examine the following three quotes again selected from popular quotes on the web.[3]

> "People don't change, they just have momentary steps outside of their true character."

—Chad Kultgen

"We do not escape our boundaries or our innermost being. We do not change. It is true we may be transformed, but we always walk within our boundaries, within the marked-off circle."

—Ernst Jünger, *The Glass Bees*

"The only time a woman really succeeds in changing a man is when he's a baby."

—Natalie Wood

The Kultgen quote embodies the common sense notion that there is only the appearance of change. Given time and varying experiences, individuals will regress back to their "essential" self and their basic identity. The Wood quote may have an amusing character but it emphasizes the idea that by adulthood all real ability to change is gone and we need to accept people as they are.

In fact, this concept of the stability of the self and resistance to change is so prevalent it has been formalized and reified in the psychological literature; people who can't change or have an extremely difficult time changing—even when their lives are profoundly dysfunctional—are called personality disorders.

(a personality disorder is) [a]n enduring pattern of inner experience and behavior that deviates markedly from the expectation of the individual's culture, is pervasive and inflexible, has an onset in adolescence or early adulthood, is stable over time, and leads to distress or impairment. (DSM IV)

In this definition of personality disorder, one can see the characteristic dilemma of change carried to the extreme. The individual with a personality disorder holds on to their sense of self in spite of the fact that it deviates from strategies that predict success. In other words, they are committed to staying the same even if that choice is regularly and repeatedly punished by their social group and results in significant pain and distress. In professional psychology the debate about personality disorders lies between advocates who believe that some personality disorders can change slowly and gradually if they are given lots of time, massive amounts of therapy, and behavioral incentives, and practitioners that believe it best to accept the personality disorders as they are—they aren't going to change; one should, therefore, teach their family members to cope with them and the individual to suffer minimally given their fixated state.

All of the above seems to be common sense until one contrasts it with the actualities of human existence on the planet. Examine the following popular quotes again harvested from the internet.[4]

"It is the greatest mistake to think that man is always one and the same. A man is never the same for long. He is continually changing. He seldom remains the same even for half an hour."

—G. I. Gurdjieff

"The fact is that five years ago I was, as near as possible, a different person to what I am tonight. I, as I am now, didn't exist at all. Will the same thing happen in the next five years? I hope so."

—Siegfried Sassoon

"Change is inevitable—except from a vending machine."

—Robert C. Gallagher

In truth, everything is in flux around us all the time. Even more importantly our physical, mental, and emotional bodies are moving relentlessly through a developmental process from birth to death. Moreover, since there is no unified, internal self, our own personality varies significantly from moment to moment as different ego states sequentially take the stage.

People change effortlessly and profoundly simply when they get a new job, or move to a new city, or get a new boyfriend or spouse. Financial success or failure, the presence of disease or disability, or the loss of a significant other often makes us completely different people. Individuals get exposed to a new idea, or spiritual belief, or political affiliation and they vow to reorganize and transform their lives accordingly and, voila, they do.

The problem in life is not the difficulty of change; rather, it is the difficulty of staying the same. Is it harder work to evolve or harder work to maintain stability?

Imagine writing a new *Informed Consent Form* without the implicit Apollonian bias against change. It might go something like this.

Welcome to the psychotherapy change process. You are about to embark on a modern version of a human experience as old as time and as natural as a youth becoming an adult. You begin with a positive prognosis. First, even without making a conscious effort—such as the one you will exert as a psychotherapy client—many psychotherapy issues resolve by themselves. Second, research suggests that therapy helps about 75% of participants. In sum, while there is no guarantee of success, given your efforts and the efforts of your therapist, it is likely that the change you desire will not only happen, but happen much more quickly and profoundly than you might imagine. Moreover, most clients report experiencing additional positive changes that occur through therapy beyond their initial target.

Psychotherapy is the safest process in the medical field in terms of side effects. In comparison to other approaches such as surgery, medicine, or physical therapy, there are few risks. And the downsides of therapy are fairly obvious and expected: sometimes a client will be urged to talk about uncomfortable feelings; occasionally she will be confronted by the therapist regarding life choices; and at other times the client might experience some regrets. Other than these, the biggest risk is that you will fall into the less than 20% of clients who do not find therapy beneficial and feel they have wasted their time and money.

In this informed consent example, the actual risks and benefits of therapy are presented without the negative Apollonian slant. It is clearly more accurate than the actual *Informed Consent Form* and, from the standpoint of instilling positive expectations, it becomes a document that might actually serve clients instead of acting as a barrier to growth and change.

Some might argue that psychology is required to have a negative and conservative *Informed Consent Form* to avoid law suits. Yet we are told in our mandatory ethics classes that our real risk of being sued only arises secondary to much more serious faults than using an encouraging *Informed Consent Form*; we are going to get sued if we operate outside our competence or sleep with our clients, not because we tell them quite accurately that psychotherapy outcomes tend to be positive. Do ethics require us to offer a negative and conservative consent form? On the contrary, ethics requires us to serve the client's highest needs and clearly that includes encouraging them to be open to the benefits of psychotherapy. In sum, our existing *Informed Consent Form* is clearly an attempt by Apollonian forces to sustain stability; the ethics of a profession dedicated to healthy change mandates a far different form.

The *Informed Consent Form* is a simple and concrete example of Apollonian influence. However, the real genius of the Apollonian approach is to convince therapists—as opposed to clients—about the slowness of change and the relative ineffectiveness of psychotherapy. Essentially, the more training a therapist has, the less they believe that change is easy and possible. A life coach believes change is easier than a master's level clinician. The doctoral-level clinician knows many more factors that preclude change than the two lower levels of training. Duncan et al. comment:

Too many pathology-based prognostications about clients pervade the field. It would seem that a field dedicated to helping people change would believe that change is not only possible but probable. Believing in the client's propensities for change seems to follow the data presented in this chapter. Given the amount of variance accounted for by the client relative to models, allegiance to this belief is perhaps more important that any commitment to a given approach. (Duncan, Miller, Wampold, & Hubble, 2010, Kindle Locations 2706–2709)

Apollonian influences are also apparent in research priorities. At present, the research that most excites interest and most attracts funding is the neuroscience of mental health. There are almost daily articles in leading papers and on the internet discussing the latest discoveries that show that complex behaviors and choices are actually determined by genetics or, sometimes, by a dysfunctional part of the brain. As pointed out in chapter 3, a number of the neuroscientists—who are deeply committed to the "intricate machine" theory implicit in pragmatism and most of science—question if there is any free will at all. To such theoreticians, change is impossible by definition as there is no independent consciousness to "stand in" to serve as a foundation for change and growth. In sum, there is a culture-wide campaign for stability, structure, and permanence. And greater training in the mental health field correlates highly with more exposure to material that argues against change or limits change to slow, modest, and partial.

Returning to the discussion of placebo, there is a sense that placebo is a powerful force in its own right; when we succeed in activating the placebo effect, we are enabling a strong mental force that can serve positive or negative ends. However, when placebo is examined from a Reality B perspective it is more helpful to think of it as a power that can disable the Apollonian forces. In this sense, the belief that placebo mobilizes powerful inner resources is a misunderstanding. The actual strong effects are Apollonian; Kahneman's System 1—plus social concordance—acts to keep clients stable even though the stability is not in their best interests. If they are sick, they remain sick; if they are depressed, they remain depressed, and if they have an anger problem, the problem continues. The client wants to be healthy or in a positive mood or calm but they cannot because if "simply wishing made it so," reality would become unstable and fragile.

Feeling the power of the Apollonian forces in every moment is a vital part of cultivating beginner's mind. Understanding that individual identity is fluid and barely held together by social concordance and beliefs is necessary to function therapeutically in constructed reality. Why is this definition so important? Because it highlights the fragility of the Net, emphasizes the ease of change, and helps focus interventions.

The ability to work effectively with Apollonian forces by adopting a Dionysian perspective is well illustrated by the following dialog from the Matrix. In the following scene, Neo, the protagonist, encounters a young adept who is capable of bending metal spoons with his mind.

*Boy:* Do not try and bend the spoon. That's impossible. Instead only try to realize the truth.
*Neo:* What truth?
*Boy:* There is no spoon.

*Neo:* There is no spoon?
*Boy:* Then you'll see that it is not the spoon that bends, it is only yourself. (Silver, Wachowski, & Wachowski, 1999)

The simple interpretation of this dialog is that since they are in the Matrix, there is no actual spoon; in truth there is only a computer program's representation of a spoon. Within the reality of the program, the spoon is real. To understand "no spoon," change yourself by recognizing that the program is not reality. Once you know the spoon is not real, it is easy to bend it.

Returning to Reality B, the seeming solidity of the spoon corresponds to the seeming solidity of the clinical syndrome. The sense of "I am sick," "I am neurotic," is difficult to move because of the stabilizing Apollonian forces. The therapist negates the reifying power of the Apollonian forces by recognizing they are constructed—they are "made up." This negation requires altering normal reality or "bending yourself."

When one asks, "is change easy or hard?" in truth, one is not actually asking about the difficulty of change. In reality, one is asking the professional to identify as an Apollonian or a Dionysian. Apollonians are required to answer this question with the assertion that change is hard and it takes a long time and much effort. Dionysians have just the opposite experience. Gifted therapists move through the therapeutic world with a sense that it is highly likely that they are going to be helpful to the client. Moreover, they delight in helping clients who have confounded standard therapeutic approaches and love to show how people are more capable of change than might be expected. Such therapists cultivate beginner's mind and recognize implicit Apollonian messages.

> The real difference between God and human beings, he thought, was that God cannot stand continuance. No sooner has he created a season of a year, or a time of the day, than he wishes for something quite different, and sweeps it all away. No sooner was one a young man, and happy at that, than the nature of things would rush one into marriage, martyrdom or old age. And human beings cleave to the existing state of things. All their lives they are striving to hold the moment fast. . . . Their art itself is nothing but the attempt to catch by all means the one particular moment, one light, the momentary beauty of one woman or one flower, and make it everlasting. (Dinesen, 1991, p. 121)

In this final quote, Dinesen discusses the fundamental inevitability of change and the natural Apollonian tendency to resist it. The Net requires ongoing maintenance, like any living structure, and it is healthy and right to do so. However, for the professional dedicated to change, Apollonian priorities, while appropriate and helpful in the correct context, are the embodiment of resistance in psychotherapy. Recognizing their hidden and constant presence is vital. And a formal commitment to seeing reality as fluid and mobile is central to enhancing therapist efficacy.

## NOTES

1. All identifying details have been altered in this case and subsequent cases in order to protect the confidentiality of my clients.

2. It is well known that the internet quote sites are not entirely accurate. Since the quotes are typically posted by individuals, quotes may have mistakes and they may even be attributed to the wrong author. I gathered quotes from internet sites because I was attempting to sample pop culture. In other words, such quotes represent what an average individual might think about change.

3. It is well known that the internet quote sites are not entirely accurate. Since the quotes are typically posted by individuals, quotes may have mistakes and they may even be attributed to the wrong author. I gathered quotes from internet sites because I was attempting to sample pop culture. In other words, such quotes represent what an average individual might think about change.

4. It is well known that the internet quote sites are not entirely accurate. Since the quotes are typically posted by individuals, quotes may have mistakes and they may even be attributed to the wrong author. I gathered quotes from internet sites because I was attempting to sample pop culture. In other words, such quotes represent what an average individual might think about change.

# Chapter 8

# Wizards among Us

Everyone goes with the flow . . . but the one who goes against the flow becomes someone remarkable in life.

—Swami Vivekananda, *The Complete Works of Swami Vivekananda* (1907)

What is real and what is unreal is not an easy question to answer once constructionism is accepted as an organizing principle. Human suffering is, of course, real to a therapist. Without the perception of suffering, there is no compassion, no motivation to be of service, and no ability to make a connection or build rapport. However, being entranced by the client's current identity results in the therapist losing the ability to move fluidly and creatively; even more important, she can start to believe that her client's dilemma is "real" and have significant difficulties imagining her in any other state.

Since the Net is socially constructed and culturally defined it is both real—in the sense that it works to stabilize an individual and to have opportunities for health and growth—and unreal in the sense that there is no right or wrong shape or construction. Because of the fluidity of reality, the exact shape of our own Net is highly determined by social and cultural conventions and especially influenced by high status people—people who exercise disproportionate influence over how we structure our net. Wampold puts it this way.

The point here is that a claim could be made that psychotherapy is a social healing practice. Or perhaps better said, psychotherapy utilizes evolved human propensities to help clients change (Wampold and Budge 2012). Lieberman, in his review of the "hard wiring" of the social nature of humans, notes . . . [o]ur brains are designed to be influenced by others. (Wampold & Imel, 2015, Kindle Locations 1280–1284)

From a constructionist point of view, every human being comes with the innate ability to be socialized into the prevailing reality. Every successfully socialized human has a capacity to take direction from the culture in general and from key individuals in particular. And this direction is not simply about learning a language or acquiring social customs; rather, we have the ability to take direction about the basic formation of the fabric of reality. No one has to learn how to do this. We are all already prepared to take our cues from our social group and key individuals. If we didn't have this ability we would not be fully capable of socialization—in short, we would not be fully human.

People are always marveling about the foolishness—or even insanity—of cult behavior. How did Jones get his followers to drink the poison Kool-Aid; why did the Heavens Gate followers employ castration and eventual mass suicide to reach their spiritual goals? Of course these stories are human tragedies, but they also document how profoundly reality can be altered given the combination of a charismatic leader and a validating peer group. In Germany, regular citizens participated in the Holocaust. In the famous Milgram experiment, normal students administered electric shock at seemingly horrific levels. Examples like these demonstrate that humans are remarkably capable of shifting reality when the conditions are right and a charismatic leader provides direction.

This human ability to take direction suggests a new definition of the highly effective therapist: the effective therapist is one who is recognized by clients as having the innate authority to reformulate our existing view of reality simply because he directs us to do so. Of course, it is not that easy to be recognized as this kind of key individual; the need to be stable requires us to be discerning about who we empower as an authority figure and reality definer. If we allowed just anyone to affect us, the world and our identity would be in a state of constant turmoil. This is where the concept of "status" becomes important. From a Reality B point of view, status can be defined as the amount of power we give the other to define and redefine our reality. Obviously parents were the original high status people although, as time passes, parental status tends to shrink. Similarly bosses, mentors, famous people, rich people, and powerful people may become high status people to us.

The problem with using the term "high status" to refer to therapeutic wizards and their power as change agents is that status is so associated with wealth and fame. Wealth and fame are often criticized as shallow and ultimately meaningless; in contrast, the kind of personal power we are discussing here is deep and profound. From the Tillichian point of view, status is associated with idolatrous ultimate concerns and the healing power of therapists needs to flow from authentic ultimate concerns.

"Charisma" tends to be a more useful term than status. Often defined as "personal magnetism," it also has spiritual connotations dating back to its

Greek origins which are connected with "grace" and "gift." In some spiritual traditions it refers to a divinely bestowed power. And, while the term is often used for leaders, politicians, and even actors—and hence can bring up the same shallow, idolatrous associations as "status"—the primary references are to magnetism, grace, and spiritual power. While some of its connotations are imperfect, we will use it to describe the characteristic that highly effective therapists possess that sets them apart from the more common kindness and wisdom possessed by ordinary therapists.

The concept of "if I say it, it becomes so" is a magical idea. It is a statement that affirms that reality is directly created by thought, intention, and action. And, of course, in constructionism this kind of magical thinking is literally true. Since virtually everything is made up—and validated by mutual consent between myself and others—the therapist is capable of creating a reality where the client is healthy and generative simply by fiat. If the client concurs with this new view of reality, then it exists. And this new reality is just as real as any other view of personhood, identity, pathology, or health.

In this sense, constructed reality is a kind of "Wild West" where laws hold no sway and reality is created by social contract and the power of remarkable individuals. Given that this is so, such individuals should stand out; we should be aware of their presence because they are not bound by the laws that "we mortals" need observe. In reviewing their work and results, we will have trouble making sense of how they operate since we try to describe their patterns and results using words and concepts from fundamental reality.

However, what makes them remarkable is that they have somehow discovered that they are not bound by socially constructed limits and have gone on to create their own rules. Exceptional therapists will achieve remarkable results. How they work will be shrouded in mystery. And analyses based on fundamental reality—including attempts to distill general principles and replicable techniques—will fail to capture their essential functioning. This failure is due to the fact that they are operating in constructed reality and, hence, are operating outside of Reality A rules and limitations.

Let's begin by looking at several examples of therapeutic wizards in action. The first example, from Milton Erickson, has been chosen as a simple demonstration of the power of a therapeutic wizard to alter reality with a simple suggestion.

As an example, I recall a demonstration Erickson once did before a large audience. He asked for a volunteer and a young man came up and sat down with him. Erickson's only trance induction was to ask the young man to put his hands on his knees. Then he said, "would you be willing to continue to see your hands on your knees?" The young man said he would. While talking with him, Erickson gestured to a colleague on the other side of the young man, and the colleague lifted up the young man's arm and it remained in the air. Erickson said to the young man, "how many hands do you have?" "Two, of course," said the young man. "I'd like you to count them as I point to them," said Erickson. "All right," said the young man, in a rather patronizing way. And Erickson pointed to the hand on one knee, and the young man said, "one." Erickson pointed to the vacant other knee, where the young man had agreed to continue to see his hand, and the young man said, "two." Then Erickson pointed to the hand up in the air. The young man stared at it, puzzled. "How do you explain the other hand?" asked Erickson. "I don't know," said the young man. "I guess I should be in the circus." That hypnotic induction took about as long as it took me to describe it here. (Zeig, 1982, p. 11)

Now, it is certainly possible to explain the suggestibility of the young man by noting that he was a volunteer for a hypnosis demonstration and hence, might be particularly open to manifesting trance phenomena. In addition, he was in front of a large audience and the presence of that many people focusing their gaze on him could put anyone in an altered state. Moreover, he had probably heard that Erickson was a famous hypnotherapist and that might have made him particularly open. Even given these and other factors conducive to an altered state, Erickson's rapid trance induction was still remarkable.

Erickson used no overt induction techniques. And yet he effortlessly achieved the very advanced trance phenomena of a positive hallucination. Clearly Erickson was capable of influencing a great many individuals with a simple "wave of his mind."

This is an interesting vignette not only in terms of illustrating Erickson's skill and charisma, but also in the way it points to Kahneman's System 1 and System 2. This vignette is an almost perfect parallel with the optical illusion of the figures on the train track. In this vignette, System 1 is clearly in trance and sees three hands and System 2 is having great difficultly explaining the results. The manner in which System 2 is an apologist for System 1 is illustrated clearly. Recalling that System 1 is also responsible for sustaining the Nomological Net gives us another perspective on why intellectual understandings so often fail to help clients improve. The insight is limited to System 2 and never touches System 1. Since clients' misconstruals, self-deprecations, and the source for virtually all symptoms lie in System 1, System 2 insights are unlikely to be helpful.

Erickson had an early understanding of the difference between the two systems and oriented almost all of his interventions to System 1. This, of course, often made his work look magical, inexplicable, and unpredictable—all words which describe confusion between fundamental and constructed reality. From the point of view of charisma and being remarkable, however, this kind of nonintellectual approach was very helpful. Now let us examine a second Erickson example.

*E:* I like volunteers and I also like to pick my volunteers. The one I'd like to pick is the pretty girl wearing the white hat who keeps hiding behind the pillar.

*S:* All the way from Colorado Springs my husband urged me to act as a subject. I told him I didn't want to.

*E:* Now, notice that you thought you didn't want to. And now that you've come out entirely from behind that pillar, you might as well come all the way to the platform.

*S:* (As she steps forward) But I don't want to.

*E:* While you continue to come forward please, don't go into a trance until you sit all the way down in this chair. As you are on the platform, you know you are not in a deep trance but you are getting closer to that chair and you are beginning to recognize you don't care whether or not you are going into trance. The closer you get, the more you can recognize the comfort of going into a trance. But don't go all the way in until you sit all the way down in the chair. All the way down. (said as she is in the process of sitting down.) You are all the way down in the chair all the way from Colorado Springs.

You know you did not want to go into a trance. You knew you would prefer something else. As you think it over there is something else. So why don't you look at it?

*S:* (looking at a blank wall) I get so much pleasure watching those skiers through my kitchen window.

*E:* What else enhances it?

*S:* I always keep the hi-fi on while I watch the skiers. That is the easiest way to wash the dishes. . . .

*E:* I think you might like to include hypnosis in your future. Suppose you ask me about it after you are awake.

*S:* (She awakens and looks around the platform.) I told my husband I would not volunteer as a hypnotic subject! I was hiding behind that pillar and now I'm here?! I must have been in a trance. (Erickson, Rossi, & Rossi, 1976, pp. 118–121)

Rossi makes a number of comments about Erickson's work with this woman. He emphasized the way in which Erickson would highlight truisms (you are on the platform) and link it to suggestions (you are not in a deep trance). He noted embedded suggestions (whether or not *you are going into a trance.*) and contingent suggestions (but don't go all the way in until you sit all the way down). And "over there is something else" becomes an invitation to review a meaningful memory. Rossi's commentary is interesting and instructive; at first glance, it appears accurate and helpful. However, underlying this commentary is the implication that Erickson's words are why the client went into trance and experienced certain trance phenomena.

Here's the problem. Imagine that you are on the stage and invite someone up using Erickson's exact dialog. What the probability that they will be in deep trance as they sit in the chair? Low probability, right? That's

because you're aware that you won't have sufficient confidence and charisma to ensure that she goes into trance. And you also suspect that the
client will somehow read your lack of confidence. This will result in the
client simply walking up to the chair and sitting down in a normal state of
consciousness.

Erickson was not only famous for achieving change using trance and hypnosis, he could be equally effective using straightforward, direct suggestions.
Take a look at the following example.

> A woman came to see Erickson because she wanted to lose weight and quit
> smoking. She said, "I can't resist eating and I can't resist smoking, but I
> can resist exercise, and I do." Erickson learned that she was religious and so
> extracted her most solemn promise that she would follow his instructions. She
> lived in a two story house. Whenever she wanted a cigarette, she was to go to
> the basement where she kept her matches and set one on top of the box. Then
> she was to run up to the attic where she would keep her cigarette, then run back
> down to the basement to light and smoke it. If she wanted some cake, she was to
> cut a thin slice, then run around the outside of her house before she ate it. If she
> wanted a second slice, she was to cut a thin one, then run around the house two
> times before eating it, and so forth. Soon she cut down on cigarettes and began
> reducing nicely. (Zeig & Munion, 1999, p. 74)

Here we have a case where a single, short intervention cured both a smoking
and a weight issue. Zeig and Munion speculate that an important therapeutic
factor is that Erickson changed how the eating and smoking would occur
without forbidding the behaviors. From the case study, Erickson apparently
gave some credit to the religious nature of the client and the motivating factor
of a solemn promise. Those are interesting theories. But, ask yourself again,
if you followed these instructions exactly, what is the chance that you could
do one session cures of weight and smoking? If solemn promises and changing how a behavior occurs are the active factors, then all of us should be able
to replicate this successful case. However, if the research is correct—and
there is no inherent power in techniques—then the active factor in these two
cases is Erickson's charisma. The active factor isn't what he did but who he
was. Put another way, Erickson could apparently do pretty much anything he
wanted and still get good results.

Now let us examine a different example of a therapeutic wizard, Frank
Farrelly. As can be seen below, Farrelly seemingly works without formally
creating altered states.

> A young woman was referred for therapy who had a variety of problems
> in both task performance and relationship areas. She was gradually able to
> achieve much better in her work but still continued not to date. She finally

confessed with some embarrassment that when she was a young girl and her breasts begin to develop, she went to her mother and told her about her problem. The problem was that, though her right breast fitted her bra, her left breast "rattled around like a goober pea in a fuel oil barrel." Her mother took her to her family physician who took the bra off the frightened young adolescent, looked first at one breast and then at the other and issued this dictum, "this is not an uncommon phenomenon." She then was told to dress and return home. Horror struck, she felt that she had a combination of leprosy, polio, and various venereal diseases. When she began to date boys, she immediately ran into the problem about their wanting to pet; her response was simply to avoid the situation and, as a result, she usually had only one or two dates with each boy.

*Therapist:* you mean you're embarrassed and ashamed for them to find out that you got that weird left tit?
*Client:* (embarrassed, hanging her head) I don't like the way you put it but, yeah, that's about it.
*Therapist:* so that's why you've been avoiding half the human race! (He pauses for a moment) well, hell, now that I think of it, your behavior makes sense. Because if you were to go out on dates with guys—guys, being guys, would naturally want to pet and get all they could off of you (the client nods), and once they got your blouse open, there could only be three possible reactions that a fella could have toward you.
*Client:* (curiously but simultaneously embarrassed) what are they?
*Therapist:* (very seriously) well, one reaction would be that he would hastily button up your blouse and say in an embarrassed manner, "I'm sorry, I didn't know you were a crip." A second reaction might be that he would get all heated up and say, "Whoopie, I've always wanted to do it to a crip!" And the only other possible reaction that a guy could have would be that, once he had unbuttoned your blouse, he would stare at your weird left tit and exclaim, "hold it right there, will you? Let me get my Polaroid swinger—the guys back at the frat house will never believe it when I tell them."

The patient stared at me throughout this and finally with a weak grin stated, "yeah, that's what I feel would happen, but I'll never really find out if I just sit here and talk and talk about it with you." I got anxious at this point and told her that time was up and that we'd have to discuss it further the next time. As she was about to leave I remarked, "I like to name my interviews, so I thought I would call this "the weird left tit interview." She laughed and said, "that sounds like an appropriate title for it."

The next interview she came in looking like the cat that swallowed the 400 pound canary. I greeted her with, "well, gorgeous, what the hell have you been up to since I saw you last?" Quite briefly, she explained that she had gone out and, with much fear and trepidation, had "hustled" a guy and had gone up to his apartment with him. They had shed their clothes and, while in their birthday suits, were having fun and games. Right in the middle of the proceedings she called his attention to the fact that her left breast was smaller than her right one. His response was to look at one and then the other and give a client centered response: "oh, yeah, you feel that it is, huh?" and immediately resumed his activities. She felt like an immense, eight year old lead weight had suddenly been lifted from her shoulders and she experienced a marked sense of relief at his acceptance of her. (Farrelly & Brandsma, 1981, pp. 67–69)

Farrelly calls his approach "provocative therapy," and this case clearly illustrates the meaning of that title. His behavior was entirely provocative; put more specifically, it was rude, inappropriate, lacked empathy, and was insulting. Of course, it could also be interpreted as Farrelly consciously acting out the inner voice that had been tormenting the client all these years. However, any therapist who hoped that the young woman would see things this way is taking quite a gamble.

From a Reality A perspective, Farrelly was acting in a socially inappropriate manner, particularly for a therapist-client relationship which is typically characterized by kindness, empathy, and understanding. This was confusing behavior, particularly from a high status mental health professional, and understandably threw the woman into a range of uncomfortable emotions—embarrassment, the "weak grin," and hanging her head. In short, Farrelly, without any kind of formal induction, quickly put his client into an altered state.

The "normal" reaction to such unexpected behaviors from the therapist would be either anger or complete collapse. In this situation, however, she somehow quickly rallied and left with a laugh. What made that possible? Obviously the woman somehow discerned that Farrelly's strange behaviors were designed to help her and left with resolve and positive intentions.

Did Farrelly develop a new technique? Hardly—most therapists attempting such an intervention would discover that their efforts were rewarded by clients who fail to return and/or malpractice lawsuits. Clearly Farrelly "got away" with such behaviors because the client recognized him as a key individual—an individual who has a right to break any rules because such individuals essentially make all the rules. In sum, the client somehow sensed Farrelly's charisma and decided to allow him to guide her.

Like many therapeutic wizards, Farrelly's own explanations of his work are both helpful and obfuscating. First, he believes that "expert mind" often leads to false conclusions.

Doom and gloom prognostic statements regarding clients' lack of ability are rampant in the clinical field and are probably much more a reflection of the individual clinician's subjective reaction of helplessness and hopelessness than any objective statement regarding the client. (1981, p. 41)

Second, he shows the characteristic optimism of most therapeutic wizards. Regardless of the client's apparent psychopathology, Farrelly expects a positive outcome. Change is seen as relatively easy and the client's identity is relatively fluid.

> The Client's maladaptive, unproductive, antisocial attitudes and behaviors can be drastically altered whatever the degree of severity or chronicity. (1981, p. 43)

Farrelly believes that clients can respond to reality, are not as fragile as they seem, and the limitations of a traumatic childhood can often be ignored.

> People make sense; the human animal is exquisitely logical and understandable (1981, p. 47). . . . The psychological fragility of patients is vastly overrated both by themselves and others (1981, p. 42). . . . (And) . . . Adult or current experiences are as at least if not more significant than childhood or previous experiences in shaping client values, operational attitudes, and behaviors. (1981, p. 44)

Farrelly has discovered that his clients are not bound by their past traumas, that change is possible, and that substantial change—even with badly traumatized clients—is relatively easy. He seems to have freed himself from the limiting nature of various psychological assumptions. Of course, his experiences as a key individual—more specifically, that his clients change pretty much no matter what he does—are likely to make him an optimist, an optimist who can afford to discount preexisting conditions and client frailties.

Then with the next quote, Farrelly gives the credit for his successes to a specific technique: "The expression of therapeutic hate and joyful sadism toward clients can markedly benefit the client" (1981, p. 48). Later in his book he takes this same idea and expands it into what he calls his "Central Hypotheses."

> If provoked by the therapist (humorously, perceptively, and within the client's own internal frame of reference), the client will tend to move in the opposite direction from the therapist's definition of the client as a person. . . . (And) if urged provocatively (humorously and perceptively) by the therapist to continue his self-defeating, deviant behaviors, the client will tend to engage in self- and other-enhancing behaviors which more closely approximate the societal norm. (1981, p. 52)

Now, it is unlikely that Farrelly had ever carefully reviewed the outcome literature and understood that techniques are not responsible for change. Moreover, much as Farrelly's successes with his unorthodox approach argued that he and the clients were operating in constructed reality, it seems likely that he continued to believe that therapy occurred in fundamental reality; in short, he thought he had found a technique—therapeutic hate and joyful sadism—that was responsible for his positive results.

Subsequent technique developers agreed and renamed Farrelly's central hypothesis, "paradoxical therapy." Weeks and L'Abate (1982) wrote an entire book about paradoxical therapy. Here is their definition of the term.

> Like a contradiction, a pragmatic paradox gives a person no choice. "Thus, if the message is an injunction, it must be disobeyed to be obeyed; if it is a definition of self or other, the person thereby defined is this kind of person only if he is not, and is not if he is." Accordingly, paradoxical therapy is based on the principle that a person is expected to change by remaining unchanged. The classic example of this principle and of the pragmatic paradox is the paradoxical injunction, "be spontaneous." As soon as one attempts to act on this command, one cannot. It is only when one gives up that one can behave spontaneously. The most common form of the pragmatic paradox or therapeutic paradox is to prescribe the symptom—in other words, to encourage the client to become even more symptomatic. (p. 5)

And here is a typical paradoxical therapy technique used with the common complaint of anxiety.

> A client who was anxious and worried chronically was told to set aside one hour a day to worry. She was told she worried constantly because she had always avoided thinking about troubling matters, and consequently never made any changes. She was further told that she would have to become a competent worrier if she could ever hope to resolve her anxieties. Effective worrying meant she had to think the worst possible thoughts and keep a list of everything that might worry her for her "worry time." Moreover, she was told to worry the full hour even if she felt like stopping early. (p. 121)

Weeks and L'Abate report that the client found the first couple of days of this exercise painful in that the worrying increased. However, after just a few days she found the assignment onerous and boring and wanted to cut it short. Finally, she reported that she was no longer worried and had decided that all that worrying she used to do was absurd.

Like Farrelly, Weeks and L'Abate got good results with paradoxical techniques. Unfortunately when used by less gifted therapists, the results were mixed at best. Many clients found the approach insulting, others failed to understand it, still others agreed to try practicing it at home but failed to follow through. Paradoxical therapy is always Dionysian and, when employed correctly, typically generates an altered state. Generating altered states is always somewhat of a gamble—a gamble between succeeding and supercharging the technique and failing and being perceived as an eccentric, strange, and confused therapist. Less charismatic therapists avoided paradoxical therapy, especially if they failed in their first few tries. As a result, despite the impressive stories from Farrelly and Weeks and L'Abate, it never gained the popularity of more Apollonian techniques such as CBT.

CBT and other Apollonian techniques do not require altered states. They are not supercharged in the same way that paradox or hypnosis is supercharged. In that sense, they are safer albeit less powerful. If a CBT therapist fails to engage the client, he is simply seen as boring or detached or a poor listener. He is not reviled as an eccentric wacko.

Farrelly succeeded for the same reasons Erickson succeeded: an abundance of charisma. Farrelly's explanations—which were in part responsible for the brief popularity of paradoxical techniques—failed to ensure replication of his results. This failure to replicate is the standard outcome when average therapists believe they can achieve the outcomes of the wizards by copying their techniques. At the end of the day, these failures are always due to a confabulation of fundamental reality with constructed reality.

## WIZARDS AND ALTERED STATES

> If the doors of perception were cleansed, everything would appear to man as it is: infinite.
>
> —William Blake, "A Memorable Fancy,"
> *The Marriage of Heaven and Hell* (1790–1793)

There is a deep and inevitable connection between therapeutic wizards and altered states. If you are a key individual who is recognized by others as empowered to define reality, wouldn't it behoove you to supercharge your rituals with altered states to ensure that your clients change more profoundly with each encounter? From another perspective, simply the act of quickly and profoundly rearranging the strands of one's Net at the direction of a key individual is, in itself, an altered state. Any way you look at it, therapeutic wizards are always associated with altered states.

Constructionists have done interesting and insightful work demonstrating just how fragile the collective Net is for each of us. In fact, the Net is so fragile that we are constrained to reinforce it constantly via tightly defining many of our social interactions. In the following examples, students are asked to disrupt this constant level of support and thereby reveal how easily the Net can unravel.

The importance of the continuity of everyday routine is well exemplified in Harold Garfinkel's (1963; 1967) experiments with everyday conversation. Garfinkel asked his students to monitor their friends' and relatives' reactions when taken-for-granted ways of conversation were suddenly called into question by the student conducting the experiment.

(Here is a carpool member telling the student) about having had a flat tire while going to work the previous day.

*Carpool member:* I had a flat tire.
*Student:* what you mean, you "had a flat tire?"
*Carpool member:* (momentarily stunned, replies hastily) what you mean, "what do you mean?" A flat tire is a flat tire. That is what I meant. Nothing special. What a crazy question.

(In a second case) the victim waved his hand cheerily.

*Acquaintance:* how are you?
*Student:* how am I in regard to what? My health, my finances, my schoolwork, my peace of mind, my . . . ?
*Acquaintance:* (red in the face and out of control) look! I was just trying to be polite. Frankly, I don't give a damn how you are. (Hjelm, 2014, pp. 28–29)

Note that in these examples, the subjects responded with some level of aggression. To understand these responses, imagine what kind of person steps outside the well-recognized boundaries of conventions, politeness, and expectations. The first category would consist of children, disabled people and strangers from another culture. By and large, when these people violate conventions they are dismissed as individuals of insignificant status and knowledge and their behaviors are essentially ignored or corrected. The second category, illustrated in these examples, occurs when peers who are acculturated respond atypically. The assumption here is that they are teasing or taunting and the common response is aggression and/or intimidation.

The aggression has a double meaning, however. The first meaning is "stop taunting me." The second meaning, and probably the more important one from the point of view of the experiment, is "stop unravelling/destroying my world." This sense of how quickly reality unravels, and how aggressively individuals operate to stop "unravelling" behaviors, is helpful to witness for Reality B therapists. Anything that demonstrates how the seemingly solid is one interaction away from becoming fluid and chaotic encourages therapists who are oriented toward change and growth.

In the Farrelly examples above, he was a high status person both by definition—he was a professional—but even more so by behavior and nonverbals: Farrelly had learned to conduct himself so that others perceived him as an authority figure. In addition, Farrelly had also developed the ability to project caring and compassion to others; he was not simply high status, his clients also had the feeling that his behaviors were emitted with the purpose of helping others. In the examples above, Farrelly generated words and behaviors that significantly violated cultural norms. And, as he emphasized, these cultural norm violations were emitted in the context of a caring relationship. Finally, he clearly intended to violate the norms in the hope that unraveling the client's sense of a solid identity would facilitate change. In the vignette above, Farrelly's subtle guidance allowed the client to recover from her altered state and return with a sense of resolve.

Note that the first response of his clients was confusion. Those familiar with Ericksonian Therapy will immediately remember Erickson's repeated emphasis on "confusion technique" as an important adjunct to therapy. Steve de Shazer (1985) points out that the confusion technique is used to shake clients out of a restricted state of consciousness.

[M]y confusion technique is a development of Erickson's work. . . . While Erickson's technique was developed in an experimental setting, he did use it in hypnotherapy with individual patients "desperately seeking therapy but restricted and dominated by their clinical problem." (p. 9)

In the classic Ericksonian definition the confusion technique consists of contradictory, inconsistent, and irrational statements in trance which served to deepen trance. The confusion technique works because the client becomes uneasy when the high status person—the therapist—unweaves the social fabric by emitting a series of statements that no one can decipher. Obviously the client can choose to discount the therapist as crazy or foolish at that moment. However, when the therapist is a high status person, the client takes the second option and decides to believe the fault is somehow with him. He becomes anxious and chooses to do something to please the therapist. Since the therapist is hypnotizing him, he pleases the therapist by going deeper into trance.

De Shazer (1985) points out that it can be used outside of trance as well.

While Erickson's technique involves the therapist using highly complex verbal skills and ambiguity in meaning, mine involves exploring in detail each and every possible point of difference between the two people without any attempt at closure or resolution and then openly admitting my confusion in the face of their confusion. In either case, the idea is that the therapist develops rapport and cooperation through utilizing the client confusion in such a way that the client's need to construct meaning in the therapy situation is frustrated and thus the setting of a goal, which gives the situation meaning, is necessitated. (pp. 9–10)

In this example, the therapist analyzes the couple's interactions carefully and professionally. Then, strangely enough, he openly declares his impotence and incompetence. The client is confused by this contradiction and tries to resolve the confusion state by doing something to please the high status therapist; in this case they are required to set a goal that gives the situation meaning.

Put another way: the best way to flee the uncomfortable and confusing situation is to leap to a solution to the presenting problem. In summary, the confusion technique exists whenever a high status person operates out of the bounds of acculturated expectations. Especially when this occurs in the context of a caring relationship, the client has a tendency to resolve the confusion by feeling and acting in accordance with the implicit or explicit expectations of the therapist.

Frankly, if even the explanation sounds confusing, you're in good company. Confusion techniques are like lots of techniques employed by therapeutic wizards; they work great when they perform them and are mediocre or ineffective when the average therapist tries to replicate them.

Now, suppose you are a high status therapist who can also project a sense of caring and connection. You would discover that virtually anything you did would result in the client attempting to please you. Moreover, if you instill confusion by operating outside the bounds of cultural expectations, you would tend to see rapid client change as they become hyper motivated to do whatever is necessary to return the world to a solid and comfortable state. If you have this "therapeutic wizard" power, it gives a whole new meaning to beginners mind. When Erickson says (as quoted in the preceding chapter), " I always invent a new treatment in accord with the individual personality," he is literally recording his experience that pretty much anything he does—given his status, warmth, and willingness to operate outside of convention—will work with most clients. Similarly, when Farrelly recommends that "The expression of therapeutic hate and joyful sadism toward clients can markedly benefit the client," he is recording his experiences as he moves through the therapeutic environment. In the quote below, de Shazer provides a different angle on the experience, "everything I do seems to work."

> For an intervention to successfully *fit*, it is not necessary to have detailed knowledge of the complaint. It is not necessary even to be able to construct with any rigor how the trouble is maintained in order to prompt solution. Given all of my previous work, this at first seemed counter-intuitive, but it does seem that *any* really different behavior in a problematic situation can be enough to prompt solution and give the client the satisfaction he seeks from therapy. All that is necessary is that the person involved in a troublesome situation *does something different*, even if that behavior is seemingly irrational, certainly irrelevant, obviously bizarre, or humorous. (1985, p. 7, italics in original)

Note how perfectly de Shazer makes the Reality B case. He says that knowing the past and/or the details of the case are not important. All one needs to do is generate any different response, preferably one which is unexpected and outside cultural norms. Of course, what de Shazer leaves out is that such situations are only resolved positively—in the direction of therapeutic healing—if the client is motivated to resolve her "confusion state" in a manner that pleases the high status, compassionate therapist.

## CLIENT POWER

[N]ever try to follow another's path for that is his way, not yours. When that path is found, you have nothing to do but fold your arms and the tide will carry you to freedom.

—Swami Vivekananda, *The Complete Works of Swami Vivekananda* (1907)

The emphasis in this chapter is on the power of the therapeutic wizard. While that is appropriate in a book focused on increasing therapeutic efficacy via enhancing charisma, it is always vital to remember the centrality of the client in the therapeutic process. While the proceeding few sections may make it appear that a wizard can move effortlessly through the therapeutic environment making changes with a "wave of her mind"—and indeed that is literally what this chapter argues—it is simultaneously and paradoxically true that all of these changes are completely dependent on connection with and feedback from the client.

Scott Miller and many of his colleagues have argued that psychology needs to deemphasize techniques and focus on enhancing the therapist. However, his emphasis on therapist enhancement is client centered. Miller (2007) points out that client factors are vastly more important than therapist factors in determining outcome and suggests that the best road forward is to develop practices—such as formal feedback mechanisms—that explicitly focus the therapist on client feedback. He notes that most therapists report that they prioritize client feedback; however, Miller believes that in actual practice, they miss many cues. In response, Miller has developed his own approach to therapy—Feedback Informed Treatment—to specifically redress this issue.

This chapter, of course, is about therapeutic wizards; these wizards, of course, operate at the highest level of functioning. In this sense, they are not only capable of being recognized as key individuals and superb at creating Dionysian experiences, they are also expert at reading and responding to client feedback. Obviously there are many ways to become expert at incorporating feedback; we will highlight one particular approach that is derived from hypnotherapy.

It can be argued that hypnotherapy is the one of the best training models in terms of learning to read clients' nonverbal cues. Trance inductions and trance deepenings are completely dependent on pacing the client's current experience and leading them toward an altered state. When the therapist fails to read the client effectively, this process fails. This kind of immediate and drastic feedback enhances therapist awareness and connection skills.

In this sense, some of the most useful work on reading clients has been done by hypnotherapists. In the Ericksonian model, this kind of client "reading" is called the utilization approach. The concept of utilization developed out of hypnotherapy and its earliest definition was something like "use whatever the client is currently doing as the basis of a trance induction." For example, if a client blinks during an induction, the therapist might say, "you'll notice that your eyes have a tendency to blink on their own and with every blink, it gets a little harder for the eyes to stay open." As you notice the breathing slowing and quieting, the therapist might say, "as you relax, your breathing slows and with every exhalation you find more and more tension leaving the body." As the person becomes more still, "the body becomes quieter and quieter and you find yourself sinking deeper into the chair. You notice your limbs becoming heavier as if it were impossible to move them." Noticing the nonverbal allows the therapist to comment on them. Correctly describing them allows the therapist to suggest moving deeper and deeper into a trance state.

Ericksonians build on this literal ability to work with feedback in trance introduction and extend it into an awareness of client feedback in every aspect of therapy. The following two quotes—the first by F. William Hanley and the second by Stephen Gilligan—explain the extension of the utilization approach into traditional verbal therapy.

> Erickson was prepared to use any behavior that the patient offered in working toward the therapeutic goal for the patient. "*In rendering aid, there should be full respect for, and utilization of, whatever the patient presents.*" Every manifest behavior, every psychological state, understanding, attitude, and resistance that the patient brings into the situation has a positive potential and can be used, wholly or modified, to lead to new, more adequate behavior. This is done by introducing new ideas (changing perception and meaning). For example, a cut on the lip of a child can become a source of satisfaction and even of prestige because of the number of stitches it requires. (Hanley, 1982, pp. 31–32)

Gilligan continues,

> [Y]ou take what the person gives you and use it. That becomes your strategy. One of the profound consequences of this way of thinking and acting is that there really is no such thing as "resistance" in a utilization approach. Everything the person is doing is exactly what you would like him to be doing. Your task is to generate communications that use ongoing experiences. When you are not fully using them, the subject will tell you, usually indirectly and nonverbally. You will find yourself accusing the person of being "resistant" or branding him\her as "non-susceptible." You are reacting to communications from

the subject that are saying, "what you're doing is not pacing me at this time. You're not using some behavior or experience of mine." Neither the hypnotist nor the subject is a "bad person" or "wrong" or "sick" or "crazy." "Resistance" is just a message that you need to synchronize yourself with the subject again. I think this is a radical concept that is incredibly useful to the clinician. (Gilligan, 1982, p. 92)

Essentially these two quotes extend the utilization approach from a method of trance induction to a method of observing and then working with every communication—verbal and nonverbal—emitted by the client. The therapist practicing utilization is not delivering a lecture about rational versus irrational cognitions or the dangers of enmeshment; rather, everything they say and do is tightly intertwined with the last message from the client. The therapist attention remains focused on the client. And in this sense, the client's current state in large part guides the therapeutic process.

The fundamental benefit of the utilization approach, of course, is that with an awareness of active feedback the therapist can modify her approach until it achieves client resonance. Whether one is a therapeutic wizard or simply an average therapist, the Frank model is clear that every therapeutic ritual requires client concurrence. Wizards have more power than the rest of us and that power allows them to influence clients in ways unavailable to the average practitioner. But we should recall that charisma is equal parts wisdom and connection. This implies that the power of the wizards comes both from the client recognizing the wizard as a key individual with unique authority and from the wizard being uniquely capable of reading and responding to the client. At the end of the day, these expressive and receptive gifts unite as one. Even the most charismatic therapist will be quick to note that her actual power is completely dependent on her ability to read, respond and defer to the essential client message.

## MAPPING AND MODELING

How many legs does a dog have if you call the tail a leg? Four. Calling a tail a leg doesn't make it a leg.

—Abraham Lincoln, *Reminiscences of Abraham Lincoln by Distinguished Men of His Time* (1886)

The most natural response to a therapeutic wizard is the attempt to understand what they are doing so that we can emulate them. Unfortunately, this wish to map the wizards runs into a simple problem; if we are trying to map them in fundamental reality and they are actually operating in constructed reality, we're going to have some difficulties. As de Shazer (1985) discusses below, this mapping process has encountered the predictable obstacles.

> Starting with Haley and Weakland's efforts, Erickson's work has been mapped in great detail by many map-makers, using a wide variety of map-making tools. It is tempting to think of the process as progressive and cumulative, map 2 being an improvement on map 1, and map 3 an improvement on both. However, as Kuhn has pointed out, this is not always the case, particularly during a paradigm shift. The degree of fit between or among the many maps may stop at a very broad and abstract level: This map is a map of Erickson's work. For instance, a glance at Haley's and Weakland's maps, Bandler and Grinder's maps and de Shazer's maps might lead the reader to wonder if the same territory is being mapped after all. (p. 49)

This level of confusion is an expected result if the actual law of constructed reality is: "a high status, caring person can do virtually anything and it will work." The map makers are trying to create Reality A-type maps that can be used by normal therapists—therapists with normal status and a normal capacity for relationship. Maps and the mapping process are essentially Apollonian; these are attempts to outline the complex machine-like processes that underlie fundamental reality. The hope is that the maps will lead to techniques which possess their own implicit power and which can be replicated by any trained person.

Unfortunately, constructed reality is resistant to mapping. Reality B change is dependent on co-created rituals that are fluid and malleable. Change occurs through passage through meaningful experiences. Put another way, while it appears that wizards are using techniques in therapy, they are, in fact, doing nothing of the kind. In sum, the search for a map that describes Farrelly or Erickson or de Shazer so effectively that an average therapist can achieve their results is doomed to failure. No techniques can be derived. These master therapists literally shape reality with their will and their interventions. They are not using techniques that can be replicated by normal therapists. This is Reality B, not Reality A.

We have already discussed the fact that wizards often break the rules during normal therapeutic interactions. Many of them also break social rules outside of the therapy room. For example, Erickson often dressed in all purple clothing and it was explained that this unusual attire was somehow related to his colorblindness. This ability to mark oneself as outside the norm is often found in shamanic healers and therapeutic wizards. Bill Maher often makes humorous references such as "the difference between you and a holy man is that he wears a pointy hat." Maher's belief is that the pointy hat is no guarantee of spiritual authority and, of course, he is literally correct. But when one reviews the lifestyle choices between a charismatic figure like Truman

Capote and a normal person, it is clear that wizards often break the rules in more ways than simply peculiar conduct in the room.

These outer signs are attempts to mark the wizard as an emissary from "sacred space"—a person who no longer dwells in the conventional world—a visitor from another reality. This is well illustrated by a scene from the movie, *The Matrix*. In this particular scene, the mentor figure, Morpheus, is teaching the beginner, Neo, about his powers and limitations in the Matrix. He explains that the Matrix is an interactive computer program which is so seductive and compelling that, when you are inside it, it cannot be distinguished from reality. However, because it is a program—and not reality—humans who understand and accept that they are in a program will have extra powers and potentialities. As the dialog evolves note that Morpheus moves from an instructional role to a more active, exhortation-type role. He repeatedly admonishes Neo to relinquish the sense that he is constrained and limited. The dialog occurs in the context of a martial arts encounter.

*Morpheus:* This is a sparring program, similar to the programmed reality of the Matrix. It has the same basic rules, rules like gravity. What you must learn is that these rules are no different that the rules of a computer system. Some of them can be bent. Others can be broken. Understand? Then hit me, if you can.
(Morpheus defeats Neo in the first round)
*Morpheus:* How did I beat you?
*Neo:* You're too fast.
*Morpheus:* Do you believe that my being stronger or faster has anything to do with my muscles in this place? You think that's air you're breathing now? Hah . . .
*Morpheus:* What are you waiting for? You're faster than this. Don't think you are, know you are. Come on. Stop trying to hit me and hit me.
*Neo:* I know what you're trying to do.
*Morpheus:* I'm trying to free your mind, Neo, but I can only show you the door, you're the one that has to walk through it. (Silver, Wachowski & Wachowski, 1999)

This is the fundamental challenge that constructionism offers therapists: can we let loose of the limitations on our minds established by prior programming? Fully absorbing this concept allows the therapist to create new realities with the "wave of her mind" subject only to the concurrence of the client. Constructionism offers therapists the opportunity to be free from the normal restrictions of programmed reality: "Some rules can be bent. Others can be broken. . . ." The key is to let go of preconceptions and all one has learned about limitations.

The second implication from the Matrix example reinforces the idea that clients do not change by techniques or psychological principles that have been discovered: "Do you believe that my being stronger or faster has anything to do with my muscles in this place? You think that's air you're breathing now? Hah. . . ." It is important to understand that techniques never create new realities. New realities are created out of whole cloth by a respected person—the therapist—and validated by the agreement of the client. Techniques and interventions are simply the dialog that occurs between therapist and client as they are co-creating a new reality. They are vehicles that carry the intentions of the therapist to the client and vice versa—vehicles that are credible and acceptable.

Returning to our process of mapping and modeling, we know the wizards are charismatic—key individuals who are recognized as having the power to define reality. This recognition arises from their acceptance—like Morpheus—that they are strangers in the conventional world and that they have been given/earned the ability to bend some rules and break others. They can be recognized by their ability to flout conventional rules, inwardly and sometimes outwardly, their abilities to cultivate altered states, and their superb capacities to connect to and read the client. Finally, they have a relentless optimism about the possibility of change and often seem to ignore limiting factors that daunt the rest of us—factors such as history and the presence of trauma, and self-destructive behaviors.

These, then, are the aspects we are attempting to model. Being distracted by techniques distilled by map makers—or even being distracted by techniques recommended by the wizards themselves—will slow down the modeling process.

Arguing that even the wizards are incapable of explaining what they do is certainly a peculiar thought. Simply because the wizards have learned to be effective does not imply that they know the basis for their own effectiveness. Every brilliant artist is not necessarily capable of describing the essence of how to be a brilliant artist. This is particularly true because every wizard is not necessarily aware of the difference between constructed and fundamental reality. In the example above from the Matrix, Morpheus knows this difference and is trying to teach it directly to Neo. But other masters, however accomplished in practice, fail to achieve that level of conscious awareness.

Thirty years ago, as a beginning psychologist, I was attempting to learn from and model myself after the wizards. At that point in my career I still believed in techniques and in training workshops. Fortunately for me, prior to studying and becoming a psychologist, I had been exposed to a vast amount of Eastern thought and been particularly attracted to the constructionism that lies at its core. I had also formally studied the phenomenology of religion which also included a great deal of constructionism as well as emphasizing a method of study embodied by the phrase "the thing in itself." One of the primary concepts in phenomenology is to simply describe something and show up for that without putting too many preconceived frames around it.

Of course, such a practice is impossible to do perfectly but it pushed me in the right direction and dovetailed nicely with my training in constructionism.

In the following example I attempt to replicate some of the qualities I had studied in the wizards. In a formal sense, what I did with the client might be labeled paradoxical therapy or perhaps ordeal therapy[1]. In truth, what I feel I was attempting to do was to encounter a client without focusing much on history, trauma, or resistance. Put most basically, I was attempting to change him via a simple request.

> A 34-year-old presented with complaints of excessive shyness around dating. He confessed that although he was successful in his profession career, and was reasonably attractive, he was so shy around women that he had never had a date and he was a virgin. His goal in therapy was to be able to date women and, ideally, have a first sexual experience.
>
> I decided to prescribe an ordeal. I explained that his problem was that he had an excessive fear of rejection which he could cure by placing himself in a situation where he was bound to be rejected. He lived near a resort town and I told him to go to the most upscale bar in that town and ask the prettiest women to dance. I predicted that he would be rejected fairly often and asked him to meditate in exquisite detail on how he made these rejections unbearable.
>
> He returned the next week and said that he had only been rejected a few times and didn't feel that his dancing experiences or his meditations on rejection had accomplished much. I replied that we needed to "up the ante" and asked him to stand outside of a coffee shop in his home town and ask every attractive woman to come inside and share a cup of coffee with him because she "looked interesting." He seemed appalled by this directive and left the session with a worried look.
>
> Next week he returned with a different look on his face. He told me that he had gone home with lots of ambivalence about his assignment. Instead of completing it, he had decided to ask a woman out at work. He had seen her three times since the last session and, on their last date, he had had sex with her.

This is a simple and straightforward example of ordeal therapy (Haley, 1993). In ordeal therapy, the therapist prescribes an ordeal with an implicit message that they can either do the ordeal or choose to resolve the presenting problem. In this case, the client needed to perform the coffee shop ordeal or make the ordeal unnecessary by dating a woman. Analyzing the vignette, it appears as if the prescribed ordeal had something to do with the outcome, particularly because the client eventually explains his success as an attempt to avoid the ordeal.

In reality, of course, the ordeal had little to do with the successful therapeutic resolution of the case. If the client had not perceived me as a relatively high status therapist who was genuinely invested in him getting better, he could easily have decided that my prescription was a silly idea and simply disregarded it. That is, in fact, what often happens when attempting to pre-scribe an ordeal. The client simply ignores the intervention and the sessions involved are more or less wasted. This case example could also be called paradoxical therapy in that I prescribed the symptom. Farrelly might have called it Provocative Therapy since I went into great detail about how pretty the women were in the resort town and how likely it was that they would reject him given his modest appearance.

I saw it at the time as an example of how easily people change. It seemed to me that all the techniques I was using were beginning to blur together. I think this insight was facilitated not only by my study of constructionism but also because I had recently completed a dissertation evaluating the efficacy of a certain neurolinguistic programming (NLP) technique. In the disserta-tion, I had to perform the same technique over and again multiple times. As I attempted to adjust the technique to meet client needs, the protocol started varying significantly from case to case. I began to believe that the outcome was much more dependent on whether the client saw me as effective versus whether I had performed the technique well.

Now I know I wasn't using a constructionist model perfectly—I still believed I was doing a technique. But every time I looked at the wizards and their work closely, I believed in the power of techniques less and less. Every time I saw a traumatized or treatment resistant client change without much fuss, the less I believed in the importance of history. My own work seemed to be pushing me in the same direction; my charisma felt vastly more significant than the techniques. Moreover, the more I learned new techniques, the more they seemed to be variations on each other.

Returning to this specific client: it should be emphasized that he was actu-ally quite anxious and certainly reported that he felt full of shame, guilt, and embarrassment. He felt terrible about being a virgin and had never had one real date. These feelings were exacerbated by his age and the fact that he lived in a resort town where everyone came to party. Moreover, he had a reason-able social life and participated in many activities each month. He was always wondering what was wrong with him. For me, it was tempting to explore his past and find out what kind of trauma or misconstruals might have led to his restricted sexual functioning.

When he resolved the issue in only two sessions, as a relatively new thera-pist I, of course, felt proud of my success; maybe this new career was going to work out after all. But more important than the ego gratification, was the sense that something different was going on. The more I practiced, the more I felt the presence of some kind of anomaly; the models of change I had learned weren't really fitting my experience. All my studies, and the particular results of this case, were piquing my curiosity. Something different was occurring here. The world seemed more fluid than I had been led to believe and for me, the door had opened to what Kuhn calls the "awareness of anomaly."

> Scientific development depends in part on a process of non-incremental or revolutionary change. Some revolutions are large, like those associated with the names of Copernicus, Newton, or Darwin, but most are much smaller, like the discovery of oxygen or the planet Uranus. The usual prelude to changes of this sort is, I believed, the awareness of anomaly, of an occurrence or set of occurrences that does not fit existing ways of ordering phenomena. The changes that result therefore require "putting on a different kind of thinking-cap," one that renders the anomalous lawlike but that, in the process, also transforms the order exhibited by some other phenomena, previously unproblematic. (Kuhn, 1977, p. xvii)

## NOTE

1. In ordeal therapy the client is required to choose between two alternatives: the healthy option and an "ordeal" that they must complete if they refuse the healthy option.

*Chapter 9*

# Apollonian Power

## *The Primacy of the Conscious Mind*

If it is not right do not do it; if it is not true do not say it.

—Marcus Aurelius, *Little Classics* (1912)

The Net is a wondrous thing. And the Apollonian forces that maintain it are serving everyone in the culture. This is a book about change; hence, the Dionysian is emphasized and the Apollonian is implicitly criticized for its conservative and stabilizing biases. But it should be clear that the Net is necessary to raise children, to enable society to have shape and stability, and to create individual continuity. In addition it provides a hundred other services without which human community would be impossible.

Just as there are therapeutic approaches that are primarily Dionysian, there are other approaches that are primarily Apollonian. The following light bulb joke discusses some of the differences.

*Q:* How many Constructionists does it take to change a light bulb?
*A:* At least ten, as they need to hold a debate on whether or not the light bulb exists. Even if they can agree upon the existence of the light bulb they still may not change it to keep from alienating those who might use other forms of light.
*Q:* How many Apollonians does it take to change a light bulb?
*A:* CHANGE??

Joking aside, of course Apollonians are committed to change, just as long as the change consists of a safe developmental path that is congruent with the existing culture's Net. Often this takes the form of moving successfully to the next level of life: the teen becoming an adult, the single person succeeding at marriage, and so on. In this sense, it can be argued that most human change is Apollonian change and the majority of clients who present are either

befuddled with Apollonian issues, have had trouble achieving full membership in the culture (e.g., young adults who are failing the adolescent/adult
transition), or individuals who have been overwhelmed by a breakthrough of
the Abyss (e.g., divorce, health problems, loss). In sum, while it may be vital
for the therapist to be comfortable with Dionysian principles and courageous
and skilled when it comes to encountering the Abyss, the majority of the
clients will be operating within the Net and focused on Apollonian developmental concerns.

There are a number of therapies which can be characterized as Apollonian but it is more useful to think that there is an Apollonian or Dionysian
approach to every therapeutic intervention. For example, hypnotherapy, a
profoundly Dionysian therapy emphasizing altered states, can be done in an
Apollonian manner.

> You're getting sleepier and sleepier and your eyes are closing sending you into
> a deep trance where you can only hear the sound of my voice. Next time you
> take a drag on a cigarette, it's going to taste like camel dung and you will have
> a vision of your lungs turning black and becoming cancerous.

In this sense, regardless of the natural tendency of any therapy to be Apollonian or Dionysian, the difference is more in the approach than the actual
qualities of the technique. However there is one particular area where there
is a consistent difference between the two: how they deal with the hierarchy
between conscious and unconscious processes.

The first challenge of psychotherapy is how to help individuals control
feelings, compulsions, and misconstruals that appear to be autonomous—
unconscious material that invades and disorganizes our lives. This is the
primary task of the Apollonian therapies: helping the individual regulate
affect and all the autonomous psychological processes so that he can function as a healthy citizen, family member, and individual. More Dionysian
therapies might discuss cooperating with the unconscious, or working with
the shadow, or experiencing the transformative nature of sacred space. Apollonian therapies focus on simple self-mastery and especially on the kind of
self-mastery that facilitates accomplishing culturally validated goals and
success experiences.

Apollonian approaches are, of course, deeply grounded in the prevailing
cultural Net. To be Apollonian implies a sense of right and wrong and good/
bad; hence Apollonian therapists are more authoritarian and directive. Compared to a Dionysian therapist, an Apollonian feels empowered to instruct a
client, to direct her, and to use her own sense of guilt and shame as a motivator. To understand how this plays out in real time, examine a classic Apollonian therapy, reality therapy.

In 1965 William Glasser wrote a small but important book entitled *Reality Therapy*. The system presented therein is deceptively simple but has profound implications for how people change and the usefulness of extant therapeutic maps. His ideas were especially creative and innovative fifty years ago when most therapy was still dominated by psychodynamic ideas and concepts.

Here are his basic principles: first, like Farrelly, Glasser (1965) neither believes in the concept of mental illness nor the unconscious mind; moreover, he does not feel that it is useful to explore the client's past.

> Because we do not accept the concept of mental illness, the patient cannot become involved with us as a mentally ill person who has no responsibility for his behavior.
>
> Working in the present and toward the future, we do not get involved with the patient's history because we can neither change what happened to him nor accept the fact that he is limited by his past.
>
> We do not look for unconscious conflicts or the reasons for them. A patient cannot become involved with us by excusing his behavior on the basis of unconscious motivations. (p. 44)

In place of old assumptions about mental illness and the importance of the past, Glasser proposes that a meaningful relationship with a responsible person can lead to healing and positive change. The essence of reality therapy is that a patient should begin from where he currently stands, examine the pros and cons of his situation, and then make effective plans that result in meeting his needs in the future. This is accomplished by straightforward, logical discussions with the therapist, who needs to be both a responsible person in his own right and someone who has formed a significant relationship with the client. Finally, the emphasis is on behavioral changes not ideas, feelings, and trauma.

> We emphasize the morality of behavior. We face the issue of right and wrong which we believe solidifies the involvement, in contrast to conventional psychiatrists who do not make the distinction between right and wrong, feeling it would be detrimental to attaining the transference relationship they seek.
>
> We teach patients better ways to fulfill their needs. The proper involvement will not be maintained unless the patient has helped define more satisfactory patterns of behavior. Conventional therapists did not feel that teaching better behavior is part of therapy. (1965, pp. 44–45)

Finally, the reality of the patient's current situation is examined not only from the standpoint of right and wrong, but also from the standpoint of workable or dysfunctional. Reality therapists are quick to question the client's feelings, cognitions, and plans in terms of: "Will this get you where you want to go?"

and "you're not accepting the truth of how things work here." Following is a typical reality therapy case.

> Sent to us as the last resort, she was a pretty but extremely tense 16-year-old who, when I first saw her, demanded that I do something to make her less nervous. She evidently had been taking a variety of different tranquilizer drugs at the previous institution, and even before I took her into therapy she cornered me in her cottage where I was eating lunch and demanded medication for her nerves. With the demand she gave me a lecture on the varieties and activities of tranquilizer drugs that would've been a model for a pharmacologist. I refused, explaining that no tranquilizers of any kind were used at Ventura because I did not believe they help the girls. Tranquilizers help people escape from facing reality; they should only be given to people who are in good control or to those who are so far out of control that they need physical restraints, such as a violent patient in a mental hospital who may need cuffs. We have neither type of girl at Ventura. I told her that I was the only person who could prescribe tranquilizers so that throwing a tantrum for someone else would not help. I explained that if she thought acting upset would get me to prescribe tranquilizers, now was her chance. She could throw her best tantrum and I would be glad to sit with her and we would discuss it, but there was nothing in terms of bad behavior that I hadn't seen 1000 times previously and I had long since given up prescribing drugs for temper outbursts.
>
> My remarks surprised her greatly. Previously, professional people had responded to her nervousness and threats of acting out by unwittingly, but from her viewpoint solicitously, relieving her of the responsibility for her behavior with large doses of tranquilizer drugs. As she continued to threaten to break windows and fall apart from nervous tension, I told her something that I believe started our involvement.
>
> "Terri," I said, "Ventura is different from any other place you have been. Here you have the right to suffer, and we will respect your suffering. You probably have good reason to feel bad, but you will not learn anything if we give you pills. In fact, I'm sure that the more pills you received in the last institution, the more you misbehaved and then blamed it on the pills. You do the same thing yourself with liquor and reds and yellows (illegally obtained Seconal and Nembutal) when you're at home, but you won't be allowed to here." Adding that I would welcome her into my group therapy where I would help her find better ways to behave so that she could feel better, I emphasized that in Ventura we believe that what you do, more than what you feel, is important. I am not beyond explaining reality therapy, in a sense, to the girls because they understand, more than most of us, the truth in stressing behavior over feelings. She agreed, as have countless other girls, that the pills increase their acting out by giving them an excuse for it (they say their pills make them goofy so they can't control themselves), and she never asked for them again. (Glasser, 1965, pp. 83–84)

Perhaps the single most striking aspect to reality therapy is its simplicity. Fundamentally, it argues that all that is necessary to perform effective psychotherapy is to place a client in relationship with a caring and "responsible" mentor who will help her face the dysfunctional nature of her current choices and replace them with better plans and behaviors that lead her toward actual need fulfillment. Reality therapy, of course, works as well as any other form of therapy (Wubbolding, 2011). Moreover, I suspect that when Dr. Glasser was the therapist, he achieved a level of effectiveness much higher than the standard therapist.

Glasser is the archetypal Apollonian therapist. He is serious, motivated, judgmental, confident, and somewhat intimidating. His goals have to do with helping his clients meet their needs in the context of fulfilling successful roles in the dominant culture. In this sense, he is likely to confront clients to face or accept "reality" and to move forward in their life by playing by the rules implicit in that reality.

Apollonian therapists are experts in the Net. In that sense, they not only direct their clients to make choices that lead to success, they are also highly aware of secondary gains. Glasser's interactions with Terri around drug seeking behavior is a good example. Apollonians would be just as direct and forthright discussing getting off disability or the downsides of misbehaving with authority figures.

Therapists who are cultivating the Apollonian will utilize both outer symbols of success and power as well as inner attitudes of confidence and certainty. Outer symbols include an upscale office, impressive diplomas on the walls, expensive clothes and haircuts, and references to past associations with high status people. Therapeutic recommendations are couched in terms of impressive research. Better to be a doctor than a master's degree therapist; better to be an MD than a PhD; and better to be a psychopharmacologist than a psychiatrist.

Interventions are delivered with confidence and with more of a black and white style. Doubts are refuted and ultimately destroyed. Glasser emphasized the importance of the relationship but noted that the most helpful client-therapist relationship often starts with the therapist telling the client the truth about how confused they are in terms of their values or choices. "I care about you enough to tell you the truth about how mixed up you are." Moreover, the charismatic Apollonian must have confidence that what they are recommending will, in fact, improve the lives and options of their clients.

Above all, the Apollonian therapist must be clear about her role as an authority figure that represents the dominant culture. As an Apollonian, a therapist is presenting herself as the power of the culture "made flesh" in the form of a psychotherapist. The client needs to have the feeling that when the therapist speaks, the entire culture is 100 percent behind the therapeutic pronouncements. "Resistance is futile" is a phrase made famous by *Star Trek* and the *Borg;* however, it is also the hallmark of the confidence projected by the Apollonian therapist.

When reality therapists are arguing that their effectiveness is due to something beyond the therapeutic relationship, they are stating that they are using the entire power of the culture and the internally programmed ideas of "should," "ought," and right and wrong. To become an effective Apollonian, to actually use reality therapy, a therapist must become comfortable with being the embodiment of these kinds of concepts.

## THE FEAR OF APOLLONIAN POWER

Be sure that you are right, and then go ahead.

—David Crockett, *The Handbook of Illustrated Proverbs* (1855)

The most controversial aspect of reality therapy and other Apollonian therapies is the implicit hierarchy between therapist and client; the Apollonian therapist accepts the hierarchy and uses it to achieve results. All of the concepts like "right and wrong" and "good and bad" rest on the foundational idea that "I know" and "you are confused" and you need to accept my help.

These assumptions can be problematic. It is easy to imagine a hundred scenarios where the assumption of such power could go astray and injure the client. Moreover, once one is comfortable with judgments, what is there to keep the "confident" therapist from using coercion and force to impel that client toward the desired goal?

A therapist cannot be an effective Apollonian without a foundational sense of confidence in his own judgment. Yet such confidence flies in the face of "client-centered therapy" and its implication that the power lies in the client not in the therapist. Moreover, many therapists have a substantial percentage of their clients who have been wounded by judgment. These clients come into therapy filled with guilt and shame because they have failed to fulfill family or cultural expectations. Is it right to "go Apollonian" and exacerbate this shame by joining with those who have judged the client as lacking and insufficient? Finally, one of the primary points of this book has been to present constructionist arguments that document that all Apollonian worldviews are arbitrary and invented. Knowing this, why would a therapist endorse a worldview that she knows is ephemeral and constructed?

Conversely, there are just as many situations where the expert needs to take control. A doctor coming upon a motor vehicle accident with significant injuries is justified—nay, mandated—to take control, order helpers about, and disregard feelings and other's ideas in response to the needs of the emergency. All therapists are mandated reporters when it comes to suicide and participate in forcing clients into care against their will.

The key, of course, is to determine when the situation is emergent, and when a client is sufficiently disabled that the therapist has the moral right and obligation to use whatever means available to force—or at least coerce—a client in a certain direction. It is easy to judge the extremes and difficult to judge the cases in the middle. The solution embraced by most therapists is a relative one. The more evolved and mature the client, the more the therapist defers to him. The more emergent, young, or disabled, the more the therapist is comfortable assuming control.

Glasser is fine with this in principle, but he had so many experiences where therapists were loath to take control when they should that he formally designed reality therapy so that it would be easier for therapists to confront and lead. In the following case—which Glasser credits as instrumental in the formation of reality therapy—he is forced to explicitly reject psychodynamic psychotherapy in order to use Apollonian power effectively. The case not only documents reality therapy principles, it serves as a cautionary tale warning therapists that their excessive respect for client self-determination can backfire and result in outcomes that actually hurt the client.

Apparently the boy in this case had had a number of psychodynamic therapists before Glasser who had concentrated on making interpretations and cultivating transference reactions. Glasser himself reported that his supervisor urged him to continue on that same course. While Glasser began his work with the boy with the intention of following that advice, the frustration of working in that manner pushed him toward the Apollonian intervention described below.

Aaron was the highly intelligent 11-year-old son of an unemotional, overly intellectual divorced woman who worked as a mathematician at one of the Los Angeles missile and space laboratories, and a father who lived in another part of the country and had no contact with him. Aaron was often left home in the care of the neighbor when his mother went away on weekends with her boyfriend. At the time I saw him he had been seen by two other therapists over the previous two years, both third-year resident in the psychiatric training facility. He was assigned to me for treatment when I was also a third-year resident and was my first child outpatient. The other therapists had treated him conventionally with play therapy. Most of their time was spent interpreting the meaning of his play to him. For example, if he struck a female doll repeatedly, the therapist would ask him if he wouldn't like to hit his mother and hope Aaron would confirm the truth of his guess. Having also been trained in traditional psychiatry, I attempted at first to follow in the footsteps of the previous therapists. When Aaron confirmed his anger and hostility against his mother I wondered, as they must have, why this insight did not help him. He wanted to learn better ways to act, but up till then all of us had avoided teaching him what he needed to know.

One way to describe Aaron and his behavior is to say that although he was pleasant in appearance, he was the most obnoxious child I have ever met. I dreaded Monday and Thursday mornings because those days started with Aaron. He had evidently been treated very permissively by his previous therapists who, besides interpreting his behavior to him, accepted everything he did. And what he did was horrible. He ran pell-mell from game to game and toy to toy, never letting me help him to enjoy what he was doing. He seemed to be almost desperately avoiding my offer to play as if my joining in the play might deprive him in some way of some of his pleasures. He acted aggressively in a completely haphazard, unpredictable way, crying for my attention but turning nasty and withdrawing when I gave him some warmth. He discussed his mother in a highly critical way, making her into an ogre of psychiatric rejection. . . . He also rattled on about all the destructive things he did and was planning to do at home.

He blamed his failure to be happy on his mother, her boyfriend, his missing father, or his previous therapists. His school did not escape his critical wrath: it was very bad, his teachers did not understand him, and the other kids picked on him.

Regardless of how he behaved, no one had ever attempted to put a value judgment on his behavior, no one had ever told him he was doing wrong. Everything he did was accepted as something to be explained or, in psychiatric terms, "interpreted" ad nauseum.

. . . It was some time before I began to realize that he was well aware of his behavior, even to the extent that in his own erratic, impulsive way he devised new tests for my patience. He actually planned some of his misconduct, which must have been exhausting and difficult for him to keep up as long as he did.

His mother was an impersonal, detached individual who raised Aaron as an object rather than a person. Instead of reacting to his behavior and setting some limits, she discussed it with him objectively. Essentially a cold woman, she did contribute to his frustration, but if our hope was for her to change, Aaron had little chance. . . .

Although Aaron was desperate for some change, I was advised by my supervisor to continue to work with him in play therapy and to interpret his "anal retention and oral regression." A firm believer in psychoanalytic theory, my supervisor was convinced that the child needed to know "why."

Although it was to be many years before reality therapy became definite in my mind as a method of treatment, it was with Aaron that I first discovered the dramatic force of confronting a child with present reality. This confrontation, fortunately made after we had gained some involvement, solidified a relationship into a deeper therapeutic involvement which produce great changes in Aaron.

I realize dimly that in following the principles of orthodox therapy I was contributing to Aaron's present desperation rather than relieving it, and I made up my mind to change my approach. Against all my training and reading, and without telling anyone what I planned to do, I began a kind of reality therapy.

The explaining was over. From now on we were going to emphasize reality and present behavior.

When Aaron arrived the following morning I took him into my office, nudging him gently past the playroom when he tried to stop there as usual. Telling him to sit down and listen, I explained that I wasn't interested in anything he had to say, only that he listens to me this morning. He whined and tried to get away, but I held them and faced him toward me. I told him to shut up and for once in his life to listen to what someone had to say. I informed him that the play was over, that we would sit and talk in an adult fashion, or if we walked we would walk as adults. I explained clearly that I would not tolerate any running away or even any impolite behavior while we were walking. He would have to be courteous and try to converse with me when I talked to him. He was to tell me everything he did and I would help them decide whether it was right or wrong.

When he immediately attempted to leave, I forcibly restrained him. When he tried to hit me, I told him I would hit him back! After two years without restraint, it was probably the suddenness of this approach it shocked him into going along with me. After some brief initial testing, he did not resist much, probably because he had been anxious for so long to be treated in this realistic way.

I wanted to know what he did in school and at home, and what he could do that was better. When I told him frankly that he was the most miserable and obnoxious child I have ever met, he was greatly surprised. He had thought all therapists must automatically love their patients. I informed him that if he stayed in therapy he was going to have to change because neither I nor anyone else could possibly care for him the way he was now.

What happened next was most dramatic. First of all, he became likable, talking to me courteously. He seemed to enjoy being with me and surprisingly I began to look forward to seeing him. . . . Rapidly Aaron and I grew more involved. Criticizing him for all his old weaknesses but praising him when he did well, I stood in his path whenever he tried to revert to his old ways.

In about six weeks he changed remarkably. I heard from school that his work at suddenly risen to straight A and that his behavior had also become excellent. The teachers couldn't understand what had happened. (Glasser, 1965, pp. 135–139)

In this case study, Glasser not only presents a masterful example of Apollonian therapy, he also illustrates his own ability to deconstruct the imbedded psychodynamic programming which was limiting his therapeutic effectiveness. His frustration with Aaron's lack of progress is palpable; it is easy to feel Glasser chafing at the bit—impatient with the limitations imposed by the psychodynamic approach. When he finally uses this frustration as a guide, and gives in to his impulse to "go Apollonian," his work takes on the vital and powerful style so characteristic of this approach. Glasser becomes confident, confrontive, and fully prepared to instruct Aaron about what is right and wrong, constructive and destructive.

Effective Apollonian interventions are rooted in the therapist's sense that the client is capable of acting according to social norms and goals. It is unlikely Glasser would have felt the frustration or used an Apollonian approach if Aaron had a history of good behavior that only went downhill after a head injury in an automobile accident. Glasser emphasizes that rapport with the client is enhanced by confronting him about his inability to behave well; implicit in the confrontation is the therapist's belief that the client can choose to behave well and that he is capable of being a full member of society if he simply decides to adopt conventional values, choices, and aspirations. And finally, Glasser is secure in the idea that it is both his duty and his obligation to impel his clients into a more effective relationship with society.

More specifically, depending on the evolution of the client, the most important goal in his current life might be to join the dominant culture, move up to the next developmental stage or fulfill his social role more successfully. Statements such as "he needs to be a better father if he is going to get over his guilt," or "she needs to take a risk and have a success if she is going to make her life work," or "he needs to stop using cocaine if he wants to keep his marriage and his job" embody these kinds of judgments.

The "reality" in reality therapy refers, of course, to the idea that clients who are not fulfilling the cultural norms—having social skills, working hard, taking healthy risks, delaying gratification and so on—are unlikely to accomplish their dreams and ambitions. Reality therapy gives its practitioners a good map to assess and guide their interventions. Using this map, they not only can point out when clients are making bad choices—"how's that working out for you?"—but they are also not shy about intervening and using whatever pressure is available to them to help the client understand that there is actually only one way to go: fulfill your needs via adapting to cultural norms. In this sense, for example, a reality therapist is probably more likely than a standard therapist to recommend "tough love" for a teen or encourage a spouse to confront a husband who is underemployed.

Assuming Apollonian power is not only occasionally required in the midst of therapy; sometimes it is a necessary precursor to beginning therapy. It is a form of "bringing the client to the table." Often, therapists encounter situations where a family member could benefit from therapy but is too frightened to come in for a meeting. Sometimes they hide this fear by disparaging therapy, but it takes little insight to realize that they dread exposure to their feelings, believe they lack power in their relationships, or fear they will be proven inadequate when it comes to mastering the next developmental stage in their life. This resistance is, of course, a form of hyperstability. Common examples include a husband who is afraid to come into therapy because he will have to deal with his wife's dissatisfactions and the teen that is afraid to take the next step in a maturation or healing process.

Often clients with this level of fear and hyperstability will only enter therapy through an Apollonian intervention—they need to be forced or pressured out of their constricted position. Sometimes a family cannot move forward without one spouse stating, "unless you do X, I will withdraw my affection from you. And I may escalate this threat to include withdrawal from the relationship."

Therapy with teenagers frequently needs to blend Apollonian interventions with the Dionysian. Some teens will not even begin to process their feelings until they experience an Apollonian boundary that forces them out of their hyperstable position. The case of the anorexic teen that was featured in the previous chapter had an Apollonian preamble which illustrates exactly this point.

Prior to meeting the teen, my original session was with the parents. As mentioned above, they detailed a history where the teen was essentially running the household via a combination of temper tantrums, suicide threats, and physical attacks on her mother. She would then promise she would behave better if her parents would accede to some wish such as letting her go to a certain summer camp, taking her on a surfing or snowboarding trip, or allowing her to attend private school.

The mother was in favor of requiring the teen to eat as prescribed by the nutritionist; the father doubted that such a direct approach would work. The mother was physically afraid of the teen and wanted to use more discipline or send her to a treatment program; the father kept pointing out that the mother, with her more direct confrontations, fanned the flames of the teen's anger, and refused to support more discipline until the "mother issues" were resolved. Both parents hoped that she would get better every time they said "yes" to another request.

Finally, the situation was complicated by the fact that the teen was enrolled in a highly desirable boarding school and both parents were loath to do anything that might interfere with her functioning at school. It should be added that her behavior at this school was polite, respectful, and well controlled; in fact, the only sign that she was different than her peers was that she tended to avoid most carbs and high fat foods in the cafeteria.

Given this situation the teen saw little likelihood that attending therapy or cooperating with her parents and the rest of the treatment team would improve her position. She was already in the private school she desired and fundamentally dominated family decision making via her combination of threats and promises. It seemed unlikely that she would be invested in change as long as the status quo was maintained.

Moreover, anyone who has experience with teens understands that they often see therapy the way Berger and Luckmann frame it: as a way to compel them to behave according to cultural norms. The teen had been seeing another therapist for months—and the reports of her interventions from the parents made her sound competent and caring—but she had been unable to build meaningful rapport with the teen, much less succeed in helping her reexamine her poor choices. Not wishing to suffer her fate, I decided that the teen needed to be less comfortable with the status quo in order to increase her motivation to participate in therapy.

I met with the parents three or four times with the explicit purpose of motivating them to change the household rules. There were two cards they could play. First, her misbehaviors had reached a level where the police could be called and, if she did not moderate her behaviors, she would become involved with the juvenile justice system in terms of probation and other consequences. Second, and more important, the teen desperately wanted to continue to attend her boarding school. In fact, she had the same feeling about the boarding school that she had about her eating: if she could succeed at this high status boarding school somehow all would be right with her life. In short, attendance at this school, like eating a "pure" diet, had become linked with her ultimate concern.

These facts made it easy to counsel the parents. I simply told them they needed to require their daughter to eat exactly as the nutritionist had prescribed and that she would be consequented if she did not. Moreover, if she continued to act out violently or with threats of suicide, the police or mental health team should immediately be called. I also asked the parents to tell the teen that if she did go on probation—or get hospitalized for a suicide threat—that it was highly likely that her private school would ask her to leave.

Given that her commitment to attending the school was unconditional, and given that she had already shown an ability to control her emotions and behaviors while in the boarding school, I was confident that the teen would choose to comply with her parents' reasonable requirements. Of course, it took several sessions of meeting with the parents to set up the plan given that they were polarized into the father being permissive and enabling and the mother punitive and authoritarian. Moreover, both parents were nervous that the girl would make bad choices and lose her chance to finish the year at the school, an outcome that both parents dreaded. Be that as it may, the parents were both capable people with sincere love for their child, and they found the current situation unbearable; in sum, after 3 sessions discussing a plan to enforce compliance and all the things that might go wrong, they committed to using the new approach over Christmas Break.

They did have some conflict with their daughter—the police had to be called once—but by the time of my first session with the teen the first week in January, she was eating more normally and essentially behaving according to family rules. The parents reported that the teen's mood was more stable than it had been in months and that there was a general feeling of relief in the family.

Like many Apollonian interventions, this one was easy to design but challenging in terms of the implicit conflict. I was confident that it would succeed given the factors enumerated above but the parents were terrified that the teen would choose the self-destructive option and refuse to comply. Just as Dionysian interventions often require creativity and high levels of compassion, Apollonian interventions require clarity and courage. Sometimes, as in this case, the intervention must be executed by the parents or a spouse. They have to do the hard and emotionally dangerous work. Their fear and dread of such work is palpable. They need to lean on the clarity and courage of the therapist to set the boundaries, require compliance, and administer consequences.

Clarity and power, of course, are often the difference between a successful therapeutic intervention and just another session of talking on and on and on. It is the therapist's responsibility to discern how powerful an intervention the client can handle, but reality therapy enjoins us to believe that clients can step up to more than we think they can. Many people remember Jack Nicholson's famous line in the movie *A Few Good Men*: "The TRUTH! You can't handle the TRUTH" (Reiner, Brown & Scheinman [Producers] & Reiner [Director], 1992). Glasser and the Apollonians are confident that clients can not only handle the truth, they can flourish when they are exposed to it. Their confidence that their clients can "rise to it" upwardly redefines the limits of human change and adaptability.

In this situation it was not only ethical to use pressure with a client, but avoiding the use of this kind of pressure was probably unethical. The teen was firmly fixed in her negative stance and was unlikely to change without the parents changing the family rules. In addition, it was improbable that she would bond with me regardless of any brilliance I might have manifested in individual therapy. I felt certain that no significant progress could occur until the parents had forced the teen out of her hyperstable position.

In truth, most therapists make stronger—more Apollonian—interventions whenever they trust their "map." Paradoxically, the ability to discern between fundamental and constructed reality often enhances the therapist's trust in her own judgment. One might think that Reality B therapists would be more confused about when and how to use therapeutic power given that they know "it's all made up." Instead, this discernment leads to an understanding of just how important it is to succeed at Apollonian challenges without any real attachment to certain aspects of the Apollonian.

In the case of the teen above, I acted more Apollonian than the previous therapist. The girl excelled at the Apollonian value of achievement but was woefully lacking in the areas of responsibility and respect. This imbalance quickly jumps out of the story. The previous therapist was limited by her overvaluing of the concept of client self-determination; in a sense, that had become her "ultimate concern." Conversely, for the Reality B therapist, all Apollonian values are seen as necessary and helpful along the road of personal evolution but none are seen as ultimate. This creates a kind of "light touch"; good judgment and courage are facilitated because of a lack of attachment. In other words, I was better able to be Apollonian because my Reality B stance allowed me to support the principle without becoming lost in it.

But Glasser did not write *Reality Therapy* to tone down excessive Apollonians; rather, he believed that too many therapists had given up their power and effectiveness because of an excessive attachment to being client centered. It is interesting—and somewhat surprising—to find him joined in this opinion by two of the most Dionysian therapists in this book, Frank Farrelly and Carl Whitaker. Farrelly, who is of course famous for his humorous and unconventional interventions, has this to say about pressuring clients.

> To sum up, then, frequently in clinical practice as in life, a distinction must be made between short term "cruelty" with long term kindness on the one hand versus short term "kindness" and long term detriment on the other. There is a strongly prevalent myth in the field of child rearing (where the half-life of "truth" has been estimated at 10 years) that punishment or negative reinforcement or irritation toward another whose behavior the helper is supposed to be shaping will have an infallibly negative effect. Yet the socialization of children in any culture is invariably implemented with love, tenderness, and massive counter-force, violence, punishment, withholding of food, forced social isolation, and similar "dog obedience training" methods. In our opinion punishments will always be used; the question is whether they will be effective and explicit or ineffective and apologetic. In all probability there will always be sadists in many walks of life including the mental health professions, but a distinction has to be made between sadism and taking pleasure in venting long overdue, justifiable anger towards the client or patient and enjoying the consequent changed, prosocial behavior in the "subject." If love is not enough, neither is punishment; the two together can be remarkably effective in changing behavior. (Farrelly & Brandsma, 1981, p. 51)

And in that same spirit, let's examine a quote from Carl Whitaker—another famous therapist with a marked Dionysian style.

> The secret of being a good parent is in the enjoyment of being hated at times, rather than fearing it. (Neill & Kniskern, 1989, p. 367)

Clearly both of these "therapeutic wizards" are suggesting that many therapists have a blind spot when it comes to using "dog obedience training" with clients. And both are arguing that therapy is more effective when such tools are included in the therapeutic armamentarium. Finally, both are urging therapists to move through their fear of conflict and judgment when it will benefit the client. Both Whitaker and Farrelly embody the principle that the most effective wielder of Apollonian power is the least Apollonian therapist.

In sum, Apollonian interventions are required in numerous situations with clients. Many therapists have hesitations about using these interventions. Some of the key reasons for hesitation include compassion for clients who have been injured by expectations, ethical stances against pressuring clients, fear of conflict, and a humble resistance to donning the mantle of Apollonian power. Working through such hesitations is facilitated by having a "clear map" such as the one offered by reality therapy, or—in a much more nuanced and holistic way—by the Tillichian hierarchy. Finally, even when hesitations are removed by study and experience, the therapist will need to manifest courage and, just as importantly, step up to her symbolic role as the emissary from the dominant culture.

## THE BASIC MODEL

If a temple is to be erected, a temple must be destroyed.

—Friedrich Nietzsche, *On the Genealogy of Morality* (1887)

The clarity and simplicity of the reality therapy model offers a number of insights into the provocative and baffling outcome research results. Counter intuitive as it might be, we know that beginners are as effective as experts. This equivalence in results suggests that beginners need no training; they arrive at the starting gate of their therapeutic career already prepared to be effective. Second, their preexisting knowledge of an effective change model implies that the model must be simple and reflective of common sense. For beginners to match experts they must already have an internalized map of change—something that is readily available to any cultural member.

Reality therapy is certainly simple; it can be explained in a sentence and understood in five minutes. A responsible and caring therapist helps a client understand his current status in the culture—his current position in the Net— and tells him that he can more effectively meet his personal needs by a certain plan that will advance his cultural position. The reason that it takes even five minutes to explain the reality therapy model is that the teacher needs to take a moment to show why preexisting ideas about diagnosis, mental health, and trauma must be discarded. And that's it.

More important, however, is the concept that the new therapist arrives with the model already internalized—that they are already aware of factors such as the client's position in the culture and what is required to fulfill the client's needs more effectively. Edward Wilson, the evolutionary biologist whose work was briefly reviewed during the discussion of faith and doubt, has reflected on this issue of human social competence for years. He believes that humans specifically evolved to achieve advanced social skills, the very skills required by therapists. Moreover, as he points out in the quotes below, many, many humans are so fixated on mastering these skills that they rehearse and practice them incessantly. Wilson begins his thesis by discussing the rapid evolution of the human brain required to achieve this level of social competency.

> Prior to the habilines the prehumans had been animals. Largely vegetarian, they had humanlike bodies, but their cranial capacity remained chimpanzee-sized at or below 600 cubic centimeters (cc). Starting with the habiline period the capacity grew precipitously to 680cc in *Homo habilis*, 900cc in *Homo erectus*, and about 1400cc in *Homo sapiens*. The expansion of the human brain was one of the most rapid episodes of complex tissue evolution in the history of life. (Wilson, 2015a, pp. 23–24)

Next Wilson discusses what these new humans did with their enhanced brain capacity.

> Today, at the terminus of this evolutionary process, our immense memory banks are smoothly activated to join past, present, and future. They allow us to evaluate the prospects and consequences of alliances, bonding, sexual contact, rivalries, domination, deception, loyalty, and betrayal. We instinctively delight in the telling of countless stories about others, cast as players upon our own inner stage.
> . . . People are intensely interested in the minutiae of behavior of those around them. Gossip is a prevailing subject of conversation, everywhere from hunter-gatherer campsites to royal courts. The mind is a kaleidoscopically shifting map of others inside the group and a few outside, each of whom is evaluated emotionally in shades of trust, love, hatred, suspicion, admiration, envy, and sociability. (2015a, pp. 22–24)

Wilson is arguing that we have an enormous capacity to measure, predict, and respond to our social world. To give just one example of the level of social skills and sensitivity of an acculturated human, examine the following experiment that Malcom Gladwell shares in his book *Blink*. The experimenters were attempting to determine whether an analysis of doctor patient conversations could predict which surgeons would be sued for malpractice. Not surprisingly, the researchers found that the doctors who had never been sued spent more time with their patients, laughed more, and made more active listening comments. But Gladwell (2007) was most interested in how the next researcher extended these findings.

> The psychologist Nalini Ambady listened to Levinson's tapes, zeroing in on the conversations that had been recorded between surgeons and their patients. For each surgeon, she picked two patient conversations. Then, from each conversation, she selected two ten-second clips of the doctor talking, so her slice was

a total of forty seconds. Finally, she "content-filtered" the slices which means she removed the high-frequency sounds from speech that enable us to recognize individual words. What's left after content-filtering is a kind of garble that preserves intonation, pitch, and rhythm but erases content. Using that slice—and that alone Ambady did a Gottman-style analysis. She had judges rate the slices of garble for such qualities as warmth, hostility, dominance, and anxiousness, and she found that by using only those ratings, she could predict which surgeons got sued and which ones didn't. (p. 42)

Socialized humans are so adept at interpreting subtle social clues that they do not even require content to discern the essence of a social interaction. And they can make that determination after listening for only forty seconds.

Individuals who choose to be therapists are likely to be even more skilled at these social cues than the average member of the culture. So when it comes to reality therapy, therapists and coaches are going to be expert at discerning and understanding the "dysfunctional nature of her current choices." They are already experts at establishing rapport and already understand how the culture operates and what kind of plan might fulfill client needs more effectively. In sum, the new therapist arrives at the beginning of her professional career with a high level of pre-established proficiency. She is an expert before she walks in the door and, as someone who is already fully developed, more training in the areas of her expertise is unlikely to significantly enhance her social competency.

This preexisting clinical expertise of the new therapist—and even lay people—is often witnessed by the experienced therapist. Who has not done family therapy or group therapy and had untrained individuals generate case conceptualizations every bit as deep and meaningful as anything developed by an experienced therapist? And it is even more common for a group of beginning therapists to produce theories and interventions identical to and sometimes superior to the ones created by their supervisors and teachers. The new therapists may not be as skilled at couching the interventions in the language endorsed by a certain psychotherapeutic system, but they are usually terrific at grasping the main ideas and the central issues.

To review, the first reason that beginners achieve results equivalent to experts is that they never were beginners in terms of advanced social and cultural competence; they are only beginners in terms of learning the details of therapeutic systems (whose contributions do not enhance therapeutic effectiveness). Moreover, as experts, their effectiveness in this area is unlikely to increase with more experience.

And, in addition to shedding insight on why beginners get results equivalent to experts, reality therapy provides a gut-level understanding of why the various psychological systems provide no added value in terms of outcome.

When reality therapy can be learned in five minutes, and when its outcomes are as good as much more complex systems such as psychodynamic psychotherapy, one can have an inner sense about the futility of developing intricate psychological systems. In truth it feels "wrong" that reality therapy is as effective as Family Systems therapy or Jungian therapy—both of which are characterized by deep and moving texts that are highly nuanced and which require careful review to fully understand—but there it is. More complex, deeper, more impressive and more thoughtful does not translate into more effective.[1]

Occam's Razor argues that when there are two competing theories describing the same phenomena, it is best to pick the simplest unless there are compelling reasons to choose the more complex. The implications of this are so important and so provocative that it is worth repeating the basic argument. The equivalence of reality therapy to more complex schools of therapy suggests that all therapy boils down to a wise and caring person telling a client that they ought to behave in ways that meet their needs more effectively. Everything else consists of bells and whistles; when it comes to outcomes, everything else is extraneous fluff. And, worst of all, pretty much any socially competent member of the culture can pull this off.

Why is this empowering? Because when the basic model is defined, it highlights what must be superseded in order to achieve above-average performance. In the case of therapy, no techniques have ever been developed that are superior to simply telling a client that they ought to do something better. But the way that this message is delivered—in other words, the charisma attached to the message—results in a significantly different impact on the client.

Finally, we need to discuss how embracing an Apollonian stance can be helpful in terms of enhancing therapist charisma. Recall the question from chapter 6: "What if the focus shifts to how the experiences in the room facilitate or diminish therapist charisma?"

For the development of charisma, the emphasis must be on mastering the essence of the Apollonian approaches. The essence of Apollonian therapies is the domination of the conscious over the unconscious. The essence of being an Apollonian therapist is the ability to embrace one's role as a designated representative of the culture with the corresponding ability to be directive, success-oriented, and have an appropriate sense of right and wrong.

Of course all these factors are constructed, relative, and culturally variable; however, from the standpoint of developmental needs—Tillich argues that individuals need to master the Apollonian before proceeding to the Dionysian—there is integrity in playing such a role. Put another way, mastery of the basic goals of life are so central to human functioning that the attempt to cultivate therapeutic charisma without a grounding in the Apollonian is futile.

It was no accident that Farrelly and Whitaker, two overtly Dionysian therapists, were so adamant about the importance of boundaries and the ability to support/impose them.

An enhancement in charisma occurs when the therapist internally owns the essence of an approach. When we read Glasser's story about confronting the boy with his own behavior—and feel the power and certainty running through the story—we have an opportunity to develop our Apollonian power; when we manifest that same energy in our own practice, we enhance our charisma. At the end of the day, we are not trying to learn reality therapy, we are trying to experience in our own process what Glasser felt the moment he blurted out to the boy:

> I told him to shut up and for once in his life to listen to what someone had to say. I informed him that the play was over, that we would sit and talk in an adult fashion, or if we walked we would walk as adults. I explained clearly that I would not tolerate any running away or even any impolite behavior while we were walking. He would have to be courteous and try to converse with me when I talked to him. (1965, p. 138)

## NOTE

1. Lest Realty therapy be portrayed as a superior psychological system, it should be clear that it has significant issues. For example, while reality therapy offers the benefits of a clear map and empowers its therapists to make powerful interventions, it is built on shaky foundations. The first problem, obviously, is that Glasser never questions his use of the word "responsible" and his assumption that operating inside the culture will lead to needs fulfillment. In many ways, of course, Glasser's assumptions in this area are appropriate. In most of the case studies presented in this book, simply helping a client to master the next developmental stage as defined by the extant culture would suffice as a moral "place to stand."

Constructionists, of course, respond that such simple ideas of responsible behavior eventually betray the less enfranchised members of that culture. Feminist therapists argue that these kinds of traditional ideas violate a woman's sense of self, her freedoms, and her right to choose. Similarly, advocates for virtually all cultural minorities point out that clichéd ideas of right and wrong, especially when advanced by high status members of a culture, often lead to inequity, injustice, and mistreatment for the lower status person. Chapter 3 went over detailed examples of how easily an imperialistic psychology can oppress minorities and representatives of non-dominant subcultures. For these reasons, constructionists argue for disassembling all the assumptions in a culture. A therapist who has taken the cultural assumptions apart has a better chance of avoiding an imperialistic stance.

# Chapter 10

# Identity

> Do I contradict myself? Very well, then I contradict myself, I am
> large, I contain multitudes.
>
> —Walt Whitman, "Song of Myself" (1854)

Confusion about the nature of the Self is one of the defining aspects of the Abyss. Not surprisingly, therefore, it also becomes one of the central focuses of the Net. Working effectively with the concept of the Self is one of the hallmarks of a Reality B therapist. And one gets far more interesting answers if the first question is not, "What is the nature of the Self?" but rather, "How many selves exist?"

This question of "how many selves?" is less a function of truth and more a function of pragmatism and usefulness. Common experience supports the existence of one self and the existence of multiple selves. Everyone, of course, has the sense that "I" exist. The "me" that went to sleep seems identical to the "me" that wakes up. The "me" from childhood is united with the "me" of adulthood.

Conversely it is just as common to recognize the multiple selves within. The statement, "A part of me wants to marry him and a part of me doesn't" is so common as to be unremarkable. "I have to talk myself into going to the party" of course implies multiple selves. And "my angry part takes over and makes me do things I regret" has the same implications. G. I. Gurdjieff comments:

> Man has no individual i. But there are, instead, hundreds and thousands of separate small "i"s, very often entirely unknown to one another, never coming into contact, or, on the contrary, hostile to each other, mutually exclusive and incompatible. Each minute, each moment, man is saying or thinking, "i." And

211

each time his i is different. Just now it was a thought, now it is a desire, now a sensation, now another thought, and so on, endlessly. Man is a plurality. Man's name is legion. (Ouspensky, 2001, p. 59)

Apollonians love the concept of the unitary self. Since one of their primary values is responsibility, and multiple selves by definition allow a person to escape personal responsibility, the Apollonian has a strong tendency to affirm the unitary self. Moreover, the unitary self implies stability, continuity, and permanence—other key Apollonian values.

Dionysians, conversely, are enchanted by multiple selves. This view gives them more freedom to respond with fluidity, creativity, and spontaneity. The Whitman epigraph above is classically Dionysian and emphasizes acceptance of contradiction, complexity, nuances, and shades of gray. Conversely, the Apollonian concept of responsibility is relatively black and white, clear, discerning, and judging.

The contrast between these two models became very clear to me early in graduate school. I had chosen to attend the University of Montana for my doctoral studies in clinical psychology for a variety of reasons, but one of the main ones was the presence of Dr. Jack Watkins on the faculty. Dr. Watkins has had a long career and made a variety of significant contributions to psychology, but he is most renowned for his development of clinical hypnosis and ego state therapy. Subsequent to World War II, Dr. Watkins, along with other luminaries such as Erickson in Arizona and Hilgaard at Stanford, was instrumental in introducing hypnosis into clinical psychology and helping it become accepted as a valid therapeutic technique. As part of his work with altered states, hypnotic amnesia, and related concepts, Dr. Watkins undertook studies of multiple personality disorder (MPD) and became an expert in that area. Not surprisingly, his expertise with hypnosis and MPD interested the justice system and he often functioned as a forensic psychologist and expert witness.

One of his most famous trials involved Kenneth Bianchi, the Hillside Strangler. Bianchi was denying any memory of the murders and Dr. Watkins was asked to examine him. He met with Bianchi, put him into a trance, and determined that Bianchi was a multiple. This news was not greeted positively by the prosecution who of course believed that Bianchi was dissembling about the MPD in order to receive a reduced sentence for his crimes. The prosecution essentially argued that, at worst, Dr. Watkins had been taken in by a con man; and, at best, Dr. Watkins had "created" the MPD as a result of the hypnotic trance. Dr. Watkins supported his position via submitting tapes of his hypnotic sessions and providing other supportive material such as a sculptured bust made by Bianchi with a normal face on one side and a hideous face on the other. Given the heinous nature of his crimes, it was not surprising that judge and jury resolved the issue by ruling in favor of the prosecution.

This case is a perfect representation of the struggle between the Apollonian and the Dionysian in terms of defining reality. Virtually every therapist is familiar with this struggle. For example, I have a fair number of college students in my practice and almost every semester I receive a request or two for a letter stating that the reason that the student failed her course was because of depression, or panic disorder, or overwhelming stress. The professor, of course, has the default Apollonian position that the student should master herself sufficiently to complete the course work; my letters, conversely, essentially state that the well-intentioned student part was overwhelmed by a mental health-related part.

Who is right: Watkins or the prosecution, the professor or the psychologist? Constructionists respond that neither the Apollonian perspective nor the Dionysian are superior; the "truth" is utilitarian and relative. The professor can defer and change the "F" to an incomplete without harming much of anything. The culture pays a much bigger price when it condones murder— especially serial murders—secondary to a mental health condition. Multiple selves removes responsibility; unitary self emphasizes it. When it comes to justice, Apollonian is usually superior. When it comes to change, multiple selves and the Dionysian perspectives are generally more effective.

The interaction between psychology and the justice system has been used to illustrate one aspect of the struggle between the unitary-self and the multiple-self models. The "truth" is that there is neither a unitary self nor a fixed number of multiple selves. Personal identity is an area where the constructed nature of reality is seen most clearly. Without thinking of the philosophic implications, people in general, and therapists in specific, create and destroy parts, selves and identities every day. The same student who asks me for a letter in the morning, explaining how his responsible "student self" got overwhelmed by his "anxious self," presents himself at a job interview in the afternoon promising to be responsible and reliable. Later in the day, he tells his girlfriend that he intends to be faithful to her while simultaneously knowing that his "player" self will be out that same evening when he goes drinking and dancing with his friends. Martin Buber said, "The origin of all conflict between me and my fellow-men is that I do not say what I mean and I don't do what I say" (as cited in Wooster, 2016, p. 117). This quote implies self-knowledge—who is making the promise and who is keeping it—and self-mastery—"I choose to honor what was promised by my one self although I may no longer be that self."

The "unitary self versus multiple self" dilemma is not only one of the primary characteristics of the Abyss, it operates throughout daily life. Individuals alter their identities frequently and casually and are so comfortable with the process that they take little note of it unless it gets them in serious trouble (e.g., with illegal activities or breaking a promise to a lover). Certain misbehaviors generate wrathful Apollonian judgment but most variability in the self is considered "normal" and excused and overlooked. Finally, since shifting the Self implicitly participates in the full power of the Abyss—both for constructive and destructive purposes—it is included in some form in almost all therapeutic systems.

## EGO STATE THERAPY: DIONYSIAN DISSOCIATION

> I am a forest, and a night of dark trees: but he who is not afraid of my darkness, will find banks full of roses under my cypresses.

> —Friedrich Nietzsche, *Thus Spake Zarathustra* (1896)

Many psychologists believe that attachment theory—with its compelling explanations of the mother-child bond and its subsequent predictions of healthy human functioning—is the central theory of human development. To constructionists—who are most focused on how an individual is socialized into a culturally constructed reality—the most important developmental process is how one learns to see reality from a certain shared and socially validated perspective. While there are many benefits to being initiated into a social reality, there are also drawbacks. One of the chief drawbacks is that every member of the culture is forced to struggle with guilt and shame. The old saying "no one gets through childhood unscathed" applies here. Virtually everyone has experiences where they internalize feelings that imply that they are bad, inadequate, or deviant because they fail to master a certain cultural value or perspective. Ram Dass, the clinical psychologist and spiritual teacher, finds this relationship with guilt and shame so central that he summarizes it with, "Your problem is you are too busy holding on to your unworthiness" (as cited in Ducey, 2015, Self Love).

Shame and guilt require a unitary self; I am responsible for my mistakes and my resulting shame and guilt. Conversely, releasing shame and guilt either requires some sort of penance and making amends—working our way out of shame and guilt through good deeds and right action—or releasing the dark feelings by attributing poor judgment and bad behavior to another part of myself. "I" know better but this confused or traumatized or miseducated part of me did the bad deeds.

This concept is so powerful that it essentially becomes part of almost every psychotherapeutic system. When paralyzed by guilt and shame, adopting a multiple-self perspective is not only Dionysian, it is like stepping on the accelerator in a car: change happens relatively easily when the client is no longer frozen with remorse. Conversely, adopting a unitary-self perspective is like stepping on the brakes; everything is stabilized and locked into place. To illustrate how this operates in a therapy office, let us examine how one school of therapy, developed by the same John Watkins discussed above, works with shame and guilt.

In addition to his forensic interests, Watkins continued to develop his interests in MPD via creating a new way to do therapy that he called Ego State Therapy (EST) (cf. Watkins, 1993). EST is an approach which allows a client to touch his traumas, failures, and poor choices without being overwhelmed by a personal sense of responsibility or identification with those negative memories. In EST, a client is invited to imagine that he has an inner family of "ego states" which, although separate parts, collectively form his complete identity. The client is then asked to understand the perspective of each part, mediate between conflicted parts, and suggest that certain parts change or make compromises. Sometimes this work is done in trance and other times it is done as a form of "chair work" with each part being placed in a seat and the client moving between seats.

The parts are described and experienced as autonomous both from each other and from the main personality. Therefore, if these autonomous parts have been responsible for bad choices or reprehensible behaviors, the primary self can feel relatively free of guilt and shame. Typically, the main personality is urged to move toward the misbehaving parts with love, understanding, and acceptance. It is a form of "embracing the shadow." And, as a result of the reduction of guilt, the increase of the sense of agency and personal power, and the presence of love and forgiveness toward the "dark" ego states, the average client paradoxically reports feeling more integrated, more empowered, and possessed of great insight. Following is a case example of EST from my own practice.

A 26-year-old, Caucasian male presented in therapy with complaints of anxiety, anger outbursts, and general confusion and agitation. The client had reported that he had been popular in high school and had been a gifted football player. Since high school he had essentially drifted through life, drinking on a daily basis, partying hard on the weekends, and only able to work part-time. He had primarily been raised by his divorced mother, with the help of her parents, and had been rejected by his biological father who was an officer in the military. His mother was very moody and would alternate between being supportive, abandoning, and, on occasion, abusive (e.g., she once threw hot tea on him when he was sleeping).

The therapy began with a referral to Alcoholics Anonymous. The client felt at home there and was quickly able to commit to and achieve sobriety. Approximately six months later, he decided to address his under employment issues by trying to become a firefighter. This choice required him to enroll in the local community college for some basic courses and for the fire academy. Unfortunately, when he stepped on campus to register, he experienced a severe panic attack and had to come home immediately. He felt discouraged and was certain that any attempt to return to the campus would rekindle his panic feelings. He exhibited marked shame and guilt, reported that he had always known that he was a "loser," and stated that he would never amount to anything in life.

At his next session, the client was introduced to the concept of ego state therapy and a list of important parts was co-created between the two of us. A label describing each part was put on each of 6 seating locations in the room and the client was instructed that when he occupied each seating position, he could only think, feel, and speak as that part of his personality. A dialogue was conducted between the therapist and the various parts which helped him understand the nature of each part and allowed him to practice quickly switching from part to part. This, of course, not only provided insight but fostered dis-identification from each part.

He had named one part "Marie," which was his mother's name, because he felt that this part was weak, confused, dependent and fearful just like his mother's personality. He noted that he hated this part of his mother and felt ashamed that he had internalized an equivalent part. Not surprisingly, he also had a part he named, "Colonel Critical," which he believed symbolized his father. This Colonel part was actively critical of the Marie part and repeatedly heaped shame and abuse upon her.

The next session he accessed a part, which he called the "big brother," which embodied all the ways that he had helped and supported children and other people in his life. This part was able to move toward the Marie part and explain to her that her fear and sense of worthlessness was natural given what she had experienced in life. The big brother part also pledged to protect the Marie part from the Colonel.

In the weeks following the sessions the client was able to return to campus. While he felt some initial anxiety, the anxiety quickly faded and he was able to register for classes. He went on to complete the fire academy and got a desirable internship with a local fire department.

This is a fairly classic example of EST. As has been demonstrated, once the parts model is adopted, it is relatively simple and straightforward to resolve problems and conflicts. Simply work with the individual using basic family therapy techniques.

EST and most dissociative techniques are a kind of constructionism-in-action. For example, suppose a client presents with social anxiety. It is simple to gesture toward a chair and state, "when you sit here, I want you to be the part that protects you from being hurt at a party. When you sit in that chair, be the little boy that was scared, and when you sit in the final chair, be the wise part that knows what to do to integrate these parts and to solve your anxiety issues." Did the parts exist before? In truth, the client had never considered his behavior from that perspective. But they exist now and the client is likely to congruently play out each part with insight and appropriate affect simply because I asked him to do it.

Experiences like this help the therapist "feel" the malleability of reality. A client who had no insight about the origin of their social anxiety is discussing it articulately and with feeling within five minutes of sitting in the chair. Was there really a childhood origin to the anxiety? Perhaps it only existed because I suggested he sit in the "little boy" chair. But if the client tells a healing story about the interaction between these three parts—and then can start attending social events—who really has the right to complain that the healing is unsubstantiated because it was implicitly suggested by the therapist?

In this sense, accepting multiple selves leads directly and indirectly to constructionism. Once the new self is created—by therapist, by client, or serendipity—it becomes as "real" as the preexisting self or selves. Yet it was created "ex nihilo" and is composed simply of intention. Moreover, there are no limits about how many selves can be created or for what purposes.

Multiple selves versus the unitary self is one of the defining characteristics of being Dionysian, being a constructionist, and, paradoxically, of being integrated. Multiple selves are not only helpful in terms of reducing or removing guilt and shame, they not only facilitate change and growth, they also are necessary to encompass the complexity of human experience. As Whitman argues in the quote at the beginning of this chapter, to be fully human is to embrace multitudes. Awareness of the fluidity of self and the capacity to use this consciously and thoughtfully is transformative both for client and therapist.

## APOLLONIAN APPROACHES TO DISSOCIATION

Consistency is the last refuge of the unimaginative.

—Oscar Wilde, "The Relation of Dress to Art,"
*The Pall Mall Gazette*, February 28, 1885

Returning to the Berger and Luckmann argument that all cultures are required to socialize their children into the prevailing cultural reality, it is not much of a stretch to understand why shame and guilt are so widespread and so paralyzing. Apollonian enculturation requires use of rewards and punishments. It is difficult for some members to become high functioning and successful. And with each failure and disappointment, the acculturating individual feels increasing shame and guilt for her inadequacies. Of course, the hope is that this shame will be motivating and result in an increased effort to master socialized behaviors. Unfortunately, for a certain percentage of individuals, the increased shame simply results in hopelessness and passivity. Instead of increased motivation and a good outcome, there is a collapse into helplessness and self-deprecation. Often this guilt and shame is accompanied by anger that the individual is being forced to play a game that they can never win.

Therapists, of course, see a good many clients who have never socialized successfully and who are imprisoned by this sort of helpless, hopeless, self-deprecating experience of life. While it is possible to use direct techniques with such clients, even the most Apollonian therapist will be drawn into the use of dissociative techniques to deal with this level of self-hatred and deprecation. James Hillman discusses the importance of dissociation.

> [M]ultiplication of personas may be used as a therapeutic tool in order to bring home the realization that "the ego complex is not the only complex in the psyche." By actively imagining the psyche into multiple persons, we prevent the ego from identifying with each and every figure in a dream and fantasy, each and every impulse and voice. For the ego is not the whole psyche, only one member of a commune. Therapy works through the paradox of admitting that all figures and feelings of the psyche are wholly "mine," while at the same time recognizing that these figures and feelings are free of my control and identity, not "mine" at all. (Hillman, 1997, p. 31)

In this sense, it is not surprising that virtually all schools of psychotherapy have some technique which embodies dissociation and multiple selves. For example, when a cognitive therapist tells the client that he adopted his irrational or unproductive beliefs because he was mistaught or had bad modeling or had traumatic experiences, he is inviting the client to view his poor choices and beliefs as inevitable—something any "normal" person would have done if they had had the same experiences. This normalization is designed to decrease the shame and guilt implicit in being a mental health patient whose presenting problem (e.g., anxiety or depression) marks him as a different and inferior type of person. Then the client is invited to dissociate. "You are going to keep having these feelings but you shouldn't worry about them because they come from another part of you that was confused from earlier experiences. Stand in the place that is healthy and have compassion for the part of you that still has these old cognitions and feelings." Or even more commonly, "dispute these irrational ideas that come from one part of you by standing in a healthy place and asserting a more rational interpretation."

Obviously, it doesn't take much work to substitute authenticity—from a humanistic perspective—for irrational beliefs. This process of normalization—to minimize guilt and shame—and then dissociation—to reduce overwhelming negative affect—also occurs with treating trauma and negative or inadequate childhood experiences. Being part of a rape survivors' group or a post-traumatic stress disorder group ensures that the client will repeatedly and credibly hear, "Any normal person who went through what you experienced will feel what you feel. Be kind to each other and to yourself. Suspend judgment and replace it with compassion and understanding. When one part of you can comfort the hurt part, you're well on the way to healing."

Family systems theory has its own particular variation on the dissociation approach. Often the individual is not even referred to as a self but as an "identified patient." As an "identified patient," the person is not only not responsible for his misbehaviors, in family systems theory the misbehaviors of the individual are framed as unconscious attempts to help someone else in the family system or as actions done for the greater good of the entire family. Often the individual is asked to "give up" this helpful attitude—the misbehavior—and let the family take care of its own issues. In sum, the person did not perform the misbehaviors; they were performed by a different part that wanted to be helpful.

Biopsychiatrists also use dissociation and disidentification when they offer their genetic model and assert something like "you can't really help being depressed (angry, anxious, ADD, etc.) because you have three other family members with the same disorder and research has proven that these disorders are fundamentally genetic. It's like diabetes: you have a disease that we can partially control with medication but never cure. Don't be so hard on yourself for all the things you have done as a result of having this condition; your genetic predisposition left you with no other choice than to feel and act as you have."

Perhaps, though, the major school of therapy which uses dissociation most effectively is the psychodynamic model. Not only did Freud talk about the urges of the id and the critical lectures of the superego, but the very concept of the unconscious mind—with its autonomous feelings and associations—simply begs the individual to dissociate into a "me" and "not me" perspective.

One of the most powerful uses of dissociation, however, comes from AA and its concept of the inevitability of bad behaviors that arise as a result of an alcoholic/addict using drugs or alcohol. In AA, the alcoholic/addict is completely responsible for whether he takes a drink or not, but he is not responsible for the negative behaviors he emits once he has begun drinking. This, of course, is because an alcoholic is defined as someone who will inevitably emit bad behaviors if he starts drinking. Given that many alcoholics have misbehaved fairly profoundly, this definition goes a long way toward removing the shame and guilt associated with those bad behaviors. And, of course, alcoholics then target releasing shame and guilt even more thoroughly via their "making amends" process. One can know the dissociation process is well accepted when one attends meetings and hears the stories—told with great pride and even glee—of just how badly the speakers behaved when drinking. They can tell these stories without shame because "they" did not perform the bad acts; it was their "drinking self" who created such havoc.

Using dissociation is not limited to trained therapists. The life coach who has just hung out her shingle a month ago after taking a weekend workshop is also likely to use some form of dissociation with her clients. For that matter, your friend who is discussing your potential marriage is likely to say, "It sounds like you really love this part of her but can't stand the other part." Or "given how you were raised and what you went through, you shouldn't be so hard on yourself."

Even the most Apollonian systems and therapists are forced to use a dissociative model to deal with guilt, shame, and self-deprecation. The upside, of course, is that the clients get better. The downside is that with the introduction of multiple selves, both clients and therapists begin to experience the implicit ephemerality of reality. They begin to sense the background rumblings of the Abyss.

Once a therapist or client begins to disassemble reality, nothing is really stopping her from going all the way. If a therapist instructs her client to let go of shame and guilt because the misbehaviors were caused by another part of her psyche, where do these assumptions start and stop? If some of my behaviors are done by a part of my identity that is "not me," which of my behaviors are done by me? The therapist in the middle of the clinical moment may answer that all one's positive behaviors are done by the "real me" and all the negative ones are done by the "false or conditioned or traumatized me," but it does not take much thinking to realize that following this argument to its logical conclusion gets one into incongruences pretty quickly.

The Apollonian response to these intimations of ephemerality is to move the client back into a unified self and a clear identity as quickly as possible. Perhaps it was necessary for therapeutic progress to move into a multiple-self model, but the Apollonian needs to reassert the primacy of the unitary self. This "reassociation" process is just as important as the progress that was made via disassociation. The new identity created after therapeutic progress solidifies the therapeutic gains and has important implications both for sustaining those gains and opening the client for further growth.

Often the new identity is formalized via a label. The most obvious examples of these are identities such as "recovering addict," "survivor," and the genetically vulnerable. Every therapist has had new clients walk into the office for a first session and explain that they are destined to be anxious because "many people in my family are anxious." Or "I have to stay on antidepressants for the rest of my life because I have a biochemical deficit." Or "I'm going to have problems in relationships because my last therapist told me that I have borderline traits." Moreover, even when the new identity is not formally defined in terms of psychopathology, there can still be residual definitions left over from encounters with mental health professionals. For example, statements such as "I have a hard time adapting to change," and "I typically have intimacy issues in relationships," may have originally been generated with good intentions but can have significant negative consequences over time.

Of course, many of these labels carry a measure of relief when they are first applied. They often act to normalize behavior and the client often feels, "My symptoms would have happened to anyone who went through my experiences. They are not due to the fact that I am a substandard person." But it is possible to limit this kind of normalizing to the early stages of treatment. It is not necessary to discharge a client with a pathologized label defining his identity.

The second good reason for such identities is that the client continues to have symptoms and they need an ongoing, pathologized identity to understand the continued symptoms and to accept them. An obvious example might be a woman recovering from a rape experience who uses her identity as a survivor to explain to herself why she has hesitancies, or even full scale flashbacks, with her new lover.

Such identities can help clients avoid falling back into negative patterns. Some substance abusers need to be in lifelong recovery because abandoning the pathological identity of an addict exposes the client to destroying their life by thinking that they can use drugs and alcohol "like a normie."

The obvious downside to such labels and identities are that they limit a person's capacity to define himself as "normal, strong, or healthy." This dilemma is often exacerbated when the therapeutic world tells the client they are in denial, or ignoring reality, or are riding for a fall when they attempt to change their identity from pathologized to normal. They are often enjoined to keep the identity of a recovering person and are informed that they are never allowed to resume the identity of a recovered or fully functional individual.

There are darker sides to this as well. Gergen argued in chapter 3 that the proliferation of mental health diagnoses are not secondary to better science and the careful discovery of how reality is structured. Rather, he saw this proliferation as an attempt by a profession to maximize its status, power, and finances. In this sense, "experts" in certain areas are most likely to reassemble clients' identities with pathological labels. The ADD expert is more likely to discharge his patients with a lifelong ADD label and the psychopharmacologist is more likely to recommend lifelong medication for an underlying, genetically based disorder. Such experts are often supported by cultural and business forces such as 'Big Pharma' who work hard to apply pathological labels to clients and to pathologize normal behaviors such as grief and hormonal fluctuations.

Some therapists have personal identities that are somewhat shaky. Such therapists are Abyss avoidant and frequently use hyperstabilizing strategies in their own life. The shakier my identity is, less likely I can tolerate ambiguity in my client's identity. Moreover, they will have a tendency to impose their own worldview on my clients in a kind of "If you believe what I believe than my identity is safer and more stable." As a result, such therapists are prone to assigning black and white labels to their clients after dissociation and at discharge. And the clearest labels are the ones which are pathology centered.

A shaky identity is one thing but an even darker outcome occurs when the mental health professional has hidden fear of the "abnormal." It was previously observed that one of the benefits of diagnosing individuals who are dysfunctional by conventional cultural values is that the label creates a boundary between "them" and "us." In the face of the threat of the Abyss, separating ourselves from those who are at risk of being devoured by darkness is always tempting.

Achieving superior effectiveness as a therapist always begins with the therapist having the ability to imagine that the client has the capacity to change and, preferably, has the capacity to change relatively quickly and profoundly. As has been demonstrated above, even Apollonians are forced to use a multiple-self model when clients are seriously blocked and immobile. However, it is vitally important to understand that Apollonian reassembly of self is almost always characterized by a labeling process that will slow and limit healthy change. While it is important to support some pathologized labels for certain clients—such as those who are self-labeled alcoholics who wish to maximize their motivation for sobriety—in general such labels should be viewed suspiciously and probably do more harm than good.

## MAKING IT REAL

There are no facts, only interpretations.

—Friedrich Nietzsche, *Beyond Good and Evil* (1907)

Nothing quite illustrates psychological constructionism as effectively as the unitary- versus multiple-self dilemma. The more one examines the possibilities, the more one works with it with clients, the less real and more constructed it appears. Take an old joke as an example.

*Question:* How do you drive an Apollonian crazy?
*Answer:* Put him in a round room and tell him there is a penny in the corner.

This simple joke implies that Apollonians need to see the world as full of straight lines and corners instead of its true nature: round and curvy.

Moreover, they seek for false treasure in the arbitrarily constructed corners. In this case, the penny represents the idolatrous promise of happiness offered by the illegitimate ultimate concern.

Make the same joke a bit more psychological.

*Question:* How do you drive an Apollonian crazy?
*Answer:* Tell him his next client has exactly 6 parts. He needs to discover the parts and then create an authentic alignment with the healthy part.

Of course the next client cannot have six parts. He has one self or as many sub-personalities as the client and the therapist co-create. A part does not shine with its own "authenticity"; rather, the authenticity is derived from the relationship that exists between the therapist and the client and between the client and his life.

Approximately twenty-five years ago there was a surge of interest in multiple personality disorder. Clinics were established and a number of therapists specialized in treating it. The clinics produced discharge summaries that detailed the twenty-two multiple selves in the patient, what each part was like, and made recommendations for how to work with the parts in an ongoing fashion. Not surprisingly, this heyday of MPD was short-lived as many other therapists made the obvious critique: why should we take your work seriously when you've obviously made it up?

Keep going with the same joke but make it institutional.

*Question:* How do you drive an Apollonian crazy?
*Answer:* Tell them they are the Commissioner of Psychology. Their job is to discover the 174 different mental health diagnostic categories that are truly independent and unique. Next they are to develop a specialized manual for each category that efficiently and effectively treats the extant disorder.

The more a psychologist works with EST or internal family systems, the more that psychologist is thrust into constructionism and has a personal experience of "making it all up." This experience quickly generalizes to related experiences; hence the evolution of the Apollonian joke from the Apollonian attempt to make the world full of straight lines, to the Apollonian tendency to make the next client fit into a preexisting pattern, to the Apollonian wish to make the diagnostic world fit a simple typology. Take the following case.

A 47-year-old single businessman presented with depression and anxiety secondary to being rejected by his current girlfriend. The business man was handsome, wealthy, and had many friends—the epitome of success. He had a history of difficult relationships with women primarily characterized by lying and cheating. He had been married for 5 years but cheated on his wife almost constantly because he didn't love her and had only married her because she was pretty and helped him impress his business clients. When he left his wife after a long term affair was revealed, he tried to have a relationship with his mistress but left her because he felt that she was "not quite right for me."

He then started dating another woman but lost interest in her when he learned that his mistress was dating someone new. He did everything he could to win back the mistress while simultaneously continuing to date the girlfriend but the mistress wouldn't have him back. The girlfriend discovered his campaign to reacquire the mistress by checking his phone and dumped him.

Upon being dumped, he decided that the girlfriend was actually his true love. He begged her to take him back and she told him that he needed to do therapy to discover why he was so compulsive and desperate in relationships.

In the first session, his childhood was reviewed and he explained that his father was a highly successful CEO who was almost never around. His mother was passive and loving and his father was judgmental and demanding. When the father made his brief appearances in the family, he typically criticized his son citing character flaws and a lack of discipline. The son responded by rebelling with alcohol and minor misbehaviors—a strategy that got him sent off to military school. He came out of college with a burning desire to achieve, a sociopathic layer of self-centeredness, and an almost complete lack of self-knowledge and self-awareness.

The client was told that he had 3 main parts: a wounded child desperate for attention, a tough achiever/protector, and a healthy part that wanted real intimacy. Because he had disowned the child, he needed to reclaim and integrate it. Similarly the unethical choices of his tough side need to be acknowledged but he was also asked to cultivate self-compassion because many of the misbehaviors had been done to protect the sensitive child.

In the next several months, he came for individual therapy and for conjoint sessions with the girlfriend. The girlfriend, not surprisingly, brought up numerous examples where she had been lied to or misled. The client was required to fully acknowledge the truth of these accusations and demonstrate, by the quality of his apologies and subsequent behaviors, that he both owned the bad choice but simultaneously forgave himself for it. He had to own it because he had hurt the girlfriend and behaved unethically, but he had to forgive himself because that "self-forgiveness" would demonstrate that he was finally accepting his child part. In addition, he had to avoid any further unethical behaviors and be especially kind to his girlfriend's mother and child to allow his "sweet side" (child part) to come out.

While there was a bit of up and down in the relationship over the next few months, the client fulfilled his requirements and felt, by doing so, that he was healing both the wounded nature of the child and the sociopathic tendencies of the "tough guy." They were engaged eight months later and married a year after that. There were no more indications of sociopathy although the childlike "desperation to be loved" returned on occasions. The client was able to have some normal fights with his wife but had to be careful not to give away too much power to her.

First of all, this was a seriously conflicted client with a history of significant misbehaviors and violations of others. Psychodynamic therapists would emphasize his narcissism and his sociopathy. As I write this, there has been a major development in psychology similar to the MPD fad that existed thirty years ago; this development conceptualizes individuals like this client as "sex addicts" or "love addicts." In fact, the girlfriend was warned by her friends that he needed to attend a thirty-day inpatient treatment program for sex addiction—and be in an ongoing sexual addiction support group—to have any hope of changing his poor behavioral choices.

The choice of three parts was, of course, somewhat arbitrary. I could say that I picked "3" because that seemed the minimum necessary to create a frame where he could both take responsibility and forgive himself. From a constructionist point of view, I could have divided the protector part into two parts: a healthy protector and a sociopathic protector who felt that his father's critical behaviors justified his lying and cheating. Of course, I could have added three or four other parts if I had believed that they would have contributed significantly to the healing ritual.

This case was chosen to illustrate the ambiguity of constructed reality. It was also chosen because it seems to have generated good results with a man who had a truly terrible history of poor choices and poor behaviors. Are his good behaviors fleeting and ephemeral—doomed to failure because his core issues of sexual addiction and narcissism have yet to be addressed? Perhaps. . . . In truth, even if he were behaving well after two years of sexual addiction treatment and in an ongoing group, a man with this history might go back to his dysfunctional behaviors at any time.

Why did my more minimalist intervention work? The client's explanation is that he felt qualitatively different about this woman: "somehow I just really love her in a way that I've never felt before." I, of course, jumped on this feeling as a justification of a more minimalist intervention: "given the gravity and long-term nature of your unethical behaviors around women, most men with your record would need years of treatment. But the quality of your love is so profound that it may serve as a significant shortcut—a path to personal transformation that allows you to change rapidly and deeply." His feeling and my endorsement allowed and supported the rapid change. If I had responded differently, and predicted a long and slow recovery with many setbacks, it seems likely that the negative prediction would have defined the course of therapy.

Just as significantly, the division of self into three parts, and the understanding that his sociopathic behaviors were emitted by the part that suffered from his father's critical behaviors, allowed him to touch his negative behaviors without being overwhelmed by guilt and shame. Is this a technique? The previous chapter on reality therapy emphasized that the minimum model for change consists of asking a client to behave better. Does this chapter on multiple selves imply that guilt and shame are always present and we always need to deal with them with dissociation?

Not exactly. The purpose of this chapter is to illustrate that whenever we move from the unitary self to multiple selves reality is altered. Multiple selves align with the Abyss and with Dionysian change. Having only a unitary self implicitly created a dire situation; his poor choices made him the embodiment of a sexually addicted personality disorder. Staying in the unitary self gives him only two choices: he can opt for long-term penance for his unethical behaviors—a penance seasoned with guilt and shame, or he could choose denial of his issues, leave his girlfriend, and recommit to treating women like objects. Conversely, going to a multiple-self model changed his reality the moment he started viewing his choices and misbehaviors from that perspective. He wasn't a bad person, he just had a part that had been criticized so often that it justified sociopathic behaviors. It was only a child part after all. It hardly knew better. You might have chosen the same if you had gone through what he went through.

And, in that new perspective, healing quickly was an option. He simply had to include the ritual behaviors of sincere apologies, generous behaviors to his mother-in-law and step-daughter, and frequent acts of self-compassion. Because he was no longer bad at a core level, anything was possible.

In this sense, it is appropriate to argue the a multiple-self model is just as central to therapy as the direct request to change that is derived from reality therapy. The purpose of the Net is to stabilize. The purpose of therapy is to change. The Net only allows licit changes like the adolescent/adult transition. Most of therapy concerns illicit feelings and behaviors. Staying Apollonian—staying committed to the unitary self—condemns the therapist and the client to slow and painful change. Going Dionysian—adopting a multiple-self perspective—allows more rapid movement unfettered by the past and by guilt and shame.

Of course, the approach doesn't seem strong enough or long enough to take care of the scope and extent of his confusion and misbehaviors. Note the Apollonian implications: since the client behaved very badly over a long time, he will require an equivalently long period of treatment—and preferably one with lots of painful work—to make up for his mistakes. Sexual addiction therapy, with its assumption of a humiliating label and its required confession of "I am a deviant," will always "feel" like the more appropriate treatment for such egregious misbehavior. Of course, adopting such an Apollonian perspective—especially if it is adopted unconsciously—will limit the therapist's choices and the client's ability to change.

Dissociation and multiple selves are one of the easiest concepts to understand—they hide in plain sight in daily life—and yet one of the most powerful. The arbitrariness about the number and the nature of the ego states creates a palpable sense of the fragility and ephemerality of reality. Switching from the responsible unitary self to the understanding/forgiving nature of multiple selves effortlessly lightens that Apollonian sense of seriousness and heaviness. And the fact that this can be created so easily is significant. We are only able to move clients into a multiple-self model so effortlessly because dissociation is so pervasive in our daily functioning.

## THE BASIC MODEL EXTENDED

Re-examine all that you have been told . . . dismiss that which insults your soul.

—Walt Whitman, *Leaves of Grass* (1855)

The dissociation approach described in this chapter is a natural complement to the reframing/reality approach described previously. Reframing is based on the fluidity of reality; dissociation is based on the fluidity of identity. Fully understanding and experiencing the concept that reality is constructed does require understanding the feeling "it's all made up"; full mastery also requires understanding the feeling that my Self and identity are enormously fluid and malleable—in other words, identity is also "all made up."

If one reflects on the history of human culture, communication, and healing, it can be argued that there is probably no other practice as effective at exposing the fluidity of identity as psychotherapy. What other practice or experience allows an individual to witness the shifting of identity easily and profoundly multiple times per day? What effect does it have on the consciousness of the therapist to realize that identity can be radically altered simply by uttering a few sentences? Merely saying, "how does your child part feel when the angry part is out?" creates a profoundly altered state—in both client and therapist—in one sentence. Absorbing the implications of how easy identity can be altered—and the resulting changes in "reality"—is like working in a laboratory that allows for constant, ongoing experimentation.

There are levels to this understanding. Even an elementary school student can say that part of me is a "good boy" and another part of me wants to do whatever I want whenever I want. This kind of identity fluidity is important—it does ultimately point toward the Abyss—but it is such a common experience that it fails to be transformative. To gain from the experience of client dissociation, the therapist must allow every shift of identity to be a potentially profound event. Even more importantly, they must cultivate the capacity to communicate this to the client. Returning to the elementary student, simply acknowledging that he has spoken of his two parts leads to little benefit. Conversely, the therapist can say, with full concentration and seriousness, "Well, has the good boy ever had a conversation with the part that does as he wishes? And in that conversation, did the good boy make any headway at changing the willful part?"

Simply with this intention, the entire situation is now in play. There is a good chance that the boy will be able to talk about his willfulness without being paralyzed by shame, guilt, or defensiveness. Simply with a question—a question asked with intensity—the door opens for the boy to move forward. But it requires the therapist to have a depth of commitment to multiple selves. The boy will know when the therapist is serious and will respond accordingly.

Dissociation also makes an important contribution to the basic model. Reality therapy postulates that therapy works when a wise and caring practitioner urges a client to move in a healthy direction. Because reality therapy embraces right/wrong it has a capacity to move hyperstable clients—clients who are frozen by fear. Some clients, however, resist being moved directly even through the urging of a wise and caring therapist. For these clients some form of dissociation is the answer. Fear is markedly reduced when the shame-based part is seen as "not me."

It is not a stretch to argue that deep work in psychotherapy is virtually impossible without some mastery of dissociation. We are all familiar with the client who is afraid to look inside—to acknowledge and experience some of his shadow-related feelings. In truth, however, all clients—and ourselves as therapists—gain much of our ability to move through the world of affect and the world of the unconscious because we can disassociate. If we had to take personal ownership for every shadow feeling we encounter, every sojourn into the subconscious would be a journey filled with terror.

The Apollonian forces will always resist dissociation, of course, at least at some level. It threatens the Net and summons the sense of the underlying Abyss. They will argue that "really" there is only one solid client in the room and that these seeming shifts in identity are simply symptomatic manifestations of pathology and trauma. This harkens back to Bill Maher's "bubble" and Kahnman's System 1; if we "know" that all people have a unitary self, we will miss the obvious experience occurring in front of us. And in the missing, we remain entranced by the Net and mistake constructed for fundamental reality.

Conversely, the Reality B therapist understands that this sense of multiple identities takes one to the chaotic edge of the Abyss. This is one of the purest forms of "dancing with the Abyss." It is achieved fairly effortlessly in that the client and the therapist can get there with one sentence. When attention and mindfulness are brought to the process, it enhances both the therapist's consciousness as well as her charisma.

*Chapter 11*

# Heart and Soul

We were together. I forget the rest.

—Walt Whitman, *Leaves of Grass* (1902)

Affect has a special role in constructed reality. Just as cognitive control of feelings defines the Apollonian, affective emphasis defines the Dionysian. This chapter focuses on what is experienced when the Abyss breaks through the shelter of the Net. Primarily, these breakthroughs are characterized by feelings, typically negative feelings like self-deprecation, anxiety, and meaninglessness. Working with these breakthrough feelings—shadow work and soul making—can transform these negative feelings into new beginnings or even guidance and epiphanies. Apollonians repress and control feelings; Dionysians cooperate with, listen to, and are transformed by them.

This chapter will also look at affect from other perspectives. The therapeutic relationship is as dependent on caring and heart as it is on wisdom. Some therapists particularly focus on working with feelings. Moreover, some of the Abyss breakthroughs are considered oracular and we will look at one form—dream work—as a way to work with messages from the Abyss. Finally feelings—and the heart that symbolizes them—are not simply objects, events, problems, and opportunities, they are also ways of knowing. Many of the Dionysians featured in this chapter recommend knowing through the heart over knowing with the head.

But we will begin with an advocate—the Dalai Lama—who sees the two forces as equivalent and as essential to the therapeutic relationship. In a recent anthology of Buddhist psychology, the Dalai Lama (2012), in his foreword, described his sense of the healthy therapeutic relationship as follows.

In the Buddhist tradition, there are two qualities seen as essential both to our own well-being and to being able to be of appropriate help to others. These are compassion and wisdom. They are said to be like the two wings of a bird or the two wheels of a cart, for the bird cannot fly and the cart cannot roll with only one. Compassion involves wishing to free someone else from suffering, recognizing that she or he wishes to be happy and to avoid distress and misery just as we do. Wisdom involves seeing things as they are, with clear, open eyes, appreciating the interdependence and constantly changing nature of people, things, and events. (p. iii)

In a literal sense, these two factors—wisdom and compassion—are different. Wisdom implies knowing, being mature, understanding. This is more the left brain or "head" attribute. Compassion, of course, comes from the heart and is a right-brain attribute. While this head/heart split is a frequently used typology in psychotherapy, the Buddhist psychologists believe that, in truth, the two are essentially the same and that one flows into the other.

Wisdom and compassion are also inseparable; one simply cannot exist without the other. Most of us notice that when we have a multilayered understanding of a patient's problem, our hearts open. Conversely, when we feel warmly toward a client, our minds can see many more treatment possibilities. This book explores how wisdom and compassion comingle at both the relative level—in the day-to-day experience of psychotherapy—and at the absolute level—in our fundamental, unconditioned nature. Depending on our perspective, we may say that compassion emerges out of wisdom or that wisdom emerges out of compassion, but either way, these two qualities are indistinguishable at the deepest level of experience and understanding. (Siegel & Germer, 2012, p. 3)

From this quote, we can see that it is not only important to see clearly but to be equally open to the guidance of the heart, the emotions, and intuition. Therapists attempting to understand the nature of constructed reality have to be guided by feelings as much as discernment. And, of course, all agree that real therapeutic change is always dependent on heart, connection, and trust.

We should also recall that wisdom and compassion not only describe the ideal therapist-client relationship, they are also the core components of therapeutic charisma. As mentioned above, one of the weaknesses of using the term, charisma, is that it can become confused with status, fame, and power. To define it as embodying wisdom and compassion eliminates this confusion.

When speaking of charisma, however, it is important to differentiate the wisdom and compassion that characterizes the average therapist from the qualities that characterize the superior therapist. For wisdom, the dividing line is fairly clear: Apollonian wisdom consists of wisdom about how to flourish inside the prevailing view of reality; it is expertise in terms of the rules of the Net. Dionysian wisdom sees beyond the prevailing Reality via willing immersion in the Abyss; it is the ability to discern between the constructed and the fundamental. The superior therapist encompasses both types of wisdom; the average therapist primarily embodies the Apollonian.

The dividing line for compassion is similar. On the surface, both the average therapist and the superior therapist have caring, compassion, and good will toward their clients. We perceive suffering and sorrow all around and move toward clients and others with kindness and concern. The superior therapist, however, moves beyond this perspective and practices compassion from a stance at the edge of the Abyss. Becker tells us we are all going to die. That fact makes our lives meaninglessness and contributes to the sense that we are essentially alone. The compassion of the superior therapist incorporates the implicit despair of the Abyss and, like Buber, continues to choose connection in place of alienation.

It is difficult to discern between average compassion and superior compassion. Martin Buber, fortunately, wrote a book, *I and Thou* (1970), which focuses explicitly on this discernment. Here is a quote from that work.

> When I confront a human being as my Thou and speak the basic word I-Thou to him, then he is no thing among things nor does he consist of things. He is no longer He or She, a dot in the world grid of space and time, nor a condition to be experienced and described, a loose bundle of named qualities. Neighborless and seamless, he is Thou and fills the firmament. Not as if there were nothing but he; but everything else lives in his light. (p. 59)

Buber believes that most of the time, humans relate to the objects in the world as "things." He calls this the "I-It" relationship. This is a condition of alienation, fear, distance, and separation. It embodies the kinds of connections that are part of the Net. Buber contrasts this world of objects with the world of relationship. In spite of our apparent existential alienation, everything is actually in dialog—there is a connection running through everything. Participating in this reality requires an action—"speaking the basic word "I-Thou." For Buber simple perception always belongs to the world of I-It; it is only when we extend that we have the opportunity to actualize the relationship. This action transforms reality—it participates in the oracular aspect of the Abyss and then "everything else lives in his light."

Discernment is the key. With wisdom, the awareness of the constructed nature of social reality is the basic metric. Buber's definition allows us to reach for a similar level of consciousness with compassion—it allows us to check the quality of our compassion using I-It versus I-Thou.

Psychology also has a special contribution to make in this area in the form of the development of attachment theory. It is somewhat hard to believe that this theory was ever in dispute as, in hindsight, it seems so reason-able to assume that children that are provided with a safe environment for attachment—an environment which provides security, affective regulation, and appropriate stimulation and exploration—would be better off than rela-tively impoverished children. Theorizing that children who lacked healthy attachment in childhood would have difficulties connecting to others as adults seems obvious. But the situation became even more compelling when neuroscientists began to look at attachment. Their first question that arises neurologically from attachment theory focuses on functionality: since human brain development continues for many years after birth, does poor attachment suggest poor brain development? Is there literally lasting brain damage in humans raised in poor attachment situations?

The neuroscientist who is perhaps most identified with these questions is Alan Schore. He has not only provided neuroscientific support validating the centrality of attachment theory for brain development, he has extended that work to look at the implications of attachment theory for the psychothera-peutic process in general. Differing from the Dalai Lama, Schore apparently believes that when it comes to therapeutic healing, "heart" is more important than "head."

> An attachment-based clinical approach highlights the unconscious nonverbal affective factors more than the conscious verbal cognitive factors as the essen-tial change process of psychotherapy. Thus, at the most essential level, the inter-subjective work of psychotherapy is not defined by what the therapist does for the patient, or says to the patient (left brain focus). Rather, the key mechanism is how to be with the patient, especially during affectively stressful moments (right brain focus). (Schore, 2012, p. 44)

The heart is not simply a basis for intervention and connection, it also has its own epistemology—its own way of knowing. This knowing is referred to by various names—intuition, gut feelings, felt sense—and it is independent from the cognitive epistemologies. Antoine de Saint-Exupery particularly lauds the heart's way of knowing: "And now here is my secret, a very simple secret: It is only with the heart that one can see rightly; what is essential is invisible to the eye" (2000, chapter 21). Pascal agrees and states: "The heart has its reasons which reason knows not" (Kegan, 1885, p. 307).

Sometimes the heart and head support each other; at other times, they are in conflict. Heart knowledge is more Dionysian; the head embodies the Apol-lonian approach. Heart material seems more unconscious and it is difficult to trace its antecedents. Like most Dionysian approaches, it is more numinous because it feels less under conscious control. Rainer Maria Rilke agrees and states, "Our heart always transcends us" (as cited in Gilbertson, 2014, p. 200).

And, finally, Noah Benshea believes: "My heart knows what my mind only think it knows" (as cited in Mejabi, 2016, p. 59).

In spite of the Dalai Lama's assertion that heart and head are equivalent and that they meet in the depths of the soul, most of the quotes above urge us to understand the unique contributions of the heart. It seems likely that an understanding of this uniqueness is a necessary preliminary step before the ultimate unity of the two principles can be fully understood.

## NEUROSCIENCE AND THE HEART-TO-HEART CONNECTION

All love is expansion, all selfishness is contraction. Love is therefore the only law of life. He who loves lives, he who is selfish is dying. Therefore love for love's sake, because it is the only law of life, just as you breathe to live.

—Swami Vivekananda, *The Complete Works of Swami Vivekananda* (1907)

Schore began his neuroscientific quest to understand the "heart" or right-brain aspect of the therapeutic relationship by exploring the neuroscience of attachment theory. He is particularly famous for his theory of affective regulation. This theory postulates that a person who has attachment deficits when young fails to develop the requisite ability to regulate their own feelings. His research demonstrates that the effects of early abuse and neglect essentially inhibit the development of the right brain which leads to a propensity to develop problematic behaviors and mental health disorders later in life.

Essentially Schore is arguing that the child's brain requires healthy attachment—primarily to the maternal figure—in order to develop appropriately. Without this healthy attachment, the evolving person essentially has "brain damage" when it comes to regulating his own affect. Fortunately Schore is optimistic and supports the concept of neural plasticity—the brain can continue to develop even much later in life. And, not surprisingly, he sees the process of therapy as the ideal opportunity to accomplish that kind of repair work.

When discussing effective therapy, however, Schore introduces a new concept. Therapy can be done from a right-brain/primal process point of view or it can be done from a left brain/verbal perspective. Since Schore believes that the trauma is centered in the underdeveloped right brain, he recommends a "right brain-to-right brain" emphasis in therapy.

Implicit right brain–to–right brain intersubjective transactions lie at the core of the therapeutic relationship. They mediate what Sander (1992) calls "moments of meeting" between patient and therapist. Current neurobiological data suggest that "While the left hemisphere mediates most linguistic behaviors, the right hemisphere is important for broader aspects of communication" (van Lancker & Cummings, 1999). . . . (J)ust as the left brain communicates its states to other left brains via conscious linguistic behaviors, so the right brain nonverbally communicates its unconscious states to other right brains that are tuned to receive these communications. Regulation theory thus describes how implicit systems of the therapist interact with implicit systems of the patient; psychotherapy is not the "talking" but the "communicating" cure. (Schore, 2012, p. 39)

Schore's extension of attachment theory postulates that all humans are aware of this right brain-to-right brain relationship because this is the same mechanism used by parents—especially mothers—during the developmental process. The infant and young children are unable to self-regulate their own affect. The right-brain-connected mother responds to this deficit by creating an environment of safety. When the infant is stimulated—and especially when the child is overstimulated or stressed—the maternal connection functions to regulate his excessive affect, and models to the child ways to handle uncomfortable feelings. Initially, the parent holds/modulates the child's feelings for him and later his developing right brain learns to do it on his own.

Schore believes that this same holding and modeling process is at the heart of psychotherapy. Therapists and mothers develop the capacity to make this right-brain connection via their own ability to live productive lives and their own abilities to regulate affect. Interestingly, he proposes that this process is unconscious both for the mothers/therapists and for the infants/clients. In support, Schore cites certain mother-infant studies where the mother begins to respond to infant needs in less than 130 milliseconds, an interval that is so short that it precludes conscious deliberation. In sum, the unconscious/primal nature of the right brain-to-right brain connection clearly differentiates this process from the more cognitive, verbal, and conscious left brain form of psychotherapy.

Unfortunately, in situations where the maternal bond was inadequate, the adult client lacks the ability to handle life stressors without experiencing some type of decompensation. When this kind of client enters therapy, his minimal requirement for progress depends on the therapist-client relationship's ability to recreate the environment of safety that was absent in childhood. As the client discusses traumatic events, the healing relationship with the therapist replaces the dysfunctional maternal relationship; this healing relationship is capable of regulating client affect and eventually results in new and more functional neural pathways in the client's brain.

Clearly Schore is discussing the "compassion" side of the therapeutic relationship. Somehow the right brain of the therapist signals to the right brain of the client that they will be safe and secure in the therapeutic environment. This is often experienced by the therapist as an openhearted presence with the client. Conversely the client senses the unconditional availability of the therapist and the implicit permission to lean into that space. Siegel and Gerner, who are Buddhist psychologists with a research focus on developing compassion, agree with Schore that there can be a neuroscientific description of compassion. Note the similarities between how they see the right brain-to-right brain relationship and how Schore describes it.

> Neuroanatomically, social emotions like compassion engage regions in the brain well below the cortex, including the hypothalamus and the brain stem, that are associated with basic metabolic processes and evolutionarily old emotions such as fear (Immordino-Yang, McColl, Damasio, & Damasio, 2009; see also chapter 8). Compassionate brain states also appear to activate the mesolimbic neural system, which may explain why compassion is intrinsically rewarding (Kim et al., 2011). The fight–freeze–flight and competition–reward subsystems in the brain are balanced by a "safeness" subsystem (Depue & Morrone-Strupinsky, 2005; Gilbert, 2009b; see chapter 18). The safeness system is associated with compassion—caregiving and soothing—and appears to be related to the neurotransmitters oxytocin and vasopressin.
>
> Compassionate mind states are typically calming and are characterized by decelerated heart rate (Eisenberg et al., 1988), lower skin conductance (Eisenberg, Fabes, Schaller, Carlo, & Miller, 1991), and vagus nerve activation (Oveis, Horberg, & Keltner, 2009; Porges, 1995, 2001)—the opposite of what occurs in sadness and distress (Goetz et al., 2010). We also have mirror neurons that continually register what others are thinking and feeling (Rizzolatti & Craighero, 2004; Rizzolatti & Sinigaglia, 2010; Siegel, 2007), prompting us to relieve the suffering of others to make ourselves feel better. Finally, it appears that many individuals, especially women, have a "tend and befriend" response to stress, rather than fight and flight (Taylor et al., 2000). In sum, numerous elements in our nervous system predispose us to feel compassion. (Siegel & Germer, 2012, pp. 18–19)

Client recognition of this client-therapist bond is primarily unconscious although it may eventually rise to conscious awareness. It may occur rapidly or even instantaneously. Recall the rather shocking provocative therapy examples from Farrelly, where he moved quickly and in a socially inappropriate manner; such movements are only possible if he has somehow connected to the client so profoundly that the client feels the compassion in spite of the provocative words.

Schore explains these kinds of results by referring to primary process communication. He believes that primary process is essentially a nonverbal communication consisting of items like tone, posture, facial expressions, and so on. The right brain of the therapist conveys its presence via these sorts of communications to the right brain of the client which is designed to receive them. Schore is arguing that it matters little what one says; rather, the therapist's presence and ability to connect to the client on a preverbal level is the most important factor in healing.

Finally, Schore takes an initial look at what is happening inside the right brain of the gifted therapist that enables her superior results. The following quote, which describes therapeutic intuition, is strongly reminiscent of the Rilke and Benshea quotes above which praise the superior wisdom of the heart.

> With regard to implicit cognition, I have recently suggested that primary process cognition underlies clinical intuition, a major factor in therapeutic effectiveness (Schore & Schore, 2008). Indeed, the definition of intuition, "the ability to understand or know something immediately, without conscious reasoning" (Compact Oxford English Dictionary of Current English, 2005), clearly implies right and not left brain processing. Psychological theoreticians now assert that intuition depends on accessing large banks of implicit knowledge formed from unarticulated person—environment exchanges that occur between environmental input and the individual's phenomenological experience (Narvaez, 2010). It operates on a nonverbal level, with little effort, deliberation, or conscious awareness, and is thus characterized as "phenomenally unconscious." (Schore, 2012, pp. 122–123)

Schore is a strong advocate for the unconscious, nonverbal, heart-centered aspect of psychotherapy. He makes a compelling case that the initial "instructions on how to be human" which occur between mother and infant are the correct metaphor for therapeutic relationships in adults. Finally with his invocation of therapeutic intuition, he aligns himself with the quotes above which refer to the innate/superior wisdom of heart over head.

Interestingly, in his discussion of right-brain attributes, Schore includes implicit references to Kahneman's System 1.

> In fact the right brain appraisal of safety or danger in the social environment is essentially performed implicitly at very fast time frames below conscious awareness (see Schore, 2003b, 2004, 2005). Thus, cognition also refers to the right-lateralized social cognition of face processing, which in a relational intersubjective context allows for the appraisal of exteroceptive social cues. In addition, interoceptive sensitivity (Barrett, Quigley, Moreau, & Aronson, 2004)—the tracking of somatovisceral information coming up from the body—is also a cognitive process. Both of these cognitive functions are operations of the right hemisphere, the locus of implicit learning (Hugdahl, 1995). (2012, p. 291)

Kahneman, of course, agrees that the appraisal of danger is done quickly and holistically. If you put together Schore and Kahneman, it is possible to argue that right brain-to-right brain bond is equivalent to a System 1-to-System 1 connection. In this sense, Schore is recommending that the System 1 of the client, which is prone to experience danger in many social environments, can be held, calmed, and soothed via exposure to the System 1 of the therapist. The calmness in the face of real-world challenges moves directly from the unconscious of the therapist to the unconscious of the client—a right brain-to-right brain connection.

The rapid and unconscious nature of the right brain-to-right brain connections make it appear that the therapist either has it or doesn't have it—he is either gifted at unconsciously creating this kind of bond or not. Fortunately the situation is not quite this simple. Therapists are familiar with the sense that they are effectively connected to one client and unable to connect to another. Similarly, even when they have a good history of connection with a certain client, they can become confused or threatened, and "close their hearts" to that client. For example, in the following quote, Gerner describes a situation with an old client who has returned to therapy after a series of life reversals. Note how Gerner becomes aware that he has lost his relationship with the client and what he does to repair it.

Ethan was a middle-aged, previous client who returned to therapy during a life crisis consisting of divorce, financial stress, failing business, and loss of a house. He had the full spectrum of depressive symptoms including insomnia, weight loss, suicidal ideation, and anhedonia. His medications were no longer helping.

I had known Ethan for almost 10 years and had never seen him in such a state. Our previous pattern had been to brainstorm together about his life problems. But this time I became frustrated because each question I raised was met with a web of problems that rendered it meaningless. Eventually Ethan stopped me and asked if I had grown tired of him. He added plaintively, "I know we've known each other for almost a decade, but have you stopped liking me?" That's when I slowed down and took the time to just be with Ethan—and to be with myself. I gave up the rush to fix him and prevent a possible suicide, to avert foreclosure on the home his wife was living in, or to keep him from becoming emotionally disabled. I said to myself, "This is the only moment of our lives, no matter how painful it may be. It's just Ethan and me." I allowed myself to enter Ethan's reality and let his pain become my own.

When I did that, I began to realize how overwhelmed I was feeling and how incapable of helping Ethan I felt. I suspected that Ethan was feeling exactly the same way. Our conversation became much simpler:

*ETHAN:* I don't know what to do.
*CKG:* Neither do I. Certainly not now.
*ETHAN:* I'm really alone here— no wife, no job, nobody.
*CKG:* It's pretty bad, I know.
*ETHAN:* I'm just so overwrought. I wake up in terror.

*CKG:* Terror?

*ETHAN:* Mostly about money, how I'll survive.

*CKG:* Can you feel the terror in your body?

*ETHAN:* Definitely . . . here in my belly. I wake up with a knot in my stomach almost every morning.

I had suspected that Ethan felt fear in his belly because I was feeling the same sensation at the time. As Ethan spoke about his experience, I waited for the muscles in my abdomen to relax—to stop resisting— before I felt ready to return to the subject of how Ethan could safely get through the day. Ethan beat me to it. He stopped calling himself a "complete failure" and wanted to discuss how to stay out of the hospital by nourishing himself with regular meals and going to bed when he felt tired. . . . When Ethan made me stop and pay attention to my own experience in this way, the therapy began to move forward again, this time with much less effort.

Compassion is a skill that allows us to open to sorrow. When we resist the sorrow that arises in our own lives, or fight the pain we feel for others who are suffering, we cannot be compassionate. In the case of Ethan, I was grieving that his life was falling apart, I was afraid he would commit suicide under my watch, and I was vainly trying to recreate the happier times we'd had together in the past. I simply wasn't willing to feel fear and sorrow, both his and mine. (Germer, 2012, pp. 94–95)

This case study suggests that when the therapist gets off center, a "deep breath" and reflection on the possible presence of fear should be the first step. Clearly Germer had lost his ability to establish Schore's right brain-to-right brain relationship although he had experienced it regularly with Ethan in the past. Fortunately he was able to reestablish it fairly easily once he became aware of his level of attachment to outcome.

Germer reports that he was feeling grief, a need to fix Ethan, fear about the suicidal ideation and a general sense of being overwhelmed. This is a common state experienced by therapists as they work with the liminal members of our culture—clients that exist near the edge of the Abyss. As mentioned earlier, it is tempting in such situations to distance ourselves from our discomfort by judging these clients, or diagnosing them, or using some other means of protecting ourselves from the anomic feelings they engender. Germer makes that most difficult of therapeutic maneuvers: turning to face fear and softening toward it when every cell in our body pushes us to fight it or run from it.

Germer's example is, of course, excellent therapy. Moreover, from a Schore perspective, it provides a concrete example of how to reestablish the right brain-to-right brain relationship. It documents that such relationships are fluid and come into and go out of existence. These relationships are not a "you can do it or you can't" kind of thing. They are available in each moment of therapy. Unfortunately, without mindfulness, these relationships can also be lost in the next moment of therapy.

Schore's work provides a different perspective on the development and manifestation of heart and compassion. Perhaps most importantly, by supplying a neurobiological explanation for heart, Schore makes the sense of connection more real, more basic and more achievable. The concept of a right brain-to-right brain connection implies that to be human is to be connected. Moreover, it suggests that focusing on alienation and responding effectively is a basic act in psychotherapy. It implies that we all have an awareness of our level of connection to each other and an assessment of the degree the other is safe, helpful, beneficent or the opposite.

Notice just how many quotes in this chapter laud the superiority of heart over head, of wisdom over compassion. Clearly the Dalai Lama, with his commitment to the equivalence of the two, disagrees. But recall that Western culture is in the midst of a battle between the Premodern and the Modern, between the faith of spiritual revelation and the rationality of the scientific model. Given that the entire culture leans to the right—toward the rational, the empirical, the scientific, and the verbal—is it any wonder that so many deep Western thinkers urge us to emphasize the heart.

In this spirit, Schore points out that certain kinds of abilities are only available to therapists who prioritize heart over head.

Attachment studies strongly support Panksepp's (2008) bold assertion of the primacy of affective neuroscience: "Now cognitive science must re-learn that ancient emotional systems have a power that is quite independent of neocortical cognitive processes" (p. 51). In other words, what is learned cognitively and stored in the left hemisphere has little to do with the affective relational, two-person experiences stored in the right hemisphere. Clinicians can only assess these patterns through their own implicit right brain connections with their clients, that is, by accessing their own bodily-based instinctive responses. (Schore, 2012, p. 400)

Finally, it should be obvious that Schore's work has implications for the concept of charisma. Virtually every use of "heart" in the section above can essentially be replaced by "charisma." The perception of charisma is a right brain-to-right brain experience. Heart helps a client be safe and to regulate dystonic affect; charisma does the same but also works to help a client resolve issues by accepting explanatory mythology and transformative rituals. Recognition of the therapist as a key individual with the right to define reality is a right brain-to-right brain experience.

## LOVE AND THERAPY

One cannot be spiritual as long as one has shame, hatred, or fear.

—Ramakrishna, *The Gospel of Sri Ramakrishna* (1910)

Returning to the chapter on therapeutic wizards: charisma is dependent on the client feeling that the therapist has access to the "secret knowledge," a knowledge that is "divinely bestowed," a knowledge that "licenses" the therapist as a key individual who can change a client by will and suggestion. This secret knowledge is both left brain—discerning the real from the unreal—and right brain—a preverbal and unconscious manifestation of heart connection. Charisma is as dependent on the ability to make a provocative and radical heart connection as it is dependent on the sense that the therapist has access to "the secret."

The following clinical examples are attempts to tell stories that illustrate this level of radical connection. Since heart is present in virtually every clinical interaction, and especially because heart connection is dependent on a right brain-to-right brain recognition, it is difficult to pull out case examples that are "pure heart" or "have more heart." That said, the following vignettes were chosen because they "feel" like such beautiful examples of the therapists connecting and loving. With that, let us move to our first clinical example, a conjoint therapy vignette from Richard and Antra Borofsky (2012).

Carl and Patricia have two children and have been married for six years. Patricia is a stay-at-home Mom and Carl works for a tech company and travels often. They have not had sex for over two years and the relationship is obviously strained.

*RICH:* I would like to ask you to please look at each other for a moment. (pause) Please look for a few seconds and notice how this feels.
*CARL:* (to us) It feels uncomfortable.
*ANTRA:* Could you please tell this to Patricia?
*CARL:* (after a short pause, looking nervously and hesitantly at her) I feel awkward looking at you. It's uncomfortable.
*RICH:* Where in your body do you feel the awkwardness?
*CARL:* (to Rich, looking confused) What do you mean?
*RICH:* Do you feel the awkwardness in your face, in your chest, or somewhere else? . . . Letting her see how you feel uncomfortable, will help her start to understand and care about what it's like for you.
*CARL:* I'm feeling how painful it is that we've become such strangers. (Looks away for a few seconds and then looks back at Patricia.) My face feels all stiff. Kind of like a mask. (pause) Now I'm feeling a lump in my throat.

*PATRICIA:* (beginning to tear up) I have been so angry at you because I have needed you and you haven't been there.

*ANTRA:* (kindly) Patricia, are you feeling angry right now?

*PATRICIA:* (slowly to Antra) No, not right now. (pause) No . . . right now, I'm feeling sad.

*ANTRA:* Please let him see your sadness. (pause) Can you see him seeing how you are sad right now?

*PATRICIA:* (looking at Carl while crying softly) I miss you. I really miss you.

*CARL:* (Silently and slowly reaches over to hold Patricia's hand.)

Later Antra instructs the couple on a couples exercise using a stone egg. She asks them to pass it back and forth without speaking but with a solemn attitude—as if passing something of importance. Passing the egg, the silence becomes more concentrated as they become aware of how they are giving and receiving. Rich then asks them to share with each other how they have been struggling in the marriage as they continue to pass the egg back and forth.

*PATRICIA:* I resent that so much of the burden of caring for our children falls on me.

*RICH:* (to Carl) See if you can open yourself to receiving this. Even if this is painful to hear, see if you can hold this with her. If you are willing, please say, "yes." This "yes" lets her know your willingness to hear and let in how it is for her and to let it sit side by side with how it is for you. This doesn't mean that you agree or see the situation the same way she does.

*CARL:* Well . . . Maybe . . . (pause) well, OK . . . yes . . . I can hear this. I can hold this with you. (Closes his eyes, takes a deep breath, and after a long pause looks at Patricia and reaches for her hand, gently putting the egg in her palm.) I am afraid that no matter what I do, it won't be enough. I feel like a failure.

ANTRA (to Patricia) Please let him know if you're willing to hold this feeling of being a failure with him.

*PATRICIA:* (letting this sink in) Yes. I'm willing to hear this. (pause) As long as you aren't blaming me. So, yes, I'm willing to hold this with you. (Now holds the stone that Carl gave her in both her hands, next to her chest.) (pp. 284–288)

This vignette is an example of working directly with a heart-centered perspective. The Borofskys are implicitly suggesting to the clients that fully and completely accepting and experiencing feelings is a path that will lead to healing and, ultimately, to a level of freedom, authenticity, and love. They are conveying this concept indirectly, through their own nonverbals of calmness, compassion, acceptance, and support. They do not give a lecture about the importance of these concepts; rather, they live them to their clients—they implicitly manifest them.

Emotional work is always more sacred, more frightening, and less predict-able than cognitive work. Emotions are symbolized by water and the chaotic nature of the Abyss is often portrayed as an uncharted and undifferentiated ocean. Emotions are connected with the "left hand of darkness" to use a phrase made famous by Ursula Le Guin. Emotional work tends to embody a ritual and a rite of passage; moving through the experience leaves one transformed.

Therapists who work with emotions effectively—like the Borofskys—are denizens of sacred space. Not only are they unafraid of affect, rather, they are like snake charmers, special people who have the power to touch and handle that which is threatening to most of us. As individuals who can touch the untouchable—the dangerous and forbidden—they have a kind of numinous glow.

Obviously they are using techniques in working with this couple. Initially they teach the couple how to communicate their feelings directly and how to accept them. Next they do a trust building exercise with the stone egg. Although these techniques are present, they are not the active ingredient that creates the movement in Carl and Patricia. Instead, Rich and Antra are modeling how they accept and hold emotions. The couple's vulnerability is sustained and made safe by the fundamental loving and accepting qualities embodied by Rich and Antra. Moreover, they simply "ask" the clients to respond in certain ways—for example, to hold an emotion without judgment and to share something threatening—and the clients comply. Schore would say that there is a right brain-to-right brain connection.

The clients are in an altered state similar to a hypnotic trance. When Rich asked Carl to look directly at Patricia and face their conflict, and then when he asked Carl to turn his anxious emotions into somatic feelings, an expert on hypnosis would argue that Rich was performing a trance induction. Patri-cia's ability to do the same, to take a statement and connect it to her body (the tears), demonstrated that she was completely altered as well. Later, the exercise with the egg yielded identical results. Rich and Antra modeled how to be altered with the egg and the couple quickly went into a trance when they used it as well.

This work is classically Dionysian, not only because the clients are in an altered state, but because they experience that "pop" or disconnection from the Net as they move from one state to another. An equivalent Apollonian intervention might be asking them to give each other two compliments per day. This is a kind and positive intervention but will not result in the "pop" achieved by the Borofskys relatively radical intervention.

While the remainder of the therapy session is not included, the Borofskys do use the last half of the article to articulate the principles underlying their approach. From this, one can imagine that the Borofskys interpreted the implications or meanings of the session to Carl and Patricia; they probably made the case that now that they have been vulnerable, now that they have reacted to their fear with courage and compassion, they are well positioned to have a love-centered marriage that is functional and generative. In this we see the classic Reality B framing approach: "now that you have passed through this effective ritual, you are free to change (you must change) in the direction of health and healing."

The Borofskys used simple techniques which are readily available to most therapists who are taught to explore and validate feelings. The techniques did not create the outcome; in the hands of a lesser therapist, this feelings exploration session would have been far less impactful. But in the hands of charismatic therapists, the clients were persuasively invited to behave in a manner cued by the therapists and experience tears, a wish to support each other, and mini-epiphanies of how they had missed each other and wanted nothing more than to give and receive love and support.

Our second example comes from Stephen Levine and takes place at a workshop.

In a workshop some years ago during a grief exploration focused on distrust and fear, a fellow stood in the back of the room and walked hesitantly down the aisle toward the podium. He was growling that this was not the world we could trust. His footsteps were heavy and his tone very frightened and angry. As he approached the front of the room one could sense a rising fear in some of the participants who viewed this person as "something of a madman and a danger." The group belly had tightened.

Swinging his head from side to side, as if expecting an ambush, his frightened heart screamed, "you can't trust the world! It out to get you! You got to be ready to fight!" As he approached closely enough for our eyes to meet, I said to him, "I'm glad you came here. This is a good place to work. You know, you're like someone wearing a bulletproof vest." Stopping, he pulled up his sweater, "I'm not like someone with a bulletproof vest. I am someone with a bulletproof vest." Beneath his shirt was displayed the shiny gray Dacron of his trembling heart's defenses. "But," he asked me, "what am I to do about armor-piercing bullets?" To let down his guard would have been, for him, to step off the edge of the flat world. There was no safety anywhere. He was terrified Narcissus seeking to protect the armoring of the heart from being penetrated.

It was clear that only kindness would do. Anything "rational" I might have said would've just fed into the well-established paranoia of his grief. Calling a "bathroom break" for the workshop, I walked a dozen feet to where this fellow stood, shaking. As I went to put my arms around him, he stiffened. But when I whispered, "the arms of the mother are always around you, all you need to do is put your head on her shoulder." He began to sob. His armoring broke and his enormous heart exposed itself. He was the personification of our grief, seques-tered layer by layer over the heart. He was all the parts of ourselves we have armored ourselves against. His bulletproof vest was a cast for his broken heart. He was the wounded Angel of us all. (Levine & Levine, 1996, pp. 112–113)

The boldness of Levine's intervention in this instance was remarkable. This was not a logical intervention. It was decided by the heart and carried out through the heart. One can imagine the effect on the frightened man; he manifested all of his darkness and was met in love and transformed in love.

Levine's wonderful response epitomizes so many heart interventions. There is the sense of pain and confusion in the client. There is an overt or covert message that they exist outside of the possibility of connection and compassion. There is the movement toward the person by the therapist—fully aware of the dangerous possibilities of the moment but manifesting a spontaneous courage. There is initial resistance where the therapist needs to stay the course and remain aligned with the heart. Finally there is the breakthrough where the armor is pierced, the dam bursts, and all the loneliness and hopelessness pours out. This is the essence of heart-centered therapy. This is what Schore means by the right brain-to-right brain connection.

One can certainly imagine the altered state in the client. He might have chosen to push Levine away, or could have discounted his hug as "touchy feely"; instead, he accepted it. In accepting it, he was catapulted out of his reality of being an unlovable person in an immensely dangerous world. In accepting the hug and the love it implied, he radically recreated his connections to the Net and his reality.

The final example consists of a famous story about Martin Buber's encounter with a student. The story credits this experience as central to Buber's insistence on making relationship and connection central to his own path and to his teachings.

Buber had been upstairs in his rooms meditating and praying one morning, fully engaged in deeply religious intensity, when there was a knock at his front door downstairs. He was taken out of his spiritual moment and went down to see who was at the door. It was a young man who had been a student and a friend, and who had come specifically to speak with Buber.

Buber was polite with the young man, even friendly, but was also hoping to soon get back to his meditations. The two spoke for a short time and then the young man left. Buber never saw him again because the young man was killed in battle (or perhaps committed suicide, the story is not entirely clear). Later, Buber learned from a mutual friend that the young man had come to him that day in need of basic affirmation, had come with a need to understand his life and what it was asking of him. Buber had not recognized the young man's need at the time because he had been concerned to get back upstairs to his prayers and meditation. He had been polite and friendly, he says, even cordial, but had not been *fully present*. He had not been present in the way that one person can be present with another, in such a way that you sense the questions and concerns of the other even before they themselves are aware of what their questions are. "Ever since then," says Buber "I have given up the sacred. Or rather it has given me up. I know now no fullness but each mortal hour's fullness" of presence and mystery. The Mystery, he says, was no longer "out there" for him, but was instead to be found in the present moment with the present person, in the present world. (Goldberg, 2011)

And so, charisma is as dependent on heart as it is on head. Given the nature of empirical Western thought, many writers and teachers elevate right brain over left when it comes to therapy and healing. The Dalai Lama—with his teaching about the equivalence of the two—is almost certainly right in the big picture, but when a therapist is considering her own personal development, Buber's advice about the primacy of heart is of great value.

## SOUL MAKING

Whoever fights monsters should see to it that in the process he does not become a monster. And if you gaze long enough into an abyss, the abyss will gaze back into you.

—Friedrich Nietzsche, *Beyond Good and Evil:*
*Prelude to a Philosophy of the Future* (1907)

One of the primary purposes of the Net is to shield us from the entropic, terrifying, and destructive properties of the Abyss. Regardless of the strength of the Net, the Abyss always breaks through. Sometimes the breakthroughs are external such as illness and aging, sometimes they are social such as divorce or job loss, and sometimes they are internal such as anxiety attacks and depression.

The internal breakthroughs—that is, psychological symptoms—are experienced as alien and independent. The apparent independence of such symptoms led psychology to postulate the existence of the unconscious mind, a part of the psyche that lies outside conscious control. Psychology has responded to this often terrifying and self-destructive part of the psyche by developing a myriad of approaches designed to control it, understand it, and minimize its negative impact.

Experientially and symbolically the unconscious mind is equivalent to the Abyss. Both are overwhelming and both attempt to overthrow the control of the ego. The preferred strategy for both is often denial—Becker's denial of death outwardly and the individual's denial of primal feelings inwardly. It takes courage to explore each one. Finally, there are promises that such exploration will eventually uncover the oracular and harmonious qualities implicit in the unconscious. Many depth psychologists, in agreement with the epigraph above, promise that the exploration of the unconscious will lead to an awakening—a day-break.

This book has already outlined two main paths that lead to an experience of the Abyss. The constructionists and the spiritual seekers tell us that deconstructing our social programming leads to the edge of the Abyss. The heart-centered healers tell us that choosing connection versus alienation at the most challenging life moments leads to the same place. Now we have the depth psychologists—Jung, Hillman, Campbell, and a host of others—promising that an exploration of the unconscious, and particularly, an exploration of painful affective breakthroughs, leads to the same goal.

Hillman, for example, elevates the meaning of these breakthroughs to the highest level; he calls the process of dialog with the unconscious and the Abyss-related breakthroughs "soul making" and even believes that the essential functioning of the psyche requires a kind of "pathologizing."

> The psyche does not exist without pathologizing. Since the unconscious was discovered as an operative factor in every soul, pathologizing has been recognized as an inherent aspect of the interior personality. (Hillman, 1997, p. 70)

The unconscious mind is a dark place, dangerous, uncharted, and full of demons. It is the shadow side of the conscious mind—the place where the power of the ego holds no sway. The nature of the unconscious is always described metaphorically. How can it be otherwise when, by definition, it is out of view of the conscious mind? This is important enough to be repeated: because it is completely out of view, all definitions of the unconscious mind are constructions and metaphors, most of which incorporate the concept that the unconscious is the *opposite* of the qualities of the conscious mind. It is dark instead of light; it is chaotic as opposed to ordered; and its meanings are hidden instead of apparent. As an example, examine this summary of Jung's definition of the shadow.

> The shadow, said celebrated Swiss psychiatrist C. G. Jung, is the unknown "dark side" of our personality—dark both because it tends to consist predominantly of the primitive, negative, socially or religiously depreciated human emotions and impulses like sexual lust, power strivings, selfishness, greed, envy, anger or rage, and due to its unenlightened nature, completely obscured from consciousness. Whatever we deem evil, inferior or unacceptable and deny in ourselves becomes part of the shadow, the counterpoint to what Jung called the persona or conscious ego personality. (Diamond, 2012)

The unconscious is full of everything we fear, everything we reject, everything we do not understand, and everything that shames us. Little wonder that it is impenetrable.

That said, there is general agreement among all depth psychologists that knowing one's shadow, deciphering its messages, and being open to its feedback is one of the primary keys to a successful human life. Jung believes that "(u)ntil you make the unconscious conscious, it will direct your life and you will call it fate" (as cited in Wernik, 2016, p. 171). And, in an even more serious warning, he comments:

A man who is unconscious of himself acts in a blind, instinctive way and is in addition fooled by all the illusions that arise when he sees everything that he is not conscious of in himself coming to meet him from outside as projections upon his neighbor. (Jung, 1983, p. 335)

Jung tells us that any meaningful personal growth requires dealing with this shadow.

Unfortunately there can be no doubt that man is, on the whole, less good than he imagines himself or wants to be. Everyone carries a shadow, and the less it is embodied in the individual's conscious life, the blacker and denser it is. If an inferiority is conscious, one always has a chance to correct it. Furthermore, it is constantly in contact with other interests, so that it is continually subjected to modifications. But if it is repressed and isolated from consciousness, it never gets corrected. (Jung, 2014b, p. 131)

In sum, unless an individual is aware of the darkness within, that darkness will essentially run one's life. Moreover, the power of the unconscious will be hidden from the unaware person; they will assume that all their problems are on the outside when actually these problems are projections of their own darkness. As Jung says: "Knowing your own darkness is the best method for dealing with the darknesses of other people" (as cited in Hart, 2007, p. 28).

Jung and the other depth psychologists of course recommend an exploration of the unconscious and then an integration of it into conscious life.

The shadow is a moral problem that challenges the whole ego-personality, for no one can become conscious of the shadow without considerable moral effort. To become conscious of it involves recognizing the dark aspects of the personality as present and real. This act is the essential condition for any kind of self-knowledge. (Jung, 2014a, p. 14)

Breakthroughs of the Abyss—eruptions of the unconscious—occur often. There is a constant ongoing dialog between the ego and the unconscious. The more one pays attention, the more one is aware of this dialog. The more one ignores or represses the unconscious, the more likely that the eruption will be dramatic and overwhelming or covert and sabotaging.

Conversely, the more one opens dialog with the unconscious, the more it functions as friend and ally. An individual begins shadow work with the sense that they need to master a difficult or wounded part of himself. But as one continues the dialog with the Abyss, a new conception emerges. In the following quote, Jung is not talking about mastering the Shadow, or eliminating it, or even working with the Shadow; essentially he argues that integrating the Shadow creates a new sense of the nature of the Self. After repeated dialogs with Shadow, the Self begins to live permanently in the space between the unconscious and the conscious mind. In the language of this book, the individual lives in the space between the Abyss and the Net—he is "dancing with the Abyss." And Jung is not simply recommending that therapists live in that space. He argues that becoming fully human requires placing the Self between those two seeming opposites of form and formlessness.

> To confront a person with his shadow is to show him his own light. Once one has experienced a few times what it is like to stand judgingly between the opposites, one begins to understand what is meant by the self. Anyone who perceives his shadow and his light simultaneously sees himself from two sides and thus gets in the middle. (Jung, 1970, p. 872)

Tillich would agree. The ultimate concern always integrates doubt with faith; it always points toward the Ultimate—and participates in it—but never fully arrives. Living in the space between dark and light, befriending both sides without needing to be possessed by one or the other, that is the ideal state of the depth psychologists. It is also the ideal state of the Reality B therapist.

This process of identifying the unconscious forces, understanding them, and attempting to distill their meaning and to work with them is often entitled "embracing the shadow." This process is common in therapy and several vignettes illustrating it have already been offered above. For example, the eating-disordered teen recovered quickly once she affirmed that the part that supported the eating disorder was simply an ego state that aspired to excellence run amuck. And the business man who cheated on his girlfriend secondary to his dread of ever letting a woman go essentially recovered after honoring the emotional needs of the child part. In both these examples, a part which had been vilified and rejected was approached with respect and appreciation. An exploration was conducted which revealed good intentions underlying the negative/compulsive behaviors. After validating the good intentions, the part could be integrated with the whole psyche. As a result, the negative behaviors/feelings were eliminated.

Virtually all of the dissociative techniques described in the previous chapter can be described as versions of embracing the shadow. Any time a client stands in one part of himself—often a healthy, strong, or adult part—and reaches out toward a wounded part, or a compulsive part, or a critical part—some form of embracing the shadow is taking place.

In addition to interpreting symptoms as messages from the unconscious, depth psychology famously sees dreams as another form of unconscious communication. The dreams can be worked with in varying ways from seeing them as a source of insight, or dialoging with them to release emotions or trauma, or even treating them as oracular pronouncements. The following example of dream work comes from my practice and exemplifies using dreams as oracles. What makes this example a bit unusual is that the dream—which was experienced by the husband—was adopted by the couple as a guide for both of them—a kind of road map for their marital therapy.

A married couple in their late 40s were separated but desired reconciliation. They were both beauticians; she had a steady and successful practice and his business was always struggling. Originally from France, they had moved here 20 years ago. They had two grown children who were successfully on their own.

After being married for over 20 years, they had separated a year and a half ago because of constant fighting. In the past 6 months, he had decided that he was not only still in love with his wife, but reconciliation was necessary from a spiritual point of view. He had an extensive background in studying spiritual texts and teachers. She was somewhat sympathetic to these ideas but distrusted his tendency to move rapidly from one approach to another especially because he often declared the latest ideas as "the ultimate." She also distrusted him because he was frequently critical of her and the children and was particularly outspoken whenever she gained a few pounds. Both spouses were attractive and spoke with appealing French accents. He noted that she worked all the time—she only took Sundays off—and had made a number of bad investment decisions which resulted in losing most of their savings. One big investment had been done behind his back and the other against his advice.

The first session consisted of gathering the background information above and assessing the level of commitment to reconciliation. He was very enthusiastic about reconciliation and argued that they should simply forget the past and start fresh. Dwelling on the past, he said, was simply being a prisoner to fear and he wanted her to "quit contracting." She claimed that she still loved him deeply in her heart—especially since they had been sweethearts since high school—but was clear that she didn't trust him, didn't want to live with him, and was unwilling to make love with him.

At the beginning of the second session, the husband reported the following dream.

I am in a nice house and I know that my wife is upstairs in a room. I go up a stairway to find her and notice that, although it is a very nice stairway, it is littered with large, abandoned, and broken down items that make the passage difficult. At the top of the stairs, I find the room. However the door has been recently blocked by something like masonry and the male worker inside has reduced the doorway to a small window. He is not friendly and tells me there is no passage this way but perhaps there is another way.

I pick my way back down the stairs with much effort and go outside to try and find the other way in. I see that I must cross the neighbor's property to get to the back. The neighbor is difficult and bothered by my presence. I request passage across his property and directions to the back door. I feel nervous about asking but he grudgingly gives the directions.

I proceed to the back door and enter into a large room. There are a number of people there including my wife who has taken the form of a brash and shallow male that we both knew in our childhood. On a very large TV is a deceased friend who was the embodiment of loving kindness when he was alive. He is talking to me and my wife.

Inspired by his loving words, we embrace and I find my wife in my arms, not the brash young man.

The husband reported that this dream had felt very important to him and that he had awoken with a positive feeling that somehow all would be well. He had told the dream to the wife prior to the therapy session and she also had a positive feeling about it.

We discussed the dream together and arrived at the following interpretation. The husband, who was enthusiastic about an immediate reconciliation based on "forgetting the past and having a fresh start," needed to drop that plan. Instead, he should recognize that his wife wanted to begin by reviewing key incidences in the past (stepping carefully down the stairs taking note of the debris) with a focus on processing interactions with the neighbor and the final reconciliation would be revealed as we went along. All agreed that the dream was positive and all agreed to use it as a basic guide in terms of the direction of therapy.

The next few sessions consisted of a review of key conflicts in the past that embodied his critical side. As we processed the events, he typically started defensively but was able to take responsibility relatively quickly. The wife worked hard on her willingness to be direct and assertive, even if it hurt his feelings. Both reported feeling as if there was progress in resolving the issues.

At the beginning of the next session, the husband said with some frustration, "we've been working hard but I don't feel like we are any closer. She still seems disinterested and closed off to me." As he made the statement, he crossed his arms across his chest to illustrate her "closed down" feeling. She nodded as he said this in silent agreement.

I asked whether her "closed off" stance reminded either of any part of the dream and both identified the attitude of the neighbor. Questioning her on why she felt so closed off, she quickly said that he continues to act needy in their interactions—continually questioning her on whether she feels there has been progress and wanting to know when they will be together. She reported that she found these "needy" interactions sad and didn't want to hurt him but she also experienced them as a "big turnoff." They dialoged about whether he was capable of controlling this child part of himself. Initially he said that he couldn't but when she made it clear that she was unable to be attracted to him as long as he acted this way, he made a commitment to deal with his child part. He made an individual appointment with me in this regard, and was able to make some progress in terms of healing this part.

At the next couple's session I suggested that he had done the bulk of changing and perhaps we should look at a part of the dream that offered her an opportunity to grow. We focused on her incarnation as the brash young childhood acquaintance. The couple said that this acquaintance was famous for telling stories that put him in a good light but were exaggerations. He wasn't a bad person but was untrustworthy and anything he said couldn't be counted on.

The couple agreed that the wife never told such stories but both immediately focused on the inauthentic quality of the young man. Like him, the wife had frequently supported decisions that she didn't agree with and avoided conflict from fear or self-doubt. Then, in hindsight, she would dislike herself and dislike her husband for pressuring her into the positions. Both agreed that as long as the wife avoided making decisions based on her inner truth—instead of fear-based decisions—the relationship was unlikely to prosper.

Within a week of her vowing to make authentic, inner-wisdom-centered decisions, the wife underwent a surgical procedure which resulted in some unpleasant complications that caused her to be in significant pain—and under the influence of analgesic medication—for about a week. The husband helped nurse her and was very supportive. About half way through her recovery, he asked her if he could move in—just for a few months cause he had no place to go—and she agreed. At the same time, she got very busy at work and did not come into therapy for almost 2 months.

When they resumed, their condo was in escrow and they needed to move within 3 weeks. The wife was adamant that she did not want to live with the husband and he began to alternately threaten and beseech her to change her mind. First he said that if she didn't find a place with him, the marriage was over immediately. Ten minutes later he offered to have patience if she would just let him live with her for 90 days in order to make her love him. The wife was firm about not living with him and told him that his combination of threats and begging was not only confusing, it was unattractive.

I pointed out that allowing him to live with her when she was recovering from the operation was exactly the kind of behavior the dream had cautioned against; she had abandoned her authentic feelings and given in to his neediness and begging. Moreover, letting him in under those circumstances would preclude making any progress in terms of their intimacy. Upon reflection, she agreed and stated that she had experienced a peculiar feeling over the past two months of living together where she felt self-conscious about allowing him to see her partially disrobed and completely adverse to him seeing her naked although they had been married many years. Essentially she endorsed the concept that allowing him into her house out of fear and manipulation doomed the possibility of becoming closer over the two months.

At this point, the husband began to panic at the idea that the wife might be able to stand up to him. He gave her an ultimatum, "Let me live with you or I will terminate the relationship." She held strong and they separated once and for all.

While a number of techniques were employed in the vignette, it was included to illustrate the oracular nature of the Abyss/Unconscious Mind. All three of us treated the dream like a symbolic instruction manual that, if followed correctly, offered a plan for reconciliation and enhanced intimacy. Their refusal to follow it during the surgery phase slowed the process down enormously. And, while they were busy during those two months selling their condo, both agreed that dropping out of therapy at that exact moment was primarily due to their knowledge that—because of the roadmap inherent in the dream—I was unlikely to endorse their plan of living together. The wife regrouped and began to follow the implicit instructions of the dream. The husband, conversely, in choosing to disregard the dream instructions, moved in a direction that led to terminating the relationship.

This case can be framed as a failure of marital therapy, an empowerment experience for the wife, or a tragedy for the husband. Each is true from its own perspective. A more interesting question, however, is the accuracy/helpfulness of the dream material.

Constructionism sees waking and conscious life is a construction; therefore, it is consistent to argue that dream material—and especially dream interpretations—are even more constructed. But dream material, because it comes from the unconscious, always has a numinous quality that suggests some kind of validity beyond mere constructionism. In spite of this numinosity, it seems absurd to argue that dreams are true and accurate instructions from the unconscious. The fact that different therapists interpret the same dream differently destroys that thesis.

The Jerome Frank model offers a solution to this dilemma. Rituals that are invested with belief by therapist and client are both more powerful and more effective. The numinosity of dreams suggests the presence of a kind of existential validity—a validity which often seems to infuse the resulting ritual. In this sense, anything that encourages client and therapist to revere the power of dreams and the accuracy of the interpretation will make the dream work more effective.

Even more important, however, is that with soul making, shadow work, and heart connection, the numinosity points beyond itself. Apollonian work celebrates the primacy of the conscious mind and the worth and the importance of the individual. The work in this chapter moves past the individual and endorses a feeling of powers beyond self. To put it another way, depth psychology and shadow work offer the opportunity to relate to the oracular side of the Abyss; there is a sense of connection to something existential and, perhaps, something spiritual.

In sum, affect in constructed space can be understood from a variety of perspectives. Apollonian therapies see affect as essentially dangerous and attempt to subordinate it to conscious control and the ego. Affect is close to the Abyss; it is dark, unconscious, and threatening. Apollonian forces necessarily take vows to resist affect, correctly sensing that it is implicitly committed to undermining order and predictability.

Reality B psychologists, however, are committed to working with Dionysian forces without subordinating them to the ego. Moreover, they understand that charisma ultimately flows from the Abyss. In pursuit of the accumulation of charisma, it is necessary to experience the affective nature of constructed reality in itself without attempting to reduce it to irrational thoughts, trauma, and mislearnings. And, of course, the best way to master a field of study is to choose to teach it to another.

## THE ABYSS AS ORACLE

The "kingdom of God" is not something one waits for; it has no yesterday or tomorrow, it does not come "in a thousand years"—it is an experience within a heart; it is everywhere, it is nowhere.

—Friedrich Nietzsche, *The Antichrist* (1895)

The Abyss is typically seen as terrifying and destructive. Yet in the last section, the depth psychologists argued that when the Abyss is approached appropriately, it can be a force for empowerment, understanding, and meaning. In this sense, a breakthrough of the Abyss can have an oracular quality.

That said, the Abyss is never to be touched lightly given that its most prominent qualities are anomia and disintegration. Paradoxically, that is what is potentially most attractive about it. The Net is so solid and substantial, that the only way to "wake up" is to be shaken out of sleep, often violently and painfully.

In that sense, the Abyss has always had a special place in mysticism and spiritual life; it is feared and respected—seen as the great threat and the great blessing simultaneously. Martin Buber has written about this generative aspect of the Abyss. In the quote below Buber shows his reverence for the Abyss and particularly emphasizes the part it plays in moving from the secular to the spiritual.

Buber underlined the fact that the collapse of the secure and harmonious world of childhood would come sooner or later to every person and the abyss at his feet would suddenly become visible. "All religious reality," . . . Buber was to state many years later, "comes when our existence between birth and death becomes incomprehensible and uncanny, when all security is shattered through the mystery." (Friedman, 1988, p. 155)

Moreover, Buber calls us to voluntarily cast ourselves into the Abyss.

> (Y)our motto will be: God and danger. For danger is the door of deep reality, and reality is the highest price of life and God's eternal birth. . . . All creation stands on the edge of being; all creation is risk. . . . You must descend ever anew into the transforming abyss, risk your soul ever anew, ever anew dedicated to the holy insecurity. (Buber, 1964, pp. 98–99)

In these two quotes Buber discusses the evolution in consciousness from the "secure world of childhood" to the experience of the Abyss. He lauds "holy insecurity." Buber is urging man to move beyond "joining the tribe" and fulfilling simple human needs. At some point, in order to proceed further along the Tillichian path, an immersion in the Abyss becomes necessary.

Buber suggests that after one becomes a fully enfranchised member of the culture, the next task is the "collapse of the secure and harmonious world." Premature collapse into the Abyss only generates terror and decompensation. Staying too long in the culturally sanctioned world invites idolatry. Joining a culture in the wrong way can lead to a violation of the soul. In Tillich's words, the healthiest ultimate concern can become idolatrous if pursued in the wrong way or at the wrong time.

Hillman, Jung, and other depth psychologists believe that the breakthroughs of the Abyss, in the form of pathologizing, dreams, or terrifying epiphanies, serve as maps and "marching orders." Of course, they would agree, the oracular instructions in the experiences are symbolic and often hidden—they need interpretation and working through—but at the end of the day, they are messages that show the way. Campbell agrees and also notes the secret qualities of the Abyss.

> The separateness apparent in the world is secondary. Beyond that world of opposites is an unseen, but experienced, unity and identity in us all. (Osbon, 1995, p. 25)

The perennial philosophy has been mentioned previously; advocates of this approach argue that philosophers and seekers from all cultures across all time periods come up with common principles for living deeply and thoughtfully. One of the common terms in the perennial philosophy is the concept of the "secret knowledge." The most common form of the secret knowledge is constructionism itself—the concept that all we hold dear and believe in so passionately is essentially "made up." A second form of secret knowledge is what Campbell has just referred to: the hidden connections that unite us all. A final form is the one emphasized in this chapter: the Abyss is outwardly horrible but inwardly oracular and healing. The meaninglessness is paradoxically the source of meaning.

This chapter asks the therapist to shift from an affiliation with the Net to a stance which is much closer to the Abyss. The clarity, simplicity, and mastery of the Net recedes to be replaced by feelings that lead without clear direction, shadow work that may be soulful but rarely results in complete resolution, and a pervasive mystery that refuses to be dispelled. This is, indeed, a different place in constructed reality—a location older, more fecund. Those who can make such a place their home must evolve from the relative daylight of the Net.

Some therapists have problems with shadow work and emotions; just as many may be challenged by assuming the mantle of power implicit in the Apollonian therapies. Enhancing charisma requires a commitment to move forward regardless of the comfort level. Lest this seem too heavy, Walt Whitman has some reassuring words. "Keep your face always toward the sunshine—and shadows will fall behind you."

# Chapter 12

# The Other Royal Road

## Social Determinants of Change

Dreams are the royal road to the Unconscious.

—Sigmund Freud, *The Dream Problem* (1916)

No therapist can explore the geography of constructed reality without exploring one of the strongest forces that sustains it: social validation. Understandably, this book has concentrated on the power of charismatic individual to change the structure of reality. This chapter puts that focus aside and examines how to work with the social forces that sustain the Net and the individual.

Constructed reality is dependent on social concurrence. In that sense, reality is structured, supported, and changed by the client's interactions with his primary social group. To belong to a group is to adopt its values and worldview. This can be a force for evolution or devolution, of course, but when it is positive, it results in a kind of graceful and relatively effortless change.

In this sense, the "royal road" of change is through understanding and working with the social aspect of clients. Therapists understandably focus on the kind of right brain-to-right brain connections that occur in individual therapy, but it is just as heart-connected to focus on the interconnections between the client and his social groups.

This is particularly true because the "I" that exists when I interact with one group is often quite different than the "I" that is present with a different group. The chapter on identity offered many examples of how easily a person can shift personas with the correct cues and there are no cues more important than social cues. The question of whether the "I" at work is truly different than the "I" at home has already been explored; what is more important is that constructionism allows us—nay, requires us—to work effectively with all the implicit possibilities. More specifically, being heart connected as a therapist requires us to feel all of the connections between the client and others and have a willingness to creatively intervene when appropriate.

The chapter on identity examined how the Self manifested at different places in constructed reality. The unitary self was championed by the Apollonians; Dionysians prefer multiple selves both to release shame and guilt and to enhance the possible. Eastern spirituality tells us that there is another form of self—no self or universal self—that fits the more Abyss-centered aspects of constructed reality. In the same way, therapists are enjoined to work with the social forces that surround the client. One can use structured groups and social roles to meet Apollonian goals, process groups and high impact retreats to meet Dionysian goals, and Sanghas to work with spiritual ends. Social endorsement is the glue that holds everything together. Working effectively and consciously with social determinants is a primary goal of the constructionist therapist.

And we will typically be delighted at the possibilities that open up when we do. I recall an example from my own practice that will probably sound familiar to most therapists.

> Some years back a young man in his mid 20's was referred to me by his parents. It seems that this young man had done well in high school and received adequate to good grades and had many friends, but at present he was disinterested in going to college. Instead, he had found a job in construction. He continued to live at home, worked diligently at his job, and partied hard every weekend. The parents were worried about his lack of interest in adult goals and so had referred him to me to work on his values and maturity.
>
> The young man was a pleasant person and, even though he was being "forced" into therapy, had resolved to make the best of it; after 3 or 4 sessions we were making steady, albeit modest, progress towards clarifying his attitude towards "growing up."
>
> Now this young man had a best friend, who worked with him at his construction job and who partied with him every weekend. He was more-or-less a carbon copy of the person I was working with. Around the fifth session with my client he came in with some news. It seemed that the friend had accidentally gotten his girlfriend pregnant. After some reflection, he had decided to marry her. He had approached his parents about helping him go back to school because, of course, now that he was about to be a father, he needed to step up and be a responsible provider.

Of course this was more of a change due to accepting a new social role versus direct influence from a group. But role acceptance is a form of group influence; the role is defined by group expectations and in stepping up to "being a father," the friend was doing what was necessary to maintain the respect of his social group.

Without any attempt to set up an experiment, I had been presented with evidence bearing on the relative power of changes secondary to role acceptance versus changes due to therapy. Certainly no psychotherapist would be surprised at my story; what is important, however, are the implications of it. Stepping up to a role change transformed the friend profoundly in a week's time. I was going to need ten or twenty weeks of therapy to achieve the same result and, even then, I suspected that my psychotherapy result would not be as solid as the changes engendered by role acceptance.

These kinds of changes are familiar to every therapist. For example, a high school student who goes off to college is often exposed to a different peer group with different worldviews. Typically such exposure results in inculcating new values, choices, and behaviors in a fairly effortless manner. These changes often involve beliefs that are radically different than the values implicit in one's family of origin. The new beliefs result in different behaviors and in choosing different experiences and often culminate in the individual living a completely different life than they might have experienced if they had stayed in the original home town. These changes happen fairly rapidly and often last for the rest of the individual's life.

Similar changes can occur if a person picks a certain profession or moves to a certain city. For example, getting a position in a major Wall Street firm on graduation from college is likely to result in far different worldview alterations than taking a position at a home town bank. Working as an international journalist will create a radically different personality than selling insurance in Topeka. And virtually everyone has a story about a person who "found religion" and almost overnight adopted changes that were permanent or at least lasted for many years.

Like the example above, adopting certain roles in life typically generates profound changes. We say, "becoming a father made him grow up" referring to adopting a new worldview associated with maturity, other-centeredness, and stability. Similarly, a leadership role at work or at church can create significant changes in confidence, risk taking, and social functioning without much effort whereas a similar demand by one's psychologist might be met by resistance and slow growth. Finally, possibilities of reward—whether it be monetary reward, a desirable marital or social position, or fame/recognition—will often result in meaningful changes that are accomplished rapidly and with little resistance. Significant "carrots or sticks" often create changes in values, behaviors, choices, and maturity much more effectively and effortlessly than psychotherapy.

Such examples not only affirm the power of the social group, they also speak to the ease of change and the essential fluidity of constructed reality. As was discussed above, the Reality B therapist is marked by his belief that change is easier than commonly thought. Conversely, the Apollonian therapist argues that change is difficult or slow. The relative ease of change seen in via the influence of a new peer group—particularly when it is associated with significant rewards or punishments—completely supports the concept of fluidity and ease of change.

Therapists typically create or contribute to social change in a straightforward manner—that is, they directly recommend that the client become affiliated with a new group or they urge that the client adopt the new and more constructive set of values. In contrast to that kind of directness, there is a well-known story of Milton Erickson making such a suggestion but in his own, characteristically indirect, fashion.

Erickson was asked to visit the aunt of one of his colleagues because he was concerned that she was seriously depressed. The aunt was wealthy, and lived in an old family mansion; she was in her 60s and medical problems had put her in a wheelchair. Unmarried and without any close relatives, she was socially isolated and had had some suicidal ideation.

The aunt met Erickson at the front door and gave him a tour of her dark and old-fashioned house. At the end of the house tour, she showed Erickson her greenhouse.

The aunt saved the very best for last, however, and finally ushered Erickson into the greenhouse nursery attached to the house. This was her pride and joy; she had a green thumb and spent many happy hours working with the plants. She proudly showed him her latest project—taking cuttings from her African violets and starting new plants.

In the discussion that followed, Erickson found out that the woman was very isolated. She had previously been quite active in her local church, but since her confinement to a wheelchair she attended church only on Sundays. Because there was no wheelchair access to the church, she hired her handyman to give her a ride to church and lift her into the building after services had started, so she wouldn't disrupt the flow of foot traffic into the church. She also left before services had ended, again so she wouldn't block traffic.

After hearing her story, Erickson told her that her nephew was worried about how depressed she had become. She admitted that it had become quite serious. But Erickson told her that he thought depression was not really the problem. It was clear to him that her problem was that she was not being a very good Christian. She was taken aback by this and began to bristle, until he explained. "Here you are with all this money, time on your hands, and a green thumb. And it's all going to waste. What I recommend is that you get a copy of your church membership list and then look in the latest church bulletin. You'll find announcements of births, illnesses, graduations, engagements, and marriages in there—all the happy and sad events in the life of people in the congregation. Make a number of African violet cuttings and get them well established. Then repot them in gift pots and have your handyman drive you to the homes of people who are affected by these happy or sad events. Bring them a plant and your congratulations or condolences and comfort, whichever is appropriate to the situation." Hearing this, the woman agreed that perhaps she had fallen down in her Christian duty and agreed to do more.

Twenty years later, as I was sitting in Erickson's office, he pulled out one of his scrap-books and showed me an article from the Milwaukee Journal (or whatever the local paper was called). It was a feature article with a large headline that read "African Violet Queen of Milwaukee Dies, Mourned by Thousands." The article detailed the life of this incredibly caring woman who had become famous for her trademark flowers and her charitable work with people in the community for the ten years preceding her death. (O'Hanlon, 2000, pp. 6–8)

If Erickson had been more direct, he would have suggested she become an important person in the church—perhaps some sort of a "designated greeter"—but it is likely that this idea would have been rejected by the depressed woman as "too demanding." He worked around this potential resistance with his characteristic elegance and grace; his skillfulness is the usual reason that this example is cited. But for our purposes, he simply connected her to a group in a way that ensured that she would be in a powerful and meaningful role that had the potential to be self-sustaining. Erickson's skill and charisma got her going but it was the power of the healthy group and the meaningful role that proved healing and transformative in the end.

The important point is not how the client is motivated to connect to the healing group experience; rather, one should think hard about how powerful these kinds of experiences are in comparison to the traditional hour of therapy. In most cases, these interventions are much more powerful and long lasting than the effects of therapy. That being true, it is probably worth investing a significant amount of time in the room planning and carrying out such referrals.

Most of these kinds of referrals result in Apollonian changes: evolutions in social roles, connections to more motivated and high status people, and exposure to values that allow the client more mobility, fluidity, and hardiness. While this is true, it is also possible to refer to groups that explicitly cultivate Dionysian experiences and growth. In the case below, I worked with a young person whose world was so dominated by ideas of "should and ought" that he hardly had room to breathe.

Mark was a 20-year-old Caucasian male was referred to me by his mother for treatment of depression. It seems that the young man had gotten lost in high school and had a poor experience characterized by no significant friends, no girlfriends, lots of video games, and lots of marijuana. He eventually dropped out of high school and started abusing his Adderall and later graduated to full scale methamphetamine use. In the eight months before I saw him, Mark had become sober, was attending AA, and had gotten a GED. He still hated school, was socially isolated, and felt he had no sense of direction. He was working in a restaurant but barely made enough to pay his bills and was living with his mother.

At the initial session he presented with a "heavy" demeanor—characterized by lots of "shoulds and oughts"—mixed with a sense of fatigue and purposeless. He told me that he was very committed to his sobriety but hated his current work in the food industry and thought that going to school more than part-time would be unthinkable due to his residual dislike of education from high school. He had no plan beyond a vague—"I want to make a lot of money"—and was essentially doing nothing beyond working and video games. He was modestly interested in getting a girlfriend but he had no idea of how to find one and was disinterested in the girls at his job. Finally Mark had no friends and did nothing for fun.

I suggested that he had a "fun deficit" and told him that he would benefit from a summer working in Yosemite Valley. He quickly researched the available jobs and was hired within 3 weeks and started 3 weeks after that. Our four sessions before he left were focused on discussing how to get the most out of his summer job and what kinds of fears needed to be dealt with to maximize his experience.

He worked in Yosemite Valley from May through September and came back into therapy upon his return. He reported that his social life had been intense and rewarding; when he wasn't out having adventures, he had a nonstop stream of friends coming by his tent cabin. He had a summer girlfriend and it was clear to him that he could have had several others if he had wished. Finally, he went on a series of adventures—from climbing 5.10 rock, to belaying from a hanging belay, to leaping into hidden pools and waterfalls, to participating in a secret "pendulum swing" off of a bolt on El Capitan. In sum, he had a summer which validated him as a friend, a lover, and a bold adventurer.

Upon his return, all talk about his inability to do well with friends and girls was gone; he had just proved that he was good at those activities in a way that even he could not dispute. Just as importantly, he had a glint in his eye and saw life more as "what's my next exciting experience?" instead of "how do I get through the next boring day as a 'good boy'"?

In many ways, this experience was Apollonian in that Mark used the Yosemite experience to make up for his lost high school experiences with friends and relationships; in short, he succeeded at accomplishing developmentally appropriate milestones which had been neglected. But it was special in that he accomplished the neglected milestones with a bang and far overshot the mark of "adequate achievement."

But the intervention had a Dionysian component as well. Mark returned from the summer believing that Yosemite Valley, and the people who live and work there, are special. The next chapter discusses the concept of "sacred space" and Mark certainly believed that he had come back from a "pilgrimage" to sacred space. Moreover, as a denizen of sacred space, he had a subtle, archetypal identity shift and no longer believed he was a normal or subnormal person. He felt touched by the mystical and transformed in ways that he didn't really try to elaborate. He simply summarized his experience with, "You needed to be there to really understand."

This encounter with the mystical left an unpredictable stamp upon Mark that was entirely Dionysian. He wasn't sure upon his return what he would do next but, somehow, he knew that it was going to be meaningful and going to contribute to the development of his life. He had walked out of the "wilderness" with an inner sense of knowing the location of his personal "north." Some of this came from Yosemite, some came from how all his new friends framed their time in Yosemite, some of it came from saying yes to experiences on rocks, beside waterfalls, and with his girlfriend. Wherever it came from, Mark somehow felt initiated into a new order of being. And this sense of being embodied a Dionysian shift.

Examining all three of the examples—the young man who got his girlfriend pregnant, Erickson's violet woman, and the Yosemite worker—the first thing that is clear is the remarkable power of such interventions, at least when they are done thoughtfully. Literally Erickson spent an hour or so with a woman in her home, but his intervention transformed her for the remainder of her life. The Yosemite intervention took a bit more than an hour and resulted in a new sense of self plus a fresh dialog with the meaning and overall direction of his life. And the pregnant girlfriend story happened without a psychological intervention but significantly overshadows typical therapeutic efficacy.

All three of the stories are straightforward and clear. Even the Erickson intervention, which is often touted as a brilliant example of indirect suggestion without trance, is—at the end—a simple referral. Most therapists are completely capable of planning and making such referrals. But, of course, prioritizing such referrals is not common. However, when one equates the power of such referrals with the power of the therapeutic wizards, then there is sufficient motivation to consider them as a primary level intervention.

Narrative therapy (Madigan, 2012) has advanced an idea that the Self exists between the individual and her social world (instead of within the individual). This implies that there is a new Self with every meaningful alteration in the social world. Using simple logic, this suggests that the client who presents with a mental health diagnosis in my office and in her current social world might not even have a diagnosis in a different social world. It is easy to argue that Mark was depressed when he walked into my office and that his successful social life in Yosemite helped alleviate his depression. It is probably more accurate from a constructionist point of view to say that the self that was generated via dialog between Mark and the Yosemite world never had depression; indeed, that self was incompatible with depression.

The depressed self was the result of Mark's dialog with his standard world. In that world, he was a recovering meth addict who needed to be serious about his recovery, being a responsible young man, and performing the hard work required to get friends and a relationship. The dialog with the Yosemite world created a self who was sociable, sexy, and up for any kind of healthy adventure. Did he gradually recover from his depression and the new qualities evolve slowly? Certainly the Apollonians, with their emphasis on ego stability, would so argue. But in reality he told me that he felt different from the moment he drove into Yosemite Valley. Did the referral allow a completely different self room to emerge? In that case, it was more than a referral; it was a profound psychological intervention. Conceptualizing social interventions in such a manner enhances therapist motivation and sensitizes them to the actual power that lies in the social approach.


## APOLLONIAN GROUP THERAPY

> The three great essentials to achieve anything worthwhile are, first,
> hard work; second, stick-to-itiveness; third, common sense.
>
> —Thomas Edison, *Men who are Making America* (1917)

Psychology seems to have created a group protocol to address almost every human ill. There are groups for assertiveness, weight loss, personal growth, parenting, anger management, divorce, cancer support and on and on. The good news is that virtually every group that is created to address a specific problem works. Recall the earlier chapter where it was argued that "everything works." When a group sets a goal of achieving any reasonable psychological change, they will succeed at it. The specific curriculum matters little. If the group members are united in their purpose, and the group leader succeeds at creating a positive milieu with healthy expectations, then the group will achieve the modest, positive outcome that psychotherapy—individual or group—reliably generates.

The efficacy of this type of group therapy rests on three main concepts: 1) support and guidance from the group, 2) support and guidance from the leader, and 3) skills training. Since the research has consistently shown that skills training is not the active ingredient in therapeutic change, that leaves the effects of the leader and the effects of the group on the client.

The leader's function in these groups is somewhat limited. First of all, many of these types of groups are "manualized"—that is, they have a set curriculum that tends to restrict spontaneous discourse and which takes up the majority of the group time. Moreover, a number of these sorts of groups are leaderless support groups—for example, AA meetings and certain divorce recovery groups—and consist of clients listening to each other and sharing their own stories without significant "cross-talk." In sum, in these types of groups, the social or subcultural aspect is likely to be the most important factor contributing to therapeutic efficacy.

Of course, the previous section demonstrated that the influences of a subgroup are, indeed, quite powerful. As Berger and Luckmann point out, humans are social animals with a strong urge to conform to their current group in terms of adopting group norms to gain approval and full membership. Given that all of these groups require healthy or healthier behavior to attain full membership, it is not surprising that clients who attend parent skill training groups become better parents and clients who attend divorce recovery groups move on from their divorces at an accelerated rate.

Moreover, even when the leader does not supply a preexisting curriculum, selected lead figures in the group will supply it for him. If it is an anger management group, the leader can count on certain members telling stories from their own lives which illustrate some of the best techniques to control anger. But the secret, of course, is not the curriculum; it is the enhanced motivation. Knowing that I am going to return to my relapse prevention group next week and share my relapse-related experiences with them motivates me to control my impulsivity and make better choices. Before my group membership I had certain forces in my life moving me toward relapse and other forces moving me toward sobriety. Now I have those same forces with the addition of pleasing the group.

The power of the group changes depending on how important affiliation with the group is to each client. Some find group membership enormously rewarding and their motivation increases proportionally; others not so much. In this sense, group leaders need to pay more attention to affiliation and caring than to curriculum and skills building.

Almost all of the groups that are centered on problems and trauma recovery are fundamentally Apollonian. In essence, their focus is on rejoining the culture (e.g., divorce recovery and relapse prevention), executing social roles more effectively (e.g., assertiveness groups and parenting groups), or symptom control (e.g., pain management). Some groups focus on helping those who have never had a role in the culture (e.g., life skills groups and DBT groups). Whatever the specifics, all of these groups have Apollonian goals and are executed in an Apollonian style. They are not intended to be transformative as much as facilitative.

That said, such groups are successful, do a great deal of good, and are generally praised by both the clients and the leaders who run the groups.

Research, unsurprisingly, finds that these sorts of groups achieve the modest, positive outcomes universally found in psychotherapy. The primary negative critique of this kind of group therapy comes from Gergen with his point about the pathologizing of the human condition. Gergen reminds us that conditions and syndromes are constructed and are "discovered" at a rate directly proportional to the number of professionals involved in mental health. Narrative therapy adds a related argument when they state that the explicit or implicit labeling incumbent in being a member of these sorts of groups moves the "authoring" of a client's narrative out of her hands into the hands of mental health professionals.

In sum, many of the groups developed by professional psychology are Apollonian in style and substance. They do succeed at helping many clients join or rejoin the culture, enhance their social roles, and become more successful. At the same time, there is some danger that the implicit pathologizing of some of these approaches may be a net negative for certain clients.

## DIONYSIAN GROUP THERAPY

> The Stars are setting and the Caravan Starts for the Dawn of
> Nothing—Oh, make haste!
>
> —Omar Khayyám, *Rubáiyát of Omar Khayyám:*
> *The Astronomer-poet of Persia* (1859)

A good therapist displays above-average charisma, but a great therapist—a therapeutic wizard—has charisma plus the ability to generate and work with altered states. Dionysian change is discontinuous and outside the net, a pop that is dependent on a significant disconnection from the normal reality. In this same sense, Dionysian group therapy uses the same power of social endorsement seen in the role evolution and Apollonian group therapy already discussed. But it adds the power of altered states.

Achieving an altered state in a group therapy context is almost ridiculously easy. Many, many writers, chief among them Irvin Yalom, have argued the presenting the intimate issues of one's life in a group context essentially creates an altered state. There are many variations on how this altered state can be created—psychodrama, encounter groups, and so on—but Yalom recommends what he call the "process group."

Yalom describes the process group as a group which has a here-and-now focus and an emphasis on process not content. This kind of unstructured environment invites clients to manifest their characteristic external behaviors and challenges in real time in the group. This often results in group members having strong feelings about certain other members who "push their buttons" and creates an accessible environment to work on the issues.

Importantly, this same recipe virtually guarantees regular altered states in the group members. Yalom points out that there is a taboo on sharing intimate feelings and experiences in public; the group requirement to do so elicits altered states in both the person sharing and in the listeners.

Yalom is unwilling to assume that simple sharing of intimate details is sufficient to create the altered states he desires. In addition, he prescribes a set of techniques which tend to enhance the probability of creating altered states. Most of these techniques encourage the client to be more vulnerable by sharing her perception of the characteristics of other group members or the group process itself.

> If a member comments that the group is too polite and too tactful, the therapist may ask, "Who are the leaders of the peace-and-tact movement in the group?" If a member is terrified of revealing himself and fears humiliation, the therapist may bring it into the here-and-now by asking him to identify those in the group he imagines might be most likely to ridicule him. Don't be satisfied by answers of "the whole group." Press the member further. Often it helps to rephrase the question in a gentler manner, for example, "Who in the group is least likely to ridicule you?" (Yalom & Leszcz, 2008, p. 158)

Yalom is a veteran of the 1960s and, as such, has experienced all of the wild escapades that characterized experiential group therapy from Esalen, to nude encounter groups, to emotional release groups. As a result of these experiences, he is quick to point out that an altered state alone is insufficient to create change.

> The mistaken assumption that a strong emotional experience is in itself a sufficient force for change is seductive as well as venerable. Modern psychotherapy was conceived in that very error: the first description of dynamic psychotherapy (Freud and Breuer's 1895 *Studies on Hysteria*) described a method of cathartic treatment based on the conviction that hysteria is caused by a traumatic event to which the individual has never fully responded emotionally. Since illness was supposed to be caused by strangulated affect, treatment was directed toward giving a voice to the stillborn emotion. It was not long before Freud recognized the error: emotional expression, though necessary, is not a sufficient condition for change. (Yalom & Leszcz, 2008, pp. 30–31)

Yalom believes that these altered states must be paired with what he calls "illumination" to actually create change. By "illumination" Yalom means that the nature of the group member's problem or challenge must be defined in such a manner that both the individual and the other group members achieve consensus about its nature and characteristics. Simple examples would include concepts such as "she is a people pleaser." Both the individual and the other group members will have seen examples in real time in the group and heard about examples of these behaviors in real life. Once the problem is illuminated—that is, defined and accepted—the group creates an experience or experiences which serve to resolve the issue. For example, the individual could stand up to another group member or share a similar experience from real life. This illumination process plus the "resolution activity"—usually carried out in an altered state—results in meaningful change.

If Yalom's prescriptions seem structurally identical to Jerome Frank's common factors theory, the resemblance is hardly accidental. Frank tells us that change begins by generating and accepting a theory that accounts for the origin of the problem and then concludes by passage through a ritual that is seen as capable of resolving the problem. In Yalom's process groups, illumination refers to group consensus about the origin theory; the ritual of resolution is implicit in the group process. Put another way, after the group achieves agreement on the core issue and its explanation, the ritual typically consists of performing behaviors either in the group or witnessed by the group which symbolize healing and resolving the core issue. The person with an "anger issue" shows control; the person who is alienated and socially withdrawn reaches out to others.

And, of course, because the group almost inevitably includes altered states, the ritual becomes Dionysian; that is, the ritual occurs "outside the Net" and it can be assumed that the client can make a rapid and meaningful change without needing to follow rules about gradual and incremental growth. A simple example from my own practice illustrates the point.

Georgia was an attractive and intelligent woman in her early 40s who worked as a title officer. She was divorced and had one daughter. A devoted mother and a diligent professional, she spent many hours working overtime and making sure that every task was done perfectly.

She joined group because she had a boyfriend who cheated on her chronically with a variety of other women. After briefly being furious at him, she would take him back and continue in the relationship until the next infidelity, which typically occurred every two or three months. The relationship had lasted for over three years and, interestingly, she tended to be somewhat amnesiac about how many infidelities and the details of each one as if she had been using some kind of primitive denial or repression to minimize her pain.

When she entered group, she reported that she had had a difficult childhood with a mother with mental health problems and a stepmother who would not allow her to live with her father. She said that she was rarely depressed but she was bothered by the fact that she couldn't leave her boyfriend in spite of his repeated misbehaviors.

As one might expect, the group reacted to this presentation with a mixture of supportive comments extolling her core self-worth and an equal number of confrontive comments about not being a door mat to the boyfriend. A number of months went by and, while Georgia reported enhanced self-esteem and more insight into the situation, she was unable to leave the boyfriend. Particularly after the group had heard several new examples of infidelity, the confrontations became stronger, but Georgia was unable to hold her boundaries and always took him back.

I had had a number of individual sessions with her before I referred her to group and was aware that the details of her childhood, especially with her mother, were truly horrific. One day in group, while she was talking to another woman about her relationship, Georgia commented that, "I always have a dream that someday some man is going to look at me from across the room and feel 'that woman would make me truly happy. I choose her.'" I commented, "but something always comes up and says 'no one could ever really see me that way. . . .' Georgia, why don't you tell the group more details about what happened in your childhood and why you can never be special?"

Georgia took a deep breath and began to describe a childhood characterized by her mother's severe mental health problems including beatings, neglect, living in filth, being locked in closets, and being shunned by her peers and their families. When her mother was finally remanded to a long term mental health hospitalization, her father's new wife wanted nothing to do with her and actively worked to kick her out of the family. As the group listened to the horrific details, one member began to cry. At the conclusion, there was silence before group members began to make supportive and empathic statements.

After the support, the Georgia shared that she always believed she would be judged and rejected if anyone knew the details of her upbringing. Different group members connected this to the sense that no man could ever see her as special.

The following week, the group checked back in with Georgia. I suggested they begin by each member sharing how Georgia's story had impacted them over the subsequent week. Each member talked about how deeply they had been moved by the awful details of her abuse, how they admired her strength in terms of creating a functional life post-abuse, and how they respected the courage it had taken to share the history. Georgia felt validated and supported by these recitations.

Within three weeks Georgia broke up with her boyfriend and a month later she began a relationship with a new man. She stated that she believed that the new relationship was the first healthy relationship she had ever had in her life.

While this vignette is an example of solid therapy, it is far from remarkable. Similar experiences occur on a daily basis in various forms of group therapy ranging from AA, to survivor groups, to process groups. However, while the therapy isn't that unusual, it clearly illustrates illumination, ritual, and altered states.

This simple example brings back the questions about whether rituals are real or constructed and invented. This ritual was based on the modern cultural assumption: "you're only as sick as your secrets." This expresses the straightforward idea that when humans carry an emotional burden on their own, especially when it is linked to guilt and shame, the act of carrying and hiding creates an inner sense of heaviness, sadness, and self-deprecation. Conversely, when this burden is shared, and when that sharing results in acceptance, then the person is set free and has more capacity for growth and vitality.

It is important to understand, however, that this intervention is a ritual masquerading as a technique. It is only "real" because a particular subculture of Western culture believes it to be real. This idea would be a hard sell in sixteenth-century Japan, for example. But for our subculture—Westerners who believe in psychotherapy—it feels like a "truth." Hence, when a client undergoes a ritual that embodies the "secrets" principle, they will be changed and the witnesses will find their change credible. It's a perfect example of creating a shared reality.

Most importantly, groups provide a "mini subculture" that supports the client's new identity. Dionysian change, rapid change, usually runs into the challenge of sustainability. Following the change, as the client attempts to reintegrate her new identity into her world, the world pushes back, insisting that her old identity is still valid. This kind of homeostatic resistance exists, to a degree, with all change but it is particularly pronounced with rapid change. The therapy group, conversely, acts to support the new change and provides social validation for the new identity.

Recall that narrative therapy postulates that the self exists in the space between us and the other. The group is a subculture that functions as a representation of the whole culture. The Self that exists between me and the rest of my therapy group has a solidity bestowed and validated by the subculture. I have not been reinvented by myself; I have not even been reinvented in the space between me and my therapist; rather, I know I am transformed because the whole culture (the therapy group) endorses the new me.

The significant difference between the Reality B view of group therapy and the traditional view is similar to the difference between the reality therapy basic model and a more complex model from, say, psychodynamic or systems psychotherapy. In the reality therapy model the client is seen as changing simply because the charismatic therapist urges him to do so. The complex techniques are not necessary—only the relationship and the urging. Similarly, in group therapy the basic power of the group influence is seen as the dominant factor. It does no harm in general to include more complex techniques such as psychodrama or DBT but the Reality B therapist keeps her focus on the simple pressure from the group to adapt to a new reality—the new reality defined by the consensus of the group.

On the one hand, assertions about the power of the group to influence the client are hardly new news; this is a factor that is acknowledged by virtually every experienced group leader. Conversely, accepting that this is *the* important factor is different. Everything seems simpler. There is a more relaxed sense in the therapist about controlling the flow of the group. And, while attempting to track the feelings and reactions of multiple individuals is always a challenge, there is also a sense of lightness as the therapist leans into the power of the group.

Therapist charisma, of course, continues to be vital especially during the "illumination" process where the client's core issues are defined and highlighted. It is also helpful when increasing or decreasing the group pressure on any particular individual. In addition, it can be very useful when meeting individually with a member either to process a group experience, work on bonding issues, or for another reason.

Process groups are an ideal environment in terms of the Frank model. With some help from the therapist, the group quickly illuminates the core issue and provides an explanation for it. The ritual grows naturally out of the group environment and typically consists of exhibiting behaviors in the group incompatible with the core issue or reporting that such has occurred outside the group. The power of the intervention is amplified by the altered states so easily achieved in the group environment. And there is the ability of a therapy group to function as a "mini subculture" in terms of socially validating a new identity.

Most important, however, is the raw power of the group to directly alter the client's worldview and identity. We are all programmed to adjust our realities to fit the social environment of our chosen groups and companions. Being fully aware of this central power—a power fully revealed as the Reality B therapist strips away distracting details like techniques and client history—allows for sustained change with relatively little effort and resistance.

## THE POWER OF SOCIAL VALIDATION

Being entirely honest with oneself is a good exercise.

—Sigmund Freud, *Origins of Psychoanalysis* (1895)

The power of social validation cannot be overemphasized. Everything that is "me" is defined, restricted, and liberated by the ongoing feedback from our social environment. Therapeutic wizards have the power to change client reality with a "wave of the mind." That power requires a gifted individual. In contrast, our social environment limits or liberates us with every encounter and interaction.

Fortunately, it is relatively easy to access this power and to work with it. This chapter illustrated many approaches that result in effortless, fluid, and long-lasting change. This is not only the source of some optimism but it helps free therapists from the crippling Apollonian assumptions that change is difficult, or change can only happen by releasing deeply ingrained traumas, or change is only temporary and will always regress back to the former state.

The power of the group and the social environment to elicit easy change is one of the "proofs" that we live and operate in constructed reality. And it also supports the concept that our essential Self is ephemeral and fluid—a realization that is a prerequisite to facilitating rapid and effective change. The chapter on shifting identity argued that psychotherapy may be the most efficient and transparent method of working with identity ever created by human culture. Similarly, the therapy group is a unique window on the essential nature of the *social* construction of reality. There are other windows on this as well, such as the study of cults and political movements, but the group therapy experience allows us to understand and work with social influence in an intimate and personalized way.

The actual environment of group therapy includes other opportunities for therapist growth as well. First, it is a perfect laboratory for illustrating the narrative therapy idea that my self exists in the space between me and others. In group therapy, the clients rapidly shift from talking about their own issues—and looking depressed and overwhelmed—to responding to the personhood and the issues of the other—and looking centered and clear. The palpable sense—to the therapist and the other group members—that these two selves are radically different concretely demonstrates the freedom of constructionism. Seeing the client transform so quickly and radically gives everyone present the sense that sustained health is possible for the client. Such shifts naturally create a belief that anything is possible and that no one is hopelessly and eternally stuck.

In addition, the group therapy environment is ideal when it comes to conceptualizing treatment as a series of rituals. The therapist co-creates the explanatory myth with both the client and the other group members. This co-creation helps the therapist feel and experience the constructed nature of explanations. And, while the healing ritual developed in group can literally be anything—just as it is in individual therapy—in most group situations, the ritual consists of demonstrating "healing" and "empowering" behaviors directly in the group environment. This allows the therapist to witness and participate in every part of the ritual, enhancing understanding and personal experience.

The fact that altered states happen so easily in group therapy can be particularly helpful for the therapist as well. Especially for therapists who are more experienced in Apollonian techniques, participating in Dionysian group therapy can stretch both abilities and awareness. Moreover, the altered states in group therapy are not limited to the clients; often the therapist gets altered as well. There is something about sharing intimate and vulnerable material in a group context that pulls everyone present into an altered state. Experiencing that and learning to channel whatever part of that is helpful also tends to stretch the therapist.

The group experience is also conducive to direct and indirect contact with the Abyss. Sharing devastating, Abyss-related life events is common in every type of therapy; however, in group therapy there is a palpable sense that sharing these difficult events results in the entire community connecting and offering to shoulder them together. It is an experiential response to the Tillichian question at the edge of the Abyss: are we essentially alone in the face of the devastating events of life or are we connected, hand in hand, as we face them?

# Chapter 13

# Dionysian Power

## Sacred Space and Altered States

They who dream by day are cognizant of many things which escape
those who dream only by night.

—Edgar Allan Poe, "Eleonora" (1841)

The concept of Apollonian versus Dionysian has played a major role in this
book. Defining Apollonian and Dionysian in terms of the Nomological Net,
one can state that everything constrained by the Net is Apollonian and everything outside of the Net is Dionysian. Culture, identity, and social interactions
are all defined by and stabilized through the Net. The Net defines normal
consciousness and secular space. Conversely, what lies outside the Net—or
what lies at the edge—can be defined as altered states of consciousness, the
Abyss, and sacred space.

At times the Abyss breaks through the Net spontaneously in the form of
epiphanies or pathologizing; at other times, humans use technologies—like
meditation, drugs, and hypnosis—to achieve these altered states. Whether
such states come spontaneously or are invoked by practices, they tend to be
disruptive. Sometimes this disruption is associated with terror, sometimes
with bliss, sometimes with knowing, and sometimes with confusion. Regardless, these purely Dionysian states are of great interest to the therapist because
they hold the power to rapidly transform the status quo and the existing identity of a client.

This chapter will focus on approaches that consciously attempt to move
the client into these Dionysian experiences. Using our analogy of the geography of constructed reality, we would say that these experiences take place at
the edge of the Abyss, the place where the Net fades away and the darkness
begins. There is another word for this location: sacred space.

Some of the most renowned work on sacred space was done by Mircea Eliade, one of the outstanding religious studies scholars of the twentieth century. Writing in books such as *The Myth of the Eternal Return* and *The Sacred and the Profane*, he developed ideas about sacred time and sacred space which are directly relevant to psychology and how people change. He begins his work on the sacred by defining a key introductory concept: hierophany.

> Man becomes aware of the sacred because it manifests itself, shows itself, as something wholly different from the profane. To designate the *act of manifestation* of the sacred, we have proposed the term *hierophany*. It is a fitting term, because it does not imply anything further; it expresses no more than is implicit in its etymological content, i.e., that *something sacred shows itself to us*. It could be said that the history of religions—from the most primitive to the most highly developed—is constituted by a great number of hierophanies, by manifestations of sacred realities. From the most elementary hierophany—e.g. manifestation of the sacred in some ordinary object, a stone or a tree—to the supreme hierophany (which, for a Christian, is the incarnation of God in Jesus Christ) there is no solution of continuity. In each case we are confronted by the same mysterious act—the manifestation of something of a wholly different order, a reality that does not belong to our world, in objects that are an integral part of our natural "profane" world. (Eliade, 1961, p. 11)

This definition of hierophany is phenomenological in that Eliade is simply asserting that humans experience the eruption of the sacred into the profane world and he is going to call these eruptions hierophanies. Next Eliade defines *homo religiosus,* the man who puts spiritual experience at the center of his life.

> For religious man, space is not homogenous; he experiences interruptions, breaks in it; some parts of the space are qualitatively different from others. (1961, p. 20)

All of us experience the grinding sameness of daily life with its predictability, its repetitive staleness, its tendency to gradually rob meaning and purpose from existence. Eliade responds that the conscious observer perceives both this process of degradation and the breaks in the fabric of reality where something else shines through. In fact, without these breaks, humans are essentially cast into a chaotic and meaningless existence.

> Life is not possible without an opening toward the transcendent; in other words human beings cannot live in chaos. (1961, p. 34)

Anticipating objections from those who reject the concept of the sacred, Eliade turns to the question of whether the non-religious man actually exists.

And in his arguments, one can hear echoes of the Tillichian statement that man is the being who is "ultimately concerned."

> A non-religious man today ignores what he considers sacred but, in the structure of his consciousness, could not be without the ideas of being and the meaningful. He may consider these purely human aspects of the structure of consciousness. What we see today is that man considers himself to have nothing sacred, no god; but still his life has a meaning, because without it he could not live; he would be in chaos. He looks for being and does not immediately call it being, but meaning or goals; he behaves in his existence as if he had a kind of center. He is going somewhere, he is doing something. We do not see anything religious here; we just see man behaving as a human being. But as a historian of religion, I am not certain that there is nothing religious here.
>
> I cannot consider exclusively what that man tells me when he consciously says, "I don't believe in God; I believe in history," and so on. For example, I do not think that Jean-Paul Sartre gives all of himself in his philosophy, because I know that Sartre sleeps and dreams and likes music and goes to the theater. And in the theater he gets into a temporal dimension in which he no longer lives his "moment historique." There he lives in quite another dimension. We live in another dimension when we listen to Bach. Another experience of time is given in drama. We spend two hours at a play, and yet the time represented in the play occupies years and years. We also dream. This is the complete man. I cannot cut this complete man off and believe someone immediately when he consciously says that he is not a religious man. I think that unconsciously, this man still behaves as the "homo religiosus," has some source of value and meaning, some images, is nourished by his unconscious, by the imaginary universe of the poems he reads, of the plays he sees; he still lives in different universes. I cannot limit his universe to that purely self-conscious, rationalistic universe which he pretends to inhabit, since that universe is not human. (Eliade, 1973, p. 104)

For Eliade the Sacred is present for all human beings regardless of tendencies to deny or dispute the presence of meaning and the existence of hierophanies. Eliade goes further and argues that humans are archetypally aware of whether they are in sacred or secular space and whether this moment is part of sacred time or secular time.

Simple definitions of sacred space are concepts such as being in a church versus outside one—or being in the wilderness versus being in the city. Simple ideas of sacred time are concepts like Lent or Mardi Gras versus the typical work week. Not content with these simple definitions, Eliade extends these ideas by discussing the concept of sacred geography. More specifically, wherever the Sacred manifests in the world becomes the center of the world, the place of the axis mundi, the spot where heaven and earth intersect.

> The experience of sacred space makes possible the "founding of the world": where the sacred manifests itself in space, the real manifests itself, the world

comes into existence. But the irruption of the sacred does not only project a fixed point into the formless fluidity of profane space, a center into chaos; it also effects a break in plane, that is, it opens communication between cosmic planes (between heaven and earth) and makes possible ontological passage from one mode of being to another. It is such a break in the heterogeneity of profane space that creates the center through which communication with the transmundane is established, that, consequently, founds the world, for the center renders orientation possible. Hence, the manifestation of the sacred in space has a cosmological valence; every spatial hierophany or consecration of space is equivalent to a cosmogony. (Eliade, 1961, p. 63)

Certain experiences in the natural world effortlessly invoke the sense of the Sacred. Philip Caputo, in the following quote, attempts to articulate the implicit sacrality of the natural world.

Directly overhead the Milky Way was as distinct as a highway across the sky. The constellations shown brilliantly, except the north, where they were blurred by the white sheets of the Aurora. Now shimmering like translucent curtains drawn over the windows of heaven, the northern lights suddenly streaked across a million miles of space to burst in silent explosions. Fountains of light, pale greens, reds, and yellows, showered the stars and geysered up to the center of the sky, where they pooled to form a multicolored sphere, a kind of mock sun that gave light but no heat, pulsing, flaring, and casting beams in all directions, horizon to horizon. Below, the wolves howled with midnight madness and the two young men stood in speechless awe. Even after the spectacle ended, the Aurora fading again to faint shimmer, they stood as silent and transfixed as the first human beings ever to behold the wonder of creation. Starkmann felt the diminishment that is not self-depreciation but humility; for what was he and what was Bonnie George? Flickers of consciousness imprisoned in lumps of dust; above them a sky ablaze with the Aurora, around them a wilderness where wolves sang savage arias to a frozen moon. (Caputo, 2004, p. 29)

Eliade agrees with Caputo and Momaday and in the following quote discusses the transmutation of the natural world into sacred space.

For those to whom a stone reveals itself as sacred, its immediate reality is transmuted into supernatural reality. In other words, for those who have a religious experience all nature is capable of revealing itself as cosmic sacrality. (Eliade, 1961, p. 12)

Humans archetypally divide the world into sacred and secular. Daily life besieges us with its dulling, deadening sense of the profane. In spite of this dulling quality, the nature of the world exposes us to breakthrough experiences of the sacred. These experiences have the capacity to become the center of our lives and to suffuse our world with purpose and meaning. However, we need to be sufficiently awake and aware to discern the presence of these hierophanies and to use the experiences to enrich our lives.

Secular space is the domain of the Nomological Net and sacred space is the place "outside" the Net. Some might visualize it as the place where the Abyss and the Net touch. Identity is fixed and solid in secular space and capable of adapting fluidly and gracefully in sacred space. Sacred space is like Never-land where a person can stay young forever. It is the Garden of Eden where all is perfect and peaceful and no sin exists. For the client, immersion in sacred space is equivalent to drinking from the Holy Grail, being enriched by the golden city of Cibola, or being healed at the Temple of the Rock. Sins, mistakes, and self-hatred are released there. One can leave sacred space with talismans of power—such as a sword or a cup—which allow one to achieve success in the secular world.

Obviously all these statements are metaphorical, not literal, but when one speaks to a person who has climbed Mount Everest, or followed the Way of St. James to Santiago, or spent a year meditating at a retreat in Southeast Asia, they often summarize their experience with phrases similar to those above. Last chapter discussed the use of rituals in group therapy. The pilgrim-ages to sacred space, the immersion in the Holy, and the treasures brought back on the return are also rituals—but the power of such rituals is amplified by their association with the numinous.

For psychologists, most examples of the Abyss breaking through the Net are associated with experiences of alienation, ennui, and despair. Eliade also talks of breakthroughs but he is focusing on the oracular Abyss and its associ-ated experiences of meaning, connection, wisdom, and bliss. Examine the fol-lowing personal experience collected by the Religious Experience Research Unit of Oxford. Note that it was a spontaneous experience; the speaker did not seek it out nor did he invoke it via spiritual practices, prayers, or medita-tion. It simply broke through the Net, just as the debilitating experiences of the Abyss come without an invitation.

> Often during my late 20s and early 30s I had a good deal of depression, not caused by any outward circumstances. . . . At the age of 33 I felt I must be going mad. I felt shut up in a cocoon in complete isolation and could not get in touch with anyone. . . . Things came to such a pass and I was so tired of fighting that I said one day, "I can do no more. Let nature, or whatever is behind the universe, look after me now."
>
> Within a few days I passed from a hell to a heaven. It was as if the cocoon had burst and my eyes were opened and I saw.
>
> The world was infinitely beautiful, full of light as if from an inner radiance. Everything was alive and God was present in all things; in fact, the Earth, all

plants and animals and people seem to be made of God. All things were one, and I was one with all creation and held safe within a deep love. I was filled with peace and joy and with deep humility, and could only bow down in the holiness of the presence of God. . . . If anyone had brought news that any member of my family had died, I should have laughed and said, "there is no death." It was as if scales had fallen from my eyes and I saw the world as it truly was. How had I lived for 33 years and been so blind? This was the secret of the world, yet it all seemed so obvious and natural that I had no idea that I should not always see it so. I felt like going round and telling everyone that all things were one and the knowledge of this would cure all ills. . . .

Psychologically, and for my own peace of mind, the effect of the experience has been of the greatest import. (Cohen & Phipps, 1979, p. 27)

Throughout history, individuals in search of healing, of redemption, and of wisdom have sought the blessings associated with scared space. Not surprisingly, a number of therapeutic and personal growth programs attempt to build on these ancient traditions to accomplish their modern goals.

For purposes of this chapter, we can talk about programs and techniques that approach sacred space externally and those that approach it internally. Internal pilgrimages to sacred space involve experiences such as meditation retreats, hypnosis, personal growth classes at places such as Esalen, and taking ayahuasca in Peru. External approaches involve programs such as Outward Bound which uses wilderness experiences to build character, service programs—especially in foreign cultures—which attempt transformation through cultural immersion and opening the heart, and literal forms of pilgrimage, such as going on the Hadj or reaching the South Pole on skis. Some approaches blend the two such as a meditation retreat (internal) where one also has the opportunity to receive the *darshan* (spiritual presence) of the "enlightened Master" (external).

## IN WILDERNESS IS THE PRESERVATION OF THE WORLD

Climb the mountains and get their good tidings. Nature's peace will flow into you as sunshine flows into trees. The winds will blow their own freshness into you, and the storms their energy, while cares will drop away from you like the leaves of Autumn.

—John Muir, *The Mountains of California* (1875)

To illustrate the nature of an external encounter with sacred space, we will use the Outward Bound program, and how it works with sacred space, as our example. Outward Bound was founded in England during World War II.

The British Merchant Marine Service was losing numerous ships as a result of German U-boat attacks. They noticed that the older seamen were surviving the lifeboat experiences better than the younger seamen. This counter-intuitive finding was explained with the theory that the older seamen were hardier than the younger. The Outward Bound program was developed to toughen up the younger seamen by impelling them into challenging experiences. After the war, Outward Bound continued but changed its focus from training young seamen to helping youths successfully master the adolescent/adult developmental passage.

Outward Bound came to the United States in 1962 and established its first school high up in the Colorado Rockies. This British import was quickly influenced by two major American themes. First, the longstanding tradition of Americans as hardy frontiersmen immediately surfaced. Second, and probably more important, the 1960s and 1970s saw the nascent environmental movement take an enormous leap as backpacking, climbing, and adventuring became commonplace. From mountain man, Japhy Ryder, in the Kerouac novel *Dharma Bums*, to climbers in Yosemite Valley such as Yvon Chouinard, the world was full of new heroes who belonged in the mountains as if they had been born there. John Denver was singing about *Rocky Mountain High* and Edward Abbey was writing *Desert Solitaire*.

Outward Bound was no longer simply about building character; it had evolved into a program staffed by idealistic Americans who did see wilderness as the "preservation of the world" and who believed that the wilderness experience had the power—through its numinosity—to transform visitors and pilgrims. These young staff members did not believe that they needed to make much of an effort with students to achieve these changes. In fact, they had a saying, "The mountains speak for themselves," which implied that they simply needed to get out of the way and allow the sacred space to directly transform the students.

To understand how an Outward Bound course functions, it is helpful to describe its essential elements. While the Outward Bound experience has been adapted for a variety of special populations, and operates in a variety of environments, the "standard" course is still conceptualized as a three or three-and-a-half week mountaineering course. Students are grouped into "patrols" and accompanied by one or two instructors. The course is divided into four phases:

1. Basic Expedition: Instructor travels with the group and teaches basic skills such as backpacking, orienteering, first aid, and climbing.
2. Second Expedition: Students begin to travel on their own. More physically demanding activities are included such as peak climbs, off trail travel, and night hiking.

3. Solo: Students spend three days alone with their journals. Most fast.
4. Final Expedition: Students travel in small groups without instructors crossing miles of wilderness.

Research on Outward Bound reveals a very strong effect immediately post course. Typical responses from students include statements like: "I found out who I am," "Having done Outward Bound, I feel like I can do anything!" and "I learned so much about myself and others that I'll never see the world in the same way." Parents report things like "my son came back a different person," or "my daughter says she really appreciates her family and we get along so much better." Psychological scales record improvements in things like self-esteem and internal locus of control and decreases on pathological measures such as depression and anxiety. The effect sizes are substantial but they have difficulty being maintained over time, a factor which is discussed in more detail in the summary section of this chapter.

These powerful outcomes are caused by a variety of factors, yet for our purpose—understanding the impact of sacred space—the archetypal nature of the Outward Bound course will be emphasized. Examine the following quote from an earlier book that I wrote on Outward Bound (OB).

The seeker always experiences sacred space as highly numinous—it is pervaded with a sense of power, mystery, and awesomeness. It clearly participates in a transcendental plane of existence. Human beings—whose home is the earth—can never stay there. In the first place, it lacks the prerequisites for normal living. In the second, the seeker almost always has something important to accomplish back in the real world.

Sacred space always leaves its mark on the seeker. Sometimes he comes away with the memento of the Sacred space—perhaps a sword or a cup—but often the mark is more internal. In any event, the seeker is irrevocably trans-formed—he has entered the Sacred Space and is forever changed. The quality of the transformation usually depends on the quality of the approach to the Sacred Space. Those who have approached it properly, with full respect and a clean spirit, are empowered in a positive manner. But those who have trifled inappropriately with the power of the Sacred Space received the power mixed with some kind of curse.

Finally, these changes are always magical and unexpected. Seekers do not earn them in the sense that they deserve their rewards. The rewards are always too great and too surprising to be anything other than free gifts from a higher power.

Anyone who has spent much time in the wilderness can easily recognize the parallels between it and the archetype of Sacred Space. Wilderness is difficult to get to and difficult to travel through. One passes a series of tests in order to exist within it. It is unlike the normal world in hundreds of ways. Above all, it is pervaded with a kind of religiosity or mysticism—one of the most compelling things about nature is that it seems to implicitly suggest the existence of order and meaning.

The power of an archetype is such that human beings are unconsciously prepared to recognize a concrete manifestation of the archetypal pattern when they encounter it in the world. According to Jung, the archetypes are literally stamped into the human unconscious. They're similar to instincts in an animal. A student is as prepared to see wilderness as Sacred Space as a bird is prepared to fly south for the winter.

The usefulness to Outward Bound of wilderness as Sacred Space is that this archetype is inextricably linked with the concept of transformation and change. Seeing the wilderness a Sacred Space means that the student has implicitly accepted the possibility—or even the probability—that some kind of powerful transformation may occur. This expectation of empowerment can exist in spite of any limitations from his past because sacred space transformations are magical and undeserved. (Bacon, 1983, p. 53)

Recall that there is a dividing line between secular space and sacred space. For OB that line is where the roads end and the wilderness begins. When students arrive at a course, the bus drops them off and they begin with a one or two mile run into the staging area just inside the wilderness boundary. Their luggage is taken in by a four wheel drive vehicle. They are given special wilderness gear (packs, clothes, tarps, and so on) and the instructors inspect the packs carefully to ensure that nothing symbolizing or embodying civilization (e.g., electronics, cosmetics) is allowed. The experience is highly similar to a pilgrimage where the pilgrim dresses in a simple (sacred) costume, travels the road on foot, and takes little or no money or food.

During the first week of the course, the students are taught the "sacred language" and the "devotional rituals" relevant to moving in the wilderness and surviving comfortably. They learn what an "arête" (ridge) is and how to move through a "col" (saddle or pass, often with no trail). They learn how to navigate, rappel and belay, stay dry in the rain, and make bread. They are often required to push themselves physically beyond their limits and not only stay cheerful while doing it, but lend a hand to another who might need it.

The experiences that make up the course are specially selected to have high emotional impact. In fact, one famous concept embodying OB in particular and experiential education in general is to attempt to "impel the student into value-forming experiences." Outward Bound loves to create moments where there is high "perceived danger" and low "actual danger." Rock climbing and rappelling are obvious examples. And there is something grand about starting a peak climb in the dark at 4 a.m., clipping in to a fixed rope crossing a knife ridge with a thousand feet of exposure, and then summiting to a view of mountains stretching in every direction as far as one can see.

The OB course includes other kinds of high impact experiences that require "adventuring in the inner world": encouraging a friend when they feel too tired to go on; confronting a difficult patrol member when their attitude becomes negative; and accepting help from another. Jumping in a lake with floating icebergs for a bath is common as is building a sweat lodge or learning to cook apple fritters when one misses donuts too much.

The students live in close proximity to the instructor who is seen as part human and part *denizen of the wilderness*—a kind of demigod. Instructors are marked as different in a variety of ways. Their equipment is better; they know the names of the flowers and animals; they can tell at a glance if the route is safe or impossible; they are effortlessly skilled at climbing and wilderness first aid, and their endurance is legendary. They speak differently and answer some questions with stories, other questions with hints, and some questions they refuse to address at all. They look different, more tanned, more fit and, most of all, they project a sense that they belong—that they are completely at home.

They are a little crazy by conventional rules. Hiking boots are required equipment on an OB course but one instructor, during a Canyonlands desert course, insisted on doing the entire course in flip flops. Naturally the students assumed she must have a special relationship with the cactus gods and the slickrock angels. One the first day of one course, the entire instructional staff introduced themselves to the students wearing nothing but loin clothes. This kind of craziness marks the instructor as a kind of divine madman—a person no longer bound by conventional rules because they are living by divine rules.

The students are encouraged to reflect on their experiences and keep a journal. The high point of this reflective activity is the three-day solo where the students are taken to an individual camp site with nothing but a sleeping bag, their tarp, their journal, and water. These sorts of "vision quest experiences" are easily recognized as one of the oldest and most traditional ways of inducing an altered state.

Most nights there are patrol meetings to reflect on and discuss the activities of the day. Often the students who have the deepest feelings about what they have experienced speak first, and longest, and talk about how profoundly they have been affected by something. This, of course, creates an atmosphere conducive to reflection; more importantly, however, such sharing inspires the other students to have their own deep feelings. This not only makes feeling and sharing safe, it actually helps create deep feelings even in students who are unused to experiencing the world on affective and existential dimensions.

As the students become dirtier, fitter, more skilled, and more independent, they begin to feel like the instructors: that perhaps they too belong in the wilderness, in sacred space. The course structure encourages this by having the students travel more and more on their own culminating in a final expedition which unfolds without any support from the instructors. By the celebration at end of course, the students know in their bones that they are no longer outsiders. They have typically forged deep bonds with other patrol members that are expressed by the classic "you have to have been there to understand." Fully belonging socially is a wonderful accomplishment on its own but it is amplified by the concomitant sense that they also belong in the wilderness. And, of course, to belong in the wilderness means that the students have recognized their implicit divine identities.

At OB—and indeed in most programs that successfully work with sacred space—the instructors are not creating the experience because they believe it is therapeutic. Rather, the instructors themselves believe that the wilderness experience is sacred, that the Outward Bound course is a full initiation into sacred space, and that the students will change in spite of themselves because they will be touched by the "Spirit." Carl Jung made the following phrase famous and prized it enough to use it as an inscription on his house and his tomb: *Vocatus atque non vocatus, Deus aderit*—Called or uncalled, God is present.

From the moment the students step off the bus they are immersed in a particular view of reality. They have come from secular space; they now inhabit sacred space. Sacred space is guarded by "monsters at the gate." At OB those monsters are the trackless wilderness, the steep fields of snow, ice and rock, and the powers of wind, rain, and night. The inner guardians are fear, doubt, lack of resolve, and inability to give and receive help. The students encounter these guardians—and with the assistance from the demigod, the instructor—gradually pass the tests and are admitted to sacred space. In sacred space their past transgressions are forgiven and rewards are bestowed. Upon return to secular space—the regular world—the students feel transformed and they exhibit signs allowing others, such as parents, to bear witness to that transformation.

Eliade's concept of the Sacred "breaking through" the Nomological Net—secular space—has remarkable implications for how people change. It is virtually identical to Becker's and the existentialists' concept of the Abyss breaking through human denial. Interestingly, examples of Abyss breakthroughs, such as the fear of death or the sense of existential alienation, are never considered constructions or the result of programming. When a person feels despair secondary to such breakthroughs, no one argues that these feelings are due to the influence of society or are the result of some kind of belief system. Instead, they are seen as the authentic experience of a person who—either wittingly or unwittingly—is facing the ultimate truth about human reality and destiny.

Contrast that with Eliade's hierophanies—the breakthroughs where humans experience the sacred directly. Such experiences are often assailed as constructions, wishful thinking, forms of denial, and the result of religious programming. There is an assumption that the dark experience of the Abyss is true and the connecting/affirming experience of the sacred must be a construction, something that only exists as a kind of reaction formation to the experience of primal terror. Obviously this double standard—if it is painful, it must be real; if it is uplifting, it must be constructed—is simply an unsupported assumption that is sustained by Apollonian ideas like "no pain, no gain."

Outward Bound and similar programs succeed at creating rituals based on sacred space immersions and initiations. Tillich might call such programs as a form of "living symbols" that point beyond themselves. For the client, they create the same modest positive effect found in virtually all psychological interventions. If the instructor is sufficiently charismatic, they can create an above-average effect.

For our purposes, however, the attempt of the instructor to master the sacred space dimension of the OB course has real potential in terms of enhancing charisma. The OB course is associated with archetypal images like pilgrimage, gates, guardians, receiving grace, reverence, and holiness. Attempting to master outer sacred space experiences requires a level of openness and surrender to accumulate the available charisma; it requires the therapist to stretch in an unusual dimension to harvest the full potential of what is available.

# TRANCEFORMATIONS

A dreamer is one who can only find his way by moonlight, and his punishment is that he sees the dawn before the rest of the world.

—Oscar Wilde, *The Critic as Artist* (1891)

The previous section described one way to enter sacred space via an outward journey—a pilgrimage that takes place in the physical world but which leads to an inner transformation. This section looks at ways to experience sacred space via an inward journey.

As mentioned above, a Dionysian experience is one that lies outside the domain of the Nomological Net. We tend to think of Dionysian experiences as unusual; we are so accustomed to secular space and normal consciousness that there is an implicit assumption that this is the default state—one that is achieved effortlessly. Of course we acknowledge that we need some help in terms of creating this "normal" state of consciousness. In large part the net is formed and sustained by social interactions; in that sense, I help you sustain your sense of identity and reality and you help sustain mine. But before becoming too comfortable with the Apollonian assumption that our natural state is secular consciousness, we might recall the research presented earlier documenting how easily the net can unravel if those around us begin to behave in unpredictable ways.

How easy is it, in actuality, to sustain the secular state of consciousness? This entire book has argued that the "basic" experience in life is the experience of the Abyss with all its chaos and meaninglessness. The net is superimposed on that. Based on this fact, it is more accurate to argue that altered states occur when we relax—that they are our native state of consciousness. As an example, examine what happens to most people when we are cut off from others—when we no longer have their help in terms of sustaining the net and supporting "normal" consciousness.

And we have the perfect—albeit horrible—natural experiment: solitary confinement in prison. Solitary confinement is considered a terrible punishment in part because it deprives the prisoner of the opportunity to have his sense of reality and identity confirmed by another. Following are some of the symptoms that can occur as a result of solitary confinement.

> There are many ways to destroy a person, but the simplest and most devastating might be solitary confinement. Deprived of meaningful human contact, otherwise healthy prisoners often come unhinged. They experience intense anxiety, paranoia, depression, memory loss, hallucinations and other perceptual distortions. Psychiatrists call this cluster of symptoms SHU syndrome, named after the Security Housing Units of many supermax prisons. Prisoners have more direct ways of naming their experience. They call it "living death," the "gray box," or "living in a black hole." (Guenther, 2012)

Clearly Guenther is portraying solitary confinement as a way to invoke an experience of the Abyss, with its dark capacities to destroy meaning, purpose, and even identity itself. In a prison, one of the most horrible consequences is forced immersion in experiences that will impel one into the Abyss. The forced and unnatural disintegration of the Nomological Net is equivalent to losing personhood, identity, and all connection.

Contrast that with experiences which are specifically designed to expose one to the oracular and meaningful aspects of the Abyss—practices such as meditation and hypnosis. The same Abyss, when invited with a willing spirit, now has the potential for healing, insight, and existential experiences. Of course this inner journey to encounter the Abyss is not without its own challenges. For example, if you ask any meditation teacher what happens when a beginner learns to meditate they will describe the experience as follows.

You will try to keep your mind focused on your breath or your mantra and you will succeed briefly. Then you will discover that your mind has veered off towards what you are going to cook for dinner, or the laundry that you have to pick up later, or how much your knee hurts or your nose itches, or how rude your boss was today. You will then remember you are trying to meditate and bring the mind back to the object of meditation. And then it will slip back into your unending stream of busy thoughts.

They say in India that the mind is like a monkey, always jumping from here to there. Upon reflection, however, it is more like a drunken monkey who is not just jumping but lurching to and fro in a stupor. And that is not quite enough: really the mind is like a drunken monkey who has been stung by a bee and is alternately jumping, lurching and screaming in pain.

In this amusing quote we see the meditation teacher describing the beginner's experience of meditation. This description can also be understood as the desperate attempt of the mind to stay involved with as many threads of the Net as possible to keep identity and reality stable. Gilligan calls this repetitive connection to the Net the "orienting response" (2012, p. 36). He cites daily life examples such as shifting postures, scratching, and looking away as behaviors that are seemingly innocuous but actually designed to maintain the dominance of the conscious mind.

Quieting the mind is not simply an experience of calmness and relaxation, it is an insidiously radical practice which disconnects us from the Net and lets us experience reality without the Net's intervening effects. Normal consciousness—staying "in reality"—requires thinking Net-related thoughts. Anything quieter, anything less Net-focused, quickly becomes an altered state. These altered states can create "Abyss breakthroughs"—as in solitary confinement—or they can open the practitioner to Eliade's hierophanies. In this sense, meditation and the practice of altered states are never "safe" practices; they always implicitly threaten the world order. Examine the following quote on the contra-indications for a meditation practice.

There are conditions and situations when meditation is contra-indicated. A useful rule of thumb is that meditation should be used with caution whenever there are concerns regarding reality testing, ego boundaries, lack of empathy, or rigid over-control. For example, when treating a schizophrenic patient with active psychotic symptoms, it may be inadvisable to include meditation as a component of treatment, as reality testing may be impaired.

Similarly, meditation may be inadvisable in treating some personality disorders (DSM-IV cluster B—antisocial, borderline, histrionic, or narcissistic) which involve lack of empathy, as it could reinforce further preoccupation with the self that characterizes those disorders.

However, an experienced therapist who has developed personal skills with meditation and other mind-body techniques can incorporate meditation into most treatment protocols, given appropriate attention to preparation of the patient. For example, the course author developed a multimodal holistic health program for schizophrenic patients at a state psychiatric hospital which incorporated meditation without any adverse effects.

Since meditation can be a powerful tool for self-reflection, it can occasionally produce an opening to the inner dimensions of experience that could be overwhelming to psychologically fragile individuals. In addition, relaxation-induced anxiety, where an individual unaccustomed to deep relaxation that often accompanies meditation and finds the resulting physiological release and attention to internal sensations, perceptions, and images, to be a source of fearful anxiety-producing apprehension, can occur in meditation as well as in other relaxation techniques used in therapy. (Lukoff & Wallace, 1986, pp. 274–282)

Lukoff et al. are pointing out that when liminal people—individuals who are poorly stabilized by the Net—meditate, they are more likely to evoke Abyss-related experiences than sacred space experiences. However, for most people who practice meditation, especially with the typical frames offered by meditation teachers (e.g., don't force anything, most people experience relaxation and inner peace, meditation is good at dropping high blood pressure and reducing pain, and you are participating in an ancient practice that leads to wisdom and bliss), there is little risk. The biggest risk for the average person is a sense of increased anxiety as they employ techniques designed to minimize their contact with the Net. The second biggest risk, of course, is boredom. Meditation usually takes a while before the practitioner begins to have significant sacred space-related hierophanies. And in a culture accustomed to intense and frequent stimulating experiences, patience is not a common virtue.

All the practices that achieve altered states do so by minimizing and extinguishing connections to the Net. Whether it is chanting, or meditating, or contemplative prayer, or hypnosis, every one of these approaches uses techniques that move the mind away from one's normal identity and conventional reality. In time, all of these practices elicit experiences of the Abyss, sacred space, or both. And, in the hands of the experienced therapist, all of these practices allow for rapid realignment of the client's identity and sense of reality.

In this section, we are going to use hypnosis as our example of an inner approach to sacred space. Hypnosis has been chosen because it is a relatively common therapeutic technique and it is not directly related to spiritual practices. Stephen Gilligan, who has been mentioned previously, is one of the foremost practitioners of clinical hypnosis in the United States. A senior student of Milton Erickson, Gilligan has worked hard to stay true to the essential

Ericksonian approach while simultaneously integrating modern ideas of constructionism, the Hero's Journey, and a more explicit approach to spirituality.

Gilligan begins his latest book on hypnosis, *Generative Trance* (2012), by defining hypnosis as a natural versus an artificial state. It is not something created or imposed by the hypnotist, rather, humans have a tendency to fall into altered states whenever they stop paying attention to their immediate experience. He calls this paying attention, the "orienting response," and notes that it is required for humans to sustain their identity. As mentioned above, this "orienting response" is the primary reason that meditation is so challenging. For therapists, it should be symbolically seen as a person chanting a mantra that goes something like: "I'm me. I'm still me. I'm me because I am mad at my husband. I'm me because my elbow tingles. I'm me because I have to shop for chicken for dinner." What is implicit in this ceaseless orientation to the Net is that if this string of thought is interrupted, the individual experiences the actual fragility of their identity and worldview. In fact, Gilligan goes so far as to say that "trance occurs whenever identity is destabilized" (p. 31).

Destabilization of identity can be positive or negative; in the sacred space of trance one can encounter the oracular Abyss or the terrifying Abyss. In this sense, Gilligan sees trauma as a form of negative trance and healing as a positive encounter with sacred space. Moreover, the definition of trance is highly culturally dependent. Put more simply, the nature of the hypnotic trance is constructed. The Christian who meditates experiences the sacred Heart of Jesus; the Yogi encounters Siva; and the modern Buddhist achieves equanimity, inner peace, and bliss. Gilligan explicitly rejects the "old-fashioned" authoritarian model of hypnosis, replacing it with a more egalitarian model of generative trance. But Gilligan could "resurrect" the state of "suggestability" if he believed it would serve a particular client. Understanding the underlying unity of the different altered states helps the therapist be more fluid and have more options.

Gilligan sees everyone as entering and exiting trance states multiple times per day whether they are aware or not. Simple examples such as driving across the city and not remembering any aspect of the journey or not feeling discomfort while we watch an engaging movie are daily life experiences. Psychological strategies like "projection," where encountering an older co-worker can bring back feelings from my father, are also considered trance experiences. Living in Gilligan's world requires the therapist to see multiple trance experiences pervading life; some individuals literally live more in trance states than "normal" states.

As a healer, Gilligan sees trance as a state full of endless possibilities. The client can go anywhere, feel anything, access any real or invented memory, and be endlessly creative. Trance is the essential Dionysian experience; there are literally no limitations on what might be imagined or developed.

The first practical question about trance has to do with inductions; how does the therapist help the client move from a normal state to a trance state.

> To develop trance, the orienting response needs to be relinquished. If you look across cultures and through time, you will find two common (complementary) trance induction principles used for this purpose. The first involves absorbing attention in a singular focus. This might involve visually focusing on a candle light, a symbolic image, a point in the environment, or an imaginary point. Sustained concentration blocks the orienting response, which would be hyper-vigilantly scanning a visual field, tense eyes moving in arrhythmic patterns. In the absence of the stress-creating orienting response, attention can widen and deepen into trance.
>
> The second, and more common, trance development principle is to entrain attention rhythmically on a repetitive pattern. This could be the chanting of a mantra, the repeating of a body movement, the beating of a drum, repetition of a prayer, singing a song, movement around a circle, the attunement to breathing, long-distance running, and so forth. The rhythmic repetition signals the brain that there is no new environmental information, so it's safe to open deeper into the world of relaxation and inner absorption. (Gilligan, 2012, pp. 36–37)

It should be clear from Gilligan's explanation that hypnotic trance, deep relaxation, self-hypnosis, and meditation are all different versions of the same state: the disconnection of the mind from its habitual movement toward the Net-defined reality. The differences between the altered states primarily come from the set-up, frames, and expectations created between the therapist and client or between the client and her culture. Meditation seems very different from hypnosis because—as Gilligan has commented above—Westerners see the altered state of hypnosis as one person, the therapist, controlling the other, the client. Meditation, conversely, seems to be a solo experience or, perhaps, a spiritual experience between the individual and their inner wisdom or between a seeker and a divine force.

In the following example, Richard Bandler works with a woman who is attending one of his workshops. The session begins with one of the client's arms elevated in midair and Bandler uses both the arm drop and the opposite arm levitation to deepen trance.

> Watch the changing focus . . . of your eyes . . . as you see the tops of your lids slowly move down . . . over . . . eyes . . . only as fast as you become aware of that need to blink. Take all the time you need, and allow your hand to go down only as fast . . . as you become completely relaxed . . . in your own special way. And it isn't important how fast that hand goes down. It's only important that it goes down . . . at the same rate . . . and speed . . . that the other hand begins . . . to lift up.

Because there's something that you want to learn about . . . and it isn't really
important that anyone but you knows what that special learning is, because
your unconscious mind has known . . . all along . . . and if you're going to learn
about it, it will be important . . . slow down! . . . to learn about it in a balanced
way. . . . And your unconscious mind knows what kind of balance will be
necessary. . . . That's right. . . . It's so useful and it's really so important . . . to
allow your unconscious mind . . . to make changes and to have a learning experience . . . and new understandings . . . which you can use . . . for yourself . . . in
some way . . . which will be . . . beneficial to you as an individual human being.

   Now, I don't know . . . whether or not . . . you could begin to dream a
dream . . . which has within it the solution that your unconscious knows . . . will
give you what you want. But I do know that if and when you do begin that dream,
it won't make any sense at all. And it's not important that you understand. . . . It's
only important that you learn . . . and you learn . . . exactly what you need to know.

   Every night . . . Liz . . . you engage in the natural process of dream-
ing. . . . Some of those dreams you're aware of . . . and some you're not aware
of. . . . That's right. . . . And I'm going to reach down now. . . . I'm going to lift up
your arm. . . . And I'm not going to tell you to put it down . . . any faster . . . than
you take all the time that's necessary . . . to begin to build a conscious understanding . . . of what that means . . . to use your unconscious creatively. And
when your hand touches your thigh, you will slowly awaken . . . and you will
take that new understanding with you. In the meantime . . . there'll be no need
to listen to anything else. But it is so pleasant to eavesdrop in a way that you
learn. (Grinder & Bandler, 1981, pp. 102–103)

Hypnosis is an ideal medium to illustrate Frank's ideas about rituals; it's also
a perfect demonstration of how new realities can be created by simple suggestions. In this example, Bandler is teaching the workshop attendees one way to
do a hypnotic induction and then providing a variety of open-ended suggestions that could be utilized to address therapeutic issues. The arm levitation
that occurs concurrently with the arm drop is both a method of deepening the
hypnotic trance and a "proof" offered to the client that, indeed, they are in an
altered state. Since they are altered, by definition they are in sacred space and
anything that occurs in trance will have sacred connotations.

   Bandler then offers suggestions that establish that the client has an "unconscious mind" that has special knowledge. This knowledge is now available
and will provide her with "special learnings" and "new understandings."
These learnings can be used to alter a negative set of unconscious behaviors.
This change may be mediated through conscious understanding or it may be
initiated via the unconscious mind in a series of dreams.

   Clearly what we have here is a Jerome Frank–style ritual. Like the group
therapy interventions, where the presence of others intensifies the experience, hypnosis creates a sacred context that amplifies the therapist's suggestions. Clearly, Bandler wasn't individualizing the experience as much as

is possible; this was a workshop demonstration, not a therapy session for a specific client. But it is easy to imagine how he might have made his suggestions more personified and accurate if this were a client who he had seen for many sessions and who was working on a set of specific goals.

Returning to Eliade, he would argue that this woman has moved into sacred space in her trance experience and been initiated into a new state of being, a place where she has an ongoing channel to divine power. She now has access to her unconscious mind; since this access is in sacred space, she essentially has access to a divine oracle. In that sense, her identity is transformed. Previously she was simply human and lived in secular space with all the fears and limitations implicit in that identity. Now, without denying the reality of her secular experience, she simultaneously lives in sacred space and can access the oracle when needed.

Now let's examine another trance experience that works with these same principles from a different angle. A forty-two-year-old woman, Joan, presented with a history of chronic migraine headaches. She had her own business as a certified public accountant (CPA) and was very successful, working long hours and making substantial amounts of money. She was married but the couple had decided not to have any children. Approximately once a week, she would get a migraine and essentially lose a day lying in a darkened bedroom and taking pain medication; in spite of years of working with different neurologists, no one had succeeded at budging this pattern. I decided to use a hypnotic approach based on a Neurolinguistic Programming technique named *6 step reframing.*

This approach begins with a hypnotic induction. Once the client is in trance, the "part" responsible for generating the headache is contacted directly via ideomotor signaling. Ideomotor signaling is a hypnotic procedure where the client is told that an unconscious part of their psyche has control of a certain part of their body, typically a finger. If the part wants to reply "yes" to a question, the index finger lifts by itself. If the part wishes to say "no," a different finger rises. This allows direct communication with an "unconscious part." In six-step reframing the client chooses the feeling that is responsible for the yes-no communication; it is not limited to a finger rising.

Of course, typically parts which are responsible for generating headaches are perceived as parts that have a dark or even malevolent relationship with the main personality. In order to get such parts into dialog, the client must begin by creating some kind of rapprochement with the alienated or dissociated part. This is generally done by urging the client to send benign and positive messages to the part.

*Therapist:* Joan, we need to begin by discovering why this part is sending you headaches. But before we uncover its purpose, it needs to be willing to talk with you. I suspect that this part feels that you hate and resent it because you have come to dread your headaches and see them as something that has, at least, partially ruined your life. So we need to send a different message.

Begin by exploring around inside and get a sense about the presence of this part. Reach out to it until you can feel it. It may reveal itself as a bodily sensation like a dark cloud in the midsection. Or it might hear a voice or see an image of it. It could be you at a younger age. Or it could simply be an amorphous feeling. Take your time and nod when you can sense the presence of the part.

(After about 30 seconds, Joan gives a nod.)

Good, That's right. OK, let's begin dialog with it. Using your own words, I want you to tell this part that you are really interested in getting to know it and, especially, getting to know the purpose of sending you these headaches. Just say that to it and wait for a response. You might sense that it is open to communicating with you or you might feel that it is blocked or held back or you might sense something else. Let me know what kind of response you get to the message offering to communicate.

*Joan:* (after about 20 seconds of silence) I gave it the message but all I got back was a kind of hostile silence.

*Therapist:* Like it doesn't trust you?

*Joan:* Yes.

*Therapist:* OK, I want you to come out of trance so we can talk about this. Take in a deep breath and slowly let it out and as you exhale, feel yourself coming back up out of trance, your eyes getting ready to open, that's right. All the way back.

Joan came out of trance and we spent a few minutes discussing all the times that she had disparaged this part and how it must feel given years of being portrayed as a malevolent force. After this brief discussion, Joan went back into a trance state and prepared to address the "headache" part again. This process—of moving out of trance and then back in—often results in subsequently deeper trance experiences.

*Therapist:* Again feeling free to use your own words I'd like you to tell this part that you understand why it might not be willing to talk to you given the many years you attacked it and put it down. But now, today, you are approaching with a different attitude. You have a curiosity about whether you've misunderstood this part. You wonder if it might have had a deeper purpose all along. And you are truly interested in listening and understanding. Say that to the part and let me know the feeling you get about its response.

*Joan:* (after a minute of silence) it really relaxed a lot when I told it that.

*Therapist:* OK, now we're ready for the next step. I want you to ask the part to send you a signal that you can detect, a signal that we can use to communicate. It could be a body signal like increasing your heart rate or sending a twinge of headache pain; it could be a visual signal like a flash of an image from your past;

it could be something else. Just be very still and ask the part to send you a signal you can detect. And let me know when you get the signal.

*Joan:* (after 30 seconds of silence) I got something. My neck muscles tightened up like steel.
*Therapist:* Oh, yes. Do you have this feeling around your headaches?
*Joan:* Yes, I almost always do.
*Therapist:* OK, that sounds like the signal, all right. But we're going to test it. Please tell the part that we want to set up a signal system. If it wants to say "yes" to a question, it should send the signal; if it wants to say "no," it shouldn't send the signal and if it agrees, it should send the "yes" signal.
*Joan:* It already did. My neck feels incredibly tight.

This signal is an ideomotor response and is used just like the finger signals described above. It is assumed that the signal is directly generated by the part and allows for direct communication with this subconscious part.

*Therapist:* That's good. So we've got a confirmation. Next question I want you to ask is whether the part is willing to tell you the purpose that underlies sending the headaches. If it is willing, it should send the "yes" signal.
*Joan:* (after 10 seconds): I've got a "yes."
*Therapist:* Great. So now make your mind a blank—create a receptive space— and ask the part to send you the purpose. Then simply observe. Something will come in like a feeling, or an old memory, or a series of images. Sometimes the parts send something literal—almost like a person talking to you. Simply be open and let the part communicate.
*Joan (after a minute of silence):* I've got a memory of a time with my father back in high school.
*Therapist:* OK, good. Take in a deep breath again and as you slowly exhale, feel yourself coming back up to the surface, allow your eyes to open.

The image was a memory of a time when Joan had presented a poor report card to her father. He was furious with her and had impressed on her that if she didn't go to a good college, her life would essentially be ruined and she would amount to nothing. There was a memorable quote in the interaction— something like "if you continue wasting your time and don't learn how to work hard, you're going to be torn apart by the world." Joan noted that ever since, she had had a terribly guilty feeling if she ever slows down and relaxes. She even added that this father wound was central to her decision not to have children; she didn't feel she could work at her current pace and find time to be a mother. She noted that her husband kept telling her she needed to relax more but she mostly ignored this advice.

*Therapist:* So it sounds like this part believes that due to the fear instilled by your father, you've been living a kind of driven life, one where any other activity besides hard work makes you feel scared and guilty.

*Joan:* That sounds about right.

*Therapist:* And do you respect this purpose? Do you like having a part that is standing up for balance in your life? Do you want to explore the side of being human that is the opposite of being driven by fear?

*Joan:* Yes, I've sort of known this for a long time and I feel ready to deal with it.

*Therapist:* OK, then. Let's go back inside. Take in another deep breath and, as you exhale, feel your eyes closing. Go right back into the presence of the headache part. And I want you to ask the part if you've understood the purpose correctly. Using your own words, repeat the idea that its purpose is to help you find balance in your life, to move you away from fear when you are not working hard, to help you say "yes" to relaxing, enjoying and creating. If this is the purpose, have it send a yes signal.

*Joan (after 30 seconds):* I got a very strong "yes."

*Therapist:* Fine, now we need to find out if it is willing to stop sending the headaches if you adopt other behaviors designed to fulfill the purpose. Ask if it is willing.

*Joan:* Another "yes."

Joan came back out of trance and discussed what decisions and behaviors she might offer the part that would embody its purpose. She settled on going to dinner and a music concert with her husband and going for a walk on the beach with her girlfriend three times a week. She went back into trance.

*Therapist:* Ask the part if it approves of each of these ideas. You should get a "yes" for each one.

*Joan:* Got 'em.

*Therapist:* Now ask the part If it will come up with one or two other things it wants you to do to embody its purpose. You aren't going to know what these other things are; the part will take care of making these things happen. Ask for a "yes" confirming that the part is adding its own new behaviors to the two you have offered.

*Joan:* (after about a minute): Another yes.

*Therapist:* Take some time to thank the part. Show your gratitude but also include your affirmation that you are serious about adopting this new life philosophy. Pay attention to the response of the part. Does it feel open/closed, tense/relaxed, whatever.

*Joan:* I got a real sense that it is very happy with this new plan.

*Therapist:* OK, one final question: but this time you need to address the whole psyche not just the part. I want you to make a general broadcast. Ask inside whether there is any other part that objects in any way to this idea of living a balanced life and alternating hard work with relaxation, creativity, and allowing life to flow. Ask the question and then be very quiet. Pay attention to anything that arises but particularly notice whether you get a sense of general relaxation and relief or some kind of tension, fear or objection.

*Joan:* It felt kind of like there was a quiet but meaningful applause.

Joan returned in a week reporting no headaches. Three weeks later she had the beginning of a headache but closed her eyes and told the part that it had promised no headaches if she did her part. She noted that she had really enjoyed the concert and the beach walks. I asked if she had any idea what the part had picked to execute and she said, with mild embarrassment, that she and her husband were having experiences in the bedroom that they had never had before.

This case can be analyzed from a variety of perspectives. The constructionists would note that I made a variety of suggestions that shaped Joan's experience as the dialog unfolded. I suggested the existence of the part, that it had a purpose, that it would communicate if it were respected, and so forth. The question of whether there really is a headache part that really had a purpose is, of course, immaterial to the outcome. Joan and I co-created the reality and it was sufficiently solid to stimulate mind-body responses that led to a diminution of her headache pain.

For this chapter, the important part of the case is that in her altered state of trance, Joan had a direct experience of dialog with her unconscious mind. In secular space, our unconscious mind in unavailable; in sacred space, we can talk to the Gods, the Spirits, and, of course, the unconscious mind. We can not only talk to it, but it responds back directly. The Oracle is the voice of the Gods. It exists in sacred space and the seeker makes a pilgrimage to hear its words. Joan made the inner pilgrimage and returned from sacred space with a plan from the oracle—from a sacred source.

## INTEGRATING THE SACRED INTO PSYCHOLOGY

To see a World in a Grain of Sand
And a Heaven in a Wild Flower,
Hold Infinity in the palm of your hand
And Eternity in an hour.

—William Blake, *Poems from the Pickering Manuscript* (1805)

Eliade tells us that we are all *homo religiosus*—the human who is predisposed to divide the world into sacred space and secular space, the human who can archetypally sense the presence of numinosity. Given that this is such a basic human experience, it is natural that psychotherapy should have evolved tools, techniques, and approaches that maximize this experience and use it for healing and growth.

There are a great many approaches in psychotherapy that include a focus on altered states, sacred space, and the Dionysian perspective. Most somatic psychotherapies have strong altered state components; EMDR is another example; most cathartic therapies also create profound altered states. Therapies that focus on rituals like sweat lodges, and group therapies that intentionally create intense emotional states like encounter or psychodrama groups, are additional examples.

At this point scientific psychology begins to be nervous. Numinosity is difficult to measure and the presence or absence of sacred space cannot be scored on a psychological test. Moreover, the hallmark of Dionysian therapies is rapid and radical change. As has been pointed out in a number of the chapters above, rapid change must be resisted by the dominant forces in the culture. Rapid change implies that everything is falling apart and that nothing is permanent. It suggests that the rules are not as solid as they seem. The illusion of stability feels threatened. Finally, hypnosis and other altered state experiences have been "owned" by fringe groups like entertainers, psychic readers, and new age healers. These approaches are so Dionysian that Apollonian scientists find them off putting at best and unethical, fraudulent and exploitive at worst.

Yet in the geography of constructionism—which locates these approaches and techniques at the edge of the Abyss—they belong to the human experience just as fully as CBT, electroshock, or communications theory. While this may be true, their forbidden/dangerous aspects will have an effect on every psychotherapist who chooses to explore the area.

The most basic approach is to simply define away the entire area. These excessively Dionysian processes cannot be part of psychology because they cannot be easily quantified by science and therefore should be left to fields that have less rigorous methodologies such as religious studies. No one can accurately determine how many psychologists endorse this approach but from the relative paucity of studies in the area and the limited number of professors specializing in altered states at major universities, it is likely that a significant number of psychologists feel this way.

Conversely there are always some that leap at the chance to go wildly Dionysian. These tools and approaches create high impact experiences that are numinous and powerful. Many of these sorts of practitioners might do well to recall Yalom's belief that high impact experiences alone fail to create meaningful change. An even more cogent critique comes from a well-known Buddhist quote: "Be somebody before you become nobody." This quote is generally interpreted as a recommendation to take care that the foundations of your life are solid before seeking Dionysian experiences. On the one hand, there is danger that the practitioner can get lost in such experiences given the lack of foundation. Even more importantly, the saying suggests that some of those who seek powerful Dionysian experiences may be afraid to build healthy foundations and are hoping that a leap into numinosity will allow them to bypass the basics. Not surprisingly, such a strategy is risky not only for the therapist, but for his clients as well.

But if the therapist has taken care of his foundations, and if he is not satisfied with the idea that science is the one and only valid epistemology for psychotherapy, then it is inevitable that he will eventually encounter sacred space and the numinous. Eliade tells us that hierophanies abound in the world. Recognizing them and responding to them allows us to experience sacred space. And these experiences inform how we do psychotherapy.

It is never necessary to become adept at the overtly Dionysian approaches described in this chapter; the research clearly indicates that one can achieve superior functioning given a sincere affiliation with any school or approach, even a school that overtly precludes Dionysian techniques. But for many, such limitations make no sense. If humans are regularly having altered states, healthy ones that lead to healing, and damaging ones—like trauma—that lead to suffering, it is natural to want to become expert in such experiences. And that, of course, is what the approaches in this chapter offer.

It should be noted that this same rapid change does not come free of charge; put another way, the faster a client changes, the more her regular world will resist the change—homeostasis—and attempt to move her back into her chronic level of functioning. The Net never supports change; it supports continuity. So after rapid, positive change, the Net operates to return the client to her previous state. Even positive forces such as caring friends or a loving family may find it difficult to accept and support rapid change.

At one point in my career, I was the head of research for Outward Bound USA. Not surprisingly, when measured over time, OB achieved the same kind of results as other therapeutic interventions: a modest, positive outcome. Of course, the estimate of the level of change at the end of the course was much higher; as mentioned above, comments such as "I'm a completely different person" and "This was the most powerful experience of my life" were very common. Unfortunately, that level of transformation was not sustained.

Once, when discussing the results in our small research unit, one person made the statement: "Outward Bound is good for the students, but it is transformative for the instructors." The act of unconsciously functioning as a "demigod" in sacred space was an even more profound experience than simply attending the course. Immersing oneself in the sacred—whether in external form or internal—can be a profoundly moving experience for the therapist. This hearkens back to the concept that performance of certain psychotherapeutic techniques has more power to change the therapist than the client.

To me, one of the great mysteries of the research literature is how a therapist fails to improve due to experience in the room. Virtually every therapist reports profound experiences of connection, wonder, open heartedness, and meaning on a more-or-less regular basis. How could repeated exposure to these experiences fail to make more experienced therapists superior to newcomers?

Perhaps it is the hesitancy about adopting a sacred worldview and the resistance to using sacred language. Once again, this is Yalom's argument: an altered state without an appropriate frame fails to lead to growth. Scientific psychology permits the therapist-client bond to exist and, of course, strongly supports it. But there are few schools of therapy that teach the therapist or the client that psychotherapy often leads into sacred space. The *Informed Consent Form* does not include a caution that "some psychotherapeutic techniques may create epiphanies and others might lead to spiritual experiences." Given that psychotherapy is part of the perennial philosophy, and that philosophy predicts that inner exploration inevitably leads to sacred space, perhaps one of our largest failings is that our scientism is hindering the maximization of our experiences—both the client experiences and the therapist experiences. It is possible that both are having "spiritual" experiences, but without appropriate expectations they occur in a vacuum—without a meaningful label they fail to be fully integrated.

Earlier chapters have pointed out that the evolutionary aspect of the Tillichian model requires one's ultimate concern to evolve as appropriate across the life span; integrating the concept of the sacred and the numinous into the ultimate concern certainly fits the evolutionary model. This Dionysian chapter also highlights the deliberate practice approach, the concept that practitioners tend to concentrate on their strengths and systematically neglect their weaknesses. In this sense, Whittaker and Farrelly urged therapists to become comfortable with the uses of power in therapy, pointing out that some therapists have neglected the Apollonian. As one might expect, other therapists have similarly neglected the Dionysian.

This chapter on overt Dionysian approaches asks us to confront our fears at a deeper level. As has been discussed, these approaches lie at the edge of the Net and the beginning of the Abyss. The edge of the world is the place where one might fall off and be lost forever. Dionysian psychotherapeutic approaches similarly lie at the edge of the psychotherapeutic world. Psychology has made certain efforts to integrate these approaches, in part by providing categories such as transpersonal psychology and hypnotherapy. This attempt to name or categorize operates partially to contain the dangerous aspects of these tools. But for many in psychology, the naming is not sufficient; the numinous continues to mark the edge of the known world, the place where "angels fear to tread."

For therapists seeking to maximize their charisma in order to be more effective with their clients these approaches mark an important fork in the road. Go forward and bear the risk of slipping off the edge or stay behind and wonder what opportunities for growth may have been sacrificed. With all the discussion of the pros and cons of Dionysian change perhaps the best guidance comes from the modeling of the therapeutic wizards. Their acknowledgment—consciously or unconsciously—of their role as key individuals inevitably draws them toward Dionysian approaches. They are compelled to push the limits of the power that comes through them, to wonder what might be possible if they cooperate with it fully.

We have already discussed fearing the power of the Apollonian; it is a tremendous responsibility to say to a client, "You're going the wrong way. Reverse course and do the right thing." Similarly, it is an equally daunting responsibility to embrace Dionysian power. To say to a client: "Infinite possibilities abound. There are doors surrounding you—doors that lead to healing and rapid change. I have been through these doors and invite you to join me on such a journey." The ability to say something like that to a client—and to say it from a firm foundation—marks the therapist who is prepared to step up to the possibilities of Dionysian healing. Pushing this experience to the limit enhances therapeutic charisma.

*Chapter 14*

# The Spiritual Path

Turn away no more;
Why wilt thou turn away?
The starry floor,
The watery shore
Is given thee till the break of day.

—William Blake, *Songs of Experience* (1794)

Continuing the metaphor of exploring the geography of constructed reality, this chapter on spirituality is centered on experiences, approaches, and practices which arise secondary to leaping into the Abyss. The last chapter on sacred space was focused on experiences at the edge of the Net and the Abyss. This chapter goes further and follows those who have fallen off the edge of the world.

Many writers have taken care to distinguish religion from spirituality. Using the language of this book, religion consists of Apollonian rules and structures that essentially work to sustain the Net; spirituality consists of experiences, insights, and perceptions that arise from encounters with the Abyss. Put in terms of Kohlberg's developmental hierarchy, religion operates at the Conventional stage of moral development and spirituality operates at the Post-Conventional. Put in Tillichian terms, religion defines faith as an unsubstantiated belief and spirituality defines faith as a relationship to an ultimate concern.

Before we can advance very far, it is important to address the resistance present in many therapists when it comes to working directly with a client's spirituality. Imposing the therapist's religious beliefs seems too much like evangelizing, too close to violating the client's individuality. In addition, using a spiritual model is often problematic because many therapists have difficulty understanding and respecting the client's specific spiritual path. Finally, religiosity is often identified with the conservative values and the oppression of certain liminal groups and these stances and actions are antithetical to many psychologists. Pargament and Faigin (2012) comment:

Helping clients access their own religious resources is unfamiliar territory for most psychotherapists. For example, as a group, psychologists are considerably less religious than the general population (Shafranske, 2001), and therefore often unaware of the wealth of resources that are contained in the world's religions. This problem is compounded by the fact that only a small percentage of graduate programs in clinical psychology provide students with any training in religion and spirituality (Brawer, Handal, Fabricatore, Roberts, & Wajda-Johnston, 2002). But the problem may go beyond unfamiliarity. From Freud to Skinner to Ellis, there is a long tradition of religious antipathy in the field, perhaps growing out of its efforts to establish itself as a "hard science" and distinguish itself from its disciplinary kin—philosophy and theology. Stereotypic notions of religion as a pacifier, a defense, or a form of denial are still commonplace among mental health professionals, even though these stereotypes are not empirically supported (Pargament, 1997). It would be more accurate to describe religion as a potential resource for many people. (p. 313)

Pargament and Faigin are, of course, correct when they document the difficulty that many psychotherapists experience when working with religion; if anything, they can be accused of underestimating the problems. For example, they fail to discuss the ongoing "war" between science and religion. In a previous chapter, the terms premodern, modern, and postmodern were discussed. These terms define the source of authority for the Apollonian task of constructing the cultural net. The modern perspective argues that science has the authority to determine the collective Net; being premodern implies that religion has the largest voice, and so on. Obviously, there is a huge struggle—particularly between religion and science—about which camp shall be granted the final authority. Premodern determined the composition of the Net before the 1700s; science gets a major say currently (although religion is certainly continuing the fight), and postmodern is simply a set of ideas—mostly at universities—that has significantly less power when it comes to defining the Net.

It is important to note that this struggle is all about the collective nature of the Net. Neither of the two dominant approaches has to do with healing, therapy, therapist efficacy, or therapist evolution. They are both about authorship of the collective agreement about how our culture defines reality and ultimate authority. Both approaches are championed by Apollonians who are interested in imposing their worldviews on the rest of the culture.

Psychology, of course, is smack dab in the middle of this war and embraces implicit assumptions that anything "scientific" is good and anything "religious" will return us to the Dark Ages. It is not a far stretch to argue that this political and existential struggle has been partly responsible for psychology's ability to ignore the research results; admitting that the research results prove that clinical psychology is "not scientific" feels like an unbearable capitulation. The collective denial of psychology about the research is ironically similar to the collective denial of certain religious authorities on evolution.

This book, of course, adopts a postmodern perspective and this chapter is essentially about spirituality, not religion, but it is almost impossible not to get caught in the "war" when discussing such topics. Put another way, spirituality exists across all three historical dimensions but it is so interwoven with religion that it is difficult to see it as sui generis—the thing in itself. And in this confusion the baby is thrown out with the bathwater and the importance of spirituality is lost in the maelstrom. Einstein (2011), who, of course, embodied the scientific perspective nonetheless managed to differentiate between the two principles when he famously said:

> Then there are the fanatical atheists whose intolerance is of the same kind as the intolerance of the religious fanatics and comes from the same source. They are like slaves who are still feeling the weight of their chains which they have thrown off after hard struggle. They are creatures who—in their grudge against the traditional "opium for the people"—cannot bear the music of the spheres. (p. 97)

Returning to Pargament and Faigin's point about the benefits of working with client religiosity, imagine the usefulness of being able to function effectively within the sphere of the client's own spiritual beliefs. Go further, and imagine being able to encourage an extension of their beliefs. Given that virtually every spiritual and religious approach urges—or commands—its followers to adopt exemplary, prosocial behaviors, the spiritually oriented therapist can align herself with these values. More specifically, therapists frequently recommend healthy choices and behaviors: be honest, persevere when you are challenged, and give to others. How helpful can it be to add, "I'm not only recommending these ideas to you but you made a covenant with God to behave this way. Don't you take that promise seriously?"

On another level, many religious teachings directly address the chronic neurotic impulses of certain clients, particularly the self-destructive strategies of personality disorders. There are spiritual teachings on topics ranging from taking responsibility, communication strategies, social isolation, dealing with guilt and self-deprecation, and how to trust. But where spirituality truly shines, of course, is in its teachings about anxiety. Whether the client is more conservative in his beliefs and endorses the idea of an afterlife or whether he believes in the concept of "no self," spiritual approaches to anxiety offer a perspective on dealing with the uncontrollable and the unpredictable that significantly outshines any psychotherapeutic approach. Being able to say something like, "You have surrendered to God and put yourself in his hands. It's normal to have doubt and fear about whether you are loveable and whether you will be supported. You can buttress your faith and your covenant by attending church and Bible Study and especially by listening to stories of other members of your faith who can testify about the protection of the Lord."

On a higher level, when clients are discussing motivation, meaning and purpose, spirituality again has something special to contribute. The humanistic and existential answers that are psychology's typical offerings pale in comparison to ideas and concepts based on thousands of years of religious contemplation. Pargament and Faigin (2012) summarize some research that bears on this topic:

> It could be argued that religion does not add anything distinctive to the mix of coping resources people can draw on when they encounter major life stressors. After all, religious and spiritual support could be viewed as merely examples of more general support. Transcendent meaning systems could be understood as simply one subset of secular meaning systems. Yet, several empirical studies suggest that religious resources make unique contributions to health and well-being, even after accounting for the effects of secular coping resources. For instance, working with a national sample of elders, Krause (2006) compared the role of emotional support received from church members with the emotional support received from nonchurch members as buffers of the effects of financial strain on self-rated health. Whereas church-based emotional support emerged as a buffer, secular support did not. Interpreting these findings, Krause emphasized the distinctive character of church-based support: It is particularly helpful because it is enacted in a group that shares a spiritual worldview and commitment to God, a common set of sacred beliefs, values, and coping methods, shared religious principles, rituals, and memories, and a support that is "imbued with the mantle of religious authority." (p. 314)

Knowledge of the religious worldview significantly assists reframing when working with spiritually inclined clients. However, while these examples may be compelling, they are unavailable to many therapists unless they can find an ethical and authentic way to access their own spiritual beliefs. Even therapists who are very spiritual can find it difficult to bridge the gap between their beliefs and the beliefs of a client that seem immature, wrong, oppressive, or limited.

This chapter has the same goals as preceding chapters: to define a set of psychological practices in the context of the geography of constructed reality and to discuss particular approaches to mastering those practices that can enhance the therapist's charisma. This chapter is somewhat different than preceding chapters in that some of the technology does, indeed, come from psychology but many of the practices have originally been developed by various spiritual traditions. Is it proper to include such techniques in a book focused on enhancing psychotherapeutic outcomes?

Three responses come to mind. First, psychology has been integrating these kinds of techniques for many years and that integration appears to be strengthening, particularly in the area of Buddhist psychology and meditation. Second, psychology is as much a part of the perennial philosophy as any other approach to understanding the human condition. The perennial philosophy argues that every serious inquiry into meaning and happiness will have much in common with all other serious inquiries. Hence, there can be open dialog between psychological techniques and spiritual techniques.

But it is the third reason that is the most important. This book has been attempting to answer the question: "if psychotherapy really operates in constructed reality, what are the full implications for improving therapist outcomes?" The moment we recognize that the vast majority of clinical psychology is in constructed reality, we are forced to discard scientific boundaries; we can no longer say that psychology can only operate in areas that can be measured, replicated, and assessed. Instead, we are forced to examine the full range of human experience and that, of course, includes the spiritual. It is no accident that in constructed reality, ritual replaces technique. And ritual is a word with profound spiritual associations and connotations. Constructionism forces us to address the place of formal spiritual practices in psychology.

## THE PATH OF WISDOM

> How can you prove whether at this moment we are sleeping, and all
> our thoughts are a dream; or whether we are awake, and talking to one
> another in the waking state?
>
> —Plato, *The Dialogues of Plato* (1907)

Every constructionist is already part way down the path of wisdom. All wisdom traditions share the concept that achieving wisdom requires learning to free ourselves from conventional assumptions and programmed thinking. Taking one's beliefs apart generates the experience of emptiness—the Abyss—and results in a perspective on normal human functioning that generally disparages simple answers to existential questions. Moreover, it brings real clarity about fundamental reality versus constructed reality. There are various words that describe the confusion that ensues when one confabulates the two; some words characterizing this distressing state include Maya (illusion), Lila (Divine play), and the Wheel of Samsara (birth and death).

Of course, there is no use in undertaking such an examination unless the result somehow leads to enhanced happiness and satisfaction. Hence, the concepts in chapter 4—"A Place to Stand"—become prominent. In all wisdom paths there is an explicit promise that pursuing wisdom—and disputing that which is programmed and impermanent—will lead to some kind of truth, bliss, and inner peace. This is typically supported by reports from advanced seekers, individuals who have achieved direct inner experiences of harmony and balance. As an example, please review the following experience described by Eckhart Tolle, the author of *The Power of Now*. Note that his experience occurred following the classic wisdom path question "Who am I?"

For most people, spiritual awakening is a gradual process. Rarely does it happen all at once. When it does, though, it is usually brought about by intense suffering. That was certainly true in my case. For years my life alternated between depression and acute anxiety. One night I woke up in a state of dread and intense fear, more intense than I had ever experienced before. Life seemed meaningless, barren, hostile. It became so unbearable that suddenly the thought came into my mind, "I cannot live with myself any longer." The thought kept repeating itself several times. Suddenly, I stepped back from the thought, and looked at it, as it were, and I became aware of the strangeness of that thought: "If I cannot live with myself, there must be two of me—the I and the self that I cannot live with." And the question arose, "Who is the 'I' and who is the self that I cannot live with?" There was no answer to that question, and all thinking stopped. For a moment, there was complete inner silence. Suddenly I felt myself drawn into a whirlpool or a vortex of energy. I was gripped by an intense fear, and my body started to shake. I heard the words, "Resist nothing," as if spoken inside my chest. I could feel myself being sucked into a void. Suddenly, all fear disappeared, and I let myself fall into that void. I have no recollection of what happened after that.

The next morning I awoke as if I had just been born into this world. Everything seemed fresh and pristine and intensely alive. A vibrant stillness filled my entire being. As I walked around the city that day, the world looked as if it had just come into existence, completely devoid of the past. I was in a state of amazement at the peace I felt within and the beauty I saw without, even in the midst of the traffic. I was no longer labeling and interpreting my sense perceptions—an almost complete absence of mental commentary. To this day, I perceive and interact with the world in this way: through stillness, not through mental noise. The peace that I felt that day, more than 20 years ago, has never left me, although it has varying degrees of intensity.

At the time, I had no conceptual framework to help me understand what had happened to me. Years later, I realized that the acute suffering I felt that night must have forced my consciousness to withdraw from identification with the unhappy self, the suffering "little me," which is ultimately a fiction of the mind. This withdrawal must have been so complete that the suffering self collapsed as if the plug had been pulled out of an inflatable toy. What was left was my true nature as the ever present "I AM": consciousness in its pure state prior to identification with form. You may also call it pure awareness or presence. (Simon, n.d.)

The Tolle experience successfully captures the flavor of the path of wisdom. Fear is gone, replaced by a sense of stillness and presence. Tolle is talking about living in the world without the intermediary effects of the "Net." Note how he repeatedly uses "Abyss" language. Life seemed meaningless, barren, and hostile; clearly, Tolle was at the edge of the Abyss. Then he falls into a vortex of energy that sucks him into the void. This is a clear example of the perennial philosophy, the philosophy that argues that mystical experiences across varying traditions are phenomenologically identical. Experiences like this are self-validating and appear to contain answers to the mystery of life.

Each great religion has its own version of the path to wisdom and the perennial philosophy suggests they are roughly equivalent. In that sense, we can assume that any path to wisdom from one of the great religions conveys the essence of seeking God via wisdom. We will use the Buddhist path as our primary example of a wisdom path, partly because it is well organized and relatively easy to understand and partly because it has made such great contributions to psychotherapy in recent years.

Understanding Buddhism begins, of course, with an understanding of the Four Noble Truths: the existence of suffering, the cause of suffering, the truth that suffering can be removed, and the way of removal. Makransky (2012) describes "suffering" as follows:

(Buddhism describes) three levels of suffering: (1) obvious suffering, (2) the suffering of transience, and (3) the suffering of self-centered conditioning.

The suffering of self-centered conditioning underlies the prior two. *This form of suffering is inherent in the mind's subconscious attempt to create from the impermanent flow of its experience the impression of a substantial, unchanging, and separate sense of self surrounded by a stable world.* The mind's ongoing attempt to fabricate such a reified, unchanging impression of self and world, in turn, conditions numerous anxious patterns of thought and reaction: clinging to whatever seems to affirm a fixed, unchanging self and its world, fearing or hating whatever seems to threaten it (see chapters 9 and 13). To oscillate uncontrollably through such feelings in reaction to our mental constructs of self and others is the suffering of self-centered conditioning. (p. 62)

Essentially the Buddhists are agreeing with Becker when they describe the "obvious suffering" inherent in being embodied and having a destiny to die. The second level of suffering describes the futility of searching for happiness by seeking pleasure and avoiding pain—indulging in strategies motivated by desire and fear.

However, it is the third level of suffering, "self-centered conditioning," which Makransky believes is the most important level of suffering—so important that it is a foundation for all other suffering. Reread the italicized sentence in the quote. Examining it closely reveals that it is virtually identical to the Apollonian commitment to sustaining and supporting the Nomological Net. This entire book is focused on understanding the implications of this definition of suffering for helping clients and for being a more effective change agent. Buddhists might argue that psychology has yet to develop a treatment system that adds value because all of its systems are implicitly founded on "clinging to whatever seems to affirm a fixed, unchanging self and . . . world." Moreover, practitioners fail to improve from practice because they do not examine the underlying assumptions of their approach—assumptions that covertly encourage "the futile attempt to get, have, and hold onto pleasant things as if they could be a stable source of security and well-being."

Following this detailed definition of suffering, Buddhism moves on to the fourth Noble Truth, the way of removing suffering. This removal consists of the concrete practices which lead to the cessation of suffering. Chief among those practices are mindfulness and meditation. Every time reality is reified, it supports suffering; every time Self and Reality are experienced as fluid—no Self and emptiness—it supports wisdom. Wisdom practitioners are enjoined to witness this dynamic in every aspect of their life from meditation, to work, to relationships.

Mindfulness begins with meditation practice where the meditator observes and witnesses all the activity of the mind and body moving across the sensorium. Through an intention to simply observe and not generate thoughts and feelings, the meditator becomes aware that the thoughts and feelings are being generated by themselves; in other words, they are coming from "non self." In this sense, mindfulness and meditation support the concept of non-identification with thoughts and feelings. Reexamine the earlier quote from Tara Brach (2012) on mindfulness:

> In the simplest terms, mindfulness is the intentional process of paying attention, without judgment, to the unfolding of moment-to-moment experience. It is the opposite of trance, a word I use to describe all the ways in which we—therapists and clients alike—live inside a limiting story about life. (p. 37)

In this quote, Brach is pointing out that the same process that is applied during formal meditation can be employed in normal life. In meditation there is a process of focusing and observing punctuated by forgetting that one is meditating and becoming caught up in the thoughts and feelings. Brach cautions against "trance," the process where one "forgets" to be mindful and begins to live as if all the thoughts and feelings are real.

The Brach quote bridges the gap between formal sitting meditation and what is often called meditation in action. Meditation in action is the practice of observing daily life using the same principles employed in sitting meditation. More specifically, the practitioner pays attention to all the experiences of daily life, both the inner life with attendant feelings, attachments, and thoughts, and the outer life with relational encounters, successes and failures, danger, and pleasures. And, just as in meditation, the practitioner regularly loses focus, identifies with the inner and outer world experiences, and "goes into trance." To minimize these distracting experiences, meditation in action builds from the simplest experiences (sitting and walking meditations), to moderately complex ones (e.g., cooking and cleaning meditation), to complex situations (e.g., workplace and relationship meditations) to the most challenging (meditation during desire, fear, and conflict).

This practice of meditation in action is available to every practitioner, twenty-four hours a day, and in every situation. Although it may be introduced in a hierarchical order from simple to complex, in reality, every moment of life has the same opportunity for presence, awareness, detachment, and openhearted compassion.

Buddhism and its chief practices essentially deprogram the world and the self. In that sense, they are an embodiment of constructionism. Interestingly, however, constructionism stops with the world disassembled. Everything is taken apart but there are no implications about what to do next. Buddhism argues that this deconstruction has implications for the heart, for connection, and for compassion. Makransky (2012) comments:

> As noted, the sufferings of transience and self-centered conditioning are mediated by unconscious habits of reification—the mind's attempt to generate and cling to a sense of permanence in self and world that the mind projects onto its impermanent experience. As our tendencies to cling to illusions of permanence are illuminated by mindful awareness, we become newly conscious of how much anxiety and unease our clinging has generated. We can then start to recognize the same subconscious layers of suffering operating in all others. Thus sympathy and compassion for self and others emerge with increasing power as we gain insight into impermanence and the constructed nature of self. Such sympathy and compassion in relation to our selves inform the gentle, accepting quality of mindful attention, giving our mind permission to open to further insight. And this, in turn, helps empower an increasingly compassionate and discerning awareness of others in their conscious and subconscious sufferings. (p. 63)

Makransky argues that awareness of our own attachment leads to self-compassion. Awareness of the same forces operating in our others—particularly our clients—leads to compassion for the other. This is one of the core tenants of Buddhism: real mindfulness is inseparable from compassion and connection. While Tillich would agree, Sartre and Becker certainly did not find this connection inevitable or even possible. The Buddhists would respond that Sartre and Becker did not go far enough; without a formal meditation practice, their deconstruction was limited to an intellectual exercise. Sartre and Becker would counter with the concept that the Buddhists were programmed to associate compassion with deprogramming. And Tillich would have the final word with his definition of faith as inclusive of doubt.

The Buddhists are so serious about their deprogramming that they try to advance a view of Reality unconditioned by fear and desire. Of course, unprogrammed reality is reality unshaped and unformed by the Net. In this book, that is equivalent to the Abyss. In Buddhist terms, it is called "emptiness." In the following quote from Sri Nisargadatta note how he also uses the metaphor of the net.

> The real world is beyond our thoughts and ideas: we see it through the net of our desires, divided into pleasure and pain, right and wrong, inner and outer. To see the universe as it is, you must step beyond the net. It is not hard to do so, for the net is full of holes. (Kornfield, 1993, p. 202)

Nisargadatta's definition of "net" aligns perfectly with the Nomological Net concept that is so basic to this book. Right and wrong and inner and outer support cultural norms whereas pleasure and pain tend to support the stable existence of the Self. "I want/fear, therefore I am" is the Buddhist equivalent of Descartes.

But Nisargadatta recommends stepping through the holes in the net to see things as they are. Stepping through the holes is equivalent to launching into the Abyss. There is no longer any net to organize the raw material of emptiness—nothing to protect us from the sense of undifferentiated chaos.

Before making this step into emptiness, the Buddhists recommend preparation. Recall that Buber agrees and urged aspirants to become strong in the conventional world before responding to the call of the Abyss. Jack Kornfield, noted Buddhist teacher, comments on the famous "be someone" quote:

> Jack Engler, the Buddhist teacher and psychologist at Harvard, put it this way: "You must be somebody before you can be nobody." By this he means that a strong and healthy sense of self is needed to withstand the meditative process of dissolution and come to a deep realization of emptiness. (Kornfield, 1993, pp. 205–206)

Kornfield goes on to caution that if one enters emptiness or encounters the Abyss prematurely, it will be experienced as meaninglessness, indifference, or depression. But if the seeker is prepared then the encounter with the Abyss will bear fruit.

True emptiness is not empty, but contains all things. The mysterious and pregnant void creates and reflects all possibilities. From it arises our individuality, which can be discovered and developed, although never possessed or fixed. The self is held in no-self, as the candle flame is held in great emptiness. The great capacities of love, unique destiny, life, and emptiness intertwine, shining, reflecting the one true nature of life. (Kornfield, 1993, p. 212)

In sum, the very force which terrifies us, which causes us to cling so tightly to the Net, is the same force that ultimately sets us free. It is a circular journey where our jailer morphs into our liberator. The Abyss is all darkness viewed from one perspective and all light from another. Makransky (2012) provides a final definition.

To realize the emptiness of the world in this way is to realize that nirvana, the empty essence of experiences, is undivided from the world of interdependent, changing appearances in the same way in which space is undivided from all the forms that it pervades. To realize emptiness thus gives one the freedom to participate in the world without clinging to it, with unconditional compassion for all who suffer by clinging and reacting to their own concretized projections of self and other as self-existent. (p. 69)

How does this play out clinically? Obviously walking the path of wisdom in whatever specific version one finds appropriate permeates every moment of therapy with every type of client. But in this chapter, we want to specifically look at how understanding and practicing a wisdom path literally affects therapy with clients.

Constructionism leads to the edge of the Abyss; the path of wisdom requires that we leap into it. The void is empty and terrifying but entering by the right portal results in the kind of outcomes embodied in the Tolle quote. The practices prepare one for the leap. Essentially they are practices of purification and mindfulness. Purification practices such as ethical behaviors and confronting fear and desire allow one to be "somebody before becoming nobody." Mindfulness, discernment, and living in constant awareness of emptiness transform the leap from a destructive and terrifying one to one that yields peace and harmony. On the one hand, the path is spiritual and takes place in sacred space; on the other hand, there is a seamless integration between the path of wisdom and all other forms of transformation starting with the most basic Apollonian practices. Tara Brach (2012) offers a summary of the path.

The lucid, open, and kind presence evoked . . . leads to the . . . freedom of nonidentification and the realization of natural awareness or natural presence. Nonidentification means that your self-sense is not fused with, or defined by, any limited set of emotions, sensations, or stories about who you are. This realization that you are "no-thing"—that there is not a static, solid self—is the ultimate expression of wisdom and the essence of freedom. Identification keeps us locked into the "small self," the self of trance. When identification with the small self is loosened, when we are no-thing, we begin to intuit and live from the aliveness, openness, and love that express our natural awareness. As Indian teacher Nisargadatta Maharaj describes it:

Love says, "I am everything."
Wisdom says, "I am nothing."
Between these two my life flows. (pp. 43–44)

The therapist who has understood a wisdom path will find that it is a kind of super charged cognitive therapy—a therapy that can easily be adapted to address virtually all client presenting problems. In place of talking about rational and irrational beliefs, the Buddhist therapist can talk about whether an experience or a feeling is representative of "big mind" versus "little mind" and of "soft belly" versus armoring. As an example, in the following vignette, I work directly with a woman who has just had a positive experience at a spiritual retreat. However, on her return home she has run into significant difficulties in her intimate life.

A 38-year-old, Caucasian female who worked as a nurse presented complaining of depression secondary to a recent break up with her boyfriend. They had only dated for about three months but she reported that they had had a remarkable connection, with both of them talking about love, marriage, and permanency after the first few dates. A week before coming in to see me, he had seemed distant, and two days later he broke up with her because "he couldn't imagine marrying her." He refused to provide any more details and cut off communication.

Her friends rallied round her and discussed what might have occurred. When she presented in therapy, she had adopted one of her friend's theories and was thinking that he must have been a sociopath to have led her on so fervently and then drop her so suddenly. She couldn't stop thinking about him and was crying so much that it was difficult to go to work.

I began by agreeing with the client that his behavior was unusual and his pattern of "leading her on and then suddenly dumping her" did suggest that he was confused in some way or another. She replied with feeling that she was sure he was a sociopath and had even read several articles about how dangerous this kind of lover can be to a woman who assumes that people are going to be honest with her. Her affect was moving rapidly between anger at him and complete personal devastation as she accessed her own inner feelings.

I complimented her on being in touch with her feelings and said that anyone would be upset with how she had been treated. I further complimented her on her knowledge of psychopathology and agreed that there are dangerous men out there that prey on women, men that are often compelled by their psychopathology to repeat the same abusive choices again and again.

I then said that I knew she had recently been to a spiritual retreat and reminded her that she had reported to me that she had gained lots of insight and inner peace. I asked her to imagine that she was in front of her favorite speaker from the retreat and had the opportunity to ask the speaker's opinion about the relationship with the "sociopath."

The client looked inward and replied after a minute of consideration, "I think she would ask me to consider 'the' suffering instead of 'my' suffering." She explained that it had been very helpful to her to consider depersonalizing suffering by holding it in "big mind" as opposed to personalizing everything by reacting with "small mind." We discussed big mind in some detail in order to deepen her connection to the memory.

She regressed back to the retreat and identified an experience of suffering that she had worked on during that time. I had her relive her retreat work and specially focused on the lightness she felt as she stayed in "big mind."

I then asked her to "wrap this consciousness around her" and move to the memory of being devastated during his breakup talk. I suggested that she allow the memory to unfold by itself and note how different it would be with this altered state of consciousness.

The client reported that his breakup still made her sad but that she had an inner sense of being supported as she re-experienced the discussion. She added that she had never let in how confused he seemed during the talk and wondered what kind of disarray and darkness might be affecting his life. She looked curious, compassionate and much lighter. We discussed some possibilities that might be affecting him and then went on to discuss healthy grieving.

In this case the client had already completed her preparatory work; she simply needed to be reminded of what she had already learned. Clearly my ability to understand what might have been discussed at the retreat and to work comfortably with that material opened the door to a rapid resolution of a devastating loss. More importantly, I not only understood what she shared about her experience at the retreat, she could also feel that I endorsed it as a "truth." Working on the spiritual dimension requires the therapist to endorse the spiritual beliefs of the client as a "fellow traveler." This is significantly different than simply understanding the concepts she was expressing.

More important than the client's improvement, however, is the ability of the therapist to "feel" the truth that the client had been wounded and traumatized and still give her an option of addressing this painful breakup from a spiritual perspective. If the client hadn't been prepared to do this—at least on an unconscious level—she would have resisted the link between the retreat and the breakup and required us to dialog further about his pathology and her vulnerability. The Frank model requires an agreement between therapist and client about the rationale for the suffering and the nature of the ritual which purports to heal it. For the client, her readiness to adopt a spiritual frame led to rapid healing. For the therapist, offering such a frame and witnessing its success supports the sense of constructed reality as well as the oracular nature of the Abyss. This kind of witnessing is a key part of dancing with the Abyss.

This case illustrates what may be the most psychologically useful aspect of the path of wisdom: the ability to resolve painful and conflicted feelings simply by recognizing that they are constructed, impermanent, and unreal. As cognitive therapy teaches, feelings arise not from the event but from our interpretation of the event. Teachings about no self and constructionism are vastly more powerful than teachings about rational cognitions; the path of wisdom is CBT plus a 2000-year-old wisdom tradition. One can argue that the entire philosophical foundation of Buddhism exists to provide a "place to stand" where the practitioner can practice discernment and nonattachment.

Complementing this powerful technology is Buddhism's recognition that it is not adequate in all cases. Psychologists have long been aware of the dangers of intellectualizing problems without actually resolving them; typically, these inadequate strategies lead to displacement, affective leakage, and impulse control problems. In the next case, Jack Kornfield works with a practitioner who has attempted to control her shadow side via meditation and spiritual discernment. While she has advanced on her path, her work has hit a familiar impasse.

> Another student, a young woman, came to practice with a tremendous sense of insecurity and fear. In the great pain of her own early childhood she had found peace by withdrawing into silence and daydreams. By being quiet, she had avoided trouble and conflict with the world around her. On entering spiritual practice she was greatly relieved. Here was a place that officially sanctioned her silence and introversion and supported her withdrawal from the world. To her teachers she initially seemed to be a very fine meditation student, having no difficulty with the rules and silence, quieting herself easily and speaking of deep insights into the transient nature of life and how to avoid the dangers of attachment. She came to retreat after retreat, but at some point it became clear that she was using her practice to avoid and run away from the world, that her meditation had simply re-created the fear of her early family life. Her life . . . was limited to certain compartments. When this was brought to her attention, she complained bitterly. Didn't the Buddha speak of solitude, of sitting under trees in the forest, living a life of seclusion? Who were we as teachers to recommend anything different?
>
> Her denial was so difficult to break through that she wandered for many years meditating in different spiritual communities. Only after 10 years, after her own frustration and dissatisfaction grew strong enough, was she motivated begin to change her life, to break out of her compartments. (Kornfield, 1993, pp. 189–190)

This sort of intervention is very common. The spiritual path can be just as idolatrous—using Tillich's language—as the path of power, safety, or money. More importantly, any time a human tries to do something great, they will run into their own "stuff." For example, if I try to be an ideal parent or an ideal romantic partner, whatever unfinished business I have will come to the surface. Because of this principle, a great deal of time and effort on the spiritual path is spent focusing on issues that are commonly classified as "psychological."

Why was my client able to let her shadow feelings go and Kornfield's student was required to face and deal with her underlying issues? Sometimes the difference is simply the charisma of the therapist; in certain situations the client gets a "lift" from the therapist's sense of what is real and is better able to release what is constructed. In this situation, however, the difference was primarily due to the disparity between the two women's foundations; my client had learned to "be someone" more effectively than Kornfield's student.

How can one discern whether the client is intellectualizing versus actually letting go? When the Dalai Lama stated that compassion and wisdom are two wings of a bird, seemingly separate but actually identical, he was showing the way. A person who lets go of shadow material through discernment and dispassion simultaneously grows in terms of compassion and connection. Conversely, the intellectualizer has the emotional signature of rigidity, distance, and subtle defensiveness.

Our third vignette was chosen to illustrate an attempt to make the therapy process itself into an embodiment of mindfulness, especially the "not knowing" aspect of mindfulness. Contemplative Psychotherapy, a version of Buddhist psychotherapy, pays particular attention to this aspect of therapy; practitioner Matthew Tomatz (2008) comments:

> Garuda exemplifies the wisdom of facing Kali, as well as the reason for acknowledging impermanence as fundamental to contemplative psychotherapy. Garuda, representing space, defines therapeutic movement as occurring in a spacious atmosphere. Habitually, we become so organized around our ego identities that we fear becoming anything more. . . . In therapy, clients are drawn to take flight and transform. To reach this goal, one must first enter the space of not knowing. . . . This is a space of vitality and texture. This space can vibrate so radically that it shatters the veil of ego and exposes an impressive and terrifying landscape of opportunity. (pp. 71–72)

Tomatz uses his work with a heroin addict as a representative example of contemplative psychotherapy. The client, James, was a widower following his wife's recent death from cancer. He had a long history of heroin addiction going back to a gangster lifestyle when younger but twenty years of marriage had enabled him to be gainfully employed, accumulate material wealth and be a father to his children. In spite of these successes, he continued to dabble with heroin. Tomatz reports that they worked on the addiction for a number of months and James had finally given up using heroin. However, he kept a secret stash of drugs that he was loathe to discard; in their discussions, James and Tomatz had labeled this stash "the hook."

> Over a few sessions, we talked about the hook, its meaning and importance. It became evident that the hook was keeping James from progressing but it was not clear why. Intellectually he understood its limiting function. James would dance between the ideas of disposing the heroin versus keeping it for posterity, "just in case." After several sessions, James was particularly close to the edge. I assumed a warrior's stance and abruptly pushed him: "you could flush it?" The room stood still. James was stunned. He was no longer looking at the hook. He was, instead, staring at his life without any hook. For a moment, James was naked, facing his life without an ego defense. The room was pregnant with opportunity.
>     . . . After few seconds of what felt like eternity, James slid down in the chair and his chest collapsed. Space evaporated. "I can't give up the hook! . . . I'm not ready. I can't face it." . . . James closed down the vitality of the present possibilities by permitting a future of stagnant sameness. For that moment, facing Kali had reified ego, but, nonetheless, a door had been opened. After several weeks, James announced he had destroyed his stash. He was standing within the unknown, eyes open to a future of possibility. (Tomatz, 2008, pp. 70–72)

In this example, Tomatz illustrates how to take the experience of mindfulness meditation and overlay it on therapy. What occurs internally gets reflected externally. An unquiet, contracted mind focused on ego attachment manifests its spiritual pathology as a substance abuse problem. The resolution of this problem requires making the same commitment to no Self and not knowing that are found along the spiritual path. The terror of living life without an ego defense—without the limiting but protecting threads of the Nomological Net—was initially too much for James. After some weeks, however, the experience of being naked—of standing at the edge of the Abyss—became transformative and he discarded his stash.

An Apollonian therapist would, of course, also have advocated for disposal of the stash. It is standard practice to remove everything drug related from one's life when attempting to be sober; in this sense, clients are asked to renounce friends they partied with, discard drug paraphernalia, and stay away from trigger environments and events. The result, as expected, is a gradual increase in commitment to sobriety.

Tomatz asks for the same relinquishment of the hook but the therapeutic experience is radically different. The passionate style of Tomatz conveys the sense that he is present at the edge of the Abyss with his client. Tomatz makes the same recommendation as the Apollonian therapist but in his hands the decision becomes primal and archetypal—infused with meaning that points well past simple sobriety. There is the sense that this decision has become a key moment in James' evolution; the decision will be definitive and life altering. The intervention is clearly Dionysian; it implicitly contains the opportunity for profound transformation.

In essence, Tomatz is on fire with spiritual passion and has imbued the moment and the decision with numinosity. This is a concrete example of charisma in action. Imagine what kind of altered state is present in both client and therapist. Everything has become possible; just one courageous decision is needed to redeem James' life. Tomatz has succeeded at bringing James to the edge of the Abyss.

Social constructionism is seen as a philosophy; the path of wisdom, based on highly similar ideas, is a centuries-old spiritual discipline. Social constructionism offers a model that provides a good fit for data and theories generated by the social sciences. The path of wisdom has gurus, disciples, sutras, scriptures, and practices that promise an end to human suffering and provide the recipe for the good life.

They seem radically different yet it should be clear from the examples and analyses in this book that they are essentially the same. Social constructionism may have roots in Western philosophy and the social sciences but it appears that asking the same questions has returned more or less the same answers. This similarity—or perhaps it is better described as, this unity—is no accident. The perennial philosophy predicts that all serious enquiries into what is real result in deepening understandings—discernment—of the dialog between fundamental and constructed reality.

The take away for psychotherapists is that once constructed reality is fully embraced, the traditional wisdom literature of various cultures becomes available. The writings may include culturally specific references, they may be structured more as poetry or other symbolic processes, but their essential contributions remain. Integrating this body of knowledge into one's own practice has the capacity to enhance charisma, particularly because many spiritual teachers have been aware of the "reading books doesn't enhance spiritual development problem" and have developed work arounds.

## THE PATH OF THE HEART

You see many stars in the sky at night, but not when the sun
rises. Can you therefore say that there are no stars in the heavens
during the day? Because you cannot find God in the days of your
ignorance, say not that there is no God.

—Ramakrishna, *The Gospel of Sri Ramakrishna* (1910)

Even as constructionism points to the path of wisdom, unconditional positive regard and therapist/client rapport points toward the path of the heart. Therapy begins with Schore's right brain-to-right brain connection, and then moves from the connection to one individual to a connection with all. Buber urges us to say "thou," first to one person, then to all persons and finally to everything. The path of the heart is first a technology to gradually expand the heart from the one to the many. Ultimately, however, it provides tools that allow us to hear the universe saying "thou" in response.

This needs to be reemphasized. It is fairly common for Western individuals to have an experience of treasuring nature and to develop a commitment to deep ecology. That is a form of saying "thou" to the natural world. But the most gifted "connecter," the "genius individual" in terms of relating to the universe and all in it, is the one who can hear the universe respond back. Such individuals have been called prophets, saints, gurus, and teachers. They get their ultimate authority from what they channel. "I heard this and now I share it with you." Of course there are false prophets and caution is appropriate. But the basic decision is subsumed in the question, "Can the universe respond or is man the only being with a voice?" It was no accident that we used Buber's dreams about a "cry" or response to illustrate Tillich's duality of faith and doubt.

The path of the heart is as radical and as straightforward as the path of wisdom. It is radical in that it critiques and displaces common assumptions; it is straightforward in that love implies connection and connection implies a two-way dialog. Once deconstructionism and doubt about the nature of the self are embraced, the path of wisdom forces us to travel to the edge of the Abyss. The path of the heart is similar. It takes us to a different aspect of the Abyss, one where we face our own worthiness and our own alienation.

It is more difficult to understand the path of the heart than the path of wisdom because most Westerners have been raised in a Judeo-Christian context of devotion. The path of wisdom seems fresh and new; there are no comparisons in common place Western religious experience to a constructionist path like Buddhism. The wisdom paths of the West tend to be part of the "secret knowledge." This is especially true because advocating for constructionism and formlessness in the context of the Religions of the Book (Judaism, Christianity, and Islam) could literally get one killed.

Because Western religions emphasize devotion, even the simplest religious references can give rise to childhood associations that have negative connotations. For example, many devotional quotes seem like authoritarian injunctions—commands that must be obeyed regardless of our response. For some therapists, it is hard to hear something like the following without some level of bristling.

And he answering said, Thou shalt love the Lord thy God with all thy heart, and with all thy soul, and with all thy strength, and with all thy mind; and thy neighbor as thyself. (Luke 10:27)

This is especially true because many Westerners conflate all prayer and meditation with the patriarchal image of a male God with a long white beard. Moreover, the concept of a "divine response" to prayer leads to an even greater sense of discomfort. Most Westerners, particularly therapists with liberal social and political leanings, have memories of fundamentalist Christians asserting that they have communicated with God and He has told them that "gays are sinners and women must be subservient." Clearly, it is generally easier to be open to the path of wisdom than the path of the heart.

That said, examine the following vignette from Phil Stutz; he and his partner, Barry Michels, wrote *The Tools*—a "self-improvement" book which has sold thousands of copies. While some of the tools are primarily psychological, others, such as the one below, are overtly spiritual.

Michels was seeing Janet, a recent college graduate, who was presenting because she was having problems with her boyfriend. She found herself unable to leave him even though he was a deadbeat financially, would flirt with other women, and would leave her for weeks at a time. Instead of being assertive, she would criticize herself and imagine that he would be good to her if she was prettier, or smarter, or whatever.

She expected Michels to give her tools to stop the self-criticism and encourage her to leave him. Instead, Michels told her that they weren't going to fight the self-deprecatory comments. Instead, he was going to teach her something called the *Grateful Flow*.

### The Grateful Flow in Brief

1. Start by silently stating to yourself specific things in your life you're grateful for, particularly items you'd normally take for granted. You can also include bad things that aren't happening. Go slowly so you really feel the gratefulness for each item. Don't use the same items each time you use the tool. You should feel a slight strain from having to come up with new ideas.
2. After about thirty seconds, stop thinking and focus on the physical sensation of gratefulness. You'll feel it coming directly from your heart. This energy you are giving out is the Grateful Flow.
3. As this energy emanates from your heart, your chest will soften and open. In this state you will feel an overwhelming presence approach you, filled with the power of infinite giving. You've made a connection to the Source.

Quickly, she began to develop a relationship with the Source. For the first time ever, she felt she was living in a universe that supported and valued her. The more she had this experience, the less accurate the self-criticisms seemed. Once she'd achieved this, she found the strength to stand up to her boyfriend and eventually leave him. (Stutz & Michels, 2012, pp. 177–179)

This is an example of a straightforward integration of psychology and devotion. The therapist tells the client to reach out to God and promises an answer. Along with the answer will come relief from the symptom and much, much more.

It is easy to interpret the successful outcome in the vignette to factors previously discussed. Clearly Michels is a charismatic therapist, a key individual who can change client reality with a word. And the Grateful Flow is a perfect example of a ritual that explains the dilemma (she couldn't leave the negative boyfriend because of lack of self-acceptance) and resolves the dilemma (Now I can leave the boyfriend because I have been affirmed by the Source).

Michels might argue that his intervention supersedes the charisma/ritual explanation in that it actually taps into a force that is always ready to respond if we simply ask for/open to it. The path of the heart frequently leads to this same dilemma—is the response real or is it programmed? We have already understood the Tillichian response to this dilemma: a dynamic Faith that is eternally interwoven with Doubt. The path of the heart essentially exists at the crux of this basic question: alone or connected, love or self-interest, meaningful or meaningless, spiritual or chaotically empty.

Many spiritual injunctions, such as the one above admonishing us to "love the Lord thy God with all thy heart," are essentially instructions for attaining a particular type of altered state conducive to hearing a divine response. The instructions show the path to the Abyss and enjoin us to jump.

The path of wisdom starts with deconstructing programming via *Neti-neti* (not this, not that) both intellectually and in the altered state of meditation. Similarly, the path of the heart deconstructs the feeling that we are alone and lost. This dilemma is embodied in the following Thomas Merton (2002) quote:

> The real reason why so few men believe in God is that they have ceased to believe that even a God can love them. (p. 213)

Wisdom seekers quiet the mind with meditation; devotees quiet the mind with service. The Dalai Lama says, "My religion is very simple. My religion is kindness." Kindness, service, "loving others as our self," these are the meditations of the Heart. They prepare the Heart to hear/feel the divine response just as meditation prepares one for emptiness and ego dissolution.

That said, it can still be difficult for certain Western intellectuals to work effectively with the path of the heart given that often its symbolism is so concrete and so connected to traditional human relationships. For example, in the quote below, Sri Chinmoy provides the following instructions:

Do not try to approach God with your thinking mind. It may only stimulate your intellectual ideas, activities, and beliefs. Try to approach God with your crying heart. It will awaken your soulful, spiritual consciousness. (Chinmoy, 2015, Kindle Locations 988–990)

This is a challenge. Chinmoy is telling us to discard our intellect and our rationality—the two elements most identified with modernism—and cultivate the attitude of a child who is "crying out." In this quote, he is consciously rejecting the idea that intellect and rationality are important in terms of the Heart. He is being intentionally offensive—literally pointing out that the road is closed to these mental approaches. Such quotes tend to disturb us in that the mental tools are so often so helpful; simultaneously the quote intrigues those of us who understand that the tools do not open every door. Examine the following quote from Way of the Pilgrim that embodies one kind of consciousness achieved by devotees.

The holy Fathers were right when they said that The Philokalia is a key to the mysteries of holy Scripture. With the help it gave me I began to some extent to understand the hidden meaning of the Word of God. I began to see the meaning of such sayings as "the inner secret man of the heart," "true prayer worships in the spirit," "the kingdom is within us," "the intercession of the Holy Spirit with groanings that cannot be uttered," "abide in me," "give me thy heart," "to put on Christ," "the betrothal of the Spirit to our hearts," the cry from the depths of the heart, "Abba, Father," and so on.

And when with all this in mind I prayed with my heart, everything around me seemed delightful and marvelous. The trees, the grass, the birds, the earth, the air, the light seemed to be telling me that they existed for man's sake, that they witnessed to the love of God for man, that everything proved the love of God for man, that all things prayed to God and sang His praise. Thus it was that I came to understand what The Philokalia calls "the knowledge of the speech of all creatures," and I saw the means by which converse could be held with God's creatures. (Sand, 1989, p. 28)

This quote illustrates a certain level of consciousness often reported by practitioners who follow the path of the heart. Their devotional practices result in a pervasive sense of love and connection. In this quote, the pilgrim feels that everything in the world is simultaneously both a sign of the divine love for man and a paean of joy arising from all of creation toward God. There is a palpable sense of connection and belonging. There is an absence of fear and desire and an ability to be fully present. The perennial philosophy documents this type of devotional experience across various cultures and historical periods.

One of the biggest obstacles to devotional practice for sophisticated practitioners of modernity is that such practice typically requires relating to what is called "God with form." As soon as the divine is conceptualized as "with form," a number of incongruences and contradictions arise. Interestingly, one of the ways to resolve this challenge comes from studying certain psycho-therapeutic techniques, particularly techniques that focus on visualizations and dissociation.

To illustrate this point, let us begin by examining a common exercise that comes from the health psychology literature. In the following example, the therapist is introducing the client to the concept of how to use imagery to evoke salivation.

> Today I'm going to teach you how to generate a somatic response that is nor-mally outside of conscious control. First, let me ask you: can you make yourself salivate via a conscious command? No? Well simply follow my directions and see what happens.
>
> Please close your eyes, sit comfortably, and take in a few easy breaths. At the end of the next exhalation, I want you to imagine that you're in your kitchen and are looking down on a lemon on a cutting board. Reach out and hold the lemon. Notice its yellow color but particularly pay attention to that slightly slippery feeling that lemons have.
>
> Now put it back down on the cutting board and pick up a knife. Carefully cut the lemon in half and notice the pungent smell released as you cut and feel a drop of lemon juice on the hand holding the lemon. Now, I want you to pick up the lemon half and hold it up to your nose and, inhaling, smell that fresh, lemon scent. Finally I want you to put it in your mouth and bite down on it.
>
> Now, tell me if your mouth is full of saliva.

In this brief example, the therapist shows the client how to use imagery to create salivation—a somatic response normally outside of conscious control. This is usually done to motivate the client to use more advanced imagery techniques to work with a chronic disease like cancer or to address a pain issue. The therapist typically tells the client that they need to become com-fortable using symbolic imagery if they wish to affect a somatic process. You can't tell your mouth to salivate; you have to imagine biting the lemon. In essence, the client is asked to imagine something that is not literally true in order to generate a desired response. Now, let us take this one step further by looking at the following example of inner child work from my own practice.

> A 46-year-old, Caucasian female recently received a promotion at work which required her to do a substantial amount of public speaking. She explained that she had enormous anxiety at the prospect of delivering these lectures and was considering refusing the promotion because she was so afraid. When questioned about her theory about the source of her anxiety, she mentioned that her mother had been a "Narcissist" who consistently demeaned and attacked her whenever

she did anything connected to a personal success. In spite of this early training, the woman had prospered in life due to her intelligence, creativity and diligence.

She was asked to remember the last time she was significantly anxious in a public speaking setting and to note how that felt in her body. Then she was asked to follow these feelings back to a memory from long ago. This process took her to a childhood experience where she was humiliated by her mother in front of her friend.

She put that memory on hold and spent the next few minutes remembering three positive experiences which embodied her own highest level of functioning; she chose one that was connected with a professional success, one that was connected with feeling loved, and a final one connected with having a wonderful time laughing with her friends.

I asked her to briefly describe the memory with her mother and then she was asked to close her eyes and return to the image. She began by describing the girl to me: her age, how she was dressed, and especially what her facial expression revealed about how she was feeling. Her breathing slowed down, she became still, and seemed very engaged in the experience. I asked her to introduce herself to the young girl as "her grown-up self from the future returned to help her deal with her feelings." She hugged and held the girl and reported that the girl felt a bit better with her there.

She was asked to take the girl by the hand and lead her to the first of her three positive experiences. After watching and re-experiencing the first memory of professional success, the client reported that the girl seemed surprised and shocked at what she had seen but was also delighted and smiling. Exposing her to the next two memories further enhanced the young girl's sense of safety and happiness.

The client was then asked to "wrap" the young girl with these memories as if they were a cloak of power or an energetic shield. Then she was asked to go to the memory of the public speaking anxiety and rewatch the memory. With this witnessing, however, she would see how that memory would change when she approached the public speaking "wrapped in the cloak of her positive memories."

As the client watched, a small smile appeared on her lips. After the witnessing, she reported that she had been able to deliver the speech with comfort and confidence and that she and the girl were delighted. Finally she gave the girl a big hug, promised to visit her again soon, and elicited a promise that the girl would help her stay centered during any further public speaking events.

The client reported feeling very optimistic that she could transfer this experience to the real world and returned in two weeks saying that her public speaking experiences were much improved and that her qualms about her new position were essentially gone.

This example of inner child work builds on the preceding example in that both require the utilization of a symbolic process. First, just like the example of the lemon, the symbolic inner child work is required because, without a symbolic experience, a client can't remove their anxiety or enhance their self-esteem through a simple act of will. She needed to use a metaphoric process—epitomized by an imaginary interaction with a child—to alter her anxiety.

This leads to the question of whether the experience was "real." Certainly there was no lemon present in the saliva example and no one believes that the client has an actual homunculus within her somewhere. But therapists would argue that the client needs to act "as if" it is real in order to contact the part of the psyche required to elicit the desired change. Moreover, therapists believe that clients who can do this effectively have a certain kind of "talent"—the ability to make an inner process "real" opens many doors to healing and understanding that are normally closed.

And then the situation starts getting a bit strange. Therapists who regularly practice inner child work commonly report that when the client becomes deeply involved in the experience, the inner figures seem to become autonomous—out of the conscious control of the client. The client cannot make the inner child happy or sad; the inner figure operates independently and appears to be an actual representation of a certain part of the psyche. The question of "real" arises again. Have the clients succeeded at directly contacting the independent, unconscious mind through their exercise or are they simply posturing to please the therapist?

With the lemon and the saliva, the answer seems clear: since salivation occurs, there is a "real" connection between the conscious mind and the salivary glands via the imaginal exercise. Similarly, since the anxiety is diminished, the inner child exercise must have provided some kind of real connection to the "unconscious mind." The client was unable to *will* salivation; now, with this imagery approach, they can. They were unable to will away their anxiety or talk themselves out of it; now, secondary to the interaction with the child, it is significantly diminished. In sum, both the lemon and the inner child examples, while "unreal" from the external reality/rationalist point of view, are completely real from both the outcome perspective and from the pragmatic perspective. And in this sense "pragmatic" implies that symbolic and imaginal communication is the most practical—and hence, most real—bridge between the conscious mind and these unconscious processes.

Returning to the path of the heart, recall that the primary aim of the devotee is to make God central in her life. Humans have various experiences of the sacred; Eliade argues that they are sprinkled throughout human experience, sometimes predictably and sometimes spontaneously. How does the devotee build a life centered on such experiences? The lemon and inner child examples demonstrate that this kind of connection is going to be symbolic and imaginal. Just as anxiety was portrayed as a "hurt child," the divine is going to be portrayed as a father, a mother, a dear friend, or counselor. It is certainly possible to have a relationship with God without using metaphoric relationships; the first section of this chapter—the path of wisdom—describes exactly how to do that. But most people are naturally drawn toward the path of devotion with its familiar relationships of father, mother, and so on. Is it easier to eliminate anxiety by metaphorically comforting and supporting a hurt child or is it easier to reduce the anxiety by affirming it is rooted in a false sense of self? In the following quote, James Hillman argues that the path of the heart requires what he calls "personifying."

> Nearer our own times another Mediterranean, the Spaniard Miguel de Unamuno (b. 1864), returned to the relationship of heart and personified images and explained the necessary interdependence between love and personifying:
>
> In order to love everything, in order to pity everything, human and extra-human, living and non-living, you must feel everything within yourself, you must personalize everything. For everything that it loves, everything that it pities, love personalizes . . . we only love—that which is like ourselves . . . it is love itself . . . that reveals these resemblances to us. . . . Love personalizes all that it loves. Only by personalizing it can we fall in love with an idea.
>
> He sums up, saying: "Our feeling of the world, upon which is based our understanding of it, is necessarily anthropomorphic and mythopoeic." Loving is a way of knowing, and for loving to know, it must personify. Personifying is thus a way of knowing, especially knowing what is invisible, hidden in the heart. (Hilmman, 1997, p. 15)

Of course, in therapy, the client is completely aware that the lemon doesn't exist in physical reality and that there are no "sub-personalities" roving around the body. In religious life, that difference has been blurred for the same reason that it gets blurred in the therapy session: the connection is much more powerful if the client or devotee becomes deeply engaged in the process and sincerely operates as if the relationship is real in the physical plane. In the religious world, priests attempt to "materialize" God with stories of miracles, incarnations, and healings. In the therapy world, the therapist materializes the experience by acting as if the child is actually there, soliciting descriptions of the child's mood and behavior, and supporting the autonomous actions and feelings of the child. This "blurring" is key to creating the autonomy of the object of meditation; when the object begins to generate independent behaviors, one knows the connection is real.

Historically, of course, this blurring of the physical world and the spiritual world has been very confusing. In physical reality, if God is my father—and he has infinite power—nothing bad should be allowed to happen to me. Conversely, in the spiritual world, acting as if God is my father enables me to have a powerful connection, a connection so powerful it can lead to actual dialog. Without this personified connection, the possibility of dialog is closed to me. So if a rationalist points out that my stance toward God the Father has implicit incongruities—nothing bad should happen to me if this is a real relationship—I will look at the rationalist with pity and say, "Try it and perhaps you will be able to understand." The rationalist leaves, confident that the incongruity has destroyed the validity of my experience. And in so doing, misses that the principle of personification is aimed at achieving connection through an altered state, not removing cognitive inconsistencies. In the following quote, Swami Vivekananda looks at this real versus unreal question from a more spiritual perspective.

> If a man can realize his divine nature with the help of an image, would it be right to call that a sin? Nor, even when he has passed that stage, should he call it an error. . . . Man is not traveling from error to truth, but from truth to truth, from lower to higher truth. To him all the religions from the lowest fetishism to the highest absolutism, mean so many attempts of the human soul to grasp and realize the Infinite, each determined by the conditions of its birth and association, and each of these marks a stage of progress; and every soul is a young eagle soaring higher and higher, gathering more and more strength till it reaches the Glorious Sun. (Vivekananda, 2015b)

Certainly, there are multiple meanings to this quote. In the context of our psychotherapeutic examples—where the autonomy of the inner child is created by acting as if the child is real all the while knowing it is not—Vivekananda is describing a hierarchy of consciousness. This kind of consciousness—seeing the devotional experience as both real and unreal—is much more natural in the East with its paradoxical embrace of the concept of God with form and God without Form.

Buddhism and Hinduism differ from the major Western religions in many ways but the one most relevant to this discussion is that they have an overt commitment to constructionism. As an example, examine the most well-known Taoist quotation.

> The Tao that can be told is not the eternal Tao.
> The name that can be named is not the eternal name.
> The nameless is the beginning of heaven and earth.
> The named is the mother of ten thousand things.
> Ever desireless, one can see the mystery.
> Ever desiring, one can see the manifestations.
> These two spring from the same source but differ in name;
> this appears as darkness.
> Darkness within darkness.
> The gate to all mystery. (Lao Tzu, Tao Te Ching, p. 80)

Virtually every line of this quotation is constructionist. It is explicitly designed to contrast the Abyss and the Net and move the reader from one perspective to another. It demonstrates Eastern religion's readiness and ability to deconstruct the literalness and the programming implicit in so many religious practices. Yet, with all that ability to take things apart, Eastern religions continue to recommend and support the path of devotion for the same reason that therapists like inner child work: the simplest and most direct relationship with God occurs through mimicking familiar social relationships. Ramakrishna states:

> The rishis of old attained the Knowledge of Brahman. One cannot have this so long as there is the slightest trace of worldliness. How hard the rishis labored! Early in the morning they would go away from the hermitage, and would spend the whole day in solitude, meditating on Brahman. At night they would return to the hermitage and eat a little fruit or roots. They kept their minds aloof from the objects of sight, hearing, touch, and other things of a worldly nature. Only thus did they realize Brahman as their own inner consciousness.
>
> But in the Kaliyuga, man, being totally dependent on food for life, cannot altogether shake off the idea that he is the body. . . . When a man does all sorts of worldly things, he should not say, "I am Brahman." Those who cannot give up attachment to worldly things, and who find no means to shake off the feeling of "I," should rather cherish the idea, "I am God's servant; I am His devotee." One can also realize God by following the path of devotion.
>
> . . . The path of knowledge leads to Truth, as does the path that combines knowledge and love. The path of love, too, leads to this goal. The way of love is as true as the way of knowledge. All paths ultimately lead to the same Truth. But as long as God keeps the feeling of ego in us, it is easier to follow the path of love. (as cited in Nikhilananda, 1984, p. 132)

And further.

> If you desire to be pure, have firm faith, and slowly go on with your devotional practices without wasting your energy in useless scriptural discussions and arguments. Your little brain will otherwise be muddled. (as cited in Abhedananda, 2010, p. 75)

Eastern religions have little trouble integrating the devotees and the wisdom seekers; they can move effortlessly from one perspective to another. With all their commitment to devotion, they are prepared to acknowledge that God with form is always God with inconsistencies and incongruences. Yet, being constructionists, they do not find these inconsistencies off putting; rather, they see them as part of the nature of constructed reality. In addition, they join with Hillman and the psychotherapeutic world in recommending personification; yes, it comes with incongruences but God with form is much more approachable for most humans.

Now, let us proceed to a brief summary of the path of the heart. In so many ways, the path of love is the simplest thing to describe: love God with all your heart and soul. Orient your life around this love. Feel His Presence constantly. Dedicate your life to serving God. Strive to imitate God as much as possible. Pray to open your heart to His Voice and to follow His Will.

This is not an affectation or an attitude but a firm decision—a complete commitment—a new pole star for one's life.

> We should fix ourselves firmly in the presence of God by conversing all the time with Him . . . we should feed our soul with a lofty conception of God and from that derive great joy in being his. We should put life in our faith. We should give ourselves utterly to God in pure abandonment, in temporal and spiritual matters alike, and find contentment in the doing of His will, whether he takes us through sufferings or consolations. (Lawrence & Beaufort, 2010, p. 5)

And, while this level of dedication can sound daunting, in actuality God places light demands on us.

> He does not ask much of us, merely a thought of Him from time to time, a little act of adoration, sometimes to ask for His grace, sometimes to offer Him your sufferings, at other times to thank Him for the graces, past and present, He has bestowed on you, in the midst of your troubles to take solace in Him as often as you can. Lift up your heart to Him during your meals and in company; the least little remembrance will always be the most pleasing to Him. One need not cry out very loudly; He is nearer to us than we think. (Lawrence & Beaufort, 2010, p. 24)

And, if you reach out to God in this manner, you will receive a response.

> Through selfless work, love of God grows in the heart. Then through his grace one realize him in course of time. God can be seen. One can talk to him as I am talking to you. (Ramakrishna, as cited in Nikhilananda, 1984, p. 109)

Living at this level of consciousness means that everything in one's life is pervaded by the divine. Everything that occurs, every person one meets, is an encounter designed and orchestrated by God. In that sense, everything that happens is a lesson sent specifically to you from God. If it is painful, it is simply "grist for the mill" to use the well-known Ram Das term. If it is a chance meeting with a person or event, it is a personal message from the divine. The Baal Shem Tov describes it as follows:

Everything is by Divine Providence. If a leaf is turned over by a breeze, it is only because this has been specifically ordained by G–d to serve a particular function within the purpose of creation. (Baal Shem Tov, as cited in Kahn, 2016, The Search for Meaning)

And what is promised to a person who chooses to live life this way: inner peace, self-awareness, and the bliss and joy of being united with the Lord.

Cleaving to G–d is the master-key that opens all locks. Every Jew, including the most simple, possesses the ability to cleave to the words of Torah and prayer, thereby achieving the highest degrees of unity with G–d. (Buber, 1995, p. 23)

This consciousness is a kind of craziness when measured by the rules of the world—a divine madness that leads to the fulfillment of human destiny. Ramakrishna tells us:

If you must be mad, be it not for the things of the world. Be mad with the love of God.

Lest this simplicity seem easy, Swami Vivekananda adds a cautionary note.

The one great advantage of Bhakti (the path of devotion and love) is that it is the easiest and most natural way to reach the great divine end in view; it's great disadvantage is that in its lower forms it oftentimes degenerates into hideous fanaticism. The fanatical crew in Hinduism, Mohammedanism, or Christianity, have always been almost exclusively recruited from these worshippers [*sic*] on the lower planes of Bhakti. That singleness of attachment (Nishthâ) to a loved object, without which no genuine love can grow, is very often also the cause of the denunciation of everything else. All the weak and undeveloped minds in every religion or country have only one way of loving their own ideal, i.e., by hating every other ideal. Herein is the explanation of why the same man who is so lovingly attached to his own ideal of God, so devoted to his own ideal of religion, becomes a howling fanatic as soon as he sees or hears anything of any other ideal. (Vivekananda, 1964, p. 35)

The path of devotion is easy to describe although, of course, it is difficult to live. Making God central in one's life requires a level of egolessness and commitment that are challenging to sustain in the real world. That said, it is the implicit extension of all that is essential in the therapeutic relationship: unconditional positive regard, compassion, and connection. Feeling connected to all others in love and service is admirable; it is a meaningful step on the path. Feeling some kind of real response from the divine—as experienced by the client with the *Grateful Flow*—is another step altogether.

Putting this into practice requires the ability to speak directly to the spiritual identity of clients, to be comfortable using religious language, and to be able to access one's own spiritual feelings. The following example, which is from my own practice, focuses on what may be the most common application of spirituality to psychopathology—laying one's worries and anxieties at the feet of the Lord.

A fifty-five-year-old nurse presented complaining that she was experiencing so much anxiety about her adult son that she could barely sleep. It seems that her twenty-three-year-old son had problems with alcohol, depression, and violence. He would try and be sober, but whenever he had some life stress, he would return to the bottle. After drinking a certain amount, he would go to the local bar and seek out fights with the other patrons. Following the fight, he would wake up with a hangover, a set of bruises, and horrible self-recrimination about his behaviors. His self-deprecation was so strong that he frequently had suicidal thoughts. The depression and self-hatred would lead to a resolve not to drink; the depression would eventually lift; the life stresses would return; and the cycle would repeat. The mother had an ongoing feeling that he was about to die, either in a fight, by his own hand, or secondary to his alcohol abuse.

The client reported that her spiritual life was very important to her and, although she only attended church once or twice a month, she had an active prayer life and felt she had a personal relationship with God. I asked her if she used the image of the "Sacred Heart" in her prayer practice and she said that she did. I suggested that she offer up her anxiety and helplessness about her son to the "Sacred Heart."

You might want to make a small altar somewhere in your house or your bedroom. On the altar you can have a candle, a picture of your son, and any other spiritual symbols that appeal to you. Every morning and every evening sit in front of the altar and light the candle. Say any prayer that appeals to you to invoke the presence of God. Many people use the Lord's Prayer or the Jesus Prayer or the Prayer of St. Francis, but use the one that feels best to you—that most easily gives you the sense of presence. After the lighting of the candle and the invocation, just sit quietly and begin to pray for your son. Again your prayers can take and shape and form that feels right to you but make sure that at least partially you pray to be relieved of the idea that you are still responsible for your son's welfare. Project the understanding that you know that his fate is in God's hands—not yours—and be asked to be relieved of the sin of Pride and Power. You know that you have no power over your son's fate and your feeling that you do have responsibility is a form of spiritual confusion. Offer that confusion to the Sacred Heart.

After a while, if you pray sincerely, you will begin to feel a sense of an answer or response. This may take the form of Grace or inner Peace, or something like that. Sincere prayers will evoke a response. . . . No one can say exactly the form of this response. Most likely it will relieve you of your anxiety. It's also possible that the response may lead you to something else you need to learn, or let go of, or respond to.

Continue this twice daily prayer practice until you see me again in 10 days.

On her next visit, the client reported that her anxiety was markedly reduced. She also said that she had felt a response that felt like a flood of inner peace—which she termed "grace." Finally, she had had an insight that she needed to discuss something with her husband, the son's stepfather, about certain comments he made about the son. She had asked him to refrain from being critical about the son's poor choices as such comments only served to agitate her. He was open to the feedback and promised to change the nature of his comments.

This vignette not only offers an example of how quickly a client can respond using a devotional approach, but it also has implications about life lessons and personal deepening. The client's symptom—anxiety—led her into an enhanced sense of her connection to God. More importantly, she had an experience where God reached back to her both with guidance and with a sense of grace and inner peace.

This question of "reaching back" is central for the path of devotion. It is one thing to discuss attempting to become a manifestation of love and acceptance but it is quite another to realize that all of us are profoundly limited in terms of that giving by our own fear and confusion. The path of devotion resolves this by repeatedly putting God or a higher power on center stage and then attempting to channel that level of love and acceptance.

This experience of love and acceptance coming through me is a common one for most therapists. There are endless stories that go something like this: "During the session I felt the pain and loneliness of the client and my heart opened. Then it felt like something outside me—larger than me—was coming through. My heart felt bigger and warmer and the client started responding differently, like they weren't afraid anymore. Afterward, when we both talked about it, we both agreed that it was a kind of magical experience."

It hardly matters whether one takes this as a construction, a documented experience of the presence of a higher power, or a form of right brain-to-right brain connection; given that such experiences are relatively common, they serve to document the human ability to manifest love and connection. And the sense that something comes through from the outside—that there is a "response" as Buber puts it—is a central feature. And, of course, it is a small step from channeling a higher power for another to prayer and the attempt to feel a personal response.

The following vignette highlights a different angle on the path of the heart. In this case, I take an Apollonian stance and challenge the client to choose behaviors consistent with her spiritual beliefs.

A woman in her late 40s presented, complaining of anxiety, fatigue and resentment. She was married, had 3 children, and worked as a midlevel executive. Her husband suffered from a variety of anxiety disorders including panic attacks and agoraphobia. His anxieties were so numerous and pervasive that they had come to dominate the family in that his level of discomfort ruled out so many family activities. He had been underemployed for a decade and was only able to work part time at a low stress, low pay job. He was adamantly against getting medication or therapy for his condition. After urging him to get some help—and getting a "no" in response—the wife had essentially accepted that he was never going to work on it. The parents were serious Christians and went to church diligently each week.

The wife reported that she was exhausted because she felt that virtually all the care of the children fell on her; it seemed that the husband was not only anxious, he somehow lacked the common sense and ability to connect required for parenthood. She was resentful because she felt she was doing all the work, providing almost all the money, and her husband was constantly pressuring her to make love more often. When asked whether she had thoughts of divorce, she answered immediately and clearly that she felt her vows were sacred, made before God, and that she would never break them. When asked about confronting her husband and asking him to get psychological help or get a better job, she replied that she was convinced that he was disabled because of a bad childhood and, even though he was a good person at core, he was unable to perform at a higher level.

She came in for a session noting that the children were going to visit their aunt the following weekend and she was dreading the incessant pressure to have sex that she expected from her husband. In response I told her that I respected her marriage as a sacred union but that she was taking the commitment too lightly.

"In a sacred marriage the vow is not simply to stay married but to view your role as a wife as an opportunity to serve God. Of course your husband is a man, but if you serve him as you would serve Jesus you will be blessed and you will have a sacred marriage. Making love is at the center of any marriage and your resistance to making love with your husband is an abandonment of a spiritual opportunity. Of course you resent him with your human side for giving in to his anxiety, not carrying his share of the load, and not getting help but it is important to put those things aside for this weekend and celebrate the sacred union.

You have also been derelict in your marital responsibilities in that you have allowed him to conduct himself in such a way that he has lost self-respect and the respect of you and the children. The marital vow includes vows about taking care of each other when ill. It is not taking care of him to allow him to continue on a course that makes him worse and results in poor relationships.

You need to begin by making love to him not as the man who has faults but as the man that was chosen for you by God. Then you need to step up and take care of him the way you would care for the divine child."

The client returned the following week reporting that the love making weekend had gone well and actually been pleasurable and connecting for her. During the session, she committed to confronting him about the burden of his anxiety on him, her, and the family. Following that confrontation, he agreed to enter individual therapy.

The important part of this intervention was my willingness to operate inside the dimension of Apollonian power. Every spiritual path has its own rules and guidelines that define the good life. By and large such rules, interpreted thoughtfully, are, in fact, helpful for the practitioners. Stepping into the role of religious authority is functionally identical to Glasser's recommendation that therapists make use of ideas like right and wrong and healthy/unhealthy. When such ideas are presented with sensitivity, they can be a great motivator for the client.

For the therapist, the opportunity to serve as a spokesperson for spiritual authority requires a high level of engagement with the relevant spiritual principles. This was both a challenging situation for me in that urging a woman to have sex with a husband she disrespects seems counter to supporting her ultimate concern. On the other hand, she had defined the rules she was playing by, and from that perspective, she had already committed both to make her husband happy sexually as well as confront him when he was lost. She created the exterior of the ritual when she reported that her Christian Faith was the center of her marriage; I merely filled in the details of the ritual.

I did suspect that my requirement that she be a "good wife" would lead to her feeling empowered to require him to be a "good husband." Obviously I laid the groundwork for this with my comments about "stepping up." What overtly appeared to be a request for her to practice "Christian submission" was paradoxically a request for Christian assertion and leadership.

In terms of my own growth, I had to understand the unity of psychological and spiritual principles. I needed to feel the constructed nature of the ritual. I also had to experience the sense of power that flows when one embraces right/wrong with integrity. Finally, I needed to feel the essential alignment with her ultimate concern that actually gave the ritual healing power. To me, this required dancing with the Abyss.

## SPIRITUAL MATERIALISM

Do not believe a thing because you have read about it in a book. Do not believe a thing because another man has said it was true. Do not believe in words because they are hallowed by tradition. Find out the truth for yourself. Reason it out. That is realization.

—Swami Vivekananda, *The Complete Works of Swami Vivekananda* (1907)

The influx of Eastern teachings in the 1970s opened a vast range of spiritual possibilities to hungry Western seekers. Not surprisingly, the Westerners approached the eastern ideas from the context of their own culture; while this approach occasionally created a kind of symbiotic positive effect, in the main it diluted and altered the Eastern teachings in an unhelpful and inappropriate manner. This effect was so striking that one of the Eastern teachers, Chogyam Trungpa, wrote an entire book, *Cutting Through Spiritual Materialism* (2002), focusing on the ways Westerners attempt to achieve spiritual progress using methodologies and strategies oriented toward winning a prize or accomplishing a material goal. In the following quote, he emphasizes how difficult it can be to discern between genuine spiritual practice and enhancement of the ego.

> Walking the spiritual path properly is a very subtle process; it is not something to jump into naively. There are numerous sidetracks which lead to a distorted, ego-centered version of spirituality; we can deceive ourselves into thinking we are developing spiritually when instead we are strengthening our egocentricity through spiritual techniques. This fundamental distortion may be referred to as spiritual materialism. (p. 3)

Put in the language of this book, Trungpa is cautioning seekers not to treat the spiritual path like it operates in fundamental reality but, instead, recognize that it operates in constructed reality. It is so easy to superimpose fundamental ideas, assumptions, and practices into constructed space. If we operate like this, there will be an impressive show of practice, insight, and accomplishment but since the path "is a very subtle process," we will miss the main point. Since that has been the fundamental error of Western psychology—and that error has resulted in no measurable progress for almost a century—it should be easy for us to take Trungpa's warning seriously.

Western culture, of course, is the home turf for modernism, science, and rationality. This makes us particularly at risk in terms of confusing the constructed and the fundamental; moreover, it also makes us prone to reification and black and white thinking. James Hillman, who is well known for his scathing analyses of simplistic psychological practices, has a special critique of Westerners attempting to cultivate Eastern spirituality. He cautions Westerners against practicing an Eastern approach outside of a supportive cultural context.

> Another form of transcendental denial occurs in (westernized) Oriental solutions to psychopathology. . . . My characterization of the Oriental denial of pathologizing is Western, reflecting the way it is used by Westerners. For what we do with Oriental transcendent methods derives as much from the Western

psyche as it does from the Eastern spirit. In the East this spirit is rooted in the thick yellow loam of richly mythologized imagery—demons, monsters, grotesque goddesses, tortures, and obscenities. It arises within mythologized world of want and despair, chained by obligations, agonized. But once uprooted and imported to the West it arrives deprived it of its dimensional ground, dirt free and smelling of sandalwood, another upward vision that offers a way to bypass our Western psychopathologies. The archetypal content of Eastern doctrines as experienced through the archetypal structures of the Western psyche becomes a major and systematic denial of pathologizing. (Hillman, 1997, pp. 66–67)

Hillman is arguing that Eastern thought is grounded when it is practiced in the East but becomes denial, simplistic thinking, and a rationalizing, New Age pap unless we are careful. He particularly warns against the rejection of shadow that can easily occur when Eastern practices are taken out of context. Kornfield's student, and her unwillingness to work with her own psychological material, is an example of this kind of mistake. If one takes Hillman seriously, and recognizes that Eastern thought has always been grounded in a part of the world where profound suffering is experienced on a regular basis, then it is easy to accept his admonition that Eastern wisdom can lead to escape and denial unless that level of suffering is somehow factored in.

A second cultural difference is the way in which the numinous is handled by the different cultures. In the West, the numinous is separated from the human; we have sinners and saints, the pure and the impure. In the East, the numinous can manifest in an imperfect vessel. Put more specifically, Eastern saints can be full of flaws and still point toward the divine. In the West, the pope is "infallible." The East sustains respect for its gurus without requiring infallibility.

As a concrete example, take the case of Ramakrishna Paramahamsa. Imagine that you are visiting India in the middle of the nineteenth century and you hear about an Indian "saint" named Ramakrishna who is reputed to be a great devotee of the Holy Mother—a man who has achieved the highest level of God consciousness. Following is a quote from an Indian man who actually visited Ramakrishna at his home in Dakshineswar during that period.

When the meeting broke up, the devotees sauntered in the temple garden. M. went in the direction of the Panchavati. It was about five o'clock in the afternoon. After a while he returned to the Master's room. There, on the small north verandah, he witnessed an amazing sight.

Sri Ramakrishna was standing still, surrounded by a few devotees, and Narendra was singing. M. had never heard anyone except the Master sing so sweetly. When he looked at Sri Ramakrishna he was struck with wonder; for the Master stood motionless, with eyes transfixed. He seemed not even to breathe. A devotee told M. that the Master was in samadhi. M. had never before seen or heard of such a thing. Silent with wonder, he thought: "Is it possible for a man to be so oblivious of the outer world in the consciousness of God? How deep his faith and devotion must be to bring about such a state!"

. . . The song drew to a close. Narendra sang the last lines:
Caught in the spell of His love's ecstasy,
Immerse yourself for evermore, O mind,
In Him who is Pure Knowledge and Pure Bliss.

The sight of the samadhi, and the divine bliss he had witnessed, left an indelible impression on M.'s mind. (Nikhilananda, 1984, p. 142)

Most people—especially most Westerners—lack categories in their mind to organize such experiences. The simplest response is denial; Ramakrishna is simulating or faking these experiences in order to achieve something. Next simplest is concrete belief; Ramakrishna is a living embodiment of the divine—a perfected being who has achieved God realization. As Eliade pointed out in the previous chapter, human beings are archetypally prepared to respond to sacred space by attributing divine qualities to its inhabitants. If Ramakrishna has achieved Samadhi, then he must be a perfected being. There are "normal" human beings and there are holy men—humans who have "attained enlightenment" and are now embodied representatives of the Divine.

Not surprisingly, seeing teachers, gurus, and lamas as literal incarnations of the Divine generates the same kinds of problems and issues as a concrete belief in God, the father. For example, if these teachers can heal some people, and they are embodiments of compassion, why not heal all petitioners? If they are really liberated, why do they have so many flaws? For example, Ramakrishna frequently preferred the company of certain disciples over others; in addition, he could become dependent, childlike and require reassurance. And, while he honored a female manifestation of God, his disciples were almost exclusively male and he frequently said that "woman and gold" were the major impediments to enlightenment.

Ramakrishna could have all these flaws and still function as a symbol of the divine because the East is culturally prepared to support the coexistence of flaws and divine teachings. Try pulling that off in the West; for example, in the case of Ramakrishna he might be seen as a hypocritical charlatan. The Western view is prone to over idealizing or to throwing the baby out with the bath water.

Why is this important? Because this kind of literalism characterizes many Western discussions about questions such as "do you believe in God?" and "is God omnipotent?" The imposition of fundamental reality-type analysis into constructed reality will always do significant damage to our ability to understand the process that is actually unfolding.

Returning to the question of the lemon and the inner child, it is clear that neither of these objects exists in fundamental reality but that acting as if they exist gives them life, power, and independence. Moreover, unless one invests these unreal objects with life, their capacity for transformation and healing will go unfulfilled. Simultaneously, if we believe that the object we have invested with life now lives in fundamental reality, we will get into all sorts of problems. Joseph Campbell comments:

> Every religion is true one way or another. It is true when understood metaphorically. But when it gets stuck in its own metaphors, interpreting them as facts, then you are in trouble. (1998, p. 67)

Religious symbols—whether teachers, gurus, or stories of saints and founders—become vital by investing them with meaning and by acting as if they are real. If we stop there, we will suffer from spiritual materialism. But if we continue and paradoxically affirm their essential unreality—their symbolic truth—then we have a chance to avoid the materialism. We act as if the inner child is real and autonomous but simultaneously know there is no internal homunculus.

Finally, the concept of spiritual materialism has much to say about the power and independence of spiritual techniques. In spirituality, it appears—just as in psychology—that progress is dependent on practicing powerful techniques. Devotees are urged to meditate, pray, do selfless service, attend lecture, participate in extended retreats, and so on. These practices are generally good for people and the practitioners get better and improve as a result of their efforts. While these improvements are well received, they are not the essence of the spiritual path. Thinking progress is due to techniques is another form of spiritual materialism. Examine the critique in the following teaching story attributed to Dogen Zenji:

> When asked why he practiced zen, the student said, "Because I intend to become a Buddha."
>
> His teacher picked up a brick and started polishing it. The student asked "What are you doing?" The teacher replied, "I am trying to make a mirror."
>
> "How can you make a mirror by polishing a brick?"
>
> "How can you become Buddha by doing zazen? If you understand sitting Zen, you will know that Zen is not about sitting or lying down. If you want to learn sitting Buddha, know that sitting Buddha is without any fixed form. Do not use discrimination in the non-abiding dharma. If you practice sitting as Buddha, you must kill Buddha. If you are attached to the sitting form, you are not yet mastering the essential principle."
>
> The student heard this admonition and felt as if he had tasted sweet nectar.

Here we have a Zen master critiquing the usefulness of meditation and telling the disciple that as long as he "believes in zazen" his progress will be severely limited. Then he gives the admonition to "kill Buddha," a phrase that is repeated regularly in the Buddhist teaching tradition. Killing Buddha is equivalent to beginner's mind. It is equivalent to the recognition that we are operating in constructed reality and the feeling that we are in fundamental reality will continue to creep in. To repeat, the confusion between these two is the essence of spiritual materialism.

This "kill-the-Buddha" idea is so central to spiritual practice that one finds it in virtually every spiritual tradition. For example, examine the following Sufi story:

> When Yasavi started to teach, he was soon surrounded by potential disciples and people of all descriptions. They all listened to what he had to say, but they insisted more and more loudly on him enrolling them in a regular teaching curriculum.
>
> Yasavi told them that he wanted them to build a special structure, a Tekkia, in which people could carry out exercises similar to those which were found throughout Turkestan.
>
> Several hundred people worked, under his direction, for six months, making this edifice.
>
> When it was complete, Yasavi said: "All who want to enter this building for instruction please stand to the right, over there; and those who do not want to do so, stand over there, to the left."
>
> Where they were arranged in the two groups, Yasavi said: "I dismiss all those who stand to the right; there is nothing I can do for you; therefore return whence you came.
>
> The remainder may become my students. Their first task is to demolish the Tekkia."
>
> The dismissed students became disaffected, and spread tales to the effect that Yasavi was insane. But it is from the selectivity of this madman of God that the Teaching of the Masters is derived. (Shah, 2016, p. 40)

Once again we see the primary teaching; when the learner becomes attached to the form of learning, they will miss the essence—they will materialize spirituality. Like the last story, the teacher emphasizes that believing in techniques is a basic error. And getting attached to techniques—building a Tekkia—will result in missing the point so profoundly that the affected disciples must "be dismissed."

Psychology has an interesting parallel to these two stories with the research finding that therapists who are in therapy do not achieve improved outcomes with their own clients. On the one hand, this makes little sense. We know that therapy works for the vast majority of clients and, therefore, we can be confident that the therapist-clients are better than they were before therapy. Unfortunately it does not appear that this improvement correlates with enhanced charisma.

This conundrum is explained by our two "kill-the-Buddha" stories. The therapy is Apollonian; the therapists become better but not different. They continue to dwell in the Tekkia and enhancing charisma requires demolishing the Tekkia. Thinking we are trying to get better is spiritual materialism or, in this case, psychological materialism. Better is an improvement inside the Net. Different is a change outside the Net. Psychologists wishing to enhance charisma need to be different, not better.

The "kill-the-Buddha" story cautions the disciples in terms of attachment to meditation; the Tekkia parable cautions against an attachment to teachings; the therapy outcome research results require us to give up belief in the innate power of psychotherapy techniques. Spiritual materialism is equivalent to psychological materialism. Discern between the constructed and the fundamental. Work on being different not better.

It is fitting that we conclude this section with a quote from Jiddu Krishnamurti. Krishnamurti was an Eastern thinker particularly renowned for his work with spiritual materialism. In quote after quote, book after book, he repeatedly emphasizes the need to avoid the easy approach of a path defined by form, concrete structure, and techniques. Instead he emphasizes consciousness, courage, and self-awareness.

> There is no method of self-knowledge. Seeking a method invariably implies the desire to attain some result—and that is what we all want. We follow authority—if not that of a person, then of a system, of an ideology—because we want a result that will be satisfactory, which will give us security. We really do not want to understand ourselves, our impulses and reactions, the whole process of our thinking, the conscious as well as the unconscious; we would rather pursue a system that assures us of a result. But the pursuit of a system is invariably the outcome of our desire for security, for certainty, and the result is obviously not the understanding of oneself. When we follow a method, we must have authorities—the teacher, the guru, the savior, the Master—who will guarantee us what we desire, and surely that is not the way of self-knowledge. Authority prevents the understanding of oneself, does it not? Under the shelter of an authority, a guide, you may have temporarily a sense of security, a sense of well-being, but that is not the understanding of the total process of oneself. Authority in its very nature prevents the full awareness of oneself and therefore ultimately destroys freedom; in freedom alone can there be creativeness. There can be creativeness only through self-knowledge. (Krishnamurti, 1995, p. 95)

# Chapter 15

# Becoming Remarkable

Become who you are!

—Friedrich Nietzsche, *Ecce Homo* (1908)

This book has advanced the concept of key individuals—individuals who are given the power to determine what is real and what is not real. Such individuals can be identified by their "charisma"—a numinous quality which requires us to defer to their guidance and ideas. In psychotherapy, of course, the Reality B therapist is not trying to hide his charisma; in fact, he has no more important priority than to be recognized as a charismatic healer by his clients. A therapist does not want to be like Elijah, often disguised as a poor traveler, who passes through the world recognized by the few. Instead, the first task in the first session of therapy is to communicate to the client that the therapist is a charismatic person who has the power to alter identity and reality. In this sense, Glasser noted that success in reality Therapy depended on it being conducted by a "responsible" person who has achieved a certain level of success in life and is recognized as such by the client. And Scott Miller finds that most therapeutic change can be predicted by the response of the client to the therapist in the first three sessions. In fact, unless change occurs that quickly, Miller often recommends a referral to another therapist. The client quickly recognizes the therapist as someone who either has the power to help him change or as someone who doesn't.

Usually, this revelation of charisma is described as "instilling hope" or "positive expectations" in the client. While occasionally this hope is due to some information that the therapist imparts, more frequently hope rises because the client becomes convinced that the therapist has the ability to help her with her presenting problem. Often it appears as if the hope is instilled by a correct diagnosis and the prescription of the right techniques—"you're

depressed and we'll be using cognitive therapy to reduce the depression"—
but in reality the hope engendered by those words varies wildly depending
on which therapist speaks them and all the nonverbals that accompany the
enunciation. Examine the following quote from Milton Erickson:

> And he didn't think it was at all necessary to tell me that he had passed the
> law examination. Because my attitude towards patients is: You are going to
> accomplish your purpose, your goal. And I am very confident. I look confident.
> I act confident. I speak in a confident way, and my patient tends to believe me.
>
> And too many therapists say, "I hope I can help you," and express a doubt.
> I had no doubt when I told her to go into a trance. I had no doubts about her.
> (Erickson points to Carol.) I had no doubt about those two either. (Erickson
> points to two women on the couch.) I was utterly confident. A good therapist
> should be utterly confident. (Zeig, 1980, p. 61)

Erickson's critique of therapists who express a doubt is the exact point. Charisma includes confidence, a wish to help the client and an implicit sense of
wonder and awe at being part of the healing process. In this Reality B view
of charisma, it should not be confounded with egotism or arrogance. This is
an easy area for therapists to become confused. First of all, many therapists
believe strongly that the ability to change lies within the client and is simply
facilitated by the therapist. In fact, any statement that implies that people
change due to the power of the therapist is seen as self-centered and mis-
guided. Instead, better to cultivate a humble stance and be a midwife to the
birth of the client's true nature.

This kind of humbleness is a perfectly fine stance toward the therapeutic
relationship with two caveats. First, "humble" therapists must be aware that
some clients will need a different style of relationship. For example, they may
grow faster with a confident expert, or with a humorous provocative style like
Farrelly, or a mystifying shaman like Erickson. Second, they need to develop
their humbleness to the point where clients recognize it—feel it—as remarkable. The title of this chapter is "Becoming Remarkable." Humbleness, Love,
Expertise, Humor, Mysticism, and many more qualities can be the organizing
principle and the beginning point of a particular therapist's development of
charisma. Humbleness can be as charismatic as Expertise; Love and Acceptance taken to a profound place are as charismatic as Glasser's Responsibility.
Recalling the Dalai Lama quote about the unity of wisdom and compassion,
all of these stances eventually unite with the others. Start wherever you are
most comfortable; by the time your choice has flowered into charisma, you
will have encompassed many of the other styles and forms as well.

Schore makes an important contribution to the discussion of charisma. In
his language, therapeutic charisma means that the right brain of the client
recognizes the capacity of the right brain of the therapist. It happens quickly

and unconsciously. And this kind of recognition is central to establishing a "remarkable" therapeutic alliance.

Charisma is different than ordinary kindness and intelligence. Certainly, Tillich has already taught that the path is both flat and hierarchical and in that sense, all wisdom and all compassion—regardless of how ordinary they are— participate in ultimate wisdom and ultimate compassion. That said, when a therapist recognizes that she needs to be "remarkable" to achieve effectiveness beyond the norm, she has taken the first step toward that achievement.

When Martin Luther King was the primary leader of the civil rights movement, he not only contributed his individual powers of intelligence, perseverance, and hard work, he also was able to call on all the traditions surrounding justice and freedom implicit in the culture. When a listener's eyes well up with tears of inspiration as they hear King's "I have a dream" speech, the emotion experienced is not directly due to King. His words, manner, and the context have allowed the listener to access all their previously established feelings about freedom and justice—every exposure to these concepts throughout their life comes into the present. Like any inspirational speaker, he takes us into "sacred space" and invites us to feel and experience the "divine emotions." In this sense, King becomes an embodiment of the archetype of freedom and justice and is no longer simply an individual.

Similarly, when a therapist like Milton Erickson has used hypnosis to connect to higher order principles like the unconscious mind and magical healing—ultimate concerns—he is no longer simply an individual. Rather, he is both an individual and the archetypal representative of those higher values. Is it any wonder that a client will recognize such a person as empowered or authorized to shift the nature of Reality—to alter the threads of the Nomological Net?

There is a helpful contribution from the phenomenology of religion that can shed light on the nature of this kind of charisma. In 1923, Rudolf Otto wrote a short book entitled *The Idea of the Holy*. Otto was an expert in the phenomenology of religion; that is, he attempted to study and understand religious feelings and God as phenomena—as objects of experience. In so doing, he came up with a definition or a description of what humans experience—across time and culture—when they encounter the Holy.

Otto described the numinous experience of the encounter with the Divine using the following Latin phrase: *mysterium tremendum et fascinans.* The experience of God is absolutely mysterious—the wholly other; that which is irreducible and unnamable. Past the core-level mystery, the Holy is experienced by humans along two dimensions. The first is *tremendum,* an overwhelming power and awe that makes us shake and tremble. And the second dimension is *fascinans*, that which attracts and comforts, that which is merciful and gracious.

It is not a coincidence that Otto's description of the Holy is virtually identical to the Buddhists' two principles of wisdom and compassion and to the common factors definition of the therapeutic relationship. What makes Otto's definitions so helpful is that the phrase *mysterium tremendum et fascinans* evocatively encompasses the sense of charisma sought by Reality B therapists. The Latin phrase resonates with a sense of the numinous and all the implicit connotations of mystery, awe, and love.

It is certainly a form of idolatry to attribute actual *mysterium tremendum et fascinans* to a person regardless of how gifted they might be. Otto intended them to be descriptions of the divine, not the human. However, the ultimate concern always participates in the Ultimate and it is entirely appropriate for clients to experience *mysterium tremendum et fascinans* with their therapist when the therapist is consciously and unconsciously attempting to be true to, manifest, and embody their own ultimate concern. The therapist, of course, is not divine; but for the client, the therapist can channel divine energy.

Jaye Haley and John Weakland, both well-known and powerful therapists in their own right, had this to say about their experience of *mysterium tremendum* with Milton Erickson. It is both interesting and significant that they actually use the word "shake" as part of their description.

> Haley: . . . I think he got more confronting as he got older, and I think that makes people feel he was more a confronting therapist than he really was in our day. I think perhaps he confronted more when he had fewer skills of physical control. Because we really remember him as a very accepting and joining sort of a therapist, and I think a lot of people don't think of him in that way.
>
> Weakland: I certainly remember him in the early days as someone who was accepting. Also, at the same time, as someone you could readily be fearful of because it was easy to see he was powerful and penetrating even while being accepting. You could shake a little about it as a client. (Haley, 1993a, pp. 94–95)

Client recognition of these "divine" qualities will vary from person to person and one level of consciousness to another. In this next example, Stephen Gilligan documents his response to Erickson's therapy.

> Some of the most profound experiences of my life came during trance sessions with Milton Erickson. They are difficult to describe in words. I would sense myself in some amazing space of infinite possibilities, without boundaries or dualism. Each experience was perfect within itself, each moment a new learning or discovery. At some point I would find myself wondering who and where I was. I would then be startled to realize that the field that was holding me was Erickson! And his presence was clearly "inside" of me, inside the boundaries I had so carefully constructed to deny anyone access to my deepest self. My budding anxiety over this realization would be almost immediately met and

assuaged with a kind reassurance (from Erickson's nonverbal presence) that I needn't worry, everything was safe, and this was a place of unconditional acceptance. (Gilligan, 2012, p. 143)

Gilligan's experience certainly epitomizes *mysterium facinans*—"kind reassurance . . . that . . . everything was safe"—and *mysterium tremendum*—"amazing space of infinite possibilities without boundaries or dualism." Did every client experience this with Erickson? Of course not: this experience was at the intersection of Erickson's ultimate concern and Gilligan's ultimate concern. But the experience leaves little doubt of Erickson's power in Gilligan's life.

Did Erickson have the same experience as Gilligan? Almost certainly not. This experience was facilitated by Erickson but generated by Gilligan. However, Erickson "owns" part of the credit for the healing experience. His ability to cultivate his own ultimate concern—and to embody it—opened the door for Gilligan's response.

The therapist's relationship with his own ultimate concern can generate altered states that are different than the client's but equally powerful. As discussed above, postmodern therapeutic ethics must be centered in both the therapist's ultimate concern and the therapist's attempt to discern, align with, and serve the client's ultimate concern. In this sense, the effective therapist is involved in manifesting—at least in some sense—her own ultimate concern and the client's. When speaking of *mysterium tremendum et fascinans* it should be apparent that the human being that is the therapist is not being elevated; rather, the existential and spiritual forces he serves are moving through him. Barry Michels tries to describe his version of this experience.

The more I used the tools, the more clearly I felt that these forces came through me, not from me—they were a gift from somewhere else. They carried an extraordinary power that made it possible to do things I'd never done before. Over time, I was able to accept that these new powers were given to me by higher forces. (Stutz & Michels, 2012, p. 19)

In the next quote, Erickson agrees that his choices in therapy are coming through him; in contrast to Michels, he attributes this flow to his "unconscious mind."

"I don't know. I don't know what I'm going to do, I don't know what I'm going to say. All I know is that I trust my unconscious to shelve into my conscious that which is appropriate. And I don't know how they're going to respond. All I know is that they will respond. I don't know why. I don't know when. All I know is that they'll respond in an appropriate fashion, in a way which best suits them as an individual. And so I've become intrigued with wondering exactly how their unconscious will choose to respond. And so I comfortably await their response, knowing that when it occurs, I can accept and utilize it."

He paused, his eyes twinkling. "Now I know that sounds ridiculous. But it works!" (Zeig, 1982, p. 92)

What is the difference between Michels' "higher forces" and Erickson's "unconscious mind"? Obviously Michel's explanation has a religious connotation and Erickson's does not. Experientially, however, the two descriptions seem highly similar. As practices, it might be argued that Michels infuses his work with more numinosity and is more conducive to egolessness, but given Erickson's success with so many clients, it is difficult to argue that his approach is less *mysterium*. In addition, the way in which Erickson refers to the unconscious, both in this quote and in other therapeutic examples, makes it clear that he considers the unconscious an infinite repository of creativity and wisdom—in short, an ultimate concern. And Tillich reminds us that all ultimate concerns point to the Ultimate equally.

The perennial philosophy argues that both Michels and Erickson are working with the same healing principles in spite of the fact that the forms are so different. Both men are making their own ultimate concern central in the work with and relationship to the client. The clients "feel" the presence of the therapists' ultimate concern—probably through Schore's right brain-to-right brain process—and it opens access to their own ultimate concerns. Even without literally invoking God or the Divine—as Michels did in his example of the Grateful Flow in the last chapter—the clients are being invited to connect to their own ultimate concerns.

A number of therapists might be appalled by the clear hierarchy between therapist and client in this explanation. As the initiator of the experience, the therapist has a unique role and is raised above the client in a literal sense. Yet Tillich's concept that the path is both hierarchical and flat can reconcile this dilemma. In order to manifest the therapist's ultimate concern, there must be a quality of surrender in the therapist. In order to feel and evoke the client's ultimate concern, there must be a quality of egolessness in the therapist. In the Michael's quote above he emphasizes that the "forces came through me not from me" and, in that sense, Tillich's flattening of the hierarchy is paradoxically maintained even when the therapist must take the lead.

The key to generate these kinds of experiences in clients is that the therapist must feel "radical"—as if they are always coming from the edge of the Abyss. Swami Vivekananda says, "Dare to be free, dare to go as far as your thought leads, and dare to carry that out in your life" (2015a, p. 8). If the therapist lives safely inside the Net, the right brain of the client will somehow know that. The modest, positive effect will be there but not the sense of charisma. That said, humbleness, egolessness, compassion, and empathy can be as radical as confidence, penetrating questions, and the provocative trickster. The Mysterium aspect of the definition is the sense that the therapist somehow is outside this normal world. Fascinans is equivalent to Tremendum.

Virginia Satir in her time was as famous for her humbleness and open heart as Erickson was for his shamanic power. She had the ability to say the simplest things and they would impact the client as profoundly as Glasser's call to fulfill your potential. For example, the following "hug" prescription is not much in itself, but it was transformational when uttered by Satir.

> We need 4 hugs a day for survival.
> We need 8 hugs a day for maintenance.
> We need 12 hugs a day for growth. (as cited in Hudson, 2011, p. 127)

Similarly, when she invited a client or a family into a constructive and egalitarian relationship, her words had profound impact.

> I want to love you without clutching, appreciate you without judging, join you without invading, invite you without demanding, leave you without guilt, criticize you without blaming, and help you without insulting. If I can have the same from you, then we can truly meet and enrich each other. (as cited in Grotberg, 2003, p. 73)

When reading a vignette, it is easy to be more impacted by the provocation of Farrelly or the gracefulness of Gilligan yet the therapists who choose, like Satir, the Borofskys, and Levine, to concentrate on connection and the heart are just as radical, just as *mysterium*, and just as effective.

The first step toward becoming a remarkable therapist is overtly and consciously seeking charisma. The first limit to therapeutic power is the capacity of the therapist to ask for it. Clearly such a request requires the therapist to address potentially confounding issues such as egotism and self-centeredness. Erickson worked around this dilemma via attributing his power to the channeling of the unconscious; Michels recommends working with more overtly spiritual attributions. Regardless, both lean heavily on the concept of the ultimate concern.

All seeking requires following your own path and having the courage of your own convictions. Vivekananda exhorts us: "You have to grow from the inside out. None can teach you, none can make you spiritual. There is no other teacher but your own soul" (Swami Vivekanada, as cited in Chockalingam, 2014, p. 65). Radical boldness is also an ultimate concern. Perhaps one of the best descriptions of this concept comes from mythologist Joseph Campbell. Campbell was describing how to search for the Holy Grail, the cup that brings healing and Eternal Life.

You enter the forest
at the darkest point,
where there is no path.

Where there is a way or path,
it is someone else's path.

You are not on your own path.

If you follow someone else's way,
you are not going to realize
your potential.
(Campbell, 1990, p. 19)

## CLIENT-CENTERED THERAPY AND
## THE ULTIMATE CONCERN

The fabled musk deer searches the world over for the source of the
scent which comes from itself.

—Ramakrishna, *The Gospel of Sri Ramakrishna* (1910)

The lack of effectiveness of techniques and systems forces us to cultivate the
interiority of the therapist—the charisma—versus the exterior world of privileged knowledge. This is well and good from one perspective but it leaves
constructionism open to the criticism that the client is reduced to a passive
object with no real power, influence, or responsibility. It is more than possible
to accept the need for therapeutic charisma logically and continue to have a
feeling that we are heading in the wrong direction. Something that moves the
client back to the center seems required.

Historically, the first significant promotion from "patient" to "client"
was, of course, secondary to the work of Carl Rogers. His client-centered
approach emphasized the power of the person and saw the therapist as more
of a midwife.

In my early professional years I was asking the question: How can I treat, or
cure, or change this person? Now I would phrase the question in this way: How
can I provide a relationship which this person may use for his own personal
growth? (Kramer & Rogers, 1995, p. 32)

Postmodern therapies embrace this Rogerian perspective and carry it even
further. Given that Postmodernism is suspicious of simple assertions of
power, authority, and expertise—often seeing them as assumptions that
marginalize certain groups and subcultures—a simple endorsement of the

concept "cultivating therapist charisma is the key to being a more effective therapist" is an anathema.

More specifically, narrative therapy (Madigan, 2012)—arguably the pre-eminent postmodern therapy—is exquisitely sensitive to power relationships in the culture. Not only do they believe that the medical model works to stabilize the client in his current identity and dilemma, they also believe that psychology often becomes a force for oppression and inequity, particularly for liminal and disenfranchised classes of people. Narrative therapy has a commitment to identify those hidden and implicit power relationships, bring them to the surface, and dispute their validity.

Narrative therapy argues that traditional psychology not only marginalizes certain groups, its very structure implicitly creates oppression and inequality. As part of exploring this concept, narrative therapy provides one of the most profound and detailed critiques of prevailing psychiatric practices available. More specifically, since it believes that a person's pathology is constructed, it accuses psychiatry of inappropriately pathologizing patients to support guild power. In response, narrative therapy attempts to put the rights to an individual's story back in his own hands. Stephen Madigan (2012) feels that this is the central theme of his book.

> Finally, the primary question I attempt to raise in the book is based on a rather simple question: Who has the storytelling rights to the story being told? (Kindle Locations 520–535)

Put another way, narrative therapy exposes the power politics of psychology and psychiatry and asks, "What right do mental health experts have in terms of defining the identity and reality of their clients?"

As might be expected, narrative therapy has a profound commitment to flatten human hierarchies; this commitment specially focuses on minimizing the hierarchy between therapist and client.

> Early on in his therapeutic practice, Epston seemed to make it his mission to work against any form of therapy that acted as a ritual of degradation—in which one party (i.e., the professional helper) would act to make the other party feel "less than." For Epston, taken-for-granted assumptions of everyday life became a focus of inquiry and celebration. (Madigan, 2012, Kindle Locations 632–634)

To this end, narrative therapists often pose new frames to clients in the form of questions instead of statements. The aim, of course, is to emphasize that the client already has the wisdom, the power, and the answer; the therapist simply invites what is already present to manifest itself. Asking questions, of course, also minimizes the identities of the "therapist as expert/client as dependent."

Given this brief summary of some of the core principles of narrative therapy, imagine how its adherents might respond to concepts like charisma, "secret knowledge," and therapeutic wizards. Regardless of the positive intentions behind these concepts, each of them is implicitly hierarchical and each one contains seeds that could develop into ways of exploiting, diminishing, and degrading clients. Moreover, narrative therapists believe that assumptions of expertise are already deeply embedded in any psychotherapeutic system that is related to medicine and psychiatry. A psychotherapeutic system that emphasized developing therapist charisma could easily be seen as dangerous and as moving in an inappropriate and unhelpful direction.

If this is true of narrative therapy, such concerns are even more pronounced in another postmodern therapeutic system, Collaborative Therapy. In order to minimize power imbalances as fully as possible, Harlene Anderson, developer of collaborative therapy, presents her vision of the ethical client-therapist relationship.

*Conversational Partners.* The collaborative therapist and client become conversational partners as they engage in dialogical conversations and collaborative relationships. Dialogical conversation and collaborative relationship refer to the shared inquiry process in which people talk with each other rather than to each other. Inviting this kind of partnership requires that the client's story take center stage. It requires that the therapist constantly learn—listening and trying to understand the client from the client's perspective.

*Client as Expert.* The collaborative therapist believes that the client is the expert on his or her life and as such is the therapist's teacher. The therapist respects and honors the client's story, listens to hear what is important for the client, and takes seriously what the client says and how they say it. This includes any and all knowledge; for instance, whether dominant cultural discourse or popular folklore informs the client's descriptions and interpretations, and it includes the many ways that the client may express his or her knowledge. For instance, the therapist does not hold expectations that a story should unfold in a chronological order or at a certain pace. The therapist does not expect certain answers and does not judge whether an answer is direct or indirect, right or wrong. . . .

*Not-Knowing.* The collaborative therapist is a not-knowing therapist. Not-knowing refers to the way the therapist thinks about and positions themselves with their knowledge and expertise. They do not believe they have superior knowledge or hold a monopoly on the truth. They offer what they know or think they might know but always hold it and present it in a tentative manner. That is, therapists offer their voice, including previous knowledge, questions, comments, opinions, and suggestions as food for thought and dialogue. Therapists remain willing and able to have their knowledge (including professional and personal values and biases) questioned, ignored, and changed.

*Being Public.* Therapists often learn to operate from invisible private thoughts—whether professionally, personally, theoretically, or experientially informed. Such therapist thoughts include diagnoses, judgments, or hypotheses about the client that influence how they listen and hear and that form and guide their questions. From a collaborative stance, therapists are open and make their invisible thoughts visible. They do not operate or try to guide the therapy from private thoughts. . . . Keeping therapists' thoughts public minimizes the risk of therapist and therapist-client monologue—being occupied by one idea about a person or situation.

*Mutual Transformation.* The therapist is not an expert agent of change; that is, a therapist does not change another person. Rather the therapist's expertise is in creating a space and facilitating a process for dialogical conversations and collaborative relationships. When involved in this kind of process, both client and therapist are shaped and reshaped—transformed—as they work together. (Anderson, 2003)

Examining Anderson's principles, it is clear that she is seriously engaged in flattening the hierarchy between client and therapist. The therapist is not senior to the client in any way—not through training, licensure, experience, age, wisdom, compassion, or fearlessness. If one takes constructionism seriously—and believes that there is "no place to stand"—then the only authority for therapy with any individual comes from the individual herself: "the client is the expert on his or her life and as such is the therapist's teacher." When the credibility of the "expert who knows the effective technique" is destroyed by research results and deconstructionism, the only place to stand is in the truth of the client.

Both Anderson in particular and narrative therapy in general are very serious about conducting therapy without a client-therapist hierarchy. While their intentions are admirable in terms of social justice and basic human respect, the problem, of course, is that fundamental reality and constructed reality are literally suffused by natural hierarchies. Perhaps, the simplest example comes when working with a child. Given that the child has an undeveloped brain, conducting therapy without hierarchies makes no sense. Is it really appropriate to make every thought in the therapist "public" when the child lacks the capacity to understand the thoughts? Even if we grant that Anderson was speaking about adults, it is clear that adults vary developmentally and fall into a range from childlike to fully mature. Moreover, Schore's research implies that a number of adults have "brain damage" when it comes to affective regulation. Isn't there a hierarchy between such people and their (hopefully) fully developed therapists?

Even in the area of constructed reality there are hierarchies. Glasser argues that the therapist must understand how to operate in the culture, the Net, more effectively than the client if he is going to help the client move from his current position to a new one. Tillich believes that many individuals are following idolatrous ultimate concerns and are reaping painful results due to this strategy. Put in Buddhist language, these clients are being driven by fear and desire—using strategies which are characterized by avoiding what is feared and desiring what seems rewarding. The Buddhists warn that such strategies diminish long-term satisfaction and contentment. If a therapist has understood the implications of the Buddhist teachings about desire/fear and Tillich's ideas about idolatry/authenticity, and the client has not, isn't there an implicit hierarchy between therapist and client?

And the lack of research support for the effectiveness of techniques adds another twist. I will defer to an expert in a fundamental reality field, such as a contractor, because they know how to build a house. But in psychotherapy, the therapist's main ability to help me change rests on her charisma, her personal power, and/or her ability to have an open heart. Her knowledge of techniques is not going to help me. Given this fact, isn't it in my best interest to go to the therapist who has wisdom and openheartedness beyond my own? I should seek a therapist that seems in some way superior to me if I want to learn and grow.

Narrative therapists might argue that while all this is true, and makes sense from the client point of view, it can still be helpful to the therapist to drop the hierarchy between herself and her client. Certainly, decreasing hierarchy from a therapist point of view has many benefits including listening more to the client, affirming his personhood, reducing dependency on the therapist, and limiting therapist hubris. However, it is more effective to achieve these desirable results via an alternative approach versus trying to accept arguments about hierarchies that are simply not true. Hierarchies exist. Typically, clients will seek therapists that "feel" wiser, more caring and more skillful at living. This is an inevitable outcome; the problems associated with it need to be dealt with in some other manner than asserting that hierarchies are odious and destructive.

A closely related issue is the established fact that it is difficult or impossible for the therapist to avoid acting in a hierarchical manner particularly when it comes to influencing the client. Carl Rogers was famous for attempting to flatten the client/therapist hierarchy as much as possible and even his best efforts failed to result in an egalitarian relationship. More specifically, a number of research studies revealed (Fromme, 2010) that Rogers was unconsciously emitting nonverbals when working with clients—nonverbals that urged the clients to focus on what Rogers believed most helpful. In other words, even when we work as hard as possible to avoid imposing our beliefs on our clients, even when we try to defer to the concept that client beliefs are primary and that they are superior in the hierarchy, we unconsciously impose our own worldview on them.

After all of the critique of specific weaknesses in the "flatten hierarchy" arguments, it should be recognized that Anderson, the narrative therapists and Carl Rogers are not simply outlining a literal psychological technique; rather, it is more useful to see their prioritization of social justice and equality as an ultimate concern. As an ultimate concern, one can argue that it should not be subjected to the same analyses used with simple intellectual arguments. Rather, it should be seen as a conveyer of higher purpose and meaning and judged from that point of view. In this sense, the concept of flattening the hierarchy between therapist and client is fundamentally useful and helpful. The literal incongruences of the position can be disregarded and the inspirational and motivational aspects embraced.

Many, many therapists have had the sense of "no hierarchy" as they work with clients. They feel like the ultimate authority on what should be done in therapy resides in the client and the therapist's job is to listen carefully, help it come to the surface, and serve it. As the therapist operates from this perspective, they often feel as if something from the client comes through them. The therapist is not generating the concepts and directions; it all arises from somewhere inside the client. This is an experientially validated state of mind, not a carefully reasoned argument.

To the degree that narrative therapy attempts to point toward and elicit this kind of experience in the therapist, the concept of flattening hierarchies is unassailable. It is more like a spiritual experience than a psychological approach. Moving toward this kind of ultimate concern often creates an altered state in the therapist which can be communicated implicitly to the client. The client feels heard and honored; their core self feels affirmed and empowered. The therapist feels humble; moreover, they often have the sensation that they are touching a core experience of love and connection.

In sum, flattening hierarchies as an ultimate concern can be helpful to both therapists and clients. Unfortunately, if taken more literally, it can confuse therapists about the need to cultivate their own charisma, take responsibility for leadership, and manifest a healing vision.

## CLIENT-CENTERED ETHICS

> By what authority are you doing these things? they asked. And who gave you authority to do this?
>
> —Mark 11:28

The fact that techniques are not responsible for outcomes in psychotherapy creates an unusual ethical dilemma. In most professions, the healer is able to state that his knowledge of the techniques of his profession is responsible for his outcomes. Take, for example, a physical therapist. The twenty-eight-year-old physical therapist has no doubt about her authority to treat a fifty-six-year-old survivor of an automobile accident. She has the right to treat him because she has been trained in effective techniques—techniques which she can teach and techniques which will lead to recovery. She will still need a code of ethics consisting of principles such as do no harm, put the client's welfare before her own, and maintain confidentiality. But she does not need to worry about the most fundamental ethical question: what right do I have to treat this patient and how can I be confident that I am helping him?

When power lies in the technique, then I can attribute the credit for change to the technique; I am simply an ordinary man in possession of a powerful tool. If I am effective, and it is due to "standing on the shoulders of the giants that came before me," then it is relatively easy to preserve humbleness, avoid corruption and resist the seduction of power. Unfortunately, this faith in techniques is no longer available after analyzing the outcome research findings. Without effective techniques, clients only change because of my charisma and caring.

The obvious alternative—and one emphasized by many therapists, including many therapeutic wizards—is attributing change and growth as secondary to power in the client; the therapist may be the midwife at the birth of the new reality, but the client is ultimately responsible for all growth. This always sounds good, especially when one says it to a client, yet it begs the central question. If the client is actually the one responsible for change, then why did they need to come to the therapist? If there is really little or no power in the therapist, why are some therapists consistently better than others at facilitating change? The moment the change agent is significantly more effective than the average therapist, the superiority must be in the therapist, not in the client.

Moreover, when techniques are responsible for change, then it is relatively easy to sustain the relationship. The therapist simply has to care for the client, monitor the response to the techniques, and alter them when appropriate. Without techniques the situation is much more demanding. Imagine a financial planner who is selling the client a good financial product that is making money. The satisfaction of making the money virtually ensures that the client will appreciate the relationship. Contrast that with the financial planners in chapter 1 that Kahneman used as examples. Since they have no real expertise at stock picking, they will have to sustain the relationship with charm and charisma and even misinformation, especially since their stock recommendations will regularly move in the wrong direction.

Therapeutic relationships are easier given that there is an expected modest, positive result from therapy; it is kind of like the stock pickers sustaining relationships during an "up" market. Even so, it is much more challenging to work with clients when one knows that the techniques are not responsible for the outcomes. When I know that all my "techniques" are really "rituals," I am left with the feeling that I am responsible for the outcomes; this feeling can make me anxious or grandiose.

In such ambiguous situations, the person of the therapist and the person of the client loom large. One can even argue that—bereft of the ability to lean on the power of the technique—it is almost impossible to be truly client centered. Without techniques, I am compelled to take stands that are not neutral; I am required to move the client in one direction or another according to my best judgment. Gergen comments:

> Unlike traditional therapists, the constructionist realizes that there is no value neutrality in the therapeutic relationship. Every intervention will favour some form of life, while undermining others. The therapist who favours heterosexuality closes the door on homosexual options; in favouring the client's industrious productivity the joys of hedonism remain unrealized; "empower" the male and the female loses options. (Gergen, 2009, p. 138)

In sum, the inability to lean on the power of techniques forces the therapist to face the fact that therapy results in an imposition of therapist values on the client. Bereft of techniques, I must take responsibility for the conduct of therapy.

If one can't attribute the power of change to the technique, and it cannot be attributed in a straightforward manner to the client, what is left? The simplest answer to this question—and one used by most spiritual seekers—is to attribute the power to change to a higher power. You, the therapist, are an instrument of some higher power working through you. Even if techniques are not the answer, I can sustain my humbleness and my egolessness by asserting that I simply have an ability to surrender to a power that works through me. I am not better in myself than the average therapist; in fact, I am not even better than the average client. However, I can be more helpful in that I channel the source more effectively. I am only special and superior in my ability to connect to the higher power and to allow it to use me. In some ways, this is similar to giving credit for change to the powerful technique; once again, it is not me that helped you change, but something that comes through me.

But many therapists do not have a direct relationship with a higher power and this kind of religious language would feel foreign to them. Interestingly, however, if one examines Rogers' famous prescription that therapists should approach the client with "unconditional positive regard," one quickly spots the spiritual incongruity. Unconditional is equivalent to infinite. It is a spiritual tautology that only God can be loved unconditionally and only God loves us unconditionally. Yet Roger's statement is one of the most oft-quoted comments defining the ideal therapeutic relationship. Does it actually require therapists to be "God-like" to fulfill the Rogerian ideal of the therapeutic relationship? The simple answer—which is of course impossible—is: *yes*. Normally, when one rests on the power of techniques this kind of god-like ability—to love unconditionally—is rarely needed nor is it examined closely. But without the shelter of techniques, unconditional positive regard becomes the technique. And the implication is that the therapist is required to achieve an "imitation of Christ-type" consciousness.

Almost all therapists recognize that they never achieve unconditional positive regard; they simply hold it as an ideal which points the way toward a healthy therapeutic relationship. This concept of "points toward" is, of course, the heart of the Tillichian model. His core argument is that the ultimate concern—if it is authentic and not idolatrous—points beyond itself toward something Infinite.

Examining the client relationship from an ultimate concern point of view opens up a new realm of possibilities because in the area of ultimate concern, there is no hierarchy between me and the client. Recall that the Tillichian path is both hierarchical and flat. A young person's ultimate concern, which might be focused on achieving recognition by the adult world, is just as connected to the Source as the middle-aged person whose ultimate concern is focused on sustaining love in a long-term marriage. Certainly, the challenge of the middle-aged person requires a higher level of maturity and depth—hence it is hierarchical; conversely, the degree to which both challenges point toward the Source are equal.

I have my own path and my own dialog with my ultimate concern. Similarly, my client has her own path. Buber quotes a Hasidic proverb that addresses this important concept:

> The same point is made by the Hasidic rabbi, Susya, who shortly before his death said, "When I get to heaven they will not ask me, 'Why were you not Moses?' Instead they will ask 'Why were you not Susya?'" (Buber, 2014, p. vxvii)

This quote implies that each person has a unique path to individuation. Using Tillich's concepts of idolatry/authenticity suggests that the therapist is ethically responsible for discerning whether an intervention participates in the client's unique path—whether it is authentic—or whether it pulls the client off her path—whether it is idolatrous. This places the therapist in the middle of two sets of ultimate concerns: her own, with which she needs to stay aligned to allow her own creativity and power to flow, and the client's ultimate concern, which must validate and support any intervention for the therapy to be ethical and appropriate. And since both ultimate concerns participate equally in the infinite, there is no hierarchy between therapist and client.

Of course the therapist "steps down" from that level of consciousness and plans and executes an intervention in constructed reality. The planning and execution of the intervention are hierarchical. But planning and intervention rest on the ability to discern the ultimate concern of the client. In that sense, the client's ultimate concern is more important and all discernment about it is nonhierarchical. In sum, hierarchy is paradoxical; it both exists and doesn't exist in the therapeutic relationship once the client's ultimate concern becomes paramount.

The Jerome Frank conceptualization of therapeutic processes as rituals has something important to add here as well. The key to make the ritual meaningful and effective is to align it with the client's primary issue; the ritual must include an explanation as well as provide a passage through an experience which justifies the resolution of the challenge. The client's issue is connected symbolically to her ultimate concern; essentially the resolution of the issue allows for an evolutionary move toward the ultimate concern. In this sense, the client's ultimate concern is at the center of every therapeutic ritual and the therapist is always required to adapt to the client's current consciousness.

Making the client's ultimate concern central in the therapeutic process allows the therapist to put much of the power of change back into the client. It is easy to feel humble standing before the client's ultimate concern. This is useful in that the less ego, the easier to discern the client's next step on her path. And, similarly, the more humble I am, the less my own material pollutes and confuses the situation.

This does not imply that every therapist needs to be a spiritual devotee in order to be more effective nor is every practitioner required to be some kind of believer. Recall that Tillich's ultimate concerns point beyond themselves. If one therapist has an ultimate concern connected with recognizing and validating the emotional side and another is committed to embracing the shadow in a profound manner, these sorts of concerns can be every bit as empowering as directly affirming some kind of relationship to the Source.

Standing in one's own ultimate concern and attempting to discern the client's path is the only meaningful answer to "by what authority do I heal?" I heal by the authority implicit in my client's ultimate concern. It is open to me when I stand in my own ultimate concern. And, obviously, part of every therapist's ultimate concern includes her identity as a healer.

In sum, the rejection of the power of techniques creates new ethical dilemmas for therapists. If superior mastery of techniques is not the source of therapeutic power, then all that is left is something special in the therapist. Obviously, the narcissistic assumption of therapist superiority leads to a dark and confused place, both for clients and for therapists. The "way out" of the dilemma is through the ultimate concern.

It is ironic that something as deconstructive as postmodern thinking essentially forces therapists and coaches into a choice between "I heal due to my personal charisma" and "I heal because I align myself with forces greater than myself." Postmodern thought is famous for supporting the "death of God." It is strange to think of it as a force that confirms the importance of the ultimate concern. Yet the very act of entering into a relationship with another human being with the intent to be of service forces the therapist into a position where they must affirm that they heal from their personal power and superiority or they heal via channeling some higher ideal or force.

## THE EVOLUTIONARY MODEL

The only religion that ought to be taught is the religion of fearlessness. Either in this world or in the world of religion, it is true that fear is the sure cause of degradation and sin. It is fear that brings misery, fear that brings death, fear that breeds evil. And what causes fear? Ignorance of our own nature.

—Swami Vivekananda, *The Complete Works of Swami Vivekananda* (1907)

Every psychotherapeutic technique has its own implicit assumptions about the structure of reality and the meaning of life. In this sense, it is possible to construct an evolutionary hierarchy of human development using schools of psychotherapy. Whether one uses Maslow's hierarchy, or Kohlberg's sense of moral development, or Tillich's progression from idolatrous to authentic, each school of therapy can make a contribution at a different developmental stage. For example, using Kohlberg's model, reality therapy and cognitive therapy embody Kohlberg's conventional stage, narrative therapy—with its emphasis on social justice—embodies a social contract orientation, and Buddhist therapy orients itself toward Universal Principles. In this sense, the therapist who is interested in mastering new schools of thought can conceptualize this learning as an evolutionary process. And, since this is an evolutionary process, as the therapist learns to embody a new approach, he has the opportunity to develop his connection to his ultimate concern and increase his charisma.

Of course, the focus of this book is on Reality B; hence, this evolutionary model of psychotherapy schools needs to be discussed in terms of constructed reality instead of fundamental reality. More specifically, each school can be described in terms of its geographic location in constructed reality—in terms of the way in which it participates in the Net-Abyss dialog. In this sense, fully mastering any school of therapy implies that the therapist understands and is competent in terms of that particular Abyss-Net interaction—the therapist comfortably dwells in that level of consciousness. For example, to effectively perform Apollonian techniques like reality therapy or CBT, the therapist needs to be an expert on culturally defined reality and at ease with concepts such as implicit judgments about healthy/unhealthy and right/wrong. To work with psychodynamic and depth psychologies, the therapist must be comfortable with exploring the personal and collective unconscious and be able to distill meaning from pathology. Working intentionally with altered states requires the therapist to have personal experiences at the edge of the Abyss. And integrating spirituality into psychotherapy rests on one's capacity to immerse oneself in the Abyss.

Each developer of a therapy school essentially believed that they were introducing a new way to understand human beings and a new approach to healing and change. The founders felt that they were opening a new view of reality, one that would expand and complement extant views. In virtually every example of new thought, one can feel the excitement of the developer—the sense that these new ideas will push the frontiers of knowledge. Experiences such as these are easy to conceptualize as expressions of the developer's ultimate concern. The implicit excitement embodies the developer's sense that they are part of an age-old quest for knowledge and truth.

In this sense, striving to master an evolutionary progression of psychotherapeutic techniques requires the therapist to undertake an inner pilgrimage. Recall that pilgrimages occur in sacred space. Clearly, simply learning a new technique like EMDR or DBT does not guarantee that the learner has moved into sacred space. In addition to attaining the technical competence, the learner needs to attempt to recreate the initial excitement of the developer and move into sacred space by feeling that she has a new experience—a transformed sense of reality. Each of these techniques allows a pure experience of a different form of the Net-Abyss interaction. Trying to help a client see and experience that interaction will immerse the therapist fully in the same experience. In this manner, each session becomes an opportunity for the therapist to have a personal encounter with her own growth and development through facilitating the client's growth and development. The evolutionary model is not simply about moving from one technique to another. Instead, it is the attempt to master a technique through reexperiencing the developer's connection to his ultimate concern and the geography of constructed reality. And the mechanism of this connection is the attempt to introduce the experience to the client.

Returning to the example of Mother Teresa offered earlier: she was attempting to purify her heart by conducting programs for the poor. In the evolutionary model, we are attempting to master constructed reality by doing therapy with clients. Since the perennial philosophy suggests that mastery of constructed reality is essentially an existential/spiritual process, the pursuit of the evolutionary model occurs in sacred space. Eliade might argue that each mastery experience of a different therapeutic approach is a hierophany.

As an example, I practice EMDR on a fairly regular basis. I'm not too concerned about whether there are any neurological underpinnings to the technique although I am sympathetic to EMDR's continual attempt to find such underpinnings. Instead, I simply practice it as another technique—similar to hypnosis—which is conducive to clients entering an altered state. It's especially useful now because its advocates have created so much good press that many clients have strong, positive expectations about the technique.

From my point of view, I simply explain to the client that his mind has the ability to make new connections around the content of a traumatic event. These new learnings will result in the ability to integrate the event in a new manner that will result in healing and growth. I continue by pointing out that it is a process; we will begin with whatever experience his mind/feelings generate and then follow them until they eventually culminate in a good result. Then I begin to wave my hand and process the resulting experiences with him.

He is working on resolving his trauma. I am watching him and marveling at how quickly and effortlessly humans can slip into altered states and how fluid the strings of the Net become in an altered state. I am also witnessing how easily humans move toward healing when they are given permission. My client's experience has allowed me to move into my own altered state. I exist at the edge of the Net/beginning of the Abyss. Everything seems possible; often everything seems effortless. The numinosity of the Abyss surrounds me; as we work through the chain of experiences, the positive movement toward healing feels as if it affirms the oracular nature of the Abyss. Hopefully, the client has an experience of healing. Just as hopefully, I have an experience of meaning and I touch the sacred space that exists at the boundaries of the Abyss.

I don't feel concerned about the way in which my experience diverges from my client's experience. She may have the feeling that I am using a technique that has been scientifically verified as effective with PTSD. I imagine that she believes the eye movements have a neurological basis. I have explained that the research has shown that many people are helped by EMDR and, although no one knows for sure how it works, EMDR theorists postulate a neurological effect. The structure of her ritual is intact including an explanation for her suffering, an explanation of why the ritual should resolve it, and the ritual of the eye movements themselves. Hopefully the right brain-to-right brain connection between us will allow her to recognize me as a credible healer. And, certainly, my ability to be excited and moved both by her altered state and by the ways in which her psyche guides her in making new connections does nothing but enhance my relationship with her and my charisma. Our separate "truths" may appear to diverge but actually they are not as separate as they may seem at first glance.

Moving to a more pragmatic perspective, the evolutionary model does not have rigid rules. It is not necessary to literally master every major school of therapy. Indeed virtually any complex school—for example, psychodynamic psychotherapy—can be practiced from an Apollonian or Dionysian point of view. Switching schools—which symbolizes switching world views—can be seen as a potentially helpful but not necessary choice. Moreover, every therapist has their own background and their own choices about what schools of therapy they have mastered and what approaches they currently use. The evolutionary model can be adapted to any beginning point.

The secret is that the therapist must feel and believe that he is stretching himself and venturing into new territory. If the new material feels like "same old-same old," it is not part of the evolutionary model. If it feels like learning a new technique, it is not part of the evolutionary model. If it feels like adopting a new worldview; if it is a true paradigm shift; it is part of the evolutionary model. The single biggest sign that one is practicing the evolutionary model is that it feels like the practice of therapy is leading to personal evolution. This is part of accepting psychotherapy as a vocation instead of a profession; helping, serving, and personal growth become intertwined.

The efficacy of the evolutionary model rests on a simple set of assumptions. If I am already a master of Apollonian techniques such as reality therapy and CBT, and I add expertise in shadow work and the unconscious mind, this level of growth should lead to enhanced charisma. This statement of course depends on the principles enumerated above; I have not simply mastered the "technique," I have embraced the essence of shadow work and/ or I have deep, personal encounter with the unconscious. If, indeed, I can achieve that, then it should result in enhanced charisma.

Similarly, if I can work well with dissociation, or sacred space, or deeply feel the impact of groups on the individual's reality structure, I should be a better therapist/more charismatic than I was prior to my mastery. Moreover, therapists who limit themselves to one approach—whether through fear, or programming, or lack of curiosity—should have limited charisma. If these simple assumptions are true, then training programs and continuing education should recommend that therapists attempt to master approaches and schools of thought that they may be unfamiliar with, especially if they have some resistance or fear about the new approach. The evolutionary model assumes more mastery equals more charisma.[1]

The evolutionary model is not limited to learning the next psychological system that lies closer to the Abyss. It can also occur on a variety of other dimensions such as an evolutionary approach to wisdom or an evolutionary approach to self and identity. For example, wisdom can evolve from an Apollonian expertise in the prevailing culture, through the kind of wisdom that can detect the numinous qualities present when the Abyss breaks into daily life. Go further and use wisdom to discern what is constructed and what is fundamental and then proceed to understand the formlessness implicit in a "kill-the-Buddha" paradigm.

Appendix A, entitled "The Geography of Constructed Reality," is included to illustrate some of the many themes that are amenable to the evolutionary model. In truth, no one can practice one theme without simultaneously participating in at least several others. Wisdom requires heart and the evolution of the ultimate concern is connected to an evolutionary experience of the self. It is important not to get too literal while still offering enough specificity to be helpful.

In attempting to accumulate charisma, we must constantly move back toward the relationship with the client. Everything is possible whenever we truly encounter the other. Buber's I-Thou relationship is always only a breath away. While that may be true, it will be easier to experience my client as a Thou when my perceptions are facilitated by my own altered state. In this sense, practitioners of the evolutionary model are always in an altered state when they are working. It is possible to perform techniques in a standard state of consciousness, but when one is focusing on psychotherapy as practice, consciousness is always altered. Psychoanalyst Marjorie Schuman comments:

> When we are deeply present with another, transcendent subjectivity can also occur as an emergent aspect of the relational field. This can be termed a transcendent relational field; it involves an experience of transpersonal awareness. We may think of such experiences as "blood moment" in which the usual boundaries between self and other are temporarily relaxed, yielding an interpersonal experience of belonging, connectedness, and deep intimacy unbounded by the sense of separate self. The quality of relatedness can emerge intersubjectively in the transference/countertransference when mindful awareness is brought to bear on the experience of the relational field. This subjective state cannot be said to "belong to" either patient or therapist. It is felt to be emergent: arising of its own accord in the mysterious alchemy of the therapeutic relationship. (Schuman, 2017, pp. 78–79)

The attempt to master a new approach is essentially a trance induction for the therapist. To repeat, the power of the evolutionary model rests on its ability to take the practitioner out of normal consciousness and land them at the edge of the Abyss. This is not simply another day at the office. Mastering an approach is not equivalent to learning a new technique.

In the sacred space opened by the altered state everything is new and everything is numinous. Certainly, such an experience has the capacity to enhance charisma. The question is less "does the evolutionary model work?" and more "can I dive so deeply into mastery that I can achieve an altered state and move into sacred space?"

## DELIBERATE PRACTICE

There are no beautiful surfaces without a terrible depth.

—Friedrich Nietzsche, *Beyond Good and Evil* (1886)

Scott Miller has been repeatedly cited in this book because he has been a thought leader in terms of popularizing the results of the research—psychology's inconvenient truth. Not surprisingly, he has not been content with simply exposing the flaws of extant practice; he is also active in developing new models of training. Miller calls his new model "deliberate practice." Derived from the work of Ericsson (1993), in deliberate practice, the practitioner focuses on the weak points in their expertise. For example, a good basketball player, who has a relatively weak left-handed dribble, might focus specifically on the dribble through exercises and drills. Conversely, simply playing regular basketball games would take a long time to improve the dribble. It is even possible that the player consciously or unconsciously avoids the left-handed dribble so much that general play will never improve his skills in this area. Miller states:

> So, that's what led us to the concept of deliberate practice. Most of us go to work every day and, perhaps surprisingly, given that we spend so much time at our jobs—more time than we spend with their families—most of us are only average at what we do. That's pretty disturbing so, what do top performers do? The truth is, they practice in a different way. You hear people, myself included, talk about how they practice but, unfortunately, that kind of practice doesn't make them any better. For a while, people like Ericsson et al (1993) and, more recently, Colvin (2008) and Shenk (2010), have been talking about deliberate practice. Deliberate practice means that there is a different order to, and level of investment by, top-performing folks that lead them to a massive knowledge that is different. It is more nuanced and contextualized and it certainly has more breath than the average practitioners. So, that's where the whole idea came from; that's a long way around. (Miller & Hubble, 2011, p. 34)

In a variety of skills—like the basketball example above—it is relatively easy to determine one's weak points and develop a deliberate practice to improve the area. In therapy, however, the complexities and relativity of the different therapists, clients, and schools of therapy make deliberate practice more challenging. Miller has come up with a model that attempts to address these challenges:

First, know your baseline. Rachel (a gifted young pianist) is able to accurately assess what she does, mindful of what she's capable of. Second, engage in deliberate practice—a systematic and critical review during which time problematic aspects of the performance are isolated and rehearsed or, failing that, alternatives are considered, implemented, and evaluated. Third, obtain formal, ongoing feedback. (Miller & Hubble, 2011, p. 25) (Items in parenthesis added)

Miller's model begins with the concept that the focus is on enhancing the therapist not on developing systems and techniques. He requires practitioners to start with self-assessment—an assessment that pays particular attention to weaknesses. Consulting with mentors and supervisors, and reviewing the work of master therapists can be helpful at this stage. Next he builds in a formal feedback process. Miller's primary feedback process is entitled Feedback Informed Treatment (FIT). The basic practice in FIT involves administering two brief questionnaires to clients at each therapy session. The first questionnaire, given at the beginning of the session, records the client's sense of ongoing progress. The second questionnaire, given at the conclusion of the session, records the client's sense of the relevance and usefulness of the current session. The questionnaires are scored immediately and the therapist uses the results to alter her interactions with the client. In addition, in between sessions the therapist can reflect on the feedback from the questionnaires, compare the results to baselines from her own practice and the practice of others, and come up with questions and interventions for the next session.

This process not only has the potential to improve therapeutic outcomes, it also functions as a method for determining relative therapeutic weaknesses. Then these weaknesses can be addressed with deliberate practice. A colleague of Miller, Chow (2014), recently completed a dissertation that attempted to define and evaluate the deliberate practice model. As part of the dissertation, he developed the following activities aimed at addressing deliberate practice weaknesses.

The 10 (solitary) activities were the average number of hours per month spent on (a) reading psychotherapy and counselling journals; (b) reading/re-reading about core counselling and therapeutic skills in psychotherapy; (c) reviewing therapy recordings; (d) reviewing difficult/challenging cases; (e) reflecting on past sessions; (f) reflecting on what to do in future sessions; (g) writing down reflections of previous sessions; (h) writing down plans for future sessions; (i) viewing master therapist videos with the aims of developing specific therapist skills; and (j) reading case studies.

The nine (non-solitary) activities were: (a) general clinical supervision as a supervisee *without* review of audio/visual recordings of sessions; (b) clinical supervision as a supervisee *with* review of audio/visual recordings of sessions; (c) clinical supervision as a supervisee reviewing challenging cases or cases with no improvement; (d) live supervision provided during sessions as co-therapist; (e) focused learning in specific models of psychotherapy; (f) reviewing recordings of therapy sessions with peers; (g) attending training workshops for specific models of therapy; (h) case discussions with a clinical supervisor; and (i) discussions of psychotherapy related subjects with peers or mentors. (Miller, Hubble, Chow, & Seidel, 2015, p. 121, items in parentheses added)

How have these ideas fared so far? Miller, writing in his personal blog (2015) summarized the results.

> Nearly three years have passed since I blogged about claims being made about the impact of routine outcome monitoring (ROM) on the quality and outcome of mental health services. While a small number of studies showed promise, other results indicated that therapists did *not* learn from nor become *more* effective over time as a result of being exposed to ongoing feedback. Such findings suggested that the focus on measures and monitoring might be misguided—or at least a "dead end."
>
> Well, the verdict is: feedback is not enough to improve outcomes.

If feedback alone is not sufficient, what does Miller recommend? Later in the same article he argues for the utility of "deep knowledge."

> What's the best way to enhance the effectiveness of therapists? Studies on expertise and expert performance document a single, underlying trait shared by top performers across a variety of endeavors: deep domain-specific knowledge. In short, the best know more, see more and, accordingly, are able to do more.

In the spirit of cultivating "deep knowledge," another colleague of Miller, Tony Rousmaniere, wrote a book, *Deliberate Practice* (2016). Rousmaniere, like Chow, recommends a series of clinical practices to enhance therapeutic abilities. For example, he offers the following example of an effective supervision session.

> At the beginning of one video, Jon (the supervisor) noticed that the client came into the session holding his stomach. I asked the client how he was feeling, and he replied, "Oh, fine, maybe a bit sick, but I'm always like this. Probably something I ate. Let's move on, I'll get over it."
>
> Jon suggested that "the client's nausea might be a sign that he actually started the therapy session beyond his anxiety threshold before he even sat down in the chair. He might be minimizing his anxiety with you due to obedient relational patterns he had learned from his past attachment figures. But let's watch some more tape and see what happens."
>
> As predicted, the client's nausea increased as the session progressed.

"Nausea is a common sign that the client's anxiety has gotten so high that it has passed over the threshold into the parasympathetic nervous system. This can cause a client to deteriorate in therapy. Although the client may try to comply and follow you in session, proceeding while his anxiety is this high only reinforces the client's habit of self-neglect. This is a relationship based on following you rather than attending to himself. The client really wants to make progress but is simply overwhelmed with cortisol [a stress hormone] from his anxiety. What I recommend here is to pause and try to help the client downregulate his anxiety." (Rousmaniere, 2016, Kindle Locations 902–913, items in parentheses added).

It's hard to believe that this sort of excellent supervision has no impact yet, of course, that is what the outcome literature suggests. Rousmaniere attempts to get around this finding by cultivating an attitude of commitment and prioritization; essentially he suggests that therapists do all of the standard improvement practices list by Chow more and harder. In addition, he particularly recommends videotape review and solitary deliberate practice.

Would excellent supervision and extensive daily practice actually enhance therapist competence and redress weaknesses? At the level recommended by Rousmaniere, the likely answer is "yes." Given that psychotherapy operates in constructed reality, doing anything positive with firm intention—investing extensive amounts of time and focus—is likely to result in some sort of improvement/accumulation of charisma.

The insight that psychotherapy occurs in constructed reality has the capacity to enhance Miller's model of deliberate practice. First, while Miller and his colleagues have been explicit and unrelenting in their insistence that techniques have no inherent power, it is not that easy to release those beliefs. For example, examining the Chow list and the Rousmaniere supervision vignette, it appears that the inherent power of techniques peeks through the overt focus on the therapist. They cite practices such as reading journals—which are technique based—and literally reviewing techniques as methods of deliberate practice. Perhaps even more importantly, we should recall that Kahneman argues that System 1 is the "hero" of his book; System 1 believes all reality is fundamental and that clients get better because of techniques. Without a specific appeal to the constructed reality paradigm, therapists will continually fall under the spell of System 1 assumptions. And, as long as that occurs, all the Chow and Rousmaniere recommendations—which are essentially the same recommendations that have been present in the field for the last fifty years—will continue to generate the same results: no meaningful improvements. Truly accepting that psychology has no privileged knowledge—and can never amass privileged knowledge because it operates in constructed reality—is a shocking conclusion. Miller and his colleagues operate at the edge of this conclusion but are hesitant about endorsing it fully.

Second, it is difficult to identify weak points when psychotherapy operates in constructed reality and there is a bias toward a modest, positive improvement regardless of what is done. More specifically, we have competing systems describing the psyche in various conflicting ways and prescribing various incongruent approaches to remediate the problems. Once past the "relationship with a wise and caring therapist," one enters a chaotic and contradictory no-man's land. How can one know one's specific weak points—and apply deliberate practice—when techniques have no validity and when reality changes from client to client, from moment to moment, and from therapist to therapist. In other words, if all techniques are constructed and essentially equivalent, and deliberate practice requires a benchmark of knowledge about "what works," then deliberate practice will have problems with effectiveness in fields where there is a high degree of constructionism.

In an attempt to address this confusion, this book attempts to create a "map" of constructed reality. Without such a map, it is impossible to perform the assessment of strengths and weaknesses needed for deliberate practice. This map of constructed reality essentially rests on dialectic principles. Some of the primary organizing principles in use are: 1) wisdom versus compassion, 2) the Net versus the Abyss, 3) Apollonian change versus Dionysian change, 4) altered states versus ordinary consciousness, 5) authentic ultimate concern versus idolatrous ultimate concern, 6) the chaotic Abyss versus the oracular Abyss, 7) connected versus alienated/alone, 8) technique versus ritual and 9) beginner's mind versus expert mind. Because we are describing constructed reality, there can never be a complete and comprehensive list of all of its qualities. However, there can be a functional description which may have utility. And, recalling the constructionist principle about truth, the question is not "is it true?" rather, it always remains "is it useful?"

Since constructed reality allows so many choices and so many directions, it can be helpful to oversimplify matters in order to facilitate discussion and analysis. Each chapter in the clinical section makes its own contribution to deliberate practice. The chapter on beginner's mind emphasizes discernment between fundamental reality and constructed reality. It is challenging to let go of our default assumptions that we are always operating in fundamental reality; more specifically, achieving the sense that what happens in the room is a ritual, not a technique, is the basis for all progress in the evolutionary model. This central principle runs throughout all the clinical chapters. It is not accident that last clinical chapter on overtly spiritual approaches emphasizes spiritual materialism. As was documented, the perennial philosophy repeatedly returns to a "kill-the-Buddha" perspective as even constructionist seekers continually become entranced with techniques (e.g., meditation).

The vast majority of therapy sessions focus on Apollonian concerns and every therapist is required to check whether she is comfortable being a representative of the culture, urging clients to achieve basic goals, and are at ease with "right" and "wrong." A number of therapists find it difficult to don this "mantle of power" and resist such a role even when the client would benefit from it. A related difficulty arises with the relatively frequent need to help a hyperstabilized client move via organizing family and community resources to "force" the client off of their frozen stance. And some therapists are uncomfortable with the Apollonian insistence that the conscious mind must control feelings and impulses.

While every therapist and every approach uses some form of dissociation, this does not imply that all use dissociation equally effectively. Particularly, the need to restabilize the client into some form of a pathologized label such as "survivor" and "recovering addict" can be challenging. While such labels do serve the interests of some clients, it is important to notice whether the therapist's need for Apollonian stability is trumping the needs of the client.

Most important in terms of the Apollonian approaches, of course, are the Dionysian therapists who undervalue Apollonian foundations. Perhaps due to some fear in their own life, they hesitate to embrace culturally validated achievement and fail to emphasize secular success experiences. It is worth remembering Buber's admonition that one must have firm foundations in culturally sanctioned achievement before launching into the Abyss. And of course the Buddhist saying "Be someone before becoming no one" also comes to mind.

The chapters on Heart and Soul—and the one on dissociation—mark the beginning of Dionysian approaches. Feelings and shadow material always threaten the primacy of the ego and traditional rational thought. Those therapists who are challenged by the numinosity of the unconscious or who are uncomfortable with powerful feelings might feel themselves pulling back when attempting to master these approaches.

And if the early Dionysian chapters are threatening to some therapists, the one on sacred space goes even further in that direction. Now, instead of responding to breakthroughs of the Abyss in the form of feelings and psychopathology, the therapist is enjoined to create and work with experiences which lead to encounters with the Abyss. Being effective at something like hypnosis requires "putting on the Shamanic robe" and assuming a role that intertwines the identity of the therapist with the client's experience of the sacred. The quote from Gilligan about his experience of Erickson "holding him" during his trance experience is representative. A number of therapists might find threatening elements in that story.

The chapter on spiritual approaches details how difficult it can be to move beyond the ongoing war between science and religion. While the path of wisdom—constructionism taken to a logical conclusion—faces little opposition from the science/religion conflict, the perennial philosophy cautions that the ongoing effort to discern between the "real and the unreal" offers deep challenges to most practitioners. And the path of the heart, with its insistence that gifted "connectors" not only say "thou" to the universe but also hear a "thou" in response, runs into its own range of resistance. Finally, avoiding the perils of spiritual materialism is challenging for virtually everyone.

Constructionism is essentially client centered in that every ritual includes an explanation of the problem and a rationale for the healing that must be endorsed by the client. One can go beyond this idea of alignment and suggest that every healing ritual arises out of the client's ultimate concern. This requires an ability to discern the client's "truth"; more importantly, it requires an ability to surrender to the client's ultimate concern. The level of other-centeredness can also be challenging.

In sum, there are a great many ways in which our personal weak points can be discovered and delineated using the principles that define constructed reality. For those who would like further examples, Appendix A, "The Geography of Constructed Reality," attempts to explore this area in more detail.

This book has argued that therapist charisma is directly related to the therapist's alignment with her own ultimate concern. It has also argued that the therapist must stand in her own ultimate concern to discern the client's ultimate concern. At the same time, we know that therapists occasionally have their own "crisis of faith" where they lose touch with why they are doing what they are doing.

In traditional psychology, this is relatively unimportant; when techniques have power, then the inner state of the therapist is relatively unimportant. A crisis of faith—loss of contact with one's ultimate concern—is sometimes ignored and sometimes seen as a sign of burnout or compassion fatigue. In constructionism, however, it is much more serious. Without clear alignment with one's own ultimate concern there is a marked diminishment of charisma and an equivalent loss of ability to intuit the client's ultimate concern. From a deliberate practice point of view, this loss of alignment with the ultimate concern is the most serious weak point and must be addressed directly through approaches such as therapy, retreat, or meaningful change of life choices.

In sum, the geography of constructed reality outlined in this book allows therapists to identify their weak points and remediation strategies in ways that are reminiscent of basketball players and cardiac surgeons. The evolutionary model already established the need to embrace and experience the full range of therapies instead of specializing in only one. Deliberate practice complements the evolutionary model by requiring therapists to identify their unique weakness and how the weaknesses might play out when operating in constructed reality.

Deliberate practice is hard work. It intentionally urges us to practice in the area of our weaknesses—a practice that by its nature often feels foreign and uncomfortable. While this is certainly true, even a deliberate practice program can be approached with a sense of ease.

Protestant Christianity offers a particular angle on this dilemma when it argues that salvation is achieved through grace and not through good works and personal effort. Constructionism believes that many, if not all, of our personal obstacles are constructed—in essence made-up factors that have no intrinsic power unless we imbue the obstacles with power. When embarking on a path of self-improvement or enhancement of charisma it is vital to bring along a sense of humor, a basic lightness, and a fundamental humbleness. Martin Buber (2006) attempts to characterize this attitude in the following quote:

> You can rake the muck this way, rake the muck that way—it will always be muck. Have I sinned or have I not sinned? In the time I am brooding over it, I could be stringing pearls for the delight of Heaven. (p. 30)

## PERSONAL DEVELOPMENT: ENHANCING CHARISMA OUTSIDE THE ROOM

> I change too quickly: my today refutes my yesterday. When I ascend I often jump over steps, and no step forgives me that.
>
> —Friedrich Nietzsche, *Thus Spake Zarathustra* (1896)

This book focuses primarily on what can be done inside the room to enhance charisma. It is clear, however, that there are a great many things that can be done outside the room that can also enhance charisma. Exploring those possibilities in detail would require a book in its own right. In place of that, this section explores a few basic ideas that point toward out-of-the-room opportunities.

In some ways, discussing what can be done outside the room is rather an imposition on personal freedom. As has been discussed in some detail above, the standard psychological perspective is that "who I am" is my business; I should be able to be effective as a therapist regardless of my personal life choices. And, indeed, that is the assumption when one joins a profession with access to privileged information. Regardless of how appealing this argument might be, however, psychology is not a profession where "who am I" is unrelated to outcome.

In this sense, psychology is as much a vocation as a profession. The dynamic tension between vocation and profession is explored in the following quote from the perspective of philosophy, a related discipline.

There is another layer to this story. The act of purification accompanying the creation of the modern research university was not just about differentiating realms of knowledge. It was also about divorcing knowledge from virtue. Though it seems foreign to us now, before purification the philosopher (and natural philosopher) was assumed to be morally superior to other sorts of people. The 18th-century thinker Joseph Priestley wrote "a Philosopher ought to be something greater and better than another man." Philosophy, understood as the love of wisdom, was seen as a vocation, like the priesthood. It required significant moral virtues (foremost among these were integrity and selflessness), and the pursuit of wisdom in turn further inculcated those virtues. The study of philosophy elevated those who pursued it. Knowing and being good were intimately linked. It was widely understood that the point of philosophy was to become good rather than simply to collect or produce knowledge. (Briggle & Frodeman, 2016)

Briggle and Frodeman are pointing out that the impact of modernism resulted in divorcing the study of philosophy both from its influence on character and from the requirement that personal virtue is necessary in order to master the field. Applied to psychology, Briggle and Frodeman might argue that enhancing therapist outcomes requires putting cultivation of virtue at the center of the process. It follows, therefore, that those who resist seeing psychology as a vocation will be inhibited in terms of their ability to garner charisma. Conversely, equating experience in the room with an immersion in "sacred space" opens the door for an enhancement of both virtue and charisma.

Preparing for a vocation is different than preparing for a profession. Imagine that you are training yourself for an important position, perhaps something like being a military leader, or the CEO of Google, or the president. You would intentionally seek out experiences that you believe develop your character—experiences that will generate respect from the individuals you hope to lead. The therapist who wishes to achieve above-average results needs to develop charisma that is roughly equivalent to the charisma required for these sorts of positions. While those jobs may have higher status than psychotherapy, the need to be respected by those you wish to influence is highly similar.

In addition to formal education, what kinds of experiences might you find valuable in preparation for your new position? Most likely you would respond that you would seek experiences that would open your heart, bestow wisdom, or develop your character. In addition, you would hope that these experiences would leave a positive mark on you—that you would be perceived as powerful and charismatic. The list of such experiences is readily available; essentially they are the kinds of experiences that result in the respect of other cultural members. Anything that might get one invited to address the local Rotary club is such an experience. Adventurous activities like climbing mountains and skiing to the North Pole qualify, as do extended service experiences like saving gorillas or reducing famine in Africa. Certain experiences of enduring suffering qualify such as surviving many days on a life raft at sea or enduring an unusual illness. Eliade would call these experiences pilgrimages to sacred space.

It is worth recalling Mallory's famous reason for climbing Everest: "because it is there." To many people, risking one's life and enduring weeks of suffering simply to stand at the highest spot on earth makes little sense and Mallory's "reason" for climbing fails to satisfy their curiosity. But Mallory, and other adventurers who risk life and limb on overtly purposeless adventures, are shy when it comes to articulating their actual reasons. It sounds crazy to say, "I'm climbing Mt. Everest because I will ascend to 'heaven', be rewarded with divine knowledge and be transformed by the experience." While this is rarely expressed so directly, our interest in listening to lectures and reading books about the experience shows that a large percentage of cultural members implicitly feel the "truth" of such statements. We believe that certain experiences have the capacity to transform individuals profoundly and we are fascinated by their "heroic" stories.

Pilgrimages to sacred space are one of the key opportunities to enhance charisma. Clearly, such experiences are rituals—power experiences endorsed both by other members of the culture and the individual who chooses them. It would be rare for a president or a pope or a military leader to ascend to their high status position without at least some of these experiences. The therapist who aspires to superior outcomes has a similar need for this kind of transformation.

The most obvious approach to out-of-the-room enhancement is personal growth experiences such as therapy, retreats, mentoring, and spiritual practices. Similar to pilgrimages, high charisma individuals often have stories documenting the positive effects of teachers and periods of intentional reflection and transformation. The previous chapter described the benefits of such approaches but also noted the limitations; the section on spiritual materialism essentially focused on the fact that many experiences lead to improved satisfaction and esteem without leading to enhanced charisma. The secret, apparently, is to practice with a "kill-the-Buddha" attitude. To offer another angle on that conclusion, examine the following Sufi story:

*A scholar asked the great sage Afzal of Iskandariya:* "What can you tell me of Alim Azimi, your teacher, to whom you attribute qualities which have fashioned you?"
*Afzal answered:* "His poetry intoxicated me, and his love of mankind suffused me, and his self-sacrificing services elated me."
*The scholar said:* "Such a man would indeed be able to fashion angels!"

*Afzal continued:* "Those are the qualities which would have recommended Alim to *you*. Now for the qualities which enabled him to help men transcend the ordinary:

Hazrat Alim Azimi made me irritated, which caused me to examine my irritation, to trace its source. Alim Azimi made me angry, so that I could feel and transform my anger. Alim Azimi allowed himself to be attacked, so that people could see the bestiality of his attackers and not join with them. He showed us the strange, so that the strange become common-place and we could realize what it really is." (Shah, 2016, p. 21)

As in the other spiritual materialism stories, the seeker is constantly reminded not to see spiritual growth as a concrete process of techniques that inevitably lead to the achievement of the spiritual goal. Recall that personal therapy does not result in enhanced outcomes. The goal is to be different, not better.

Finally, reflect on the concept that while this kind of personal growth requires an openness to the guidance of others, it also requires holding on to one's personal sense of self. Swami Vivekananda comments:

Be strong! . . . You talk of ghosts and devils. We are the living devils. The sign of life is strength and growth. The sign of death is weakness. Whatever is weak, avoid! It is death. If it is strength, go down into hell and get hold of it! There is salvation only for the brave. None but the brave deserves the fair. None but the bravest deserves salvation. (Vivekananda, 1964, The Gita III)

With this quote Vivekananda succeeds in embodying the fierceness of spirit which is helpful when seeking charisma. Charisma is not for the faint of heart. Fear is an expected companion on the journey; in fact, the presence of some sort of fear marks a transformational opportunity. But surrendering to fear destroys the possibility of charisma enhancement.

A third approach is less traditional and predictable than the first two. Examine the following "parable" that novelist, Tom Robbins, uses to conclude one of his stories.

In a place out of doors, near forests and meadows, stands a jar of vinegar—the emblem of life.

Confucius approaches the jar, dips his finger in and tastes the brew. "Sour," he says. "Nonetheless, I can see where it could be very useful in preparing certain foods."

Buddha come to the vinegar jar, dips in a finger and has a taste. "Bitter," is his comment. "It can cause suffering to the palate, and since suffering is to be avoided, the stuff should be disposed of at once."

The next to stick a finger in the vinegar is Jesus Christ. "Yuk," says Jesus. "It's both bitter and sour. It's not fit to drink. In order that no one else will have to drink it, I will drink it all myself."

But now two people approach the jar, together, naked, hand in hand. The man has a beard and woolly legs like a goat. His long tongue is slightly swollen from some poetry he's been reciting. The woman wears a cowgirl hat, a necklace of feathers, a rosy complexion. Her tummy and tits bear the stretch marks of motherhood; she carries a basket of mushroom and herbs. First the man and then the woman sticks a thumb into the vinegar. She licks his thumb and he hers. Initially they make a face, but almost immediately they break into wide grins. "It's sweet," they chime.

"Swee-eet!" (Robbins, 1990, p. 380)

In this quote Robbins is contrasting traditional recommendations about life philosophy with his Western, counter-culture version. Essentially he is proposing that living life fully and deeply—diving into loving, feeling, expressing—is a path equivalent to older spiritual paths. His words participate in Whitman/Emerson/Thoreau transcendentalist tradition. They line up with the Campbell reference cited earlier that the greatest contribution of Western culture was the development of the concept of romantic love. Finally, Robbins' ideas are endorsed by one of the primary images of Western religion: the creation of New Jerusalem on earth. The East defines earthly existence as Maya and Samsara which must be resolved through liberation and Samadhi. Conversely, the West believes that the world can be redeemed; the image of the Holy City implies that we can recreate the "garden of Eden" on earth itself. In this sense, alignment with the elements of this redemption is, in itself, a personal spiritual path and a potential ultimate concern.

More specifically, this suggests that conscious marriage, child rearing, creativity, and authenticity can be equivalent to meditation and selfless service. The secret, of course, is not simply performing such activities but investing them with significance. In constructed reality, everything can serve as a ritual of transformation as long as it is invested with meaning by the therapist and the client. In this sense, Robbins is arguing that the connected and passionate life is as valid a path as the path of an ascetic monastic.

Robbins' parables suggest that acquisition of charisma is not limited to pilgrimages to sacred space and conscious personal development, it can also occur through living deeply and passionately. Put another way, he is recommending a different attitude toward the sacrality of the world. Living life whole heartedly—cultivating healthy desire—and connecting to the natural world deeply is as valid a path as selflessness, renunciation, and asceticism.

A final example of personal development is closely related to the concept of dancing with the Abyss. Examine the following quote from Francis Harold Cook:

Activities such as chanting, bowing, and sitting in zazen are not at all wasted, even when done merely formally, for even this superficial encounter with the

Dharma will have some wholesome outcome at a later time. However, it must be said in the most unambiguous terms that this is not real Zen. To follow the Dharma involves a complete reorientation of one's life in such a way that one's activities are manifestations of, and are filled with, a deeper meaning. If it were not otherwise, and merely sitting in zazen were enough, every frog in the pond would be enlightened, as one Zen master said. Dōgen Zenji himself said that one must practice Zen with the attitude of a person trying to extinguish a fire in his hair. That is, Zen must be practiced with an attitude of single-minded urgency. (Cook, 1999, p. 33)

At first glance, this is another "kill-the Buddha"-type quote and, indeed, that element is highlighted. But the quote also emphasizes the "reorientation of one's life" toward deeper meaning and having a feeling of "single-minded urgency." This sense that every moment offers an opportunity for consciousness, and mindfulness is one of the essential principles of the perennial philosophy.

More specifically, constructionism—fully embraced—opens the door to a level of lightness and freedom, particularly in terms of handling the distressing aspects of daily life. Put another way, the one who is free from the illusions and delusions of the Net can achieve a profound sense of freedom. Barbara Held, in a book focusing on constructionism, psychotherapy, and identity, compiled several quotes illustrating the correlations between constructionism, detachment, and freedom.

Consider these few exemplary quotations, in which liberation often takes the form of reinventing one's (ever malleable) "self" or "identity."

The doors of therapeutic perception and possibility have been opened wide by the recognition that we are actively constructing our mental realities rather than simply uncovering or coping with an objective "truth." (Hoyt, 1996, p. 1)

. . . People can (in therapy) be enabled to construct things from different viewpoints, thus liberating them from the oppression of limiting narrative beliefs and relieving the resulting pain. . . . (They) may come to transcend the restraints imposed by their erstwhile reliance on a determinate set of meanings. . . . For still others a stance toward meaning itself will evolve; one which betokens that tolerance of uncertainty, that freeing of experience which comes from acceptance of unbounded relativity of meaning." (Gergen & Kaye, 1992, p. 183)

. . . In addition to the rejection of totalizing explanations . . . postmodern thought also rejects strongly deterministic and reductionistic theories. . . . Individuals are free to choose, adopt and change self-images according to shifting life circumstances and needs. A multiplicity of images is increasingly available to everyone. They are democratic in the sense that individual life circumstances (e.g., race, class, age, etc.) provide less constraint on their adoption than in the past. (Boumgardner & Rappoport, 1996, pp. 126, 128; Held, 2007, pp. 33–34)

These quotations from Held embody the qualities of lightness, detachment, and freedom implicit in fully understanding and accepting constructionism. Since most, if not all, of the factors that define us are constructed and not part of fundamental reality, each individual is free to reframe their dilemmas, challenges, and even their basic identity in any direction they choose. All the limitations can be experienced as ephemeral and fragile, with the least touch of consciousness, they disappear. Paul Watzlawick, who was both a constructionist and a systemic thinker, wrote a book with the title *The Situation is Hopeless but not Serious*. Watzlawick reports that his title is derived from an old, central European saying and suggests that it embodies the kind of freedom that is available to anyone who is awake and aware.

Returning to the Dalai Lama's typology of wisdom and compassion, there is a quote from the New Testament that parallels the freedom of constructionism from a heart-centered perspective. "For my yoke is easy and my burden is light" (Matthew 11:30). Just as the primary choice in wisdom is real versus constructed, the analogous choice in compassion is alone versus connected. Choosing to see connections versus alienation is the "light and easy" choice. We all fear that we are alone; we relax and release into the concept we are connected.

Each moment of life allows a practice and a choice. Every breath includes an implicit discernment involving identity, meaning, and presence. In this sense, cultivating charisma is a daily practice with each life experience offering an opportunity for enhancement or constriction.

## DANCING WITH THE ABYSS

The whole life is a succession of dreams. My ambition is to be a conscious dreamer that is all.

—Swami Vivekananda, *The Complete Works
of Swami Vivekananda* (1907)

It should be clear that most therapeutic wizards and most superior therapists attained their high level of functioning without ever thinking about the Net, the Abyss, or social constructionism. They did not take part in the evolutionary model and, while they may have brought serious thought to addressing their own strengths and weaknesses, it is also unlikely they ever formally participated in deliberate practice. Some of them may have embarked on their own personal pilgrimages and others almost certainly benefited from the guidance of a mentor or a therapist but most of them developed their charisma via an intense personal relationship with their own ultimate concern. As an example, examine the following autobiographical segment from Stephen

Madigan about his early exposure to narrative therapy. It seems that Madigan had been invited to participate in an apprenticeship experience with his mentors, Michael and Cheryl White.

> To say that I took this narrative therapy apprenticeship seriously would be an understatement. For example, when observing therapy sessions with Michael White and David Epston (I would participate in anywhere from six to seven therapy sessions every day), I wrote down each and every therapeutic question in a notebook. In the evenings, I would ask Michael and David (and others) questions about all the narrative questions that they had asked that day—to get what I suppose could be called a genealogy of each question. I would ask where certain questions came from, the intent behind their use of a collapsed and mashed up temporality (past, present, future), why a certain grammar of expression was used, what theory and author a particular question belonged to, what other questions could have been asked but were not asked, and so on.
>
> Every night of my narrative therapy apprenticeship in Australia and New Zealand, and after everyone retired for the evening, I would categorize each narrative therapy question we discussed into a specific grouping. I would classify questions into relative influence questions, future possibility questions, experience of experience questions, and so on. I was fascinated with narrative therapy's unique grammar; the decentered positioning of the therapist; narrative therapy's commitment to social justice; and how narrative therapy organized around appreciation, respect, and wonder. I would then speak each question into a tape recorder and include an annotated bibliography for each one (nerd-like, indeed). (Madigan, 2012, Kindle Locations 179–292)

Reading this selection exposes us to Madigan's sense of the power and potentiality of narrative therapy. The apprenticeship embodied a quality of passion and presence that suggests that his studies had become a link to his ultimate concern. When a system of psychology becomes a symbolic stand-in for one's ultimate concern, then an ultimate commitment to that system can create an exceptional therapist. The ultimate concern has a special relationship to the Abyss and the Source. When it breaks into the Net, it is experienced as sacred and numinous. Hence, any practitioner who has truly made her system into an ultimate concern lives in sacred space, is a denizen of sacred space, and opens herself to channel something greater than her. For therapists who feel that their system embodies ultimacy, each session is a numinous experience—each connection with a client is a mythic event. Ram Dass says: "Treat everyone you meet like God in drag" (Dass, 2007, p. 13). Therapists who experience their work and their system as ultimate are having some kind of interaction with their higher power in every session.

David Brooks, the *New York Times* columnist, describes this same kind of practice from a different angle.

I suppose that people who live with passion start out with an especially intense desire to complete themselves. We are the only animals who are naturally unfinished. We have to bring ourselves to fulfillment, to integration and to coherence.

Some people are seized by this task with a fierce longing. Maybe they are propelled by wounds that need urgent healing or by a fear of loneliness or fragmentation. Maybe they are driven by some glorious fantasy to make a mark on the world. But they often have a fervent curiosity about their inner natures and an unquenchable thirst to find some activity that they can pursue wholeheartedly, without reservation.

They construct themselves inwardly by expressing themselves outwardly. Members of the clergy sometimes say they convert themselves from the pulpit. By speaking out their faith, they make themselves faithful. People who live with passion do that. By teaching or singing or writing or nursing or parenting they bring coherence to the scattered impulses we are all born with inside. By doing some outward activity they understand and define themselves. A life of passion happens when an emotional nature meets a consuming vocation. (Brooks, 2015)

In this brief quote, Brooks is offering a summary of many of the themes central to dancing with the Abyss. Charisma is only enhanced when one has an "intense desire" and a "fierce longing" that requires a "wholehearted" dedication. Their inner transformation rests on the ability to express themselves outwardly. It is a vocation, not a profession.

There are so many ways to enhance charisma. Seeing our work as a channel and an embodiment of the ultimate concern is certainly one. The evolutionary path and deliberate practice are two others. The section on personal development only briefly discussed some of the ways to gather charisma outside the room: pilgrimages to sacred space, psychological and spiritual practices, and becoming an embodiment of the Western concepts of progress, romantic love, and being present in the redeemable world.

Dancing with the Abyss is another term for meditation in action. When one is learning to meditate, formal sitting meditation is considered the best practice. The eventual goal, however, is to have the same consciousness that is embodied in sitting meditation run throughout one's life. As an intermediate step, students are taught walking mediation where they continue their meditation practice while moving. This is followed by simple tasks, such as food preparation, again with the enjoinder to continue to meditate while acting in the world. The most advanced practice is to have the same consciousness as sitting meditation when one engages in conflict situations or intimate relationships.

Dancing with the Abyss is the fourth approach to cultivate charisma. As we have shown, it rests on the ability to work consciously and gracefully with the ultimate concern. In addition it requires the ability to show up in all aspects of life—in the room with clients and in the regular world—with an implicit awareness of the nature of constructed reality and the dance between the Net and the Abyss. It means experiencing the terror and meaninglessness of the Abyss intertwined with its oracular and numinous nature. It means staying fluid and centered even as our System 1 mind urges us to become rigid and to dash for safety. Essentially it requires the therapist to transfer the meditative presence cultivated in the room into every aspect of life.

This, of course, is a goal shared by many spiritual paths. This sharing is hardly surprising given that psychotherapy in constructed reality is simply another path in universe of paths that form the perennial philosophy. And the shared characteristic of all those paths is that they conclude with the recommendation that the practitioner cultivate an inner consciousness that recognizes what is constructed and what is real and the truth about separateness versus connection. Thomas Merton tells us:

> Life is this simple: we are living in a world that is absolutely transparent and the divine is shining through it all the time. This is not just a nice story or a fable, it is true. (Thomas Merton, as cited in Brach, 2004, p. 72)

Finally we return to the place where therapists are the most privileged: the opportunity to be a witness and a participant in others' lives, dilemmas, and possibilities. Certainly, even though the research fails to support it, there must be another "royal road"—a road especially open to those of us allowed to be part of our clients' story. The primary theme of this clinical section is the paradoxical concept that therapy is performed to enhance the charisma of the therapist—to contribute to her personal transformation. Whether one concentrates on donning the robes of Apollonian power, or sensing the message and guidance from pathologizing, shadow work, and numinous dreams, or listening to that "still, small voice" that characterizes spiritual work, every encounter in the room opens the door for therapist growth. Our opportunity to serve others is the key opportunity for our own evolution.

## ONLY A BREATH AWAY

> Afoot and light-hearted I take to the open road, Healthy, free, the world before me, The long brown path before me leading wherever I choose. Henceforth I ask not good-fortune, I myself am good-fortune.
>
> —Walt Whitman, "Song of the Open Road" (1856)

This book began with the outcome research and its insistence that therapists do not benefit from training and fail to improve over time. Most importantly, the research demonstrates that clients do not change due to the inherent power of psychological techniques. Regardless of how convincing the research results might be, it is very difficult to accept the full implications of the findings. Those who can integrate this information have a significant edge on those who continue in denial.

We have discussed this material from so many angles: beginner's mind, placebo, identity, dissociation, sacred space, constructionism, and breakthroughs of the Abyss. For now, however, simply return to the simple and stark research results. Return to the argument that psychology, along with related fields like leadership and education, is not a science. Science functions in fundamental reality. Human satisfaction, happiness, disappointment, and depression—these all function in constructed reality. Healers will always heal in constructed reality. They will always use rituals and ritualistic change will always have a magical, unpredictable, and indefinable quality.

Clinical practice seems predictable because everything works. But when everything works, we really know nothing about the subject area. In fundamental reality something always works better and other things work worse. Constructed reality is not like that.

We have experts—superior therapists who generate superior results. Our attempts to distill their patterns come to naught. These studies are fruitless because even the gifted healers fail to discern the patterns in their own work; many of them lack conscious awareness of how they achieve their exceptional outcomes. They also find that everything that they do with clients works. It's just that when they do it, it works better. And in shifting our attention from looking for their "patterns" to looking at them and their charisma, new pathways open.

Is this a dismal situation? Yes, when one is committed to imposing fundamental reality tools on constructed reality. But, in truth, it is the opposite of a dismal situation. Knowing that the vast majority of suffering is in constructed reality—and that reality only seems solid when it is actually fragile and brittle—is the farthest thing from a dismal situation. There is always a sense that Becker is right and death and chaos are always only a breath or a thought away, but simultaneously the oracular Abyss and the sense of connection and meaning are also only a breath away.

Healers will always study healing. We are all rightfully concerned—perhaps even obsessed—with being better at what we do. The secret to becoming better is to become different. All the "kill-the-Buddha" stories show the way. Jiddu Krisnamurti comments:

> I maintain that Truth is a pathless land, and you cannot approach it by any path whatsoever, by any religion, by any sect. . . . The moment you follow someone you cease to follow Truth. (as cited in Weeraperuma, 1996, p. 3)

Throwing oneself into the Abyss—killing psychological science—seems like an invitation to chaos. Yet the perennial philosophy assures us that such an action is paradoxically the way forward. This requires a level of boldness. Rumi comments:

> Run from what's comfortable. Forget safety. Live where you fear to live. Destroy your reputation. Be notorious. I have tried prudent planning long enough. From now on I'll be mad.

For all the calls to be courageous and bold, the teachers are also ready to be reassuring. Joseph Campbell recommends that the seeker should "Follow your bliss and the universe will open doors where there were only walls" (as cited in Espiritu, 2016, Hero's Journey). This is essentially identical to Rumi's counsel to "Respond to every call that excites your spirit." And Krishnamurti—who so often is dour and full of warnings about the wrong direction—says: "It is only when the mind is free from the old that it meets everything anew, and in that there is joy" (as cited in Lutyens, 2005, p. 374).

Rumi reminds us of the centrality of the "different not better" maxim. Normal rules no longer apply. Mostly, though, he reassures us at last that in the "senselessness" there is also joy and hidden order.

> Beyond our ideas of right-doing and wrong-doing,
> there is a field. I'll meet you there.
> When the soul lies down in that grass,
> the world is too full to talk about.
> Ideas, language, even the phrase "each other"
> doesn't make sense any more.

And his final advice is to move forward, even if there are no clear markers to show the path.

> Keep walking, though there's no place to get to.
> Don't try to see through the distances.
> That's not for human beings. Move within,
> But don't move the way fear makes you move.

## NOTE

1. This may be logical but it runs into the research finding that all schools of therapy achieve equal results. More specifically, the evolutionary model is implicitly hierarchical; it argues that the schools of psychology that are more Dionysian and closer to the Abyss are more "evolved" than the more Apollonian schools. Dionysian

practitioners should best Apollonian practitioners. But the equality of results requires us to immediately dismiss simple ideas of better and worse. In this sense, the research results appear to contradict the implicit assumptions of the evolutionary model.

Before accepting this simple conclusion, one must examine a number of confounding variables. First, there is a hidden assumption that those who practice from a more Dionysian perspective have already mastered the Apollonian approaches that exist further down the hierarchy. Brief reflection, however, suggests that this assumption is often untrue. For example, how often does one hear critiques such as "Jungian therapists are wonderful to talk to but they just aren't that grounded with their clients." This quote suggests that some Jungians may have skipped the therapeutic basics perhaps because they are personally uncomfortable with an Apollonian focus. More specifically, it is easy to imagine a therapist who is gifted with hypnosis and yet uneasy about telling an underemployed father that he will never be happy unless he gets a better job.

Similarly, it is equally unfair to assume that overt Apollonians fail to include a range of Dionysian responses in their work. For example, many CBT practitioners are as comfortable with emotions as the Borofskys and as ready to discuss the meaning of life as a devotee of Logotherapy and Victor Frankl. In fact, the process literature repeatedly notes that many therapists who are allegedly from differing schools behave in a similar manner in actual clinical practice.

Imagine trying to design a research study that could measure whether the evolutionary model results in an enhancement of charisma. First one would need to find Apollonian therapists who essentially rejected Dionysian approaches, not simply in theory but in practice as well. Next one would need to locate Dionysian therapists who have access to a full range of Apollonian skills as well as a deep connection to their Dionysian perspective. No studies such as this have ever been conducted and, due to the difficulty of operationalizing the factors discussed, it is unlikely that such studies will ever be conducted.

My personal experience is that when I master a new way of encountering reality, I am a bigger person and, by implication, my charisma is enhanced. We are all aware that this intuition in itself fails to prove anything, especially when I feel enhanced by lots of other factors in my therapeutic world—for example, my experience and training—and they fail to improve my outcomes.

Even with this justified caveat, it remains appropriate to argue for the efficacy of the evolutionary model. When we reflect on our own mentors and teachers—people we invest with charisma and see as key individuals—they seem to emanate the qualities associated with the evolutionary model. They have lived more deeply, felt more profoundly, have the ability to see from more perspectives, and embody the compassion and acceptance that lets us know they have owned their own shadow material. Anything that helps me feel like one of my own teachers is likely to be a valid source of charisma enhancement. The secret, of course, is to ensure that my mastery of the next model truly gives me the experiences I attribute to my mentors. And, if my exposure to the unconscious, or my work with altered states, or anything else new to me feels as if it has been a journey into sacred space, then I suspect it really has been.

*Chapter 16*

# The Way Forward

Now and then we had a hope that if we lived and were good, God would permit us to be pirates.

—Mark Twain, *Old Times on the Mississippi* (1875)

In 1965, when I was on summer vacation with my family, I ran out of books to read. I was so desperate that I decided to read a new book that my step-mother had brought on the trip entitled *Games People Play*. This book pretty much blew away my thirteen-year-old mind. For those readers unfamiliar with this venerable work, *Games People Play* was a pop psychology book by Eric Berne (1996) where he introduced the ideas of the ego, superego, and id and then talked about stereotypic interactions—"games"—that could occur when individuals neglected to operate from their "adult" ego state.

I believed that the book was written by an incredibly wise man who had given me the ultimate map describing how human interactions really work. I felt liberated and empowered, confident that with this new information I could not only refrain from making interactional mistakes on my own part, but would also be competent to understand the mistakes made by others. It seemed to me as if I had been transported to a higher plane of knowledge that would transform my life completely and permanently.

Of course, many years have passed since that first psychological book, and I suspect that I have failed to sustain my identity as a neo Freudian, but I still relish the memory of the freedom and empowerment implicit in Berne's "map." Obviously, I've been equally excited by many subsequent maps since then—a number of which I've incorporated into this book—but I guess that none of these subsequent models can ever quite equal the excitement that arose from my "first." All joking aside, however, the sense of power and freedom implicit in an existential map is one of the great gifts available to seekers with intellectual curiosity and the passion which can accompany that sort of curiosity.

That said, maps run into an immediate problem. As mentioned earlier, Alfred Korzybski coined the famous phrase: "The map is not the territory." He was a constructionist in that he argued that humans do not directly encounter reality; rather, they make a representation or "map" of it within the psyche. This map is constructed both culturally and individually and hence, varies from person to person. In this sense, each person lives within their own constructed reality and these "multiple universes" form limitations to communication and agreement.

Constructionists laugh at maps while simultaneously respecting their usefulness. Maps bring to mind a relevant Nasrudin parable.

> Nasrudin walked into a teahouse and announced, "The moon is more useful than the sun."
> "Why?" he was asked.
> "Because at night we need the light more."
> (as cited in Blenkiron, 2011, p. 43)

Korzybski essentially argues that since we cannot experience the "sun" directly, the "moon" or map becomes more important. Since we cannot live in the midst of the Abyss—except briefly in altered states—the Net is more important than the absolute reality against which it is projected. Kahneman tells us that System 1 is the "star" of his book and the Net and constructed reality is the star of this one. As Nasrudin points out, we are night denizens and therefore dependent on what we can grasp of the world by the limited light we can get from a moon. We should, therefore, honor the moon while never forgetting it is not the sun. Funny, paradoxical, sad, and true all in one small story.

Constructionists remind us that maps are not judged as true or untrue but rather as useful or useless. In addition, they caution us to always be aware of their essential insubstantiality. Similarly, the material in this book needs to be taken lightly—seen as one attempt to create a useful map of what therapy, and enhanced therapist effectiveness, might look like from a constructionist point of view.

In order to make this concept of mapping more concrete, let us compare the Reality B model with some of the other major models reviewed in this book. The Introduction stated that the purpose of this book was to recognize that psychotherapy operates in constructed reality instead of fundamental reality and to examine the implications of that shift for improving outcomes. The first implication is that a helping profession must have a "place to stand" if it is going to operate in constructed reality. Tillich's concept of the ultimate concern provides that foundation and simultaneously addresses issues such as the source of charisma and equalizing hierarchy between clients and therapists. A geography of constructed reality was proposed allowing for the development of the evolutionary model and deliberate practice.

Now compare this Reality B model to existing models. Almost all extant psychological models ignore the research implications about training, experience, and techniques; in addition, they fail to address whether psychotherapy operates in constructed or fundamental reality. This twin level of ignorance is primarily responsible for the failure of psychology to achieve significant progress over the past century. More sophisticated psychological models, such as Miller's deliberate practice, embrace the research findings and have a focus on enhancing the therapist; unfortunately their inability to address constructed versus fundamental reality leaves the long-term results of their work in doubt. Conversely, narrative therapy is profoundly aligned with constructionism but it fails to integrate the implications of the research. As a result, it still develops and teaches techniques as if they are powerful and effective thereby failing to fully develop the full implications of constructionism.

Buddhist psychology seems to be the most promising in theory. It is profoundly aligned with constructionism and there are many references, such as the quote from the last chapter about "killing Buddha," that explicitly warn practitioners about the fallibility of techniques. It has an evolutionary range from the Apollonian foundations of the eightfold path through the most Abyss-oriented sense of non self.

Unfortunately, when these ideas are translated into practice, most Buddhist psychologists seem to be unaware of the limitations of techniques. For example, at present perhaps the most comprehensive gathering of Buddhist therapeutic thought is represented by the book *Wisdom and Compassion in Psychotherapy* (2012). This book has over twenty chapters, each written by experts in Buddhist psychology. None of the chapters mentions the research results and, while there are a number of references to non self and ideas like killing the Buddha, there are many, many more recommendations about Buddhist techniques; moreover, there are repeated and clear implications that learning and practicing these techniques will improve the therapist and are responsible for client change. In sum, Buddhist psychology is there in theory but in practice, it appears to suffer from the same shortcomings as narrative therapy.

Clearly, what we now require are more models that integrate the full implications of both the research results and constructionism.

To all those readers who, like me, have read hundreds and hundreds of psychological articles and books, what comes next might create a smile. Virtually all of those articles end with the recommendation for additional research. Given that this book has portrayed the science of clinical psychology as "barking up the wrong tree" with its assertion that more research will eventually succeed in defining the nature of constructed reality, it is ironic to recommend more of it. To be a bit more precise, what I am actually recommending is not more research—although eventually that can be helpful in certain ways—but more thought and more dialog.

It should be clear that we have barely begun to consider the implications of the research and the interactions between psychology and constructionism. What we need now are more thinkers who are interested in answering basic questions such as the ones below.

1. What makes clinical psychology different from other professions where experience, training, techniques, and systems enhance outcomes?
2. Why are reversals and losses so much more powerful than successes and what does that mean for how people change?
3. How much of psychology is fundamental reality and how much is constructed reality and what are the implications for change and for enhancing therapeutic outcome?
4. Why do even beginners regularly achieve the modest, positive effect with clients?
5. In a constructed reality, without the ability to take refuge in reliable techniques and systems, what is the source of healing and change?
6. What do therapy techniques look like when viewed from the perspective of constructed reality?

This list of questions can be expanded and refined. What is important is that the research results and the constructionist analysis of clinical psychology have opened Pandora's box for psychology. The names of the released daemons are "meaninglessness," "disrespect from other professions," "inability to justify our practices," "need to completely revamp how we conceptualize change," and so on.

The daemon of Hope lies in understanding that psychology is not alone. Virtually all other professions that concentrate on constructed reality are in the exact same boat—law, political science, and organizational development are good examples. Many professions—such as medicine, architecture, and economics—have substantial aspects that are constructed and would benefit from the same analyses as psychology. The implication is that if psychology can work consciously with constructionism we can provide real leadership for these other fields. Psychology has at least begun to integrate constructionism. Moreover our research base allows us to reject the power of the technique much more thoughtfully than anything, for example, in education or organizational development.

Accepting that human culture and some of the most essential aspects of human experience are constructed is a major blow to the empiricists and scientific fundamentalists. The universe gets much more difficult to dissect, predict, and control. At the same time, accepting the constructed nature of culture and identity is the first step to becoming more helpful and effective. Certainly we will never get anywhere if we keep insisting that all human psychology—and related fields and professions—can be framed as fundamental reality. Rumi reminds us how challenging it can be to maintain this consciousness.

> The breezes at dawn have secrets to tell you
> Don't go back to sleep!
> You must ask for what you really want.
> Don't go back to sleep!
> People are going back and forth
> across the doorsill where the two worlds touch,
> The door is round and open
> Don't go back to sleep! (Barks, 1995, p. 37)

Let's allow Nasrudin to have the final word.

> Nasrudin was walking past a well, when he had the impulse to look into it. It was night, and as he peered into the deep water, he saw the Moon's reflection there.
>
> "I must save the Moon!" the Mulla thought. "Otherwise she will never wane, and the fasting month of Ramadan will never come to an end,"
>
> He found a rope, threw it in, and called down: "Hold tight; keep bright; succor is at hand!"
>
> The rope caught in a rock inside the well, and Nasrudin heaved as hard as he could. Straining back, he suddenly felt the rope give as it came loose, and he was thrown on his back. As he lay there, panting, he saw the moon riding in the sky above.
>
> "Glad to be of service," said Nasrudin. "Just as well I came along, wasn't it?" (Shah, 1971, p. 42)

# Appendix

## *The Geography of Constructed Reality*

The attempt to represent the geography of constructed reality through a series of figures is incongruous at best and absurd at worst. Since it is constructed, by definition what lies below is only the imaginations of one particular person in the context of one particular culture. It is not intended to be true; instead there is some hope that it might be useful.

We are all denizens of the Net. As Net dwellers, we benefit from concrete structures even as we understand their limitations. It is better to think of the figures below as a kind of poem—a poem that takes the unusual form of a set of figures. Poems are intended to be evocative, as are these figures. Taking things too literally will inhibit their usefulness.

The figures are necessarily incomplete and inaccurate. Each theme is a universe in its own right and resents being constrained by a particular box or category. Is it true that CBT or Psychodynamic systems only operate in the Apollonian confines of the Net? Of course not; even the most facile analysis reveals they operate in other areas as well. But for the purpose of facilitating a holistic understanding of the geography of constructed reality, certain liberties have been taken.

Structurally, each figure has the same left hand column; this column defines the Net-Abyss interaction. The other columns vary and should primarily be understood as representations of the consciousness of the therapist.

A different writer would have arrived at a different typology. As you read the one below, an improved typology may occur to you. That analysis and those improvements are evocative; simply creating a dialog between my vision and your sense of constructed reality is one of the primary points of this appendix.

The differences between anxiety that is pre-Net, anxiety at the Net and anxiety due to breakthroughs of the Abyss are important. Pre-Net anxiety and

**Table A.1  Psychotherapy, Identity, and Pathology**

| | Psychotherapy Systems | Self/Identity | Psychopathology |
|---|---|---|---|
| The Chaotic Abyss: Unable to connect to the Net in a functional role, too traumatized to join the Net | Mental hospitals, jails, half way houses, ghettos, homeless | Disorganized Undifferentiated | Severe decompensation such as autism, schizophrenia, severe personality disorders |
| The Nomological Net: Operating within the culture. Achieving culturally endorsed goals | Reality therapy CBT Psychodynamic | Unitary Self | Trauma, anxiety, depression, substance abuse, life issues for example, marital or job-related issues |
| Abyss Breaks Through the Net: old age, illness, and death, reversals, attacks of anomie | Shadow work Depth psychology Soul making | Multiple Selves | Anxiety and depression with existential features, existential grief, anomie |
| Sacred Space: A pilgrimage to the boundary between the Net and the Abyss | Hypnosis Somatic therapies Depth psychology | Multiple Selves | Personal growth |
| The Numinous Abyss: Leap into the depths | Transpersonal Psychotherapies | No Self Atman | Spiritual growth |

depression are related to the feeling that I have failed in my attempt to be a human being. Net-related anxiety and depression are related to failures and possible failures in terms of succeeding at culturally endorsed goals. Anxiety and depression related to Abyss breakthroughs are more existential. They are connected to meaning and purpose; they make us question our place in the universe.

The three columns in Table A.2 are all related to therapist development. There are no entries in the "chaotic Abyss" row because such individuals cannot function as therapists.

Differentiating between a "personal unconscious" and the "collective unconscious" is always a bit challenging. In this book, the personal unconscious refers to everything that is not related to the Abyss and Abyss breakthroughs. This includes social programming, trauma, mislearnings, modeling, etc. Feelings, perceptions, prejudices, and ingrained habits are all contained

**Table A.2  Wisdom, Heart, and Development**

| | Wisdom | Heart | Therapist out-of-room Development |
|---|---|---|---|
| The Chaotic Abyss: Unable to connect to the Net in a functional role, too traumatized to join the Net | | | |
| The Nomological Net: Operating within the culture. Achieving culturally endorsed goals | Expert on the Culture. Willing to make strong Apollonian interventions | Kindness, ethics, and compassion in "I-It" relationships | Successful life in terms of professional and personal accomplishments;. "responsible" individual |
| Abyss Breaks Through the Net: old age, illness, and death, reversals. attacks of anomie | Discernment between what is real and what is constructed. Sees breakthroughs as numinous communications | Work effectively with affect and emotions | Personal therapy and transformation experiences. Discern between conventional therapy and Dionysian therapy |
| Sacred Space: A pilgrimage to the boundary between the Net and the Abyss | Awareness of hierophanies | Cultivate "I-Thou" relationship | Consciously create pilgrimage experiences such as retreats and adventures |
| The Numinous Abyss: Leap into the depths | Discernment includes kill-the-Buddha level of judgment and experience | Universe says "Thou" in return | Dancing with the Abyss level of consciousness in professional and personal life |

in the personal unconscious. Conversely, the collective unconscious generates material from the Other—the Abyss or the Source. The unconscious of pre-Net individuals contains a lot of Abyss-related material; unfortunately it is so dominated by terror that it is difficult to work with directly.

The groups column is both related to what kinds of groups are useful at that state as well as what kinds of groups a therapist might choose to facilitate to master that level. The ultimate concern column similarly has the dual relationship of "what is appropriate at this level" and "what kind of client ultimate concern should be facilitated." Recalling that the therapist is asked to stand in her own ultimate concern to discern and work with the client's ultimate concern is helpful. Finally, the Tillichian paradox of simultaneously hierarchical and flat creates a background context for the ultimate concern column.

**Table A.3  Unconscious Mind, Groups, and the Ultimate Concern**

| | Unconscious Mind | Groups and Sangha | Ultimate Concern |
|---|---|---|---|
| The Chaotic Abyss: Unable to connect to the Net in a functional role, too traumatized to join the Net | The terrifying Abyss | Afraid of any group experience because of feeling of ultimate alienation | Frozen in terror |
| The Nomological Net: Operating within the culture. Achieving culturally endorsed goals | Personal Unconscious | Joins any group that facilitates motivation or skills that lead to Net-related success | Focused on achieving success in an ethical and connected manner |
| Abyss Breaks Through the Net: old age, illness, and death, reversals, attacks of anomie | Collective Unconscious | Works with groups that manifest compassion and guidance for breakthrough challenges | Interprets pathology and feelings as numinous messages |
| Sacred Space: A pilgrimage to the boundary between the Net and the Abyss | Collective Unconscious | Connects to groups that support experiences of the numinous | Attempts to create experiences of the numinous |
| The Numinous Abyss: Leap into the depths | Numinous Abyss | Part of groups that focus on kill-the-Buddha experience | Manifests the ultimate concern in each moment |

# References

Abhedananda, S. (2010). *The sayings of Sri Ramakrishna*. Retrieved from https://www.amazon.com/Sayings-Sri-Ramakrishna-Swami-Abhedananda-ebook/dp/B071P2S4LN.

Anderson, H. (2003). Postmodern social construction therapies. In G. Weeks, T. L. Sexton, & M. Robbins (Eds.), *Handbook of family therapy*, (pp. 125–145). New York, NY: Brunner/Mazel, Inc.

Anderson, T., Lunnen K. M., & Ogles, B. M. (2010). Putting models and techniques in context. In B. L. Duncan, S. D. Miller, B. E. Wampold, & M. A Hubble's *The heart and soul of change* (Kindle Locations 3795–4399). Retrieved from https://www.amazon.com/Heart-Soul-Change-Second-Delivering-ebook/dp/B004T9YTEG.

Angell, M. (2011a, June 23). The epidemic of mental illness: Why? *The New York Times*. Retrieved from http://www.nybooks.com/articles/2011/06/23/epidemic-mental-illness-why/.

Angell, M. (2011b, July 14). The Illusions of Psychiatry. *The New York Times*. Retrieved from http://www.nybooks.com/articles/archives/2011/jul/14/illusions-of-psychiatry/.

Bacon, S. (1983). *The conscious use of metaphor in outward bound*. Denver, CO: Colorado Outward Bound School.

Bandler, R. & Grinder, J. (1976). *The structure of magic*. Palo Alto, CA: Science and Behavior Books.

Barks, C. (1995). *The essential Rumi*. New York, NY: Harper One.

Becker, E. (1997). *The Denial of Death*. Retrieved from https://www.amazon.com/dp/B002C7Z57C.

Begley, S. (2010, January 28). Why antidepressants are no better than placebos. *Newsweek LLC*. Retrieved from http://www.newsweek.com/why-antidepressants-are-no-better-placebos-71111.

Berger, P. L. & Luckmann, T. (1966). *The social construction of reality: A treatise in the sociology of knowledge*. New York, NY: Anchor Books.

Berne, E. (1996). *Games people play: The psychology of human relationships.* New York, NY: Ballantine Books.

Blenkiron, P. (2011). *Stories and analogies in cognitive behavior therapy.* Hoboken, NJ: Wiley-Blackwell.

Borofsky, R. & Borofsky, A. (2012). The heart of couples therapy. In C. K. Germer & R. D. Siegel (Eds.) *Wisdom and compassion in psychotherapy: Deepening mindfulness in clinical practice,* (pp. 35–47). Retrieved from https://www.amazon.com/Wisdom-Compassion-Psychoherapy-Deepening-Mindfulness-ebook/dp/B007W4ED6O.

Brach, T. (2004). *Radical acceptance.* Retrieved from https://www.amazon.com/Radical-Acceptance-Tara-Brach-ebook/dp/B000FC2NHG.

Brach, T. (2012). Mindful presence: A foundation for compassion and wisdom. In C. K. Germer & R. D. Siegel (Eds.) *Wisdom and compassion in psychotherapy: Deepening mindfulness in clinical practice,* (pp. 35–47). Retrieved from https://www.amazon.com/Wisdom-Compassion-Psychoherapy-Deepening-Mindfulness-ebook/dp/B007W4ED6O.

Briggle, A. & Frodeman, A. (2016, January 11). When philosophy lost its way. *The New York Times.* Retrieved from https://opinionator.blogs.nytimes.com/2016/01/11/when-philosophy-lost-its-way/.

Brooks, D. (2015, October 23). Lady Gaga and the life of passion. *The New York Times.* Retrieved from https://www.nytimes.com/2015/10/23/opinion/lady-gaga-and-the-life-of-passion.html.

Buber, M. (1964). *Daniel: Dialogues on realization.* (M. Friedman, Trans.). New York, NY: Holt, Rinehart and Winston.

Buber, M. (1970). *I and thou.* (W. Kaufmann, Trans.). New York, NY: Scribner's.

Buber, M. (1995). *The legend of the Baal-Shem.* (M. Friedman, Trans.). Princeton, NJ: Princeton University Press.

Buber, M. (2006). *The way of man and ten rungs.* New York, NY: Citadel Press Books.

Buber, M. (2014). *Between man and man.* Mansfield Centre, CT: Martino Publishing.

Burr, V. (2003). *Social constructionism* (2nd ed.). New York, NY: Routledge.

Cameron, J (Producer, Director). (2009). *Avatar* [Motion Picture]. United States: 20th Century Fox.

Campbell, J. (1990). *The hero's journey: Joseph Campbell on his life and work.* Novato, CA: New World Library.

Campbell, J. (1998). *The power of myth.* New York, NY: Random House, Inc.

Caputo, P. (2004). *Indian Country.* New York, NY: Vintage Books.

Carroll, L. (1869). *Alice's adventures in Wonderland.* Boston, MA: Lee and Shepard.

Chimnoy, Sri (2015). *Beyond within: A philosophy for the inner life.* Retrieved from https://www.amazon.com/dp/B00JC8MFYK.

Chockalingam, S. P. (2014). *The life: Is it mystical or real & painful or magical?* Retrieved from https://www.amazon.com/dp/B00IR34X6Y.

Cohen, J. M. & Phipps, J. F. (1979). *The common experience.* New York, NY: St. Martin's Press.

Cook, F. D. (1999). *How to raise an ox: Pen practice as taught in master Dogen's Shobogenzo.* Boston, MA: Wisdom Publications.

Dalai Lama. (2012). Foreword. In C. K. Germer & R. D. Siegel's *Wisdom and compassion in psychotherapy: Deepening mindfulness in clinical practice*. Retrieved from https://www.amazon.com/Wisdom-Compassion-Psychotherapy-Deepening-Mindfulness-ebook/dp/B007W4ED6O.

Dass, R. (1971). *Be here now*. New York, NY: Crown Publishing.

Dass, R. (2007). *One-liners: A mini-manual for a spiritual life*. Retrieved from https://www.amazon.com/dp/B0012T6O12.

De Shazer, S. (1985). *Keys to solution in brief therapy*. New York, NY: W. W. Norton & Company.

Diamond, S. A. (2012, April 20). Essential secrets of psychotherapy: What is the "Shadow"? Retrieved from http://www.psychologytoday.com/blog/evil-deeds/201204/essential-secrets-psychotherapy-what-is-the-shadow.

Dick, P. K. (1996). *The shifting realities of Philip K. Dick*. New York, NY: Vintage Books.

Dinesen, I. (1991). *Seven gothic tales*. New York, NY: Vintage Books.

Doyle, A. C. (2000). *The complete Sherlock Holmes*. Retrieved from https://www.amazon.com/dp/B0754MF8MN/ref=dp-kindle-redirect?_encoding=UTF8&btkr=1.

Ducey, J. (2015). *The purpose principles: How to draw more meaning into your life*. Retrieved from https://www.amazon.com/dp/B00KWG5RS2.

Duncan, B. L., Miller, S. D., Wampold, B. E., & Hubble, M. A. (2010). *The heart and soul of change: Delivering what works in therapy* (2nd ed.). Retrieved from https://www.amazon.com/Heart-Soul-Change-Second-Delivering-ebook/dp/B004T9YTEG.

Eagleman, D. (2012). *Incognito: The secret lives of the brain*. New York, NY: Vintage Books.

Einstein, A. (2010). As cited in Jammer, Max (2010). *Einstein and religion: Physics and theology*. Princeton, NJ: Princeton University Press.

Eliade, M. (1961). *The sacred and the profane: The nature of religion*. (W. R. Trask, Trans.). New York, NY: Harcourt Brace Jovanovich.

Eliade, M. (1973). The sacred in the secular world. *Philosophy and Social Criticism, 1* (1). Retrieved from https://doi.org/10.1177/019145377300100105.

Ericsson, K. A., Krampe, R. T., & Tesch-Römer, C. (1993). The role of deliberate practice in the acquisition of expert performance. *Psychological Review, 100* (3), 363–406.

Eriksen, T. H. (2010). *Small places, large issues: An introduction to social and cultural anthropology*, (3rd ed.). London, UK: Pluto Press.

Erickson, M., Rossi, E., & Rossi, S. (1976). *Hypnotic realities: The induction of clinical hypnosis and forms of indirect suggestion*. New York, NY: Irvington Publishers, Inc.

Espiritu, F. (2016). *The path to awesomeness: Becoming super, being human*. Retrieved from https://www.amazon.com/dp/B01CNM4IZ0.

Farrelly, F. & Brandsma, J. (1981). *Provocative therapy*. Cupertino, CA: Meta Publications.

Frank, J. (1930). *Law and the modern mind*. Piscataway, NJ: Transaction Publishers.

Frank, J. & Frank, J. (1993). *Persuasion and healing: A comparative study of psychotherapy* (3rd ed.). Baltimore, MD: Johns Hopkins University Press.

Friedman, M. S. (1988). *Martin Buber's life and work.* Detroit, MI: Wayne State University Press.

Fromme, D. (2010). *Systems of psychotherapy: Dialectical tensions and integration.* New York, NY: Springer.

Gergen, K. J. (2009). *An invitation to social construction* (2nd ed.). Los Angeles, CA: SAGE Publications Ltd.

Germer, C. (2012). Cultivating compassion in psychotherapy. In C. K. Germer & R. D. Siegel (Eds.) *Wisdom and compassion in psychotherapy: Deepening mindfulness in clinical practice,* (pp. 35–47). Retrieved from https://www.amazon.com/Wisdom-Compassion-Psychoherapy-Deepening-Mindfulness-ebook/dp/B007W4ED6O.

Germer, C. K. & Siegel, R. D. (Eds.). (2012). *Wisdom and compassion in psychotherapy: Deepening mindfulness in clinical practice.* Retrieved from https://www.amazon.com/Wisdom-Compassion-Psychotherapy-Deepening-Mindfulness-ebook/dp/B007W4ED6O.

Gilbertson, T. (2014). *Constructive wallowing: How to beat bad feelings by letting yourself have them.* Retrieved from https://www.amazon.com/dp/B00H6UOCK6.

Gilligan, S. (1982). Erickson Approaches to Clinical Hypnosis. In J. K. Zeig (Ed.), *Ericksonian approaches to hypnosis and psychotherapy* (p. 518). Hove, UK: Brunner/Mazel, Inc.

Gilligan, S. (2012). *Generative trance: The experience of creative flow.* Retrieved from https://www.amazon.com/Generative-Trance-experience-Creative-Flow-ebook/dp/B00AAU5OZQ.

Gladwell, M. (2007). *Blink: The power of thinking without thinking.* New York, NY: Back Bay Books.

Glasser, W. (1965). *Reality therapy: A new approach to psychiatry.* New York, NY: Harper Collins.

Goldberg, E. (2011, September 29). Success is not one of the names of god Rosh Hashanah sermon. Retrieved from http://rabbigoldberg.blogspot.com/2011/09/success-is-not-one-of-names-of-god-rosh.html.

Grinder, J. & Bandler, R. (1981). *Trance-formations: Neuro-linguistic programming and the structure of hypnosis.* Moab, UT: Real People Press.

Grotberg, E. H. (2003). *Resilience for today: Gaining strength from adversity.* Retrieved from https://www.amazon.com/dp/B000QEIMR8.

Guenther, L. (2012, August 26). The living death of solitary confinement. *The New York Times.* Retrieved from https://opinionator.blogs.nytimes.com/author/lisa-guenther/.

Haley, J. (1993a). *Jay Haley on Milton H. Erickson.* New York, NY: Routledge.

Haley, J. (1993b). *Uncommon therapy: The psychiatric techniques of Milton H. Erickson, M.D.* New York, NY: W. W. Norton & Company.

Hanley, W. F. (1982). Erickson's contribution to change in psychotherapy. In J. K. Zeig (Ed.), *Ericksonian approaches to hypnosis and psychotherapy* (p. 518). Hove, UK: Brunner/Mazel, Inc.

Hart, A. H. (2009). *Knowing darkness: Reflections on skepticism, melancholy, friendship, and God.* Retrieved from https://www.amazon.com/dp/B002KQ61WI.

Held, B. S. (2007). *Psychology's interpretive turn: The search for truth and agency in theoretical and philosophical psychology.* Washington, DC: American Psychological Association.

Hill, C. E. & Knox, S. (2013). Training and supervision in psychotherapy. In Michael J. Lambert (Ed.) *Bergin and Garfield's handbook of psychotherapy and behavior change* (6th ed.). Hoboken, NJ: John Wiley & Sons.

Hillman, J. (1997). *Re-visioning psychology.* New York, NY: William Morrow Paperbacks.

Hillman, J. (2000). *The force of character: And the lasting life* (1st Ballantine Books Trade ed.). London; New York, NY: Ballantine Books.

Hjelm, T. (2014). *Social constructionisms: Approaches to the study of the human world.* New York, NY: Palgrave Macmillan.

Hudson, J, (2011). *Healthy loving relationships.* Retrieved from https://www.amazon.com/Healthy-Loving-Relationships-Joe-Hudson-ebook/dp/B004P1IZUC.

Huxley, A. (2009). *The perennial philosophy.* New York, NY: HarperCollins.

Jerome, F. D. (1993). *Persuasion and healing: A comparative study of psychotherapy* (3rd ed.). Baltimore, MD: Johns Hopkins University Press.

Jung, C. G. (1970). *Civilization in transition* (G. Adler, Ed., R. F. C. Hull, Trans.) (2nd ed.). Princeton, NJ: Princeton University Press.

Jung, C. G. (1983). *Alchemical studies* (G. Adler & R. F. C. Hull, Trans.). Princeton, NJ: Princeton University Press.

Jung, C. G. (2014a). *Collected works of C.G. Jung, volume 9 (part 2): Aion: Researches into the phenomenology of the self* (G. Adler & R. F. C. Hull, Trans.) (2nd ed.). Princeton, NJ: Princeton University Press.

Jung, C. G. (2014b). *Collected works of C.G. Jung, volume 11: Psychology and religion: West and east* (S. H. Read & G. Adler, Eds., R. F. C. Hull, Trans.) (2nd ed., Vol. 11). Princeton, NJ: Princeton University Press.

Kahn, T. (2016). *Intuition: Language of the soul: Book one.* Retrieved from https://www.amazon.com/Intuition-Language-Soul-Book-Blue-ebook/dp/B01IBWGDX6.

Kahneman, D. (2013). *Thinking, fast and slow.* New York, NY: Farrar, Straus and Giroux.

Kain, J. P. (2011), *Conversing with the spirits.* Retrieved from https://www.amazon.com/dp/B0057G2VB8.

Keen, S. (1997). Foreward. In E. Becker (Ed.) *The denial of death,* (Kindle Locations 93–189). Retrieved from https://www.amazon.com/dp/B002C7Z57C.

Kennedy, K. & Molen, G. (Producers), & Spielberg, S. (Director). (1993). *Jurassic park* [Motion Picture]. United States: Universal Pictures.

King, L. (2015). *Euphoria.* New York, NY: Grove Press.

Knafo, S. (2013, October 4). 1 in 3 black males will go to prison in their lifetime, report warns. *Huffington Post.* Retrieved from http://www.huffingtonpost.com/2013/10/04/racial-disparities-criminal-justice_n_4045144.html.

Kopp, S. B. (1976). *If you meet the Buddha on the road, kill him! The pilgrimage of psychotherapy patients.* New York, NY: Bantam Books.

Kornfield, J. (1993). *A path with heart: A guide through the perils and promises of spiritual life*. New York, NY: Bantam Books.

Krishnamurti, J. (1995). *The book of life: Daily meditations with Krishnamurti*. San Francisco, CA: HarperOne.

Kuhn, T. S. (1962). *The structure of scientific reasoning*. Chicago, IL: University of Chicago Press.

Kuhn, T. S. (1977). *The essential tension: Selected studies in scientific tradition and change*. Chicago, IL: University Of Chicago Press.

Lambert, M. & Ogles, B. M. (2004). The efficacy and effectiveness of psychotherapy. In Michael J. Lambert (Ed.) *Bergin and Garfield's handbook of psychotherapy and behavior change* (5th ed., p. 169). Hoboken, NJ: John Wiley & Sons.

Lao Tzu, Tao Te Ching. (2008). In Duker, W. & Spielvogel, J. *World history Volume I*. Boston, MA: Wadsworth.

Lawhead, S. R. (2008). *Merlin*. New York, NY: Harper Voyager.

Lawrence, B. & Beaufort, F. J. de. (2010). *The practice of the presence of God: The wisdom and teachings of Brother Lawrence*. Rockville, MD: Wildside Press LLC.

Lawson-Te, A. (1993). The socially constructed nature of psychology and the abnormalisation of Maori. *New Zealand Psychological Bulletin, 76*, 25030.

Leon, S. C., Martinovich, Z., Lutz, W., & Lyons, J. S. (2005). The effect of therapist experience on psychotherapy outcomes. *Clinical Psychology and Psychotherapy, 12* (6), 417–426.

Levine, S. (1998). *A year to live: How to live this year as if it were your last*. New York, NY: Bell Tower.

Levine, S. & Levine, O. (1996). *Embracing the beloved: Relationship as a path of awakening*. New York, NY: Anchor Books.

Lexchin, J., Bero, L. A., Djulbegovic, B., & Clark, O. (2003). Pharmaceutical industry sponsorship and research outcome and quality: Systematic review. *BMJ, 326* (7400). Retrieved from https://doi.org/10.1136/bmj.326.7400.1167.

Lucas, G. (Producer) & Kershner, I. (Director). (1980). *The empire strikes back* [Motion Picture]. United States: Lucas Films.

Lukoff, D. (n.d.). Contraindications. Retrieved from http://www.spiritualcompetency.com/meditat/lesson6.asp.

Lukoff, D., Wallace, C. J., Liberman, R. P., & Burke, K. (1986). A holistic program for chronic schizophrenic patients. *Schizophrenia Bulletin, 12* (2), 274–282.

Lutyens, M. (2005). *J. Krishnamurti: A life*. London, UK: Penguin Books.

Madigan, S. (2012). *Narrative therapy (theories of psychotherapy)*. Retrieved from https://www.amazon.com/Narrative-Therapy-Theories-Psychotherapy-Stephen-ebook/dp/B006X3F4LS.

Maher, B. (Writer) & Casey, P. (Director). (2011). Episode 224 [Television series episode]. In Maher, B. (Executive Producer), *Real time with Bill Maher*. Los Angeles, CA: Home Box Office.

Makari, G. (2016, February 23). Notes from psychiatry's battle lines. *The New York Times*. Retrieved from https://opinionator.blogs.nytimes.com/2016/02/23/notes-from-psychiatrys-battle-lines/.

Makransky, J. (2012). Compassion in Buddhist Psychology. In C. K. Germer & R. D. Siegel (Eds.) *Wisdom and compassion in psychotherapy: Deepening mindfulness in clinical practice,* (pp. 35–47). Retrieved from https://www.amazon.com/Wisdom-Compassion-Psychoherapy-Deepening-Mindfulness-ebook/dp/B007W4ED6O.

Marshall, F. (Producer) & Spielberg, S. (Director). (1981). *Raiders of the lost ark.* [Motion Picture]. United States: Paramount Pictures.

Mead, M. (2001). *Coming of age in Samoa: A psychological study of primitive youth for western civilisation* . New York, NY: HarperCollins.

Mejabi, F. (2016). *Inspired reflections on knowledge.* Morrisville, NC: Lulu Publishing.

Merton, T. (2002). *No man is an island.* Boston, MA: Houghton Mifflin Harcourt.

Miller, S. D., Hubble, M. A., Chow, D., & Seidel, J. (2015). Beyond measures and monitoring: Realizing the potential of feedback-informed treatment. *Psychotherapy, 52* (4), 449–457. Retrieved from https://doi.org/10.1037/pst0000031.

Miller, S. & Hubble, M. (2011). The road to mastery. *Psychotherapy networker, 35* (3), 22.

Miller, S., Hubble, M., & Duncan, B. (2007). Supershrinks: What is the secret to their success? *Psychotherapy networker, 31* (6).

Millham, A. (2011, February). It's not the right way: How deliberate practice can improve performance – an interview with Scott Miller. *Context Magazine.*

Moreno, J. D. (2012, April 6). Check this box: Science is getting easier/harder/both/neither? *The Huffington Post.* Retrieved from http://www.huffingtonpost.com/jonathan-d-moreno/check-this-box-science-is_b_1408938.html.

Neill, J. R. & Kniskern, D. P. (Eds.). (1989). *From psyche to system: The evolving therapy of Carl Whitaker.* New York, NY: The Guilford Press.

Nietzsche, F. (1994). *The birth of tragedy: Out of the spirit of music.* (M. Tanner, Ed., S. Whiteside, Trans.). New York, NY: Penguin Classics.

Nikhilananda, S. (Trans.) (1984). *The gospel of Sri Ramakrishna* (7th ptg ed.). New York, NY: Ramakrishna-Vivekananda Center.

O'Hanlon, B. (2000). *Do one thing different: Ten simple ways to change your life.* New York, NY: William Morrow Paperbacks.

Orwell, G. (1964). *1984.* New York, NY: Signet New American Library.

Osbon, D. (1995). *Reflections on the art of living: A Joseph Campbell companion.* New York, NY: Harper.

Ouspensky, P. D. (2001). *In search of the miraculous.* Boston, MA: Houghton Mifflin Harcourt.

Pargament, K. & Faigin, C. (2012). Drawing on the wisdom of religious traditions in psychotherapy. In C. K. Germer & R. D. Siegel (Eds.) *Wisdom and compassion in psychotherapy: Deepening mindfulness in clinical practice,* (pp. 35–47). Retrieved from https://www.amazon.com/Wisdom-Compassion-Psychoherapy-Deepening-Mindfulness-ebook/dp/B007W4ED6O.

Paul, C. (1885). *The thoughts of Blaise Pascal.* London: Kegan Paul Trench & Co.

Plato & Stock, M. A. S. G. (1899). *The apology of Plato with introduction and notes* (3rd ed., Revised ed.). Wotton-under-Edge, UK: Clarendon Press.

Reiner, R., Brown, D., & Scheinman, A. (Producers), & Reiner, R. (Director). (1992). *A few good men* [Motion Picture]. United States: Columbia Pictures.

Robbins, T. (1990). *Even cowgirls get the blues.* Retrieved from https://www.amazon.com/dp/B000FBFNVA.

Rogers, C. & Kramer, P. D. (1995). *On becoming a person: A therapist's view of psychotherapy* (2nd ed.). Boston, MA: Houghton Mifflin Harcourt.

Rousmaniere, T. (2016). *Deliberate practice for psychotherapists: A guide to improving clinical effectiveness.* New York, NY: Routledge.

Rousseau, N. (2002). *Self, symbols, and society: Classic readings in social psychology.* Lanham, MD: Rowman & Littlefield Publishers.

Rumi, J. (1995). *The essential Rumi.* (C. Barks, Trans.). New York, NY: Quality Paperback Book Club.

Saint-Exupery, A. de (2000). *The little prince.* (R. Howard, Trans.). Retrieved from https://www.amazon.com/Little-Prince-Antoine-Saint-Exupery-ebook/dp/B008QYT7DI.

Sand, F. A. (1989). *The way of a pilgrim: And the pilgrim continues his way.* (R. M. French, Trans.) (2nd ed.). Pasadena, CA: Hope Publishing House.

Sapir, E. (1929). The status of linguistics as a science. *Language, 5* (4), 207–214.

Sartre, J.-P. (1993). *Being and nothingness.* New York, NY: Washington Square Press.

Sartre, J.-P. (2007). *Existentialism is a humanism.* New Haven, CT: Yale University Press.

Sartre, J.-P., Wood, J., & Howard, R. (2013). *Nausea.* (L. Alexander, Trans.). New York, NY: New Directions.

Schore, A. N. (2012). *The science of the art of psychotherapy.* Retrieved from https://www.amazon.com/Science-Psychotherapy-Norton-Interpersonal-Neurobiology-ebook/dp/B005LW5K2U.

Schuman, M. (2017). *Mindfulness-informed relational psychotherapy.* New York, NY: Routledge.

Shah, I. (1971). *The pleasantries of the incredible Mulla Nasrudin.* Boston, MA: E. P. Dutton.

Shah, I. (2016). *The dermis probe.* United Kingdom: ISF Publishing.

Siegel, R. D. (2010). *The mindfulness solution: Everyday practices for everyday problems.* New York, NY: Guilford Press.

Siegel, R. D. (2012). The wise psychotherapist. In C. K. Germer & R. D. Siegel (Eds.) *Wisdom and compassion in psychotherapy: Deepening mindfulness in clinical practice,* (pp. 138–153). Retrieved from https://www.amazon.com/Wisdom-Compassion-Psychoherapy-Deepening-Mindfulness-ebook/dp/B007W4ED6O.

Siegel, R. & Germer, C. (2012). Wisdom and compassion: Two wings of a bird. In C. K. Germer & R. D. Siegel (Eds.) *Wisdom and compassion in psychotherapy: Deepening mindfulness in clinical practice,* (pp. 35–47). Retrieved from https://www.amazon.com/Wisdom-Compassion-Psychoherapy-Deepening-Mindfulness-ebook/dp/B007W4ED6O.

Silver, J. (Producer), & Wachowski, L. & Wachowski, L (Directors). (1999). *The matrix* [Motion Picture]. United States: Warner Bros.

Simon, T. (n.d.). The power of now and the end of suffering. *Eckhart Teachings.* Retrieved from https://www.eckharttolle.com/article/The-Power-Of-Now-Spirituality-And-The-End-Of-Suffering.

Sparks, J. A., Duncan, B. L., & Miller, S. D. (2008, September 24). Integrating psychotherapy and pharmacotherapy: Myths and the missing link. *Journal of Family Psychotherapy, 17* (3–4), 83–108.

Stossel, S. (2014). *My age of anxiety: Fear, hope, dread, and the search for peace of mind.* New York, NY: Vintage Books.

Strupp, H. H. & Hadley, S. W. (1979, September). Specific vs nonspecific factors in psychotherapy. A controlled study of outcome. *Archives of General Psychiatry, 36* (10), 1125–1136.

Stutz, P. & Michels, B. (2013). *The tools: 5 tools to help you find courage, creativity, and willpower--and inspire you to live life in forward motion.* Retrieved from ttps://www.amazon.com/dp/B006YZ285A.

Surrey, J. & Jordan, J. (2012). The wisdom of connection. In C. K. Germer & R. D. Siegel (Eds.) *Wisdom and compassion in psychotherapy: Deepening mindfulness in clinical practice,* (pp. 163–175). Retrieved from https://www.amazon.com/Wisdom-Compassion-Psychoherapy-Deepening-Mindfulness-ebook/dp/B007W4ED6O.

Suzuki, S., Smith, H., Baker, R., & Chadwick, D. (2011). *Zen mind, beginner's mind.* (T. Dixon, Ed.) Boston, MA: Shambhala.

Thomas, J. (2014, February). Therapy: No improvement for 40 years. *The National Psychologist, 23* (1). Retrieved from http://www.scottdmiller.com/wp-content/uploads/2016/09/National-Psychologist-2014.pdf.

Tillich, P. (1957). *Dynamics of faith: Faith and belief: What they are & what they are not.* New York, NY: HarperOne.

Tolle, E. (2010). *The power of now: A guide to spiritual enlightenment.* Novato, CA: New World Library.

Tomatz, M. (2008). Warriorship: A tradition of fearlessness and its impact on contemplative psychotherapy. In F. J. Kaklauskas, S. Nimanheminda, L. Hoffman, & M. Jack (Eds.), *Brilliant sanity: Buddhist approaches to psychotherapy* (pp. 65–86). Colorado Springs, CO: Universities of the Rockies Press.

Trungpa, C. (1973). *Cutting through spiritual materialism.* Boston, MA: Shambhala.

Vivekananda, S. (1964). *The complete works of Swami Vivekananda: Vol. 3 pb* (9th ed.). Mylapore, Chennai: Sri Ramakrishna Math.

Vivekananda, S. (2015a). *Lectures vol. 3: Vedanta philosophy basics.* Germany: Jazzybee Verlag.

Vivekananda, S. (2015b). *Swami Vivekanand's Chicago speech: Swami Vivekananda's speech at world parliament of religion, Chicago.* Retrieved from https://www.amazon.com/Swami-Vivekanands-Chicago-Speech-Vivekanandas-ebook/dp/B018BAOLVO.

Vonnegut, K. (2010). *Cat's Cradle: A Novel.* New York, NY: Dell Publishing.

Walsh, R. & Roche, L. (1979, August). Precipitation of acute psychotic episodes by intensive meditation in individuals with a history of schizophrenia. *The American Journal of Psychiatry, 136* (8), 1085–1086.

Walt, J. (2007, February). The future of mental health: An interview with Scott D. Miller, Ph.D. *The Therapist*, 81–87.

Wampold, B. E., (2010). The research evidence for the common factors models: A historically situated perspective. In B. L. Duncan, S. D. Miller, B. E. Wampold & M. A Hubble (Eds.), *The heart and soul of change* (Kindle Locations 1511–2360). Retrieved from https://www.amazon.com/Heart-Soul-Change-Second-Delivering-ebook/dp/B004T9YTEG.

Wampold, B. E. & Imel, Z. E. (2015). *The great psychotherapy debate: The evidence for what makes psychotherapy work* (2nd ed.). Retrieved from https://www.amazon.com/Great-Psychotherapy-Debate-Counseling-Investigating-ebook/dp/B00SYJWC6Y.

Watkins, H. (1993). Ego-state therapy: An overview. *American Journal of Clinical Hypnosis, 35* (4), 232–240. Retrieved from https://doi.org/10.1080/00029157.199 3.10403014.

Watts, A. (1966). *The book: On the taboo against knowing who you are.* New York, NY: Pantheon Books.

Weeks, G. R. & L'Abate, L. (1982). *Paradoxical psychotherapy: Theory & practice with individuals couples & families.* New York, NY: Brunner/Mazel, Inc.

Weeraperuma, S. (1996). *Living and dying: From moment to moment.* India: Motilal Banarsidass Publishing.

Wernik, U. (2016). *Nietzschean psychology and psychotherapy: The new doctors of the soul.* Retrieved from https://www.amazon.com/Nietzschean-Psychology-Psychotherapy-Doctors-Soul-ebook/dp/B01D6OTRRI.

Wilson, E. O. (2015). *The meaning of human existence.* New York, NY: Liveright Publishing.

Wooster, P. (2016). *So, you want to be a leader? An awesome guide to becoming a head honcho.* Retrieved from https://www.amazon.com/dp/B01675AE70.

Yalom, I. D. (2008). *Existential psychotherapy.* Retrieved from https://www.amazon.com/Existential-Psychotherapy-Irvin-D-Yalom-ebook/dp/B008HMAMYC.

Yalom, I. D. & Leszcz, M. (2008). *The theory and practice of group psychotherapy* (5th ed.). Retrieved from https://www.amazon.ca/Theory-Practice-Group-Psychotherapy-ebook/dp/B005GX1O1U.

Zeig, J. K. (Ed.) (1980). *A teaching seminar with Milton H. Erickson.* New York, NY: Brunner/Mazel, Inc.

Zeig, J. K. (Ed.) (1982). *Ericksonian approaches to hypnosis and psychotherapy.* New York, NY: Brunner/Mazel, Inc.

Zeig, J. K. & Munion, W. (1999). *Milton H. Erickson.* London: Sage Publications.

# Index

Abyss, 2, 9, 45, 48, 49, 52, 60, 61,
  64, 101, 103, 111, 112, 117–22,
  127, 128, 133, 135–37, 139, 155,
  156, 192, 211, 213, 214, 220–22,
  226–29, 231, 238, 242, 245–48,
  252–55, 273, 275, 279, 285–90,
  298, 300, 303, 307, 309, 312, 313,
  316, 318–20, 322, 329, 335, 348,
  361–64, 369, 370, 376, 378–83,
  386, 391–94
Apollonian, 55, 56, 120, 121, 127, 128,
  135–37, 144, 147, 153, 155–58,
  161–64, 177, 184, 191, 192, 195–97,
  199–205, 208, 209, 212–14, 217,
  218, 220, 222, 223, 226–31, 242,
  252, 253, 255, 258, 259, 261, 262,
  264–66, 272, 273, 275, 286, 287,
  300, 301, 303, 304, 310, 313, 318,
  333, 335, 341, 361, 363, 369, 370,
  381, 383, 384, 387, 391, 393

Borofsky, Antra, 240, 396
Borofskys, 241–43, 349, 384
Brach, Tara, 141, 142, 310, 311, 313,
  381, 396
Buber, Martin, 109–13, 119, 213, 231,
  244, 245, 253, 254, 312, 320, 331,
  333, 358, 372, 396
Burger, David, 46, 139

Campbell, Joseph, 67, 246, 254,
  255, 339, 349, 350, 376, 383,
  396, 401
chaos, 2, 33, 37, 38, 51, 54, 61, 65, 69,
  72, 73, 98, 100, 103, 111, 117, 119,
  126, 127, 135, 276–78, 287, 312,
  382, 383
charisma, 7, 8, 11, 60, 126, 128,
  131–37, 151, 152, 168, 170, 172,
  174, 177, 181, 183, 188, 208, 209,
  228, 230, 239, 240, 245, 253, 255,
  261, 266, 271, 286, 301, 306, 317,
  319, 322, 341, 343–46, 348–52,
  354–56, 360, 363–65, 368, 371–76,
  378, 380–82, 384, 387
compassion, 7, 54, 80, 105, 133, 167,
  178, 204, 218, 219, 230, 231, 234,
  235, 238, 239, 241, 243, 244,
  311–13, 317, 331, 338, 344–46,
  348, 353, 371, 378, 387, 393, 394,
  396, 398, 400–3
constructionism, 1, 2, 7, 9, 11, 12,
  63, 65, 67, 68, 73, 82, 86–88,
  99–101, 117, 122, 125, 127, 128,
  136, 145, 169, 185–88, 217, 222,
  223, 252, 254, 257, 298, 311,
  313, 316, 319, 320, 328, 350, 353,
  369–72, 377, 378, 382, 387,
  388, 396

dancing with the abyss, 122, 137, 228, 316, 335, 376, 378, 380
deliberate practice, 136, 300, 365–69, 371, 372, 378, 380, 387, 401
Dionysian, 55, 119, 121, 128, 135–37, 151, 155, 164, 176, 181, 191, 192, 201, 203, 204, 209, 212–14, 217, 226, 231, 232, 242, 258, 261–63, 266, 268, 270, 273, 275, 286, 290, 298–301, 319, 363, 369, 370, 383, 384, 393

Eagleman, David, 82, 83, 85, 86, 88, 397
ego state, 212, 214–16, 248, 385
Ego-state, 403
Eliade, Mircea, 276–79, 293, 297, 299, 326, 338, 362, 374, 397
epiphanies, 45, 119, 134, 229, 254, 275, 300
Erickson, Milton, 134, 146, 154–56, 169–72, 177, 180, 182, 184, 212, 260, 261, 263, 289, 344–49, 370, 397, 398, 404
Ericksonian, 179, 182, 290, 398, 404, 405

faith, 10, 40, 69–71, 103–6, 108, 109, 111, 112, 114, 115, 122, 124, 127, 205, 239, 248, 303, 306, 312, 320, 322, 329, 330, 335, 338, 356, 371, 380, 403
Farrelly, Frank, 88, 89, 172, 174–78, 180, 184, 188, 193, 204, 209, 235, 300, 344, 349, 397
Frank, 5, 7, 12, 88, 122, 123, 126, 149, 153, 155, 172, 183, 204, 252, 268, 271, 315, 359, 397

geography, 43, 54, 121, 128, 135, 257, 277, 298, 303, 306, 361, 364, 371, 387, 391
Germer, C. K., 230, 235, 238, 396, 398, 400–3

Gilligan, Stephen, 118, 182, 288–91, 347, 349, 370, 398
god, 45, 54, 55, 63, 69–73, 76, 98, 99, 105, 106, 114, 132, 164, 253, 254, 276, 277, 279, 280, 285, 305, 306, 309, 319, 321–24, 326–34, 337, 338, 340, 345, 348, 357, 360, 379, 385, 398, 400

Haley, Jaye, 38, 155, 184, 187, 346, 398
heart-centered, 236, 241, 244, 246, 378
hierophanies, 276, 277, 279, 285, 288, 289, 299, 393
Hillman, James, 61, 119, 218, 246, 254, 327, 329, 336, 337, 399
Huxley, Aldous, 12, 399

Kahneman, Daniel, 29–35, 37, 38, 69, 99, 127, 137, 236, 356, 368, 386, 399
kill-the-Buddha, 340, 341, 364, 369, 374, 377, 382, 393, 394
Kornfield, Jack, 85, 312, 313, 316, 399
Krishnamurti, J., 341, 383, 399, 400

Luckmann, T., 46, 53, 77–79, 81, 139, 201, 217, 265, 395

Madigan, Stephen, 74, 118, 263, 351, 379, 400
materialism, 335, 336, 339–41, 369, 371, 375, 403
Miller, Scott, 20–22, 28, 42, 181, 343, 365–68, 395, 397, 401–3
mindfulness, 22, 51, 52, 61, 136, 141, 142, 228, 239, 310, 311, 313, 317, 318, 377, 396, 398, 400–3

narrative, 1, 74, 118, 124, 125, 263, 266, 270, 351–55, 360, 377, 379, 387, 400
net, 117–22, 128, 133, 135–37, 139, 148, 155, 157, 163, 164, 167, 170, 177, 191, 192, 195, 205, 211, 226, 228, 229, 231, 242, 244, 245, 248, 253, 255, 257, 266, 268, 275, 279,

285–90, 299, 300, 303, 304, 309, 310, 312, 313, 318, 329, 341, 345, 348, 353, 362, 369, 377–79, 381, 386, 391–94

Net-Abyss, 135, 136, 360, 361, 391

Nietzsche, Friedrich, 1, 55, 68, 122, 126, 134, 151, 205, 214, 222, 245, 253, 343, 365, 372, 401

numinous, 110, 133, 135, 137, 156, 232, 242, 252, 279, 282, 298–301, 337, 343, 345, 346, 364, 379, 381, 392–94

oracular, 135, 137, 229, 231, 245, 249, 252–55, 279, 287, 290, 316, 362, 369, 381, 382

perennial philosophy, 12, 127, 254, 300, 307, 309, 319, 323, 348, 361, 369, 370, 381, 383, 399

pilgrimage, 280, 283, 286, 297, 392–94, 399

placebo, 24, 91, 92, 98, 124, 125, 150, 151, 163, 382

postmodernism, 49, 68, 99, 103, 350

prayer, 289, 291, 321, 323, 331–33

Ramakrishna, 52, 73, 240, 319, 329–31, 337, 338, 350, 395, 401, 403

religiosus, 105, 276, 277, 297

resistance, 121, 143–45, 158–60, 164, 182, 183, 187, 195, 200, 205, 244, 259, 261, 270, 271, 300, 303, 334, 363, 371

right-brain, 230, 233, 234, 236

right-brain-connected, 234

rituals, 128, 149, 150, 177, 184, 239, 252, 270, 272, 279, 283, 286, 292, 298, 306, 357, 359, 374, 382

sacred, 70, 126, 185, 192, 242, 245, 262, 263, 275–86, 289, 290, 292, 293, 297–300, 303, 306, 313, 326, 332, 334, 338, 345, 361–65, 370, 373, 374, 376, 379, 380, 382, 384, 392–94, 397

Schore, 32, 232–39, 242, 244, 344, 402

shamanic, 122, 123, 133, 149, 184, 349, 370

social constructionism, 1, 2, 7, 11, 63, 65, 68, 319, 378, 396

spirituality, 104, 112, 258, 290, 303–6, 332, 336, 339, 340, 361

spiritual materialism, 335, 336, 339–41, 369, 371, 375, 403

sub-personalities, 223, 327

Swami Vivekananda, 60, 81, 108, 167, 181, 233, 328, 331, 335, 348, 360, 375, 378, 403

trance, 9, 141, 147, 154, 169–72, 179, 181–83, 192, 212, 215, 242, 263, 290–94, 296, 297, 310, 311, 314, 344, 346, 364, 370, 398

Vivekananda, 60, 81, 108, 167, 181, 233, 328, 331, 335, 348, 349, 360, 375, 378, 403

Wampold, Bruce, 4, 19, 22, 23, 25, 40, 41, 123, 167, 395, 397, 403

Whitman, Walt, 129, 131, 211, 212, 217, 227, 229, 255, 376, 381

Zeig, J. K., 146, 170, 172, 344, 348, 398, 404

zen, 140, 339, 340, 377, 403

# About the Author

**Stephen Bacon** is a licensed clinical psychologist in private practice in Santa Barbara, California. He has a long history of interest in how worldview structures an individual's reality and how that interacts with the therapeutic relationship and the possibility of positive change and growth. In addition to his formal psychology training, Dr. Bacon has a degree in the phenomenology of religion, has lived in a meditation center for almost six years, and has written a book on metaphors and archetypes in experiential/adventure-based education. He has studied a variety of high impact therapeutic approaches such as EMDR, NLP, hypnosis, and the Ericksonian model, and taught workshops and retreats in the United States and Europe. In addition to his private practice of psychotherapy, he also works as a coach for nonprofit and corporate executives and leaders. Outdoor adventure has also been a major motif in Dr. Bacon's life. He was vice president for program development for Outward Bound after being a field instructor and fulfilled his personal commitment to adventuring through blue water sailing, white water kayaking, canoeing and rafting, climbing, and mountaineering and canyoneering.